Q: I can't seem to select a graphic. Why not?

A: A graphic that has its text wrap option set to **E**... select the graphic, right-click the graphic to dis... *See Chapter 12.*

Q: Why does my default folder change every time I open a document?

A: WordPerfect is automatically set to change default folders when you move to different folders using any file management dialog box. You can easily turn off this feature. Choose <u>F</u>ile, <u>O</u>pen. In the Open File dialog box, display the menus (by clicking the Toggle Menu On/Off button) and then choose <u>E</u>dit from the menu. Remove the check mark from Change Default <u>F</u>older and click <u>C</u>lose to exit the Open File dialog box. *See Chapter 3.*

Q: Why can't I set the top and bottom margin to one-quarter inch?

A: Most printers cannot print all the way to the edge of a piece of paper. Some printers have minimum distances from the edges of the page that are greater than one-quarter inch. WordPerfect generally doesn't allow you to make settings that are incompatible with the capabilities of your selected printer. *See Chapter 4.*

Q: I can see graphics in my document, so why won't the graphics print?

A: It's possible that the print instruction was set to P<u>r</u>int Text Only. When submitting the document to print again, click the Details tab in the Print dialog box, and then be sure P<u>r</u>int Text Only is not checked. *See Chapters 6 and 12.*

Q: Why does my cross-reference still contain a question mark (?) after the document is generated?

A: A target must exist for a reference to properly generate. Be sure that both the target and reference codes still exist. You may have accidentally deleted a target code while editing the document. Try marking the target again, and then regenerate the document. *See Chapter 10.*

Q: How can I quickly use the same formatting for every heading in a report?

A: Rather than creating a full-blown style, apply all formatting attributes you need to the first heading. Then select the heading text and right-click it to display a QuickMenu. Choose QuickFormat, H<u>e</u>adings and click OK. Then click each heading in the report to apply the same attributes. When all headings are formatted, right-click again, and toggle QuickFormat off. *See Chapter 5.*

Q: Is there a method to set tabs evenly across a line?

A: Yes. Right-click the ruler, then select Tab Set to open the Tab Set dialog box. If desired, click Clear <u>A</u>ll to remove all existing tabs. Click Repeat E<u>v</u>ery, type the distance you want between tabs, and click OK. *See Chapter 4.*

Q: Can I make a change to a project?

A: Well, yes and no. You can edit the template associated with the project, but you can't actually edit the project itself. Editing the template generally affects the look of the document and the toolbars, menus, macros, or keyboards available when the project is used. *See Chapter 16.*

How to Order:

For information on quantity discounts, contact the publisher: Prima Publishing, P.O. Box 1260BK, Rocklin, CA 95677-1260; (916) 632-4400. On your letterhead include information concerning the intended use of the books and the number of books you want to purchase. For individual orders, turn to the back of this book for more information.

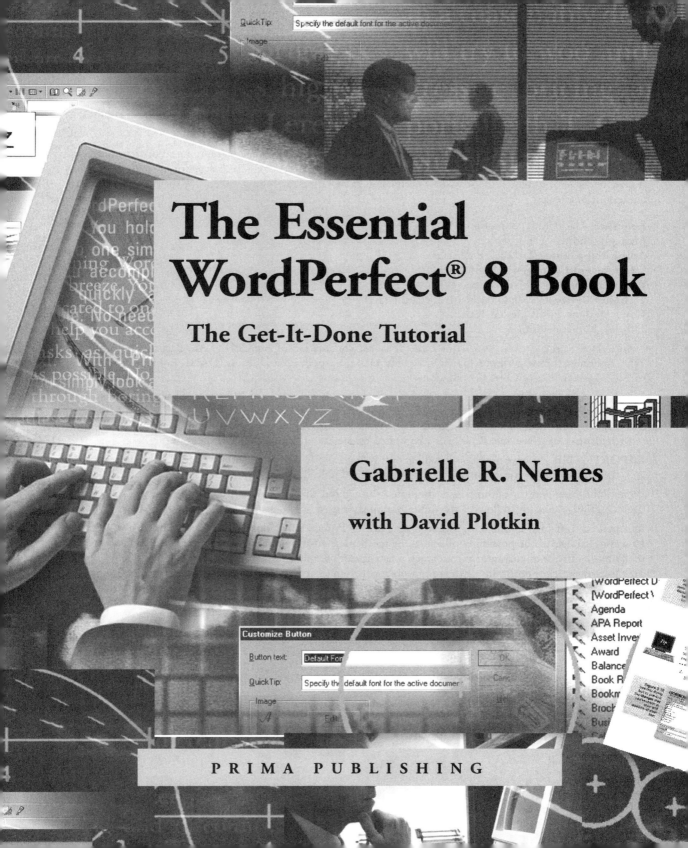

P is a registered trademark of Prima Publishing, a division of Prima Communications, Inc. Prima Publishing is a registered trademark of Prima Communications, Inc.

© 1997 by Gabrielle R. Nemes. All rights reserved. No part of this book may be reproduced or transmitted in any form or by any means, electronic or mechanical, including photocopying, recording, or by any information storage or retrieval system without written permission from Prima Publishing, except for the inclusion of brief quotations in a review.

Publisher: Matthew H. Carleson
Managing Editor: Dan J. Foster
Acquisitions Editor: Deborah F. Abshier
Development Editor: Joyce Nielsen
Project Editor: Chris Haidri
Technical Reviewers: Marla Lockhart, Richard Cravens
Cover Design: Prima Design Team
Indexer: Katherine Stimson

Corel, WordPerfect, Quattro Pro, Time Line, Versions, Presentations, CorelCENTRAL, Barista, Photo House, WEB.SiteBuilder, Envoy Viewer, Quick View Plus, Desktop Application Director (DAD), and PerfectExpert are registered trademarks of Corel Corporation.

Microsoft, Windows, DirectDraw, and DirectX are registered trademarks of Microsoft Corporation. Netscape, Communicator, and Navigator are trademarks of Netscape Communications Corporation. Bitstream Font Navigator is a registered trademark of Bitstream, Inc. Java is a trademark of Sun Microsystems, Inc. Avery is a registered trademark of Avery, Inc. Paradox is a registered trademark of Borland International, Inc.

IMPORTANT: If you have problems installing or running Corel WordPerfect, notify Corel Corporation at (801) 765-4096 or on the Web at http://www.corel.com. Prima Publishing cannot provide software support.

Prima Publishing and the authors have attempted throughout this book to distinguish proprietary trademarks from descriptive terms by following the capitalization style used by the manufacturer.

Information contained in this book has been obtained by Prima Publishing from sources believed to be reliable. However, because of the possibility of human or mechanical error by our sources, Prima Publishing, or others, the Publisher does not guarantee the accuracy, adequacy, or completeness of any information and is not responsible for any errors or omissions or the results obtained from use of such information. Readers should be particularly aware of the fact that the Internet in an ever-changing entity. Some facts may have changed since this book went to press.

ISBN: 0-7615-0425-7
Library of Congress Catalog Card Number: 97-66854
Printed in the United States of America
97 98 99 AA 10 9 8 7 6 5 4 3 2 1

To my husband, Bill

Contents at a Glance

Introduction xxi

PART I LET'S GET STARTED 1

Chapter 1 Introducing Corel WordPerfect Suite 8 3
Chapter 2 The Look and Feel of WordPerfect 8 13
Chapter 3 So How Does WordPerfect Work? 45

PART II DAILY TASKS 77

Chapter 4 The Basic Business Letter 79
Chapter 5 Fine-Tuning and Enhancing Your
         Documents 119
Chapter 6 Printing Your Document to Paper, E-mail,
         or Fax 151
Chapter 7 Same Letter to Lots of Different People! . . 171

PART III REPORTS AND PRESENTATIONS 199

Chapter 8 An Organized Report Starts with an
         Outline 201
Chapter 9 Using Tables for Powerful Data
         Presentation 223
Chapter 10 Maintaining Your Report's Organization . . . 265

CONTENTS AT A GLANCE

PART IV CREATE A NEWSLETTER 315
Chapter 11 Placing the Text and Masthead 317
Chapter 12 Adding Graphic Elements to the
            Newsletter 345

PART V TELL ME MORE 395
Chapter 13 Using WordPerfect to Connect to the
            World. 397
Chapter 14 Equations—A Special Type of Graphic 435
Chapter 15 Automating Daily Work with Simple
            Macros 449
Chapter 16 Understanding Templates and Projects . . . 481

PART VI APPENDIXES. 507
A Keyboard Shortcut Keys 509
B Predefined Toolbars and Property Bars . . . 517
C Glossary 533

Index 545

Contents

Introduction xxi

PART I LET'S GET STARTED 1

Chapter 1 Introducing Corel WordPerfect Suite 8 3
What's Included in Corel WordPerfect Suite 8? 4
Why Would I Use Corel WordPerfect Suite 8? 5
Installing Corel WordPerfect Suite 8 7
    System Requirements 7
    The Installation Process 8
Starting WordPerfect 8 10

Chapter 2 The Look and Feel of WordPerfect 8 13
What's on the Window? 14
    Windows 95 Elements 15
    Elements Unique to WordPerfect 8 18
And What You Can't See 28
    QuickMenus 28
    Reveal Codes 29
    A Few Thoughts About Customization 32

Chapter 3 So How Does WordPerfect Work? 45
The Very Basics 46
    Creating a New Document 46
    Naming, Saving, and Closing a Document 51
    Tracking Multiple Versions of the Same Document 54
    Managing Your Files and Folders 58
    Editing or Opening an Existing Document 59
Some Useful Editing Techniques 60
    How to Move Around in a Document 60

  Fixing Those Darn Typos 62
  For the Love of a Mouse 66
 Getting Help When You Really Need It 71
  Using the Windows 95-Style Help 71
  Using Ask the PerfectExpert 72
  Getting Online Help 74

PART II DAILY TASKS 77

Chapter 4 The Basic Business Letter 79

 Creating a Letter from Scratch 80
  Some Basic Layout Thoughts 80
  Starting Your Letter 84
  Adding a Date 85
  Addresses, Addresses, Addresses Everywhere! 86
  Typing the Body of the Letter 92
  Refining the Document 97
  Center, Flush Right, and Justification 108
  Numbering the Pages 110
 Using a Project to Create a Letter 114

Chapter 5 Fine-Tuning and Enhancing Your Documents ... 119

 Using Spell Checker, Thesaurus, and Grammatik Features for Accuracy ... 120
  Checking for Correct Spelling 121
  Using Thesaurus for Alternative Words and Word Meanings 129
  Checking for Grammatical Accuracy 132
 Easy Tools for Improving Speed and Consistency in Your Documents 134
  Automatic Typing Tools 134
  Using Styles for Consistency 140

Chapter 6 Printing Your Document to Paper, E-Mail, or Fax 151

 Printing a Document 152
 What About an Envelope? 156
  Creating an Envelope 156
  Printing an Envelope 158
 How About Labels? 159
  Selecting a Label Definition 160
  Typing and Printing Labels 161

Contents

Troubleshooting Printing Problems 163
    The Printed Document Looks Different Than It Did On-Screen 163
    I Sent It to Print, But Nothing Came Out! 165
Sending a Document via E-Mail or Fax. 166
    Using Your E-Mail Service 167
    Printing to Fax Services 168

Chapter 7 Same Letter to Lots of Different People! 171

Understanding Merge Terminology 172
Creating the Sales Letter Merge. 174
    Creating the Form Letter 174
    Selecting Address Book Entries and Performing the Merge. 180
    Adding Envelopes to the Merge 182
Merges Using Other Data Sources. 184
    Merging with a Database 185
    Creating a WordPerfect Data File from Scratch 190

Part III Reports and Presentations. 199

Chapter 8 An Organized Report Starts with an Outline . . 201

Choosing an Outline Definition 202
    Typing an Outline Definition. 205
    Understanding Outline Families 207
    Adding New Items to an Outline 209
Modifying an Outline's Appearance. 212
    Creating a Custom Outline Definition 213
    Saving a Custom Definition for Use with Other Documents 220

Chapter 9 Using Tables for Powerful Data Presentation . . 223

A Simple Revenue Projection Table 224
    Creating the Projected Gross Revenue Table 224
    Dressing Up the Table's Appearance 238
    Using Table Math and Formulas 245
Using Floating Cells to Include Calculations in Text. 251
    Computing Payments for a Financed Equipment Purchase. 251
Using Table Data to Produce a Chart 253
Sorting Table Entries 260

Chapter 10	**Maintaining Your Report's Organization** **265**
	Including Document References in a Report 266
	Creating a Table of Contents 268
	Creating a List of Report Items. 276
	Creating an Index. 280
	Creating a Table of Authorities 286
	Using Cross-References to Point to Other Locations 292
	Generating the References 294
	Breaking Up Your Report Into Manageable Sections. 296
	Creating a Master Document 297
	Generating References from a Master Document 301
	Rolling the Whole Report Back Together Again. 301
	Connecting Other Items to a Document 304
	Linking Objects Using OLE. 304
	Hypertext Links to Other Documents. 307
	QuickLinks to the World Wide Web. 312

PART IV   CREATE A NEWSLETTER **315**

Chapter 11	**Placing the Text and Masthead** **317**
	Creating a Newsletter from Scratch 318
	Developing an Effective Masthead. 318
	Using Columns to Control Text Flow 327
	Dressing Up Columns with Borders and Fills 335
	Creating Asymmetric Columns. 338
	Using Parallel Columns to Type a Script 340

Chapter 12	**Adding Graphics Elements to the Newsletter.** **345**
	A Few Design Thoughts 346
	Adding Images to Your Newsletter. 347
	Using the Scrapbook to Locate a Corel Clipart Image 348
	Adding an Image from a File. 351
	Manipulating the Images 356
	Sizing Graphics and Placing Them Effectively 357
	Changing Graphic Attributes 368
	Editing an Image 374
	Moving the Headline Provides the Final Touch 380

Contents

Adding a Screen Shot to Documentation................................381
    Adding a Callout to the Figure.................................382
    Adding a Caption to the Screen Shot Figure....................391
Including a Graphic on Every Page Using a Watermark................392

Part V Tell Me More 395

Chapter 13 Using WordPerfect to Connect to the World . . 397
Creating a Web Document..398
    Publishing a WordPerfect Document to HTML....................399
    Creating a New Document Using a Web Template.................402
    Working with Hyperlinks......................................420
    Adding Other Objects to Your Web Page........................429
Publishing Pages to Your Web Site.................................431

Chapter 14 Equations—A Special Type of Graphic. 435
Starting the Equation Editor......................................437
Understanding the Equation Editor Toolbar.........................437
Understanding Style and Size in the Equation Editor...............439
    Changing the Style of an Equation............................439
    Changing the Size of an Equation.............................440
Creating a Simple Equation..441
Understanding How to Edit in the Equation Editor..................444
    Setting the Graphic Properties of an Equation................445

Chapter 15 Automating Daily Work with Simple Macros . . 449
Macro Basics..451
    Planning the Macro...451
    Understanding Macro Types....................................453
    Recording and Playing Macros.................................457
Editing a Macro...462
    Understanding Macro Commands.................................464
    Recording a Change to the faxform Macro......................467
    Compiling the faxform Macro..................................470
Getting Macro Help..472
    Using the Command Inserter to Add Commands to a Macro........472
    Using Macro Help...476
Converting Macros from Previous Versions..........................478

Chapter 16 Understanding Templates and Projects. 481

What are Projects and Templates? 482
Creating the Personal Letterhead Template. 484
    Creating a Category for Your Templates. 486
    Creating the Template 487
    Using Your Custom Template 489
Enhancing the Letterhead Template with Prompts 489
Associating a Macro with the Template 496
    Adding Objects to the Template 496
    Understanding Associations 499
Managing Projects 502
    Removing a Project 503
    Adding a Project 504

PART VI APPENDIXES. 507

Appendix A Keyboard Shortcut Keys. 509

Appendix B Predefined Toolbars and Property Bars 517

Predefined Toolbars 518
Property Bars 522
    Bars for Working with Graphic Features 523
    Formatting Property Bars 526
    Internet Publisher Property Bars 532
    Tables Property Bars. 531
    Specialty Property Bars 532

Appendix C Glossary. 533

Index 545

Hands-On Topics

Hiding the Guidelines	18
Creating a Memo Using the Memo Project	46
Naming and Saving the Memo	50
Archiving a Document	53
Storing Another Version	54
Retrieving an Archived Document	55
Using Find and Replace to Change Text	63
Using Find and Replace to Change a Font Face Throughout a Document	63
Selecting a Paper Size	79
Changing Page Margins	81
Adding a Letterhead	82
Adding Today's Date to Your Letter	83
Adding Names to Your Address Book	86
Inserting an Address Book Entry in a Document	88
Using the Windows Messaging/Exchange Address Book in WordPerfect Suite 8	89
Using Tabs to Align Text	92
Creating Simple Bulleted or Numbered Lists	95
Changing Font Faces and Font Sizes for Existing Text	100
Using Keyboard Quick Keys to Add Common Attributes	102
Using the Font Dialog Box	104
Including WordPerfect Characters	105
Using Center, Flush Right, and Justification	107
Creating Headers or Footers	110
Suppressing the Header from Page 1 of the Letter	112
Using the Business Letter Project	112
Creating the Sample Document	118
Using Spell-As-You-Go and Prompt-As-You-Go to Correct Misspellings	120
Adding a QuickCorrect Entry	123
Spell Checking a Document	124
Using Grammar-As-You-Go	130

Hands-On Topics

Creating a QuickWords Entry 133
Creating a Sample Document for Style Practice 141
Using the Predefined Heading Styles 142
Editing the Predefined Styles 142
Creating a QuickFormat Style 145
Creating a QuickStyle 146
Printing the Current Document to the Default Printer 150
Creating an Envelope 154
Selecting a Label Definition 158
Typing and Printing Address Labels 160
Sending an E-Mail Message 165
Sending the Current Document as a Fax 167
Typing the Letter 173
Creating a Merge Form from the Letter 173
Associating the Address Book with the Form Letter 174
Adding Field Locations to a Form Letter 176
Selecting Address Book Entries and Performing the Merge 178
Adding Envelopes to the Sales Letter Merge 180
Using a Paradox Database as a Data Source 184
Creating a WordPerfect Merge Data File from an ASCII Delimited File ... 186
Creating a Legal Caption Data File and Defining Field Names 189
Creating a Legal Caption Data File and Adding the Data 191
Creating a Legal Pleading Form 194
Choosing an Outline Definition for a Business Plan 202
Typing the Business Plan Outline 204
Rearranging the Business Plan Outline 205
Hiding and Displaying Outline Levels 206
Adding New Outline Items to the Business Plan 208
Adding Body Text to the Business Plan 209
Hiding and Redisplaying Body Text 209
Selecting a Different Outline Definition 211
Creating and Naming a Custom Definition 213
Defining (or Modifying) Level Styles for a Legal Brief 215
Saving the Legal Brief Definition 219
Using a Saved Style File in Another Document 219
Creating a Table 223
Using QuickFill to Complete a Series of Months 227
Rotating Text 228
Adding Columns to a Table 231

Hands-On Topics

Sizing the Row Heading Column 234
Creating a Title Row. 235
Adding Fills to the Title and Header Rows. 237
Modifying Table Lines 239
Setting Number Types and Aligning Text. 242
Summing Rows 244
Creating the Gross Revenue Formula. 247
Creating a Floating Cell That Calculates Payments. 250
Creating an Effective Chart Using Table Data 252
Enhancing the Chart 256
A Simple Alphabetic or Numeric Sort 259
Sorting By the Second Word in a Column 260
Using Sort to Extract Data 261
Creating a Sample Business Plan 265
Including Table of Content Marks in a Style 270
Defining the Table of Contents Location 272
Preparing a Document for a List of Tables 274
Marking Text for a List 276
Defining the List 277
Marking Words and Phrases for an Index. 280
Creating a Concordance File 282
Defining an Index 283
Defining a Table of Authorities Page 285
Marking Items for a Table of Authorities 288
Including a Cross-Reference in a Report 290
Renumbering the Document Page. 293
Generating the References. 293
Creating a Master Document and Subdocuments. 295
Creating a Master Document 297
Generating References from a Condensed Master Document 299
Expanding and Contracting the Master Document 300
Adding an Object to the Business Plan 303
Adding a Hypertext Link to the Business Plan 306
Adding a Bookmark-Based Hypertext Link to a Document 309
Adding a QuickLink to your Document 311
Creating a Masthead Using a Table for Layout 318
Creating a Masthead with TextArt 319
Sizing and Placing the Masthead 324
Creating an Article for Your Newsletter in Columnar Format 327

Sizing the Columns and Gutter Widths	331
Locking in Column Settings	331
Adding Lines Between the Columns	335
Creating Asymmetric Columns	337
Creating a Script Using Parallel Columns	339
Adding a Clipart Image to a Newsletter	348
Adding a Scrapbook Image from the CD	350
Adding a Drop Cap and a Graphic Image from a File	354
Positioning the Graphic Elements on the Newsletter	360
Setting Text Wrap Options for the Newsletter Graphic Boxes	362
Sizing Images on the Newsletter	365
Placing the Images in the Correct Order	368
Fading the Drop Cap's Background Image	370
Rotating an Image in a Graphic Box	372
Moving and Zooming an Image	373
Adding a Gradient Fill to the Paint Splash	375
Editing the Paint Tubes Image	377
Placing the Headline Over Both Columns	380
Capturing a Screen, Then Pasting It to a Document	382
Adding a Callout to the Screen Capture	385
Adding a Description to the Callout	388
Adding a Shape to the Callout	390
Adding a Caption to the Screen Shot Figure	391
Creating a New Web Page	402
Adding Text to the Web Page	403
Adding Bulleted Items to a Web Page	405
Including Columns in a Web Page	406
Adding a Table to a Web Page	408
Adjusting the Table Dimensions	411
Adding Graphics to a Web Page	414
Adding a TextArt Button	417
Inserting Lines in the Web Page	418
Changing the Text and Background Colors	419
Adding Web Pages for Linking	421
Creating a Text Hyperlink	423
Adding a Text Button Hyperlink	425
Attaching a Graphic to a Hyperlink	426
Adding Bookmarks to Hyperlinks	427
Adding a Sound Clip to a Web Page	430

Hands-On Topics

Converting Web Pages to HTML Format 432
Creating a New Equation 441
Editing an Equation 444
Formatting the Equation. 445
Recording the Fax Cover Sheet Macro. 459
Playing the faxform Macro 461
Opening the faxform Macro File for Editing 463
Adding a Footer to the faxform Macro. 468
Saving and Compiling the Macro Changes 472
Adding an IF Test to the faxform Macro 474
Using Macro Help to Find a Particular Command. 477
Creating a Category for Your Custom Letterhead. 486
Creating the Letterhead Template 487
Using the Letterhead Template 489
Adding Prompts to the Letterhead Template 490
Using the Letterhead Template 495
Creating a File Save Macro 497
Adding a Macro to a Template 498
Associating a Macro with the Pre Print Trigger. 502
Removing a Project from the Corel WordPerfect 8 Category. 503
Adding a Project. 504

Acknowledgments

Writing a book takes an incredible amount of dedication on the part of a full team of professionals. Thank you to every person who participated in this endeavor, at both Prima and Corel.

A very special thank you goes to Debbie Abshier for not only allowing me to write this book, but for her constant support during difficult deadlines. Debbie, you're absolutely the best! Without Joyce Nielsen who kept a close eye on the content, I'm sure every single list would be numbered in error. Chris Haidri used his considerable talents to straighten out my grammar and keep the final review process moving along with sensitivity. David Plotkin stepped in and provided Internet and equations expertise. Marla Lockhart verified every step in every activity, making sure that the technical quality was absolutely top-notch! The technical team at Corel was outstanding in their willingness to answer tough questions—especially Michelle Murphy-Crouteau for keeping us informed and on schedule. And much thanks to each and every person on the production team who had to endure many, many changes as we worked our way through each beta.

Finally, and most importantly, many thanks and much love to my husband, Bill. Your encouragement and quirky sense of humor kept me at it while you very capably managed the crowd at home! Galen, Jennifer, and Ritsuko, you all cheerfully took on lots of extra chores while I locked myself in the office one more time! Oh, and thanks for walking the dog, guys!

About the Authors

Gabrielle R. Nemes is the President of MicroTutor Training Services in Kent, Washington. She has authored, contributed to, or provided technical services for several other WordPerfect books, including self-publishing almost 15 years of PC courseware. In addition to maintaining Certified Instructor status for WordPerfect products, Gabrielle is a Corel Premier Solution Partner. She's a WordPerfect devotee, regularly consulting and developing macros and office solutions for law firms and government agencies in the Seattle area. She can be reached via e-mail at **microtut@sprynet.com**.

David Plotkin is a Data Administrator for Longs Drug Stores in Walnut Creek, CA. He has written several books on computers, and over 1000 articles in various computer periodicals. He is an expert at computer system design, specializing in capturing requirements and programming database applications.

Introduction

"Just tell me how to get my work done!" is probably the most common refrain I hear when consulting or training. As a computer trainer, I've had the privilege of helping hundreds of businesses automate their daily work. With only a few exceptions (those real techies who just have to know how and why everything works!), most people just want to know the *essentials*—those indispensable, basic, how-to techniques necessary for daily use.

You certainly don't need to know everything about WordPerfect 8 before you can jump in and begin creating some pretty sophisticated documents. You just need to know what features and functions are used for the types of documents you create, and the easiest method to use them. This book shows you how to type a letter, create a memo, type a report, create a Web page, and so on, using WordPerfect 8. Along the way, you'll learn important information about WordPerfect features and functions so that you're ready to tackle other tasks on your own.

This book focuses on the easiest method to get specific tasks done in WordPerfect 8. You'll learn that other methods exist and how to find out more about them, but the focus here is on the easiest, most effective way—not every way.

WordPerfect 8 is the most important tool to completing your daily work you have on your computer. This book helps you get the most use from this tool in the shortest amount of time, so you can keep getting work done while you learn!

Can You Use This Book?

Absolutely! This book is for everyone who uses WordPerfect: busy professionals who need to create letters and reports; administrative staff who maintain an incredible amount of highly formatted written work; students who need to create research papers, complete with cross-references and tables of content; and systems managers who need to know how to best implement WordPerfect 8 in their offices.

This book will provide you with valuable insight into how WordPerfect works. Perhaps you've already used a previous version of WordPerfect, or another word processing program. If so, you'll find out how this new version of WordPerfect works and how you can effectively use the new features to lighten your workload. If you're completely new to word processing, you'll quickly pick up the basics!

Overview of Contents

Almost every chapter in this book focuses on typical business tasks rather than a set of features. In this sense, *The Essential WordPerfect 8 Book* differs from other reference books on WordPerfect. The chapters in this book are organized by grouping similar tasks.

Part I, "Let's Get Started," introduces you to the things that are essential to every WordPerfect task. You'll learn how to interpret and use the WordPerfect window elements, type and correct mistakes, name and save your documents, and locate a document you've lost. You'll also discover where to find more information and where you can go to get technical support.

In Part II, "Daily Tasks," you'll create a basic business letter and its envelope, send a sales letter using merge, and learn how to create a legal court caption. Along the way you'll discover how to format the document, create bulleted lists, and work with effective fonts. Automatic typing tools will help you speed up your work, while features such as spell checking, grammar checking, and a dynamite thesaurus will help you maintain the accuracy of your documents.

Part III, "Reports and Presentations," provides you with the tools to organize your document, and maintain that organization. You'll create a business plan while learning about outlines, tables, and charts. Then you'll learn how to use reference techniques like a table of contents, an index, and cross-references. You'll also use WordPerfect's master document and subdocument features to create manageable sections and chapters, and combine them into an organized report.

In Part IV, "Create a Newsletter," you'll start getting visual—creating a newsletter and a script, complete with columns and graphics. TextArt will be used to dress-up a masthead for the newsletter. You'll also learn the basics of using the Scrapbook to insert images to a document and how to make easy changes to clipart. WordPerfect now includes a versatile set of drawing tools which you will use to annotate screen shots for documentation.

Part V, "Tell Me More," explains how to create a Web page using WordPerfect 8 and how to include an equation in a technical document. You'll learn to create and edit a personalized fax cover sheet and custom letterhead while using macros, projects, and templates.

Lastly, and perhaps most importantly, three appendixes are included. Appendix A offers a convenient list of the shortcut keystrokes you can use to access WordPerfect 8's features, Appendix B identifies the buttons on the most commonly used toolbars and property bars, and Appendix C provides a helpful glossary defining terms unique to WordPerfect.

Conventions Used in This Book

Throughout this book, some common conventions are used so that the directions and discussions are clear and concise. As you create the sample documents, text that you should type appears in **bold**. When existing text is referred to, it appears in `monospace`. And, periodically, you'll see references to specific codes that are visible on-screen in Reveal Codes. These codes also appear in `monospace` in this book, as in `[TabSet]`. *Italic* is used to draw your attention to new terms when they are first introduced.

You can perform most tasks in WordPerfect 8 using either the keyboard or the mouse. Sometimes, you even need a combination of both. The instructions you'll see in this book often read like the following: "Choose File, Open, or click the Open button on the toolbar." Because you might prefer a different method of making menu selections than I do, here are a few ways you can interpret this instruction:

- Point with the mouse to the File menu, then click. The File menu opens. Then click the Open item in the menu.
- Press [Alt]+[F] to open the File menu. Then press [O] to choose the Open command. Notice that the letters F and O are underlined both on-screen and in this book. This designates them as *selection keys*. Whenever you see an underlined letter in a menu name, you can hold down the [Alt] key and press the selection letter to open that menu. After a menu has been opened, you can just press the selection key by itself to select a particular menu item.
- Click the Open button in the toolbar. Keep in mind that you can rest your mouse pointer on any button in any toolbar to see a QuickTip which identifies the button by name.

> YOU'LL LEARN MORE ABOUT IDENTIFYING TOOLBARS AND QUICKTIPS THROUGHOUT THIS BOOK.

Keys that should be pressed one after the other are separated by a comma. For example, "Press [End], [Home]" means that you should first press and release the [End] key, then press and release the [Home] key.

Keys that should be pressed together are separated by a plus (+) symbol, as in "Press [Ctrl]+[Home]." It's usually easiest to press and hold the first key ([Ctrl]) while you press the second key ([Home]). Then release both keys to perform the function.

Some functions require that you use both keypress techniques. For example, "Press Ctrl+Home, Home" means that you should press and hold Ctrl while you press Home. Release both keys, then press and release Home again.

Many instructions also assume that you are familiar with these common mouse actions:

- **Point.** Move the mouse so that the mouse pointer touches the item to which you are referring.
- **Click.** Point to the item, then press and release the primary mouse button. The primary mouse button is used to make selections and is almost always the left button.
- **Double-click, Triple-click, Quadruple-click.** Point to the item, then press and release the primary mouse button twice, three times, or four times (depending on the instruction) in quick succession. It may take a bit of practice to get your timing just right on these multiple-click instructions.

If you're having difficulty double-clicking an item to make a menu or dialog box selection, click it once, then press the Enter key. This performs exactly the same function as double-clicking.

- **Right-click.** This term means that you should point to the item, then press and release your secondary mouse button—usually the rightmost button on your mouse. If you've reassigned your mouse buttons, however, you need to press and release whichever button you use as your secondary button.

> YOU'LL LEARN MORE ABOUT THE SHADOW CURSOR IN CHAPTER 2.

- **Drag.** Press and hold down the primary mouse button while you move the mouse until the object moves to a new location. Typically, as you drag with the mouse, a special *shadow cursor* jumps along with you indicating where the selected item will go. Then, when you release the mouse button, the object appears in that new location.

Special Elements

Did you notice the two special elements—the gray box in the margin and the tip—in the preceding section? These are just two of the special notations used to draw your attention to important information. Special elements used in this book include the following:

INTRODUCTION

Tips provide suggestions about other ways you can get things done. They might describe little-known standard techniques, helpful shortcuts, or clever tricks for using WordPerfect.

There aren't too many, but *cautions* are important elements designed to steer you away from making critical mistakes as you work. You'll see cautions when you're in danger of losing work; many cautions will also explain what actions to take in case you do have difficulty.

Notes provide just a little bit more—sometimes of a more technical nature, and sometimes just more background information to help you understand exactly what's going on.

As often as possible, I've included locations on the Internet, such as **http://www.corel.com**, where you can find updates, new information, or even freebies. These helpful locations appear alongside a Find It Online icon.

Hands On: Demonstrating Exactly How to Get the Job Done

> A BOX IN THE MARGIN POINTS YOU TO ANOTHER LOCATION IN THE BOOK WHERE YOU CAN LEARN MORE ABOUT THE SUBJECT AT HAND.

Most importantly, hands-on activities appear for most techniques discussed in this book. These short exercises provide step-by-step instructions to accomplish the task being presented. You can follow along using the examples provided, or you can use similar documents of your own—that way you'll actually get some work done while you're learning!

> **Sidebars Provide Supplementary Information**
>
> Sidebars add interesting background or additional facts about WordPerfect. You can read them to find out all the details provided, or just quickly skim their content and then move on.

Contacting Us

Prima Publishing welcomes your feedback, and would like to hear more about the kinds of help you need, other computing topics you'd like to read about, or any other questions you have.

For a catalog, call 1-800-632-8676 or visit the Prima Publishing Web site at **http://www.primapublishing.com**.

Part I
Let's Get Started

1   INTRODUCING COREL WORDPERFECT SUITE 8 1

2   THE LOOK AND FEEL OF WORDPERFECT 8 13

3   SO HOW DOES WORDPERFECT WORK? 45

1
Introducing Corel WordPerfect Suite 8

In This Chapter

- Suite Components
- System Requirements
- Installation
- Starting WordPerfect 8

Corel WordPerfect 8 is a continuation of the long line of award-winning WordPerfect word processing programs. Corel WordPerfect Suite 8 is a gathering of Corel programs that mesh tightly to form an unparalleled solution for creative documents. With WordPerfect 8 alone, you have the tools necessary to develop complex office solutions, complete with graphics, drawings, Internet links, equations, and mathematical formulas, to name just a few features. Combine WordPerfect 8 with the remaining Suite programs and you're able to handle just about any task that comes your way.

This chapter acquaints you with each element of Corel WordPerfect Suite 8, and provides you with a few practical examples for which you might use the program features. However, this book focuses on WordPerfect 8, the central program of Corel WordPerfect Suite 8. No doubt you've installed other programs in the Suite, and, where appropriate, you'll be directed to other programs. Refer to the Reference Center on your Corel WordPerfect Suite 8 CD for a more in-depth look at the remaining Suite products.

What's Included in Corel WordPerfect Suite 8?

There are two separate versions of Corel WordPerfect Suite 8, the Standard Suite and the Professional Suite. The Professional Suite includes some additional applications and fonts for power users or those on a corporate network. Also, you'll find more features for CorelCENTRAL in the Professional Suite than in the Standard Suite. Other than that, however, the corresponding programs in each Suite are identical (for example, WordPerfect 8 in the Standard Suite is identical to WordPerfect 8 in the Professional Suite).

The Standard Suite includes the following:

- Corel WordPerfect 8, for word processing tasks
- Corel Quattro Pro 8, for spreadsheet tasks
- Corel Presentations 8, for drawing and presentation projects
- Corel Photo House 1.1, with a full set of photo-editing tools
- CorelCENTRAL, an address book with calendaring, scheduling, and a linked cardfile. At the time this book is written, a voucher for CorelCENTRAL appears in the Suite packaging. Send the voucher to Corel to receive CorelCENTRAL.
- Envoy 7 Viewer, for creating and viewing electronic documents
- Fonts with over 1,000 choices!

The first 100 fonts are automatically installed with the Suite. The remaining fonts can be selected and installed from the CD during a Custom installation.

- Bitstream Font Navigator 2.0, an outstanding tool to help you manage and install fonts
- Clipart and photos—over 10,000 images are included
- Software Development Kit, a useful tool when you develop for the Suite
- Corel Barista, a Java programming tool that lets you publish Web pages without programming
- Corel WordPerfect SGML Layout Designer tools are included to enable you to include SGML tags in a WordPerfect document (SGML is short for Standard Generalized Markup Language)
- Quick View Plus, a program that enables you to preview files without regard to their native format
- Corel Versions, archiving software that enables you to track document versions
- The Reference Center, a set of documentation manuals for Corel WordPerfect Suite 8 in Envoy 7 format

The Professional Suite includes all programs in the Standard Suite, except for Corel Photo House, plus these:

- Corel Paradox 8, a WordPerfect integrated, relational database
- Full version of CorelCENTRAL, including Netscape Communicator 4, Calendaring & Scheduling, Address Book Cardfile, Netscape Messenger, Netscape Composer, Netscape Collabra, and Netscape Conference
- Corel Time Line, a project management and scheduling program
- Corel WEB.SiteBuilder, to create and maintain a full Internet Web site
- Envoy printer driver, enabling you to create your own Envoy files

Why Would I Use Corel WordPerfect Suite 8?

Corel has done an exceptional job of combining Windows 95 programs which build on each other to help you create flexible and very powerful applications. Here's a possible scenario to give you some ideas:

Suppose that you're responsible for creating an online reference library that contains company policies and procedures. Your company has offices all over the United States. Furthermore, your company is now developing an intranet site.

There's a tremendous amount of text involved—much of which has already been created and is available on your in-office network. Some document files have been created in various versions of Word, some in the DOS WordPerfect 5.1 version, and others in WordPerfect for Windows versions 7 and 8.

In addition, several existing charts diagram product and sales flow by department. These charts are regularly updated and the desire is to include them in the reference library. The company logo has never been converted to a computer image of any kind, but the CEO wants to be sure that it's included in all online documents. Whew, quite a project! Using several of the Corel WordPerfect Suite 8 components, however, you'll be able to accomplish this formidable task easily.

Here are some thoughts about *one* method of creating the online documents. WordPerfect 8 contains superior file conversion features to allow you to accurately open and edit files from any previous version of WordPerfect, as well as from other major programs, such as word processing, spreadsheet, and graphic programs. Using this capability, it's a simple task to edit any file on your company network and publish it for inclusion on the web site.

From within WordPerfect 8 you can add links to other web pages and other documents, thus quickly tying documents together. A WordPerfect 8 file can easily provide links to other document types, such as Quattro Pro files, Presentation files, or Paradox files. Within any of these programs, you can add further links where necessary—or even add Java applets (small applications written using the Java programming language).

After all links are added and edits are complete, you can publish your document directly as a web page in HTML format. Or, here's a thought—you can even publish your documents to Envoy 7, retaining any Internet links that you have included. Now, using the embedded Envoy 7 viewer, visitors to your intranet site can view your documents with *exactly* the same formatting the documents had when created in WordPerfect 8. All headers, footers, page numbers, cross-references, and so on will be in place. A visitor can then view or print the file, and it will look exactly as it did in WordPerfect 8.

If you've purchased the Professional version of Corel WordPerfect Suite 8, you can use Corel WEB.SiteBuilder to create an entire intranet (or Internet) site, easily pulling together all the documents and files you've edited and published. WEB.SiteBuilder contains galleries of pre-built components, including backgrounds, buttons, and banners.

Don't forget the CEO's instructions to include the company logo! Using Corel Presentations, you can easily manipulate the image after you've scanned it on your company scanner. Then you can edit the image, cleaning it up or dressing it up as you desire. You can even create a full-blown slide show as an introduction to your company, then publish it to the Web using HTML, Corel Barista, or Presentation's Show On The Go.

Barista is a tool developed by Corel that allows you to publish Java-based Web documents from any Windows 95 application.

Installing Corel WordPerfect Suite 8

As with most Windows 95 programs, installation of Corel WordPerfect Suite 8 is easy and automated. You need to answer only a few questions and Corel's installation program takes care of the rest for you.

System Requirements

Before beginning the installation, however, you need to know a few things. First, is your system adequate to run Corel WordPerfect Suite 8? Minimum system requirements for Corel WordPerfect Suite 8 are:

- Windows 95 or Windows NT 4.0
- A minimum 486/66 processor
- At least 8 MB of RAM

In my opinion, more than 8 MB of RAM is essential. Shoot for at least 16 MB!

- At least 50 MB of hard disk space is required to install and run Corel WordPerfect Suite 8 from the CD. You'll need about 120 MB of hard disk space to perform a Typical installation.

I recommend having at least twice that much hard disk space. The Typical installation takes about 120 MB and you'll want some room to maneuver. If you install everything, you'll need a minimum of 300 MB.

PART I • LET'S GET STARTED

Note — Disk space requirements vary according to the sector size of your hard disk. The Setup program indicates the correct figure for *your* destination disk.

- A CD-ROM drive for installation—only minimal installations of the core applications can be ordered on 3.5" diskettes
- VGA or higher monitor
- Mouse or tablet

As with most Windows 95 programs, bigger is better. WordPerfect 8 runs reasonably well on a 486/66 system with 16 MB of RAM, but it really screams on my Pentium 200 with 32 MB of RAM.

The Installation Process

On most Windows 95 systems, inserting a CD into the CD-ROM drive automatically starts the CD. This means that the starting installation file for Corel WordPerfect Suite 8 will run and the first installation window will automatically appear. If your CD-ROM drive is not configured for autoplay, start with the first step below; if autoplay *is* active, start with step 4 below:

1. Be sure that no other programs are running. From the Windows 95 taskbar, choose Start, Settings, Control Panel.
2. Double-click the Add/Remove Programs icon.
3. Place the Corel WordPerfect Suite 8 CD into the CD-ROM drive if it's not already inserted, and then click Install. After Windows 95 locates the setup file for Corel WordPerfect Suite 8, the installation program begins.

Note — If the CD or disk isn't already inserted, Windows 95 prompts you to insert the CD or installation disk. Insert the CD or disk, then click Next. You might need to click the Browse button, locate the correct installation file (setup.exe), and select it. Then click Finish to continue the installation process.

4. Click the text button labeled Corel WordPerfect Suite Setup to begin. Corel copies a few temporary files to your Windows 95 temp directory and then prompts you to continue.

Note

> As you point to each text item, the text *jumps* forward, indicating that it really is a button. A description of the included applications for that button appears at the bottom of the installation window.

5. Step through each dialog box, reading and accepting the Corel Licensing Agreement, and completing the entry of your serial number in the appropriate fields.
6. To install the most common Corel WordPerfect Suite 8 program set, choose Typical when prompted for Installation Type.

Note

> Choose Custom instead of Typical if you want to install only specific programs, or if, for example, you plan to write your own macros from scratch rather than simply recording them. The Custom installation option allows you to pick and choose each component for each program, including the WordPerfect 8 macro help file. I usually choose a Custom installation because I like to see exactly where everything is copied and what my possible choices are for extra program goodies such as additional projects, fonts, or help files. If you're fairly new to computers, however, choose Typical and let Corel make the decisions for you.

7. After you've decided on the installation type, you're asked to verify which drive should be used for the Suite. You can change drives or change the default path used by the Suite. After you've decided where to install, choose Next.
8. The next dialog box asks you to select which components of the Suite you want to install. The most commonly used Suite components are checked. Notice that you can click any of the Suite components and see a brief description of that product. At a minimum, you want to install Corel WordPerfect Suite 8 and probably Corel Presentations 8 (so that you can easily create a slide-show presentation or edit clipart and other graphics). I also recommend that you install Envoy 7 so that you can read the Reference Center manuals. When you've made your selection, choose Next.
9. Setup asks you to verify your choices. If everything is okay, choose Install. Setup copies files from the CD to your hard drive and configures your system to work with Corel WordPerfect Suite 8.

PART I • LET'S GET STARTED

Tip

You can go back through your choices to make changes by clicking the <u>B</u>ack button.

When the file copy process is complete (this can take a long time if you've chosen a Custom installation or selected extra components), Setup prompts you to restart your computer so that file configuration can be performed. Click the Restart button; when the computer restarts, Setup completes its file configuration. When you see a dialog box indicating that installation was successful, it's time to get to work!

Note

After you click Restart, Setup restarts your computer for you. If, for some reason, Setup cannot automatically restart the system, choose Start, Shut Down, Restart Computer from the Windows 95 taskbar.

Starting WordPerfect 8

Starting *any* program in Windows 95 is easy; WordPerfect 8 is no exception. There are several methods you can use to actually start WordPerfect 8. Here are a few of your choices:

- From the Windows 95 desktop, choose Start, Corel WordPerfect Suite 8, Corel WordPerfect 8 (see Figure 1-1).

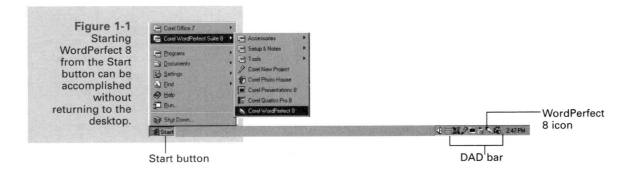

Figure 1-1
Starting WordPerfect 8 from the Start button can be accomplished without returning to the desktop.

Chapter 1 • Introducing Corel WordPerfect Suite 8

- From any file list, such as Windows Explorer or My Computer, double-click the file you want to open in WordPerfect 8. WordPerfect 8 starts with your selected file open.
- To open a file in WordPerfect that you've recently worked on, choose Start, <u>D</u>ocuments and then select the file. WordPerfect 8 starts with the file open in the document window.
- Installation of WordPerfect 8 typically loads several Corel WordPerfect Suite 8 icons to the status area of the Windows 95 taskbar. Cumulatively, these icons are called the *DAD bar* (for <u>D</u>esktop <u>A</u>pplication <u>D</u>irector). To launch WordPerfect 8 from the taskbar, click its icon.

Note — **Your selection of menu choices and icons in the DAD bar may differ, depending on your Corel WordPerfect Suite 8 installation or other programs on your system.**

Now that you've successfully installed Corel WordPerfect Suite 8 and learned how to start WordPerfect 8, you're on the way to becoming a WordPerfect 8 master!

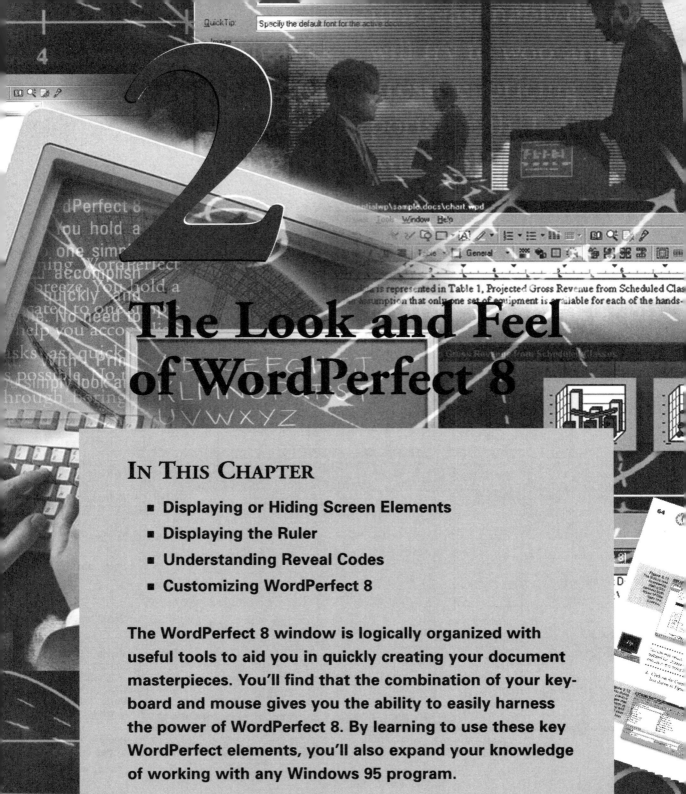

The Look and Feel of WordPerfect 8

IN THIS CHAPTER

- **Displaying or Hiding Screen Elements**
- **Displaying the Ruler**
- **Understanding Reveal Codes**
- **Customizing WordPerfect 8**

The WordPerfect 8 window is logically organized with useful tools to aid you in quickly creating your document masterpieces. You'll find that the combination of your keyboard and mouse gives you the ability to easily harness the power of WordPerfect 8. By learning to use these key WordPerfect elements, you'll also expand your knowledge of working with any Windows 95 program.

PART I • LET'S GET STARTED

This chapter guides you through the basic principals of working with the default window elements for WordPerfect 8. In addition, you'll be introduced to the steps of customizing your WordPerfect window so that it more appropriately reflects your own working habits.

What's on the Window?

Figure 2-1 displays the default window (with the addition of the ruler bar, to be discussed later in this chapter) that appears when you begin working with Word-Perfect 8. You'll want to refer often to Figure 2-1 as you read this section.

The WordPerfect window generally starts in full-screen mode, although you can work with less than a full screen by clicking the Windows 95 Restore button. Refer to the list of Windows 95 elements later in this chapter to locate the Restore button.

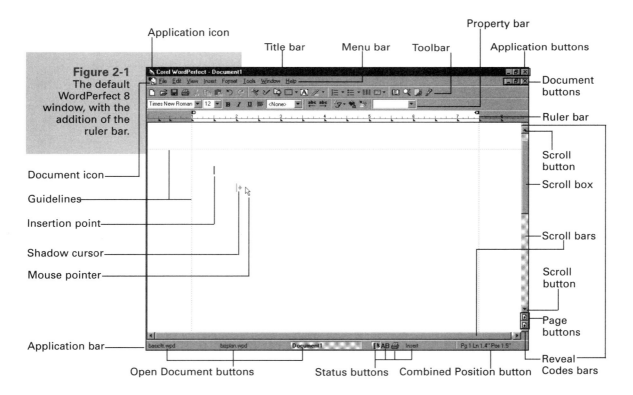

Figure 2-1 The default WordPerfect 8 window, with the addition of the ruler bar.

Chapter 2 • The Look and Feel of WordPerfect 8

The elements on the WordPerfect 8 window can be logically grouped as discussed in the next few sections.

Drafting or creating text sometimes requires an empty, non-distracting window. You can temporarily turn off all bars, whether WordPerfect or Windows specific, by choosing View, Hide Bars, or pressing Alt+Shift+F5. The Hide Bars Information dialog box appears each time you hide the bars unless you check the Do Not Show This Message next Time I Hide Bars check box. From this dialog box, you need to click OK to actually hide the bars. If guidelines were displayed prior to hiding the bars, they will appear on the resulting window. Even with the bars hidden, you can continue to use any hot key combination for a menu item, such as Alt+R to open the Format menu. To return the bars to the Window, press −.

Windows 95 Elements

Several elements appear universally in all Windows 95 applications. Figure 2-2 identifies each Windows 95 element. In addition it displays the Windows 95 taskbar.

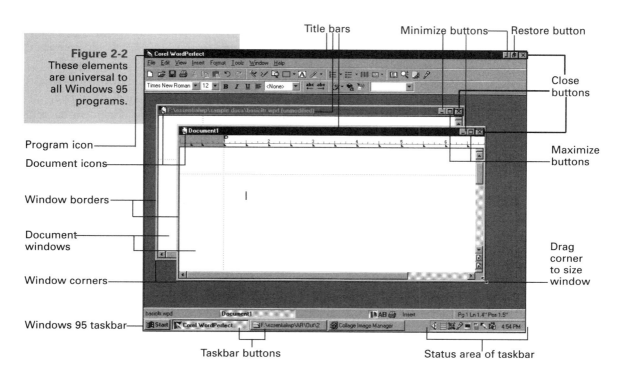

Figure 2-2 These elements are universal to all Windows 95 programs.

The following listing describes the Windows 95 elements and provides you with some thoughts about how you might use them in WordPerfect 8:

- **Windows**. All programs run in a window. Typically, a program or document opens in full-screen mode. However, both programs and documents can be placed in partial-screen mode by clicking the Restore button. This provides the capability to view more than one document window at the same time. A partial-screen window can be sized by clicking the Restore button and then dragging its edges with the mouse. Notice the double-headed mouse pointer at the lower-right corner of the document window in Figure 2-2. A double-headed mouse pointer appears when dragging a window border or corner.

- **Title bar**. The WordPerfect 8 program window and all document windows include title bars. Usually, as displayed in Figure 2-1, the document window is maximized—it takes up the entire space of the program window. With the document window maximized, the document title bar is combined with the program window's title bar. However, as displayed in Figure 2-2, a document window can be less than full size. In that case, the document displays its own title bar.

  Title bars display the name of the current program, Corel WordPerfect, and usually the name of the current document or open file. For example, a full-windowed document named `C:\MyFiles\Examples.wpd` would appear in the title bar as `Corel WordPerfect - C:\MyFiles\Examples.wpd`. WordPerfect also presents the status of a document in the title bar, where possible. For example, if no changes or edits have been made to an open document, the title bar appends `(unmodified)` after the document name. You might also see `(Read-Only)` to indicate that a file cannot be saved with the current filename.

  In WordPerfect 8, if no document has been opened, or a new document has been created which has not yet been saved and named, the title bar will display `Document1`. With the two title bars combined, therefore, the title bar would display `Corel WordPerfect - Document1`.

- **Program and document icons**. The program icon is the same one that appears in the Start menu, in a file window, on the desktop, or even in a taskbar button. It's a quick, visual method of identifying a program. The document icon, similarly, provides a visual identification of the document type. Clicking a program or document icon opens a menu of appropriate commands to minimize, restore, maximize, or close. Double-clicking a program or document icon closes the program or document.

- **Minimize buttons**. Click the program window's Minimize button to minimize WordPerfect (or any active program) to the Windows 95 taskbar. Similarly, click a document window's Minimize button to minimize that document to the bottom of the WordPerfect window. If you've minimized WordPerfect or a document, click its taskbar or application bar button to restore it to its previous screen size.
- **Restore button**. Click the Restore button to change the program window or document window size from full-screen to partial-screen, and back again. When a window is displayed in less than full-screen mode, a Maximize button is displayed in this position.
- **Maximize button**. The Maximize button is the reverse toggle of the Restore button. An example of a Maximize button can be seen in the document window of Figure 2-2. Click the Maximize button to return a window to full-screen mode.
- **Close button**. Click a Close button to close and exit the current program or document. This is a handy method of exiting WordPerfect when you are finished with the program, or of closing a document when you're finished with the document.

Note

If you click the Close button on any document window that is not in unmodified status, WordPerfect prompts you to save the file before it exits.

- **Windows 95 taskbar**. The taskbar displays buttons for each open program, along with useful information such as the status of a modem, a volume control icon, or other programs that load icons into the status area. In addition, you can start other programs or Windows 95 tasks using the Start menu, opened by clicking the Start button.

Tip

If you're a dedicated keyboard person, you can open the taskbar's Start menu by using the Windows keyboard button (if you have a newer keyboard that includes one), or by pressing Ctrl+Esc.

Elements Unique to WordPerfect 8

If you've worked with other Windows 95 applications, you are already familiar with the screen elements listed in the previous section. However, most of the elements which appear on the WordPerfect 8 window are unique to WordPerfect, although they may work and look similar to elements in other Windows 95 programs. If you're an experienced WordPerfect user but new to the Windows 95 environment, a great many of the elements are already familiar to you, but may look a little different in version 8.

Probably the best thing to remember as you explore this new version is that WordPerfect is still WordPerfect. In other words, functions and features with which you're familiar are still part of WordPerfect, although they may appear and behave in a slightly different manner. To confuse things, however, many of the features have been renamed—you'll especially notice this if you're upgrading from one of the WordPerfect for DOS versions.

Almost every window element in WordPerfect 8 can also be highly customized. To keep this section simple, customization is discussed later.

> SEE THE SECTION TITLED "A FEW THOUGHTS ABOUT CUSTOMIZATION" LATER IN THIS CHAPTER.

Document-Editing Elements

As mentioned previously, almost every element on the document window can be customized to meet your preferences. The guidelines can only be customized to the point of turning their display on or off.

SHADOW CURSOR

The shadow cursor jumps along with your mouse pointer to aid you in locating the exact position where the insertion point will reside if you click the mouse. Refer to Figure 2-1 to view a shadow cursor. Where no text has yet been created in the document, the shadow cursor is, by default, a light gray color. When you move the mouse through an existing area of the document, the shadow cursor is black.

Corel made a radical change in their approach to document creation with the release of WordPerfect 8. In the past, you were unable to move the insertion point beyond text that had already been created in a document. This meant that if you wanted to type text in the vertical middle of a page, you needed to add hard returns or select page centering to force your text to appear in that location. In WordPerfect 8, however, you can point to the rough center of a page—or anywhere on the page for that matter—and click. WordPerfect automatically adds all necessary formatting codes, such as tabs, spaces, or hard returns, in the background, thus allowing you to begin typing on the fly.

CHAPTER 2 • THE LOOK AND FEEL OF WORDPERFECT 8   19

While this seems handy, be careful. It's possible to end up with formatting instructions you don't want in your file merely by clicking the mouse at an unintended location. You can undo this unintentional formatting by immediately clicking back in the original text without having typed at the new location. All added codes will go away!

GUIDELINES

Margin guidelines appear by default when you start a new document in WordPerfect. They indicate visually where each of the margins is currently set. Additionally, guidelines will appear by default as you add headers, footers, columns or tables to your document. Using the mouse, you can drag a guideline to reposition any of the four margins. Figure 2-3 displays a document with several guidelines and the mouse pointer positioned over a guideline.

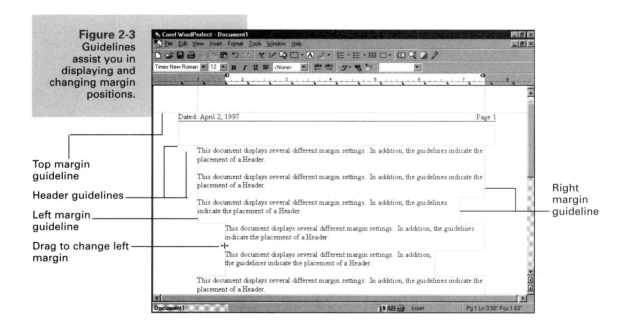

Figure 2-3 Guidelines assist you in displaying and changing margin positions.

Hands On: Hiding the Guidelines

You can turn off the display of guidelines using the steps below. When you turn off the guideline display using this method, the guidelines remain hidden for all new documents until you return to the Guidelines dialog box and select the guidelines you want to see.

1. Choose View, Guidelines. The Guidelines dialog box appears as shown in Figure 2-4.

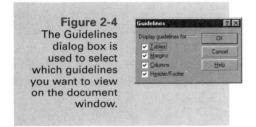

Figure 2-4 The Guidelines dialog box is used to select which guidelines you want to view on the document window.

2. Clear those check boxes for which you want to hide guidelines, and then click OK.

RULER

The ruler is one of the most useful tools of the WordPerfect window, in my opinion. It is used with the mouse to easily set tabs, change margins, manipulate columns, work with table cell margins, and so on. It's also a handy visual reminder of what the current settings are for a section of text.

Unfortunately, the ruler is not displayed by default. Once displayed, however, it remains for all new documents and WordPerfect sessions until the display is turned off again. To turn on the ruler display, choose View, Ruler. A checkmark then appears next to Ruler on the menu.

Since tabs, margins, columns, and tables are such an integral part of almost every document, you'll find references to working with the ruler in almost every chapter of this book. To get you started, however, Figure 2-5 identifies the symbols that appear on the ruler.

Chapter 2 • The Look and Feel of WordPerfect 8

Note: For ease of identifying the symbols, the paragraph symbols displayed in Figure 2-5 have been positioned away from the left and right margin symbols. On a document where no paragraph margin changes have occurred, these symbols appear with the margin symbols.

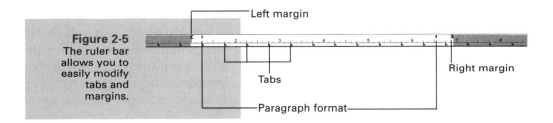

Figure 2-5 The ruler bar allows you to easily modify tabs and margins.

Symbol		Purpose
▐	Left Margin	Drag the left margin symbol to change the left margin in a document from this point forward, or for selected text.
▌	Right Margin	Drag the right margin symbol to change the right margin in a document from this point forward, or for selected text.
▐	Paragraph Format	Two symbols actually exist in the left paragraph format symbol—the top symbol sets the first line indent, and the bottom symbol sets the left margin. The right paragraph format symbol sets the right margin. All settings affect the selected paragraph(s) or the remainder of the document if no paragraphs are selected.
▲	Tabs	The tab symbols indicate where tabs are currently set. Tab symbols vary depending on the tab type—left, right, center, or decimal. Click the ruler bar to set a new tab, or drag an existing tab symbol off the ruler to delete it. Chapter 4, "The Basic Business Letter," discusses tabs in greater depth.

Tip

Double-click any of the symbols on the ruler to open its associated dialog box.

All Those Bars!

The remaining elements of the WordPerfect window can all be classified as *bars*—the menu bar, toolbar, property bar, scroll bars, and application bar. With the exception of the scroll bars, each of these bars can be customized. They provide you with a quick mouse method of editing, because you merely click a button within the bar to open a particular WordPerfect feature.

THE MENU BAR

A menu bar almost always appears immediately under the title bar in a Windows 95 program. Each program, however, has menu items that are used specifically for that program. As you saw in Figure 2-1, the WordPerfect 8 menu bar displays the currently selected main menu, along with the document icon at the far-left edge of the bar and document buttons at the far-right edge. However, as shown in Figure 2-2, these buttons appear in the document title bar when the document window is not maximized. Similar to buttons on the title bar, the document icon and document buttons provide you with easy methods of sizing the document window or closing the current document.

The WordPerfect 8 menu bar is not substantially different from those which appear in most other Windows 95 word processing packages. In fact, the main menu items are almost identical to those in other programs. The WordPerfect 8 menu is logically organized, grouping functions together under each main menu heading. For example, the items appearing on the File menu are those which deal with complete documents, not portions of documents. Under File you see items that allow you to create, open, and save documents, as well as informational functions that allow you to do tasks such as obtaining a count of all words in the file. Furthermore, you can set up margins for your entire file, send the file to another user on your e-mail system, or publish the file to the Internet.

> **EXAMPLES OF QUICKMENUS ARE DISCUSSED IN A LATER SECTION OF THIS CHAPTER TITLED "QUICK-MENUS."**

Similar to other Windows 95 programs, you can open a menu in WordPerfect 8 by clicking the menu item with your mouse, or by pressing a combination of [Alt] plus the underlined letter (known as the *selection letter* or *mnemonic*) in each menu item. For example, to open the Format menu using the keyboard, press [Alt]+[R]. An opened menu displays a list of those functions or features that can now be accessed.

As you move your mouse pointer over an opened menu, submenus or QuickTips may appear. A submenu is evidenced by a small right-pointing triangle at the right edge of the menu. Menu items that will open a dialog box are followed by an ellipsis, three dots immediately after the menu item (...). Commands that will produce a dialog box or will directly access a function display a QuickTip if you let your mouse pointer rest on the command for a moment. A QuickTip is a small box, usually with a light yellow background, that displays a phrase or two of help text describing the command to which you're pointing (see Figure 2-6).

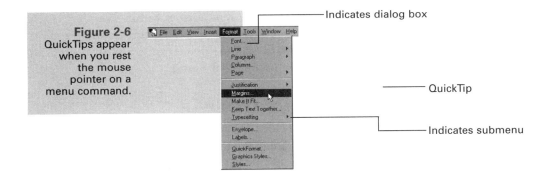

Figure 2-6
QuickTips appear when you rest the mouse pointer on a menu command.

The default WordPerfect menu bar isn't the only menu bar available to you. You can easily switch between the Internet Publisher menu, the WordPerfect 7 menu, and the WordPerfect 8 menu. Here's how:

1. With the mouse, point to the currently displayed menu bar.
2. Right-click to access the QuickMenu for the menu bar. Figure 2-7 shows the default QuickMenu. If you've added any additional menus, they also appear on the QuickMenu list.

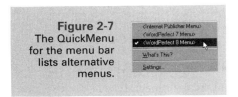

Figure 2-7
The QuickMenu for the menu bar lists alternative menus.

3. Select and click the menu you want to use. Your selected menu appears in the menu bar and the QuickMenu disappears.

You can easily switch between any defined menu using these steps.

THE TOOLBAR

As with the menu bar, the toolbar is a convenient method of accessing the most commonly used features of WordPerfect. Of course "commonly used" is a relative term, but you'll find that you frequently use features such as opening a document, printing it, cutting and pasting text from one place to another, or spell checking. These basic features, along with several others, appear on the default WordPerfect 8 toolbar.

The toolbar is a mouse-only editing aid. You cannot access a toolbar button via a keypress. Toolbars change as you access different features within WordPerfect. For example, when you work within a table, the Tables toolbar automatically appears. Similar to menu commands, resting the mouse pointer on a toolbar button displays a QuickTip to explain the purpose of that button.

SELECTING A DIFFERENT TOOLBAR

Fifteen predefined toolbars are provided for your use within WordPerfect 8. You can edit any toolbar by adding, deleting, and rearranging its contents or you can create as many custom toolbars as you need to provide easy access to all the features you regularly use. You can choose to display either pictures or text (pictures are the default), or both. You can also select up to ten toolbars for display, if you want. Of course, you may not have any room left to display the document text if you do so!

To select an alternative toolbar, use these steps:

1. Rest the mouse pointer on the currently displayed toolbar.
2. Right-click to display the toolbar QuickMenu.
3. Click the toolbar you want to use. The QuickMenu disappears and the selected toolbar is added to the window.

Similarly, return to the toolbar QuickMenu and click a checked choice if you want to remove it from the window.

CHANGING DISPLAY OPTIONS FOR TOOLBARS

The default position for a WordPerfect toolbar is immediately below the menu bar. You can easily move the toolbar to a different location on the window, or can modify its display options.

To move the toolbar, use these steps:

1. Position the mouse pointer over an unused area of the toolbar. The mouse pointer changes to a four-headed arrow.
2. Press and hold the mouse button, drag the mouse pointer to another location on the window, and release the mouse button. The mouse pointer returns to its normal appearance. Refer to Figure 2-8 to see the mouse pointer and a possible location for the toolbar.

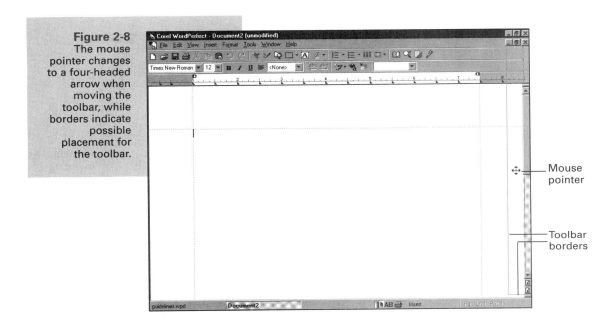

Figure 2-8
The mouse pointer changes to a four-headed arrow when moving the toolbar, while borders indicate possible placement for the toolbar.

Notice that while dragging the toolbar, its borders snap to the location where the toolbar will appear when released. If you drag to either of the four edges of the WordPerfect window, the toolbar remains a long rectangle. However, you also can drop the toolbar as a floating palette onto the top of the document window. The toolbar appears in the new location, as shown in Figure 2-9.

My work requires a lot of software customization for clients. I've defined a number of macros and other utilities that have been assigned to toolbar buttons. By now I have a *lot* of buttons, so my personal toolbar is displayed with two rows rather than the default one row. A maximum of three rows of toolbar buttons can be displayed. To change the number of button rows that can be displayed by the toolbar, use these steps:

1. Rest the mouse pointer over the toolbar, and then right-click. The toolbar QuickMenu appears.
2. Select Settings from the QuickMenu. The Customize Settings dialog box appears.
3. Choose the Options button to see the Toolbar Options dialog box (see Figure 2-10).

Figure 2-9
This toolbar now resides on the right side of the document window.

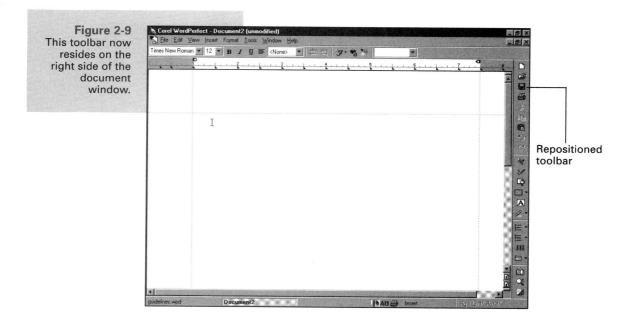

Repositioned toolbar

Figure 2-10
The Toolbar Options dialog box lets you customize the appearance of your toolbar.

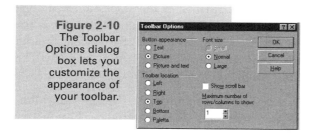

   4. Enter the number of toolbar rows or columns to be displayed in the Maximum Number of Rows/Columns to Show field. You can either type the desired number, from 1 to 3, or spin to the desired number with your mouse.

   5. Make any other changes you need, and then choose OK, Close to return to the document window.

The Toolbar Options dialog box is also used to modify the appearance of the toolbar. You can choose to display only text on the toolbar buttons, or both pictures and text. If you want, you can select an alternative font size for the button text.

PROPERTY BARS

Property bars, called *feature bars* in previous versions of WordPerfect, reside under the toolbar. They are yet another method, usually accessed with the mouse, of quickly using WordPerfect features. Almost all 42 predefined property bars are specific to WordPerfect tasks. For example, when you're creating a footnote, a property bar displays buttons for footnote functions, such as Go to Previous Footnote/Endnote and Go to Next Footnote/Endnote.

As with all other WordPerfect bars, a property bar can be edited, or have its display options modified, through its QuickMenu. For additional information on customizing bars, see the section titled "A Few Thoughts About Customization," later in this chapter.

A few property bar buttons can be accessed directly from the keyboard by pressing [Alt] plus [Shift] plus the mnemonic for the button.

SCROLL BARS

Scroll bars are the exception to the rule of customization. They are used to shift contents of a document left, right, up, or down within the document window, so that you can view the contents more clearly. Clicking one of the scroll arrows shifts the document one line or one position at a time. Dragging the scroll box shifts the document much farther, depending on how far you drag the scroll box. For example, if you drag the scroll box to the bottom of the vertical scroll bar, the document image shifts to the end of the document. You also can click the scroll bar above or below the scroll box to shift the document image one complete window.

Scrolling through a document does not move the insertion point. It merely shifts the portion of the document you are currently viewing. To edit in a location that's visible after scrolling, you first need to click with the mouse to place the insertion point in the desired position.

At the lower end of the vertical scroll bars are Next Page and Previous Page buttons, which you can click to shift the document view to the top of the next and previous page, respectively.

APPLICATION BAR

The application bar runs along the bottom of the WordPerfect window and is used to display general status information about the current working condition. Refer to Figure 2-1 if you are unsure of its location and appearance. By default, the application bar displays the current location of the insertion point, the status of the Insert/Typeover key, the currently selected printer, and the status of the shadow cursor. The application bar also displays document buttons for all open documents. Clicking a document button switches you to that document window.

Place the mouse pointer over any button in the application bar to see a QuickTip identifying the button. Click any of the application buttons to either open the dialog box associated with that feature, or to toggle a feature. For example, click the CAPS button to turn on and off the Caps Lock keyboard feature; or click the Insert button to toggle between Insert and Typeover modes.

As with every other bar on the WordPerfect document window, you can right-click while pointing to the application bar to access its QuickMenu. From the QuickMenu, you can hide the application bar or customize its settings.

And What You *Can't* See

The obvious tools on the WordPerfect window go a fair distance in providing you with methods of learning WordPerfect and using it successfully. There are two additional tools, however, which I consider significant—QuickMenus and Reveal Codes.

This chapter has referred to QuickMenus in connection with selecting, editing, or hiding various program bars. QuickMenus exist in many other locations, however, and provide you with instant access to contextually-relevant features of WordPerfect.

Reveal Codes is a WordPerfect standard, used to display, edit, or delete the formatting codes or instructions you've added to your document. In my experience, it's a feature that makes WordPerfect ultimately understandable and unique. With very little practice, you'll find that Reveal Codes allows you to become a Word-Perfect master.

QuickMenus

QuickMenus appear whenever you right-click. They display a list of menu commands that apply to the situation in which the mouse pointer is currently resting. For example, if you point to selected text, and then right-click, you see a QuickMenu pertaining to selected text (see Figure 2-11). This QuickMenu enables you to Cut or Copy the selected text. You also can Paste the current contents of the Clipboard into

Chapter 2 • The Look and Feel of WordPerfect 8

the selected area (replacing the selection with the Clipboard contents). In addition, you can <u>H</u>ighlight the text so that it's visible for review, and so on.

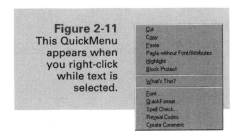

Figure 2-11
This QuickMenu appears when you right-click while text is selected.

Conversely, if you point the mouse to the left margin and right-click, the Quick-Menu that appears contains commands that apply to complete sentences, paragraphs, or pages. It also lists commands that can affect the margins, add comments, and so on (see Figure 2-12).

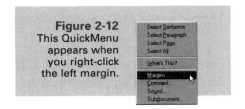

Figure 2-12
This QuickMenu appears when you right-click the left margin.

Of all the various tips and tricks I've learned since beginning to work with Word-Perfect products, this is possibly the most useful. It saves hours of time when formatting or working with tables or other complex editing tasks. Be sure to remember to explore the QuickMenus available in a variety of editing situations!

Reveal Codes

I hear all kinds of complaints when I teach Reveal Codes to new, or even experienced, users. "It's hard to read," "It's confusing," or "I just don't understand it" summarize the most common comments. On the other hand, when I work with users who've opted to change to another word processing package, the feature those users miss (and complain about not having) the most is Reveal Codes.

Reveal Codes opens a window to the formatting of the document. With it you can actively see, and manipulate, all the instructions you've included in your document. As is usually the case when using Reveal Codes, some of these instructions are included by mistake or through user error. Learning to read and work with Reveal Codes, therefore, provides you with an easy, straightforward way to correct or change complex formatting instructions.

Accessing Reveal Codes

There are several methods of opening the Reveal Codes window pane. Choose one of the following methods:

- Press Alt+F3.
- With the mouse, point anywhere within the document text and right-click; select Reveal Codes from the resulting QuickMenu.
- Choose View, Reveal Codes.
- Drag one of the Reveal Codes bars up or down to open the Reveal Codes window. Refer to Figure 2-1 to locate the Reveal Codes buttons.

You can use any of the same methods to close Reveal Codes. You don't need to repeat the same method that you used to open Reveal Codes.

When open, the Reveal Codes pane looks similar to Figure 2-13. For clarity, I usually recommend that the appearance of the codes and text be customized. To customize the appearance of the Reveal Codes pane, right-click while the mouse pointer rests in Reveal Codes to open its QuickMenu, then choose Settings. The Display Settings dialog box opens with the Reveal Codes tab on top, ready for your changes. Uncheck Use System Colors, then select Text and Background colors that are easy for you to work with. Try also changing to a different Font Face and Font Size. When your modifications are complete, click Apply to test your settings; if satisfied, click OK to return to your document.

You can make the Reveal Codes pane larger or smaller by dragging its border up or down.

Understanding the Reveal Codes Pane

The Reveal Codes pane displays text and codes that reside at the current insertion point position in the document. For example, in Figure 2-13, the insertion point in the document area is immediately before the word This. Notice that the Reveal Codes insertion point also exists immediately before the word This. As you move the document insertion point using any method, the Reveal Codes insertion point moves to exactly the same position.

Chapter 2 • The Look and Feel of WordPerfect 8

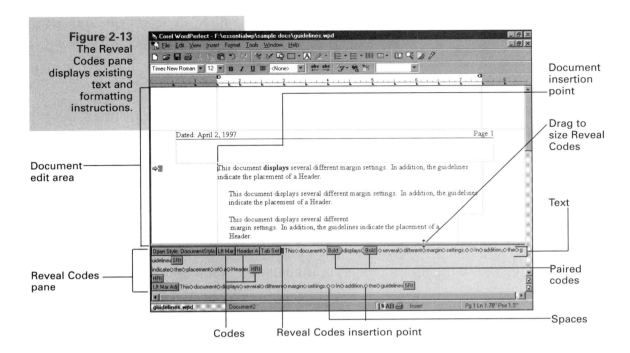

Figure 2-13 The Reveal Codes pane displays existing text and formatting instructions.

In this example, immediately prior to the insertion point in the Reveal Codes window are four codes: [Open Style: DocumentStyle], [Lft Mar], [Header A], and [Tab Set]. These four codes contain formatting instructions for the document. You can read the contents of these codes by positioning the Reveal Codes insertion point immediately to the left of each code. The easiest way to do so is by pressing ← on your keyboard. (You can click with the mouse, but accuracy can sometimes be difficult!) As you move the insertion point, each code expands so that you can read its contents. From left to right, these codes format the document as follows:

Code	Instruction
[Open Style: DocumentStyle]	All documents begin with this code. The code represents the default settings for all documents, such as default margin settings, line spacing, and so on. This code cannot be deleted.
[Lft Mar]	The left margin has been changed to 1.5 inches.
[Header A]	Header A exists in this document and was created on this page. It contains its own Open Style code, along with additional text and formatting codes that are unique to the header.

PART I • LET'S GET STARTED

`[Tab Set]` This code displays a list of the first 14 tab locations and their tab style (such as Left, Right, Decimal, or Center).

You can move the insertion point to the very beginning of a document by pressing Ctrl+Home, Ctrl+Home. This positions the insertion point prior to any typing or formatting codes, and immediately after the `[Open Style: DocumentStyle]` code.

With Reveal Codes open you can:

Do this	To
Double-click a code	Open the dialog box associated with that feature. When you make alternative choices from the dialog box and then close the dialog box to return to your document window, the code is updated to reflect your changes.
Drag the code out of the pane	Delete the code, effectively canceling any formatting instructions the code controlled. When you delete one of a pair of codes, such as `[Bold→]` or `[←Bold]`, the other half of the pair is also automatically deleted.

These two simple techniques allow you to quickly modify any layout or formatting instructions you've included in your document.

A Few Thoughts About Customization

WordPerfect for Windows versions have long been famous for their outstanding ability to let you customize your window to your own peculiar specifications. By peculiar, I mean that you can display your toolbar text in magenta if it so suits you; you can add, delete, and rearrange menu commands; and you can even change the appearance of each toolbar or property bar picture.

While you can customize the appearance of your WordPerfect window in many different ways, be cautious about going too far. It's often very difficult for another WordPerfect user, consultant, or even the Corel technical team to help you when you're having difficulty, if you've heavily customized the program!

Customizing each of the bars is done essentially the same way. Some of the choices for the bars differ depending on the purpose of that bar. For example, the application bar is not designed to hold functions (such as playing macros). With this in mind, however, you'll find that customizing the appearance of the Word-Perfect window is simple and fun.

Customizing the Bars

You can easily customize the appearance and content of the menu bar, toolbar, property bar, and application bar. To do so, start by pointing to a bar with your mouse, then right-click to access its associated QuickMenu. On each Quick-Menu, you see a command such as Edit or Settings (sometimes both). The Edit command usually allows you to add, remove, or rearrange buttons on the bar. The Settings command usually allows you to select an alternative defined bar and provides a method of getting to the Edit command. You can also access the Settings dialog box for each bar through Tools, Settings as discussed in the next section.

EDITING A BAR

Where available, the Edit command on a QuickMenu typically opens a dialog box similar to the Toolbar Editor dialog box shown in Figure 2-14. Remember that QuickMenus are accessed by right-clicking while pointing to the item to be edited, in this case one of the bars.

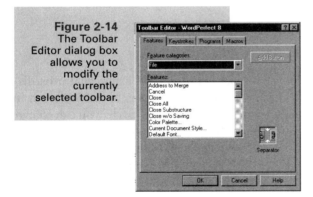

Figure 2-14
The Toolbar Editor dialog box allows you to modify the currently selected toolbar.

Notice that four tabs exist within the dialog box. These allow you to assign Word-Perfect features, user-defined keystrokes, other programs, or defined macros to the bar you are editing. The list of WordPerfect features is categorized by main menu entries. For example, the File menu is used to access commands that affect a complete WordPerfect file. Only a few file commands, however, actually exist on the predefined WordPerfect 8 menu bar. Many more file commands are listed in the Features list box. By selecting a feature command and then clicking Add Button, or by double-clicking a Feature command, you add it to the bar. Conversely, you can delete an item by dragging the button off of the bar.

Rearranging buttons on a bar is also easy. With the appropriate Editor dialog box open, point to the button on the bar you want to move; then click and drag it to its new location. You can rearrange buttons within a single bar, but you cannot move buttons between bars, such as between a toolbar and a property bar.

In addition, you can click Separator to add a separator (a vertical line) to the bar. After you add the separator, drag it to the position where you want it to appear.

As you add buttons to your bars, you can edit the Button text and QuickTip text, along with editing the bitmap picture that appears on the face of the button. To edit the assigned button text, double-click an existing button on the bar. The Customize Button dialog box opens, as shown in Figure 2-15. Type replacement text in the Button Text or QuickTip text box to change these entries.

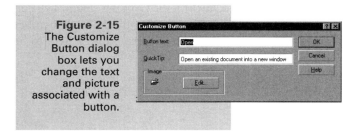

Figure 2-15 The Customize Button dialog box lets you change the text and picture associated with a button.

To modify the appearance of the button picture, from the Customize Button dialog box, click the Edit button. The Image Editor dialog box opens, as shown in Figure 2-16. By clicking the mouse in the Zoomed button image, you can change the color of each pixel. Notice that the left and right mouse buttons are each assigned a different color from the Colors palette. If you want to duplicate this button's picture, click Copy, and then click Paste while editing another button. If you're brave enough, click Clear to erase the entire button image and start over. (Of course, my favorite button is Undo!)

When you've completed your image edit, click OK to return to the Customize Button dialog box. Click OK again to return to the bar's Editor dialog box. When all changes to the bar are complete, click OK to return to the document window.

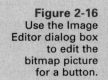
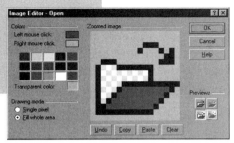

Figure 2-16 Use the Image Editor dialog box to edit the bitmap picture for a button.

ADDING KEYSTROKES TO A BAR

Adding keystrokes to a bar adds text to a button that will be inserted when you click the button. Keystrokes are just characters that appear—no formatting such as tabs, indents, or character attributes like bold and italic can be included. You can, however, include hard returns (by pressing Enter) in your keystroke text.

To add keystrokes to a button from within the bar's Editor dialog box, use these steps:

1. Click the Keystrokes tab to move it to the front of the dialog box.
2. In the Type the Keystrokes This Button Plays text box, enter the text you want to assign to the button.
3. When you are satisfied with the text, click Add Keystrokes and then click OK. A button is added to the end of your toolbar or property bar.

Note

To edit keystrokes stored in a button, from the bar's QuickMenu, choose Edit, then double-click the button. The Customize Button dialog box opens. Click Properties to open the Keystrokes for the button. Modify the text, then click OK until you get back to your document.

ADDING PROGRAMS TO A BAR

A program is a file that resides on your computer or network which will start when you click the button to which the program is assigned. Adding a program to a bar is simple:

1. From within the bar's Editor dialog box, select the Programs tab.
2. Click Add Program and locate the file that starts the program.

PART I • LET'S GET STARTED

3. Select the program file, then click <u>O</u>pen to return to the bar's Editor dialog box. A button is added to the end of the bar you're editing.

4. Double-click the new button to open the Customize Button dialog box. You then can modify the button by adding button text, adding a QuickTip, or changing the button's picture. Click P<u>r</u>operties to modify the program's path or <u>W</u>orking Folder. Then click OK until you get back to your document. That's all there is to it!

ADDING MACROS TO A BAR

A macro is a file that resides either on a disk or within the current template. Macros are simply used to record functions and repetitive tasks. They can be complex, however, and can run complete custom applications.

> FOR MORE INFORMATION ABOUT TEMPLATES, SEE CHAPTER 16.

Adding a macro to a bar is similar to adding any of the other bar functions. Use these steps:

1. Within the bar's Editor dialog box, select the Macros tab.
2. Choose <u>A</u>dd Macro to select a macro from disk, or Add <u>T</u>emplate Macro to integrate a macro that resides in the current template. Select the macro you want to include, then click Select.

Note

If you've selected a macro from disk, WordPerfect prompts `Save Macro with Full Path?`**. Click <u>Y</u>es to retain the relationship between the bar and the macro file. If you click <u>N</u>o, the macro will be compiled separately. The possibility then exists that the macro on disk may be different than the one played through the bar button. However, it's much easier to distribute to several users a bar with all macros intact than a group of macro files.**

Tip

• •
Refer to Chapters 15 and 16 for more information about macros and templates—the method by which you can distribute toolbars.
• •

3. When you're done, click OK to return to your document window.

CHAPTER 2 • THE LOOK AND FEEL OF WORDPERFECT 8   37

Working with the Settings Dialog Box

The Settings feature allows you to thoroughly customize the display, environment, location of files, document summary, conversion filters, keyboard, and each of the program bars described earlier in this chapter. What you're doing here is setting defaults—the preferences that are in place each time you start WordPerfect. Default settings for document formatting, however, occur through the File, Document, Default Font and File, Document, Current Document Style commands.

Most of the settings you make will only affect your own usage. If you work in a networked environment, however, be a little cautious about making too many environment or file location changes until you've talked things over with your network or WordPerfect administrator. To do so might affect not only your own work with WordPerfect, but perhaps your ability to work effectively in your network. This section will guide you through some settings that work well for me and some which I see in many business installations. This section is not intended to be an exhaustive recitation of each possible setting. Refer to WordPerfect's Help or Online Help commands for additional (or more specific) information.

Right-click any field within the Settings dialog box to see that field's associated QuickTip.

To open the Settings dialog box so that you can set personal preferences, choose Tools, Settings. The Settings dialog box appears, as shown in Figure 2-17. Double-click one of the icons to access the appropriate Settings dialog box.

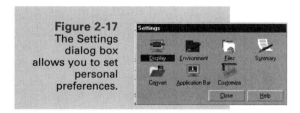

Figure 2-17
The Settings dialog box allows you to set personal preferences.

DISPLAY SETTINGS

Use the Display Settings dialog box to change the appearance of the WordPerfect window. The settings are grouped into six tabs. You should review each of the fields periodically to determine whether you can set preferences that will allow you to work more efficiently. After you complete your changes, click OK to return to your document.

Table 2-1 lists the settings grouped within each dialog tab. I've also indicated any setting that I find to be more efficient for most users than the default settings.

Table 2-1 Display Settings

Tab/field	Sets these display settings	My preference
Document	Table Gridlines	Not checked
	Windows System Colors	No preference
	Tab Bar Icons	Not checked
	Comments	Checked
	Graphics	Checked
	Hidden Text	Checked
	Shadow Cursor Color	No preference
	Shadow Cursor Shape	No preference
	Shadow Cursor Snap to:	Tabs
	Shadow Cursor	Active in white space
	Units of Measure	Inches
	Application Bar/Ruler Display	Inches
	Scroll bars	Show both when required
Symbols	Show Symbols on Current and New Documents	Not checked
View/Zoom	Default View	Page
	Default Zoom	Page width
Reveal Codes	Show Reveal Codes on Current and New Documents	Not checked
	Font	No preference
	Font Face	No preference
	Font Size	No preference
	Wrap Lines at Window	Checked
	Show Spaces as Bullets	Checked
	Show Codes in Detail	Not checked
	Window Size:	15%
	Use System Colors	Not checked
	Color: Text	No preference
	Color: Background	No preference
Ruler	Tabs Snap to Ruler Bar Grid	Checked
	Show Ruler Guides	Checked
Merge	Merge Code Options	Display Merge Codes

CHAPTER 2 • THE LOOK AND FEEL OF WORDPERFECT 8 **39**

ENVIRONMENT SETTINGS

The Environment Settings dialog box is used to set overall preferences for the way WordPerfect works. Settings identify you to other users who might edit or review your documents, set preferences for working with document reformatting when multiple printers are possible, set actions of prompts, and specify how WordPerfect works with graphics and equations.

Table 2-2 lists the settings grouped within each dialog tab. As with the Display Settings dialog box, I've indicated any setting that I find to be more efficient for most users than the default settings.

Table 2-2   Environment Settings

Tab/field	Sets these display settings	My preference
General	User information	No preference
	Ac*t*ivate Hypertext Links on Open	Checked
	*S*elect Whole Words Instead of Characters	Not checked
	Refor*m*at Documents for the WordPerfect Default Printer on Open	Checked
Interface	Display Last *O*pen Documents on the File Menu	Checked
	Display Shortc*u*t Keys	Checked
	Display *Q*uickTips	Checked
	*S*ave Workspace (documents and window layout)	Prompt on E*x*it
	Interface *L*anguage	No preference
Prompts	Prompt On *H*yphenation	Always
	*C*onfirm Deletion of Codes and Stop *I*nsertion Point at Hidden Codes	Not checked
	Confirm Deletion of Ta*b*le Formulas	Not checked
	Beep on Error	Checked
	Beep on Hyphenation	Not checked
	Beep on Find Failure	Not checked
Graphics	Drag to Create New Graphic Boxes	Checked
	Default Equation Editor	No preference
	Show the "Select Equation Editor" Dialog …	No preference

PART I • LET'S GET STARTED

FILES SETTINGS

The Files Settings dialog box is used to indicate to WordPerfect the names of your default folders for the different file types that may be used with WordPerfect. Most of these locations are completed automatically by the WordPerfect installation program. You might want to edit these locations in certain situations; for example, if you have folders or files that contain a set of label definitions or graphics from a previous WordPerfect for Windows version. Because file locations are unique to most installations, I won't list any of my preferences here.

Since WordPerfect 8 automatically sets up a new folder for documents, you'll probably want to edit the Files Settings for your Default Document Folder, naming the folder from which you most commonly save and open your files.

SUMMARY SETTINGS

Document summaries provide a method of identifying files. This information is often used when attempting to locate a missing file, or to compile document statistics. The Document Summary Settings dialog box allows you to set your preferences for whether a summary should be created each time a document is saved or exited, whether to use a long descriptive name as the document's filename when the file is first opened, or when a file is saved. You also can specify what phrase to use as Search text when looking for a file by subject and what the default descriptive type should be. In most installations I've observed, these fields either are highly customized by the user, or else not used at all. Accordingly, I have no preferences.

CONVERT SETTINGS

The Convert Settings dialog box is used primarily for importing files from other applications that use delimiters. For example, database applications often have the ability to export a file in ASCII Delimited format. When the resulting delimited file is imported into WordPerfect, WordPerfect looks for the characters that mark each field, record, and character separation.

This dialog box is also used to set the default graphic file format option for Windows. My preference is to keep the default settings until it becomes necessary in an individual situation to change them.

APPLICATION BAR SETTINGS

The Application Bar Settings dialog box also can be accessed through Quick-Menus. From this dialog box, check those items which you want to include as buttons on the application bar. Although these are personal preferences, I like to add the Select On/Off button to the application bar, finding it a convenient method of turning on or off the select feature.

The Application Bar Settings dialog box is also especially useful because it opens the method used to size or rearrange the application bar buttons. Sizing the buttons enables you to make a particular button wider or narrower. To do so, position the mouse pointer over the edge of the button you want to resize on the application bar, then click and drag it to the width you require.

CUSTOMIZE SETTINGS

The Customize Settings dialog box is also accessed through the QuickMenus for bar settings as described earlier in this chapter. One additional type of item that can be customized, the keyboard, has not yet been discussed.

I probably customize keyboards more than any other item within WordPerfect. A custom keyboard assigns key combinations to WordPerfect features, keystrokes, programs, and macros, in the same manner as with menu bars, toolbars, and property bars. However, unlike the bars, keyboards are used directly by the fingers—not with a mouse! WordPerfect 5.1 for DOS (WPDOS 5.1) was almost strictly keyboard-based, and the vast majority of WordPerfect for Windows users are previous users of WPDOS 5.1. Old habits die hard, and users like to use well-remembered keystrokes for functions. This can easily be done by customizing a WordPerfect keyboard.

WordPerfect 8 installs with four predefined keyboards: an Equation Editor keyboard with keys assigned for users who work heavily with equations, a WPDOS 6.1 keyboard, a WPWIN 7 keyboard, and the default WPWIN 8 keyboard. Of these, the WPDOS 6.1 keyboard is closest to the WPDOS 5.1 keystrokes.

I believe that everyone should make the effort to learn some of the new key combinations in order to be compatible with other Windows 95 programs. I therefore recommend that you *add* key combinations to the WPWIN 8 keyboard wherever you want to, rather than reassigning *all* the keys to match WPDOS.

The four predefined keyboards cannot be edited. Any keyboard you create, however, automatically contains all the key combinations that exist in the currently selected keyboard. Therefore, if the WPWIN 8 keyboard is selected when you create a new keyboard, the WPWIN 8 key combinations all exist in your new keyboard.

PART I • LET'S GET STARTED

To customize keyboard settings, follow these steps:

1. From the document window, choose <u>T</u>ools, Sett<u>i</u>ngs to open the Settings dialog box. Click Cus<u>t</u>omize to open the Customize Settings dialog box, then click the Keyboards tab to bring it to the front of the dialog box.
2. Select the keyboard you want to use as your pattern, and then click <u>C</u>reate. The Create Keyboard dialog box appears.
3. Type a name for your new keyboard in the <u>N</u>ew Keyboard Name text box, and then click OK. The Keyboard Shortcuts dialog box opens (see Figure 2-18). Notice that the name of your new keyboard appears in the title bar of the Keyboard Shortcuts dialog box.

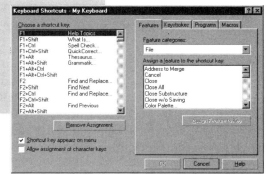

Figure 2-18
The Keyboard Shortcuts dialog box displays all shortcuts that exist for the selected keyboard.

4. From the <u>C</u>hoose a Shortcut Key list box, select an empty key assignment.

The <u>C</u>hoose a Shortcut Key list box does not contain the key combinations used to access menu entries. You want to avoid reassigning combinations such as Alt + F (which is used to open the <u>F</u>ile menu).

5. Select a feature, type a keystroke, launch a program, or assign a macro to your selected shortcut key from its appropriate tab.
6. Click <u>A</u>ssign Feature (Keystrokes, Program, Macro) to Key. If you've assigned a key combination by mistake, click <u>R</u>emove Assignment to cancel your choice.

7. When you have finished assigning keyboard shortcuts, click OK to return to the Customize dialog box. Your new keyboard appears on the Available Keyboards list.

8. Select your new keyboard, and then click Close to return to the Settings dialog box.

9. Click Close to return to your document window.

3

So How Does WordPerfect Work?

IN THIS CHAPTER

- **Creating and Saving Documents**
- **Techniques for Editing**
- **Using PerfectExpert**
- **Locating Electronic Support**

Programmers for computer software constantly strive to make software easy to use and easy to learn. That's certainly true of WordPerfect 8. But those in charge of designing software also constantly add new and improved features. This means you need to refresh your software talents periodically, even if you're an experienced

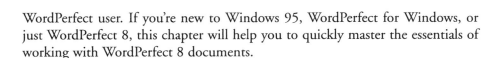

WordPerfect user. If you're new to Windows 95, WordPerfect for Windows, or just WordPerfect 8, this chapter will help you to quickly master the essentials of working with WordPerfect 8 documents.

The Very Basics

At the heart of Corel WordPerfect Suite 8 is WordPerfect 8, a word-processing program. Word processors have been necessary tools for most businesses since at least the early 1970s. In one form or another, documents have been created, named, saved, and then reopened for editing.

> ## Documents or files?
>
> You'll find both terms used throughout this book. Basically, they refer to the same thing. In general, when a file is open in WordPerfect, I've referred to it as a *document*. However, when looking for or referring to a document by name—for example, in a file management list—the document is referred to as a *file*.
>
> To be strictly correct, a *document* is any file that can be edited, but typically this term is used when referring to a word-processing file type, such as a file in WordPerfect, Word, or WordPro.

Creating a New Document

Several methods exist to help you create a new document in WordPerfect 8. The most common method is to just start typing when WordPerfect opens. But, depending on what you want to do, you might also want to use one of the pre-defined projects that are provided with WordPerfect. Some of these projects prompt you for information and then go ahead and create fancy letterhead, headers and footers, or even page numbering. Others just lay out the paper so that you can begin typing a report or presentation.

Using the Blank Document Window

This is the easiest, most common way to create a brand-new document. Just start typing! A blank document window is already open when you start WordPerfect 8. It contains the default document formatting which is stored in the [Open Style: DocumentStyle] code.

> **REFER TO CHAPTER 2 FOR A REVIEW OF REVEAL CODES.**

When WordPerfect 8 is installed, the [Open Style: DocumentStyle] code stores the settings used to define the appearance of a new document. These default settings consist of pages that measure $8\frac{1}{2}''$ x 11", one-inch margins around the perimeter of the paper, and tabs set every one-half inch.

Margins control not only the text of the document itself, but the distance which *any* element appears from the edges of the paper. For example, if you create a header (text that typically appears at the top of every page), that header can reside no closer to the edge of the paper than the current top margin measurement. If you need the header to appear closer to the top edge, make the top margin smaller. Likewise, make the top margin setting larger to force the header farther from the edge of the paper.

The guidelines and ruler illustrate the default settings, as shown in Figure 3-1.

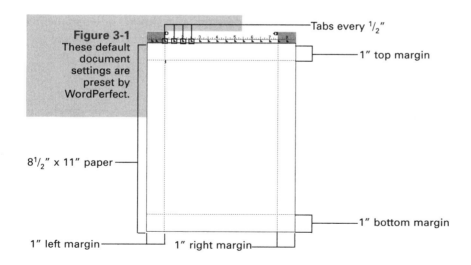

Figure 3-1 These default document settings are preset by WordPerfect.

If you close the only open document window, WordPerfect 8 automatically opens another new, blank document window with these same settings. As you learn to change document margins and other settings, you'll also learn how to change the default document settings represented by the [Open Style: DocumentStyle] code.

Using a Project or Template

> CHAPTERS 15 AND 16 EXPLAIN HOW TO CREATE MACROS AND TEMPLATES.

To put it very simply, a project, definable only by Corel or other third-party programmers, can be any document, spreadsheet, template, macro or application that can be opened when you click File, New. A project typically prompts you through the creation of various form documents. They can contain prompts to select formatting choices, prompts for fill-in-the-blank areas similar to a database form, templates, and links to the PerfectExpert (WordPerfect's version of the Windows 95 Wizard), or other programs. The templates associated with a project often contain connections to the address book, and custom menus, toolbars, keyboards, and macros. You can create personal templates for your business letterhead, memo forms, pleading papers, or other fill-in-the-blank forms such as routing slips. Projects and templates commingle on the dialog box that appears when you choose File, New.

When using a project, you might be prompted to fill in the name of an addressee, for example. Your response is then placed on a new document in appropriate locations so that you can immediately begin typing the document body and any other unique parts of that particular document.

Projects and templates are organized into categories which group the projects by task similarity. Depending on the Corel WordPerfect Suite 8 programs you installed, an individual list of categories appears for each program. Remembering that projects can use multiple programs, some projects or templates appear in several categories. For example, the project which creates a Cash Budget appears in the WordPerfect 8, Quattro Pro 8, Budget, and Business categories.

Hands On: Creating a Memo Using the Memo Project

The steps necessary for each project or template vary depending on the complexity and type of document being created. To create a memo using the Memo project, follow these steps:

1. Choose File, New. The New dialog box appears, as shown in Figure 3-2.
2. Select Memo from the project list.

    If the project you want to use does not appear on the project list, you can open the drop-down project category list and select an alternative category (see Figure 3-3).

3. Click Create. The PerfectExpert panel appears at the left edge of the document window and a new document window opens.

Chapter 3 • So How Does WordPerfect Work?

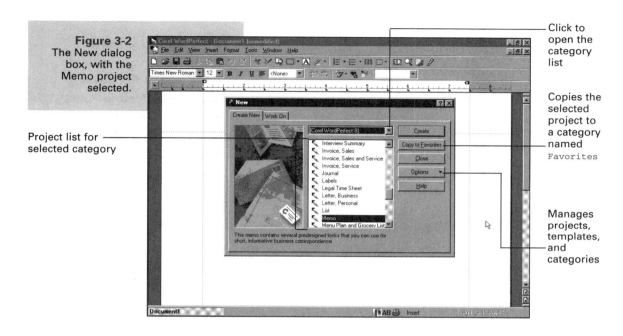

Figure 3-2
The New dialog box, with the Memo project selected.

Project list for selected category

Click to open the category list

Copies the selected project to a category named Favorites

Manages projects, templates, and categories

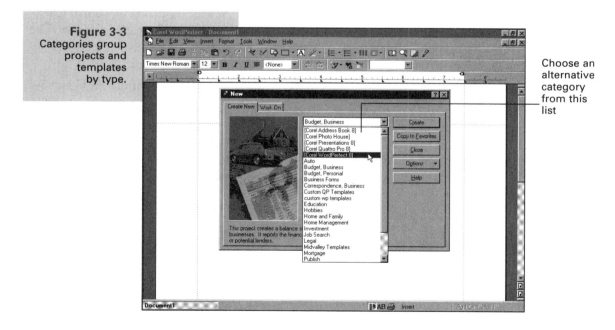

Figure 3-3
Categories group projects and templates by type.

Choose an alternative category from this list

Note

Of the 100 or so projects that reside on the Corel WordPerfect Suite 8 CD, only six projects are actually copied to your system during a default Typical or Custom installation: the Fax Cover Sheet, Memo, Monthly Calendar, Business Letter, Personal Letter, and Newsletter projects. If you select a project that does not reside on your local system, you'll be prompted to insert the Corel WordPerfect Suite 8 CD so that the project file can be accessed from the CD.

Note

If this is the first time you've used a project or template, you may be prompted to enter personal information into the Address Book, which will then be used to complete personal fields on the template.

> CHAPTER 4 DISCUSSES THE ADDRESS BOOK IN MORE DETAIL.

4. If the Personalize Your Templates dialog box appears, click OK to open the Address Book. The Address Book and New Entry dialog box open. Click Cancel, Close to avoid completing this personal information for now. The Address Book closes and the Memo PerfectExpert begins. Figure 3-4 displays the completed Memo PerfectExpert prompt box.

5. In the To, From, and Subject fields, type sample text similar to Figure 3-4.

Tip

Many PerfectExpert dialog boxes prompt for information similar to the Memo PerfectExpert. The checked prompt boxes are considered to be *required* fields—information you must complete before the PerfectExpert will allow you to go to the next step. Remove the check from the prompt field to avoid completing any of the fields.

6. In the Memo Style drop-down list, experiment with the various memo styles until you find one you like. Figure 3-4 uses the Contemporary style.

7. Click OK to close the Memo PerfectExpert prompt box. Your entries are added to the document, and the PerfectExpert panel remains open for your use.

The PerfectExpert panel varies from project to project, but remains open until specifically closed. It is context-sensitive, however, and updates to reflect appropriate choices for the document currently under construction.

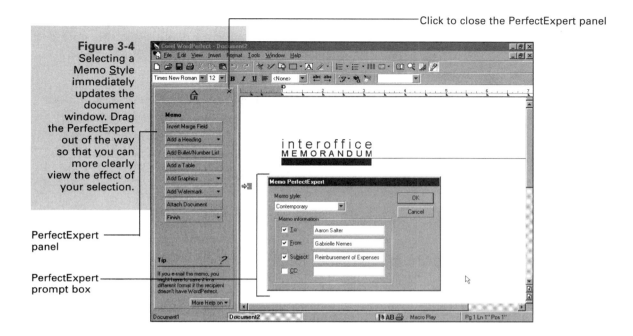

Figure 3-4 Selecting a Memo Style immediately updates the document window. Drag the PerfectExpert out of the way so that you can more clearly view the effect of your selection.

The Finish button typically appears and lists choices to check the spelling of your document, print, fax, or e-mail the document, and to save and close the document.

8. While you'd normally at least name and save the document before closing this panel, for now click the Close button on the PerfectExpert panel to remove the panel from your document window.

Naming, Saving, and Closing a Document

A new document has not been named and won't be saved until you specifically say to do so. True, there's an automatic backup feature in WordPerfect 8. But that backup is only useful if your system accidentally locks up or for some reason needs to be reset. In those cases, you can sometimes recover the document.

You should name and save your new document as soon as possible to protect your work. Of course, it isn't strictly necessary to name and save a document—you can type as much as you want, use virtually all WordPerfect features, and then merely throw the document away when you're through.

Files in Windows 95 programs can have long, descriptive names and are logically stored in folders, similar to a real-life file cabinet/folder arrangement. The first time a file is saved, you need to assign a name to the file and assign the file to a folder.

PART I • LET'S GET STARTED

Note

You can change the location and frequency of automatic file back-up by choosing <u>T</u>ools, Setti<u>n</u>gs. Double-click the <u>F</u>iles icon, then modify the backup folder and set backup options.

If you've reset your system for some reason while a document was open in a WordPerfect window, you should see a prompt the next time you start WordPerfect 8. You'll then see an option to open the file that was active when the reset occurred. You'll be able to rename or delete that recovered file if you want.

WordPerfect 8 filenames follow Windows 95 conventions. They can include spaces and some special characters, along with an optional three-character extension. You should avoid using the characters *, +, =, [,], ;, :, ", <, >, ?, /, \, and | in a filename. You should also not use the extensions .bat, .com, .dll, .exe, .hlp, .ini, .fil, .reg, .wcm, or .wpt when naming WordPerfect documents.

Note

Unless you specifically indicate *not* to do so in the Files Settings dialog box, the extension .wpd is automatically added to the end of every document you create, even if you type your own extension. For example, a document you name mydoc.gn will actually be named mydoc.gn.wpd.

Hands On: Naming and Saving the Memo

Here's how to name and save the memo you created using the Memo project in the previous hands-on activity:

1. Choose <u>F</u>ile, <u>S</u>ave or <u>F</u>ile, Save <u>A</u>s. The Save File dialog box opens, as shown in Figure 3-5.

Tip

Alternatively, press Ctrl+S or click the Save button on the toolbar. Or, if the PerfectExpert panel still appears on the document window, click the Finish button, then choose Save.

Note: The Save or Save As dialog box only appears the first time you save and name a document. As you resave your file, WordPerfect 8 automatically writes over the previously named file, updating its contents. If you, therefore, want to change the name for a file, be sure to choose File, Save As and type an alternate name or location for your document.

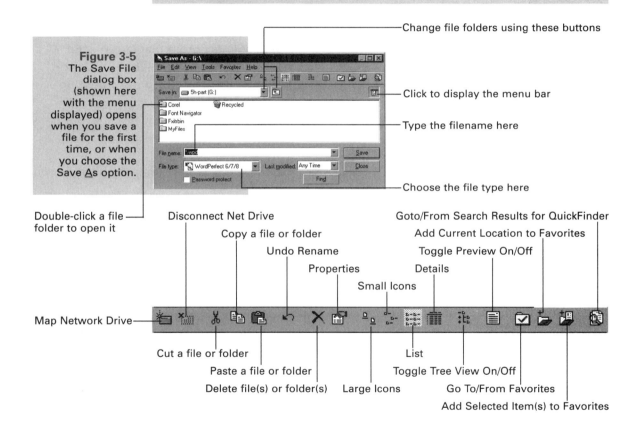

Figure 3-5
The Save File dialog box (shown here with the menu displayed) opens when you save a file for the first time, or when you choose the Save As option.

- Change file folders using these buttons
- Click to display the menu bar
- Type the filename here
- Choose the file type here
- Double-click a file folder to open it
- Map Network Drive
- Disconnect Net Drive
- Cut a file or folder
- Copy a file or folder
- Paste a file or folder
- Undo Rename
- Delete file(s) or folder(s)
- Properties
- Small Icons
- Large Icons
- Details
- List
- Toggle Tree View On/Off
- Toggle Preview On/Off
- Add Current Location to Favorites
- Go To/From Favorites
- Goto/From Search Results for QuickFinder
- Add Selected Item(s) to Favorites

2. Select the folder to which you want to save the memo by double-clicking a visible folder, or by selecting a different drive or folder tree using the Save In field. You can move to a commonly used folder by using the Favorites button.

3. Type the name for the memo, such as **Reimbursement Memo,** in the File Name text box.

PART I • LET'S GET STARTED

Note

You can also create new folders or perform other file management tasks using the Save File dialog box, or any of WordPerfect's file management dialog boxes. See the section titled "Managing Your Files and Folders," later in this chapter, for more information.

Note

If necessary, select an alternative file type from the File type drop-down list. If some users in your office still use WordPerfect 5.1, for example, you might want to save your file using that file type. Be aware, however, that older versions of the software did not support many of the advanced features of WordPerfect 8. Some formatting will be stripped from your document (but all text will be retained) if that formatting is not supported by the file type you select.

4. Choose <u>S</u>ave. The file is saved to the selected folder using the filename you entered.

Tip

As you continue to edit your document, resave it periodically by pressing Ctrl+S or clicking the Save toolbar button.

When you've finished working with a document, close it by clicking the document window's Close button, pressing Ctrl+F4, or choosing <u>F</u>ile, <u>C</u>lose. The document closes and you are returned to the next open document window or to a new, blank document window.

Tracking Multiple Versions of the Same Document

FIGURE 2-2 SHOWS THE PARTS OF THE DOCUMENT WINDOW.

Corel WordPerfect Suite 8 includes Corel Versions, a powerful solution to the problem of managing old and new versions of the same document. By automatically *archiving*, or filing a copy of the document in a special archive file, Corel Versions allows you to save changes you make to each successive version of your file. It then creates a history list of file versions from which you can retrieve, view, or delete an archived file. You can compare archived versions to determine exactly where they differ. Even better, since Corel Versions stores the name of the user who archived the document, you can track the modifications each person in a workgroup setting has made to the document.

You may not have installed Corel Versions when you installed WordPerfect 8. Generally, an easy way to tell if it's installed and active from within WordPerfect is to open the File menu. If Version Control is listed, Corel Versions is installed and enabled. If it's not listed, check your Windows 95 Control Panel for Corel Versions. If the icon appears, Corel Versions was installed, but may be disabled. Double-click the Corel Versions icon in the Control Panel, then check Enable Version Control to allow its use within WordPerfect. If Corel Versions does not appear in the Control Panel, add it by performing a Custom installation from the Corel WordPerfect Suite 8 CD.

Note

Corel Versions in the Windows 95 Control Panel allows you to set defaults for the number of temporary versions to be created, and to set up the folder where the versions will be kept. From the Corel Versions window, be sure to click the Help button to learn more about these default settings.

Archiving a Document

Archiving a document requires that you determine whether the document version you are saving should be considered the *permanent* or *temporary*. Permanent versions are retained until you specifically delete them. Temporary versions are replaced by newer versions of the document when the maximum number of versions is reached, as determined when the first archive is stored.

Hands On: Archiving a Document

To save the current document as an archive, use these steps:

1. Open any document for which you want to store various versions. Then, with the document open, choose File, Version Control, Save Current. The New Version dialog box opens, with the name of the current document displayed in its title bar (see Figure 3-6).

2. Check Make First Version Permanent to store this version permanently. (Permanent archives are in addition to temporary archives.)

Tip

You can also choose to compress the current version, which saves disk space but makes for a longer retrieval time when you need to open the file.

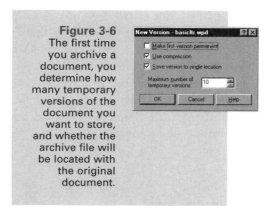

Figure 3-6
The first time you archive a document, you determine how many temporary versions of the document you want to store, and whether the archive file will be located with the original document.

3. Clear the checkmark from Save Version to Single Location to store the archive file in the same folder as the original file.

Retain the checkmark for Save Version to Single Location to indicate that you want the archive file for the document to be stored in the default folder named in the Control Panel, Corel Versions default settings dialog box.

4. Verify the number of temporary versions you want to store for the document (10 is the default), then click OK. A copy of the document is added to the archive file and you are returned to the document window to continue your edits.

Hands On: Storing Another Version

As you distribute your document, or make changes to the document yourself, you can store additional versions of the document in the archive file. Here's how:

1. At any time you want to store another version of the document, be sure the document is open in WordPerfect.
2. Choose File, Version Control, Save Current. The Version Properties dialog box opens, with the document name also appearing in the title bar (see Figure 3-7).

Chapter 3 • So How Does WordPerfect Work?

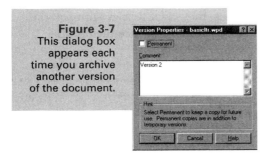

Figure 3-7
This dialog box appears each time you archive another version of the document.

3. Determine whether you want to make this copy permanent, then add any comments to the <u>C</u>omment area that will help you identify the version later.
4. When your comments are complete, click OK to add the version to the archive file.

Hands On: Retrieving an Archived Document

You can retrieve an archived version of any document at any time, so that you can review or further edit the version. It's easiest to retrieve a version for the document currently open, although you can retrieve a version directly from disk. Use these steps:

1. Open the document for which you want to retrieve a previous version.
2. Choose <u>F</u>ile, <u>V</u>ersion Control, <u>R</u>etrieve Current. The Retrieve Version dialog box opens, as displayed in Figure 3-8.

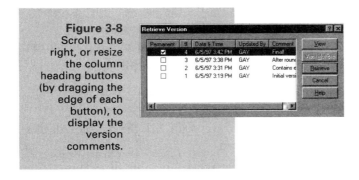

Figure 3-8
Scroll to the right, or resize the column heading buttons (by dragging the edge of each button), to display the version comments.

3. Select one or more of the listed versions, then click <u>R</u>etrieve to open the archived document. WordPerfect prompts you to replace the open document with the archived document.

If you click No, the archived version is renamed and placed in a new window. If you click Yes, the previously opened document closes and the newly retrieved archive opens.

4. Click Yes.

Refer to the Help text for Corel Versions to learn about more Corel Versions features.

Managing Your Files and Folders

Any time you see a file management dialog box—such as Save, Save As, or Insert File—within WordPerfect 8, you can perform file management tasks while that dialog box is open. For example, you might want to create a new folder for a new client. Or you might want to delete some unused files, or copy files to another drive. You can do so by opening one of the file management dialog boxes, then using the toolbar or menu choices available within that dialog box. (You need to display the menu in the dialog box by clicking the Toggle Menu On/Off button.)

Suppose that you've decided to move several files from one folder to another. Use these steps:

1. Choose the commands to open one of the file management dialog boxes, such as <u>F</u>ile, <u>S</u>ave.
2. If the menu's not already displayed, click the Toggle Menu On/Off button.
3. Select the files you want to move using one of these methods:
    - Drag the mouse pointer through the list of files to select a contiguous list.
    - Click the first file to be moved, then Shift+click the last file. All files between the two clicks are selected.
    - Click a file to be moved, then Ctrl+click any other files. This method selects files that are not physically grouped.
4. Choose <u>F</u>ile, Move to <u>F</u>older. The Select Destination Folder for Move dialog box opens, displaying a folder tree.

CHAPTER 3 • SO HOW DOES WORDPERFECT WORK?

5. Select the folder to which you want to move the files, then click <u>M</u>ove. The selected files are sent to the designated folder.

6. Click the <u>C</u>lose button to close the dialog box.

Here are a few additional techniques that I frequently use when working with files and folders in WordPerfect:

- Create a new folder for your files directly from a file list by right-clicking while pointing to a file list. When the associated QuickMenu appears, choose N<u>e</u>w, <u>F</u>older. Type the name you want to assign to the folder, then press `Enter` or click outside the folder name.

- Sort your files alphabetically by name, size, type, or when modified by first clicking the Details button on the toolbar. Then click a column heading to sort the list by that column. Click the column heading again to reverse the sort. I frequently like to sort files in reverse order by date modified. This puts the files I most recently used at the top of the list.

- Display the folder tree, then select several files or folders and move them by dragging them to another folder in the folder tree. You can hold down `Ctrl` while dragging to copy the files. Be careful here, however! Sometimes things move quickly and your files end up in an unintended location!

- Add files that you open frequently to the Favorites list. When you later want to work with the file, go directly to Favorites and double-click the filename. Similarly, add folder names to the Favorites list so that you can quickly open a folder without having to manually step through the folder tree.

Editing or Opening an Existing Document

It's inevitable. Once you've created a document, you need to make changes to it. That means you need to locate and open the file. Like most things in WordPerfect 8, there are a number of methods you can use to open an existing document for editing. Documents created with previous versions of WordPerfect, or even with other word processing programs, will usually open without additional prompting in WordPerfect 8. You might briefly see the Convert dialog box, or the Convert File Format dialog box might ask you to verify the file format for a selected file. Then the file opens.

I've listed the methods I use most commonly; my choice between them depends on how recently I opened the file I now want to edit. Here are the methods I find to be the most useful:

PART I • LET'S GET STARTED

- Choose File, Open (or press Ctrl+O, or click the Open File toolbar button). The Open File dialog box appears. You may need to change folders or use the Favorites list to locate the file. When you've located the file, double-click the filename to select and open it (or select the filename and then choose Open).

You can choose Open As Copy instead of Open to avoid accidentally modifying a critical document. An Open As Copy document actually opens as a read-only file. When you attempt to save the file, the Save As dialog box opens, requiring you to give the file a new name.

- From Windows 95's My Computer or Explorer, double-click a WordPerfect file. WordPerfect 8 starts (if it's not already running) and the selected file is opened.

These next three options are for files you've recently edited:

- Choose File, then select the filename from the list of most recently opened documents that appears at the bottom of the File menu. If the file is the third one on the list, for example, just press F3 to quickly open it.
- From the Open File dialog box, click the drop-down list button at the right edge of the File name field, select the file, and click Open.
- From the Windows 95 taskbar, click the Start button and choose Documents. Then click the file you want to edit. WordPerfect starts (if it's not already running) and the selected document is opened.

Some Useful Editing Techniques

All documents require editing—sometimes just simple corrections to mistyped words, but other times rearrangement of paragraphs or even whole sections. The ability to knowledgeably use WordPerfect's editing tools will set you apart from the casual WordPerfect user.

How to Move Around in a Document

No doubt you've already discovered that just moving the cursor arrows to get around in a document can make editing tasks very slow. Table 3-1 lists a number of quick methods—some using the keyboard and others using the mouse—that will get you where you want to be.

CHAPTER 3 • SO HOW DOES WORDPERFECT WORK? **61**

Table 3-1 Methods for Navigating a Document

Keyboard Shortcut	Mouse Shortcut	Goes to
Ctrl+→, Ctrl+←		Beginning of next or previous word
Ctrl+↑, Ctrl+↓		Beginning of previous or next paragraph
Ctrl+Home	Drag scroll box to top of scroll bar, then click in document	Beginning of document, after formatting codes
Ctrl+Home, Ctrl+Home		Beginning of document, prior to formatting codes
Ctrl+End	Drag scroll box to bottom of scroll bar, then click in document	End of document
Alt+Pg Dn	Next page button	Top of next page
Alt+Pg Up	Previous page button	Top of previous page
Ctrl+G		Opens the Go To dialog box
Pg Up		Top of current or previous screen
Pg Dn		Bottom of current or next screen
Ctrl+Pg Up	On scroll bar, click to left of scroll box	Scrolls one screen to the left
Ctrl+Pg Dn	On scroll bar, click to right of scroll box	Scrolls one screen to the right
End	Click at end of line	End of current line
Home	Click at beginning of line	Beginning of current line after formatting codes
Home, Home		Beginning of line before formatting codes
Alt+↑	Click in cell	In a table, top of cell above
Alt+↓	Click in cell	In a table, top of cell below
Alt+→	Click at top of next column	In a column, top of next column
Alt+←	Click at top of previous column	In a column, top of previous column

Fixing Those Darn Typos

As you create or edit a document, you'll likely make typing mistakes. I know I do! Sometimes, however, the errors aren't even of your own making, especially when you edit work done on another word processing program.

"As You Type" Typos

> **Refer to Chapter 5 for help with spell checking.**

Probably the simplest and most often used methods to correct mistakes are to simply backspace or delete the offending characters. Use `←Backspace` to erase characters immediately before (to the left of) the insertion point; use `Del` to erase characters immediately after (to the right of) the insertion point. I encounter a significant number of experienced computer users who always move the insertion point to the end of a word, and then press `←Backspace` to erase. Don't forget to use `Del`!

WordPerfect uses two other unique methods of erasing text so that you can type corrections:

Press this combination	To do this
`Ctrl`+`←Backspace`	Delete the entire word in which the insertion point resides
`Ctrl`+`Del`	Delete everything from the insertion point to the end of the line

"After the Fact" Typos

After you've typed a full paragraph, or even a sentence, it can be more trouble than it's worth to backspace through several lines and then retype. The "select the text first" method is more appropriate for these types of editing corrections.

SELECTING TEXT

Select the appropriate text, using one of the methods listed in Table 3-2, including any formatting codes if you want, and then press `Del` or `←Backspace`. Unless you delete or replace selected text, you need to manually turn off Select when you're through. This wonderful feature allows you to add as many formatting changes as you want without needing to continually reselect the same text over and over. To manually turn off Select, press `F8` (the Select toggle key), or click anywhere outside of the selection.

There are a number of methods of selecting text, of course, but all of them are easy and efficient! Here are some methods:

CHAPTER 3 • SO HOW DOES WORDPERFECT WORK?

Table 3-2 Methods for Selecting Text

Action	Result
Press and drag the mouse	Selects text as you drag the mouse
Double-click	Selects the current word
Triple-click	Selects the current sentence
Quadruple-click	Selects the current paragraph
Point to the left margin and click	Selects the current sentence
Point to the left margin and double-click	Selects the current paragraph
Click in the text to anchor the insertion point, and then Shift+click at the end of the text to be selected	Selects all text between the beginning click and the Shift+click
Hold down Shift while using any of the keyboard methods listed in Table 3-1	Selects the text as you move to the new location
Press F8 to turn on Select, and then use arrow keys to move through the text	Selects the text as you move through it

With text selected, you can just start typing. Your new entry replaces the selected phrase.

If you accidentally replace selected text by starting to type, press Ctrl+Z to undo your edits. (The default limit for how many edits you can undo is 10, but you can change the number of undo items stored with your document through Edit, Undo/Redo History.)

USING FIND AND REPLACE

Perhaps my favorite method of editing a document uses the Find feature. Imagine that you need to quickly position your insertion point at the beginning of a word or phrase so that you can change it. Perhaps, however, the place you want to edit is three or four pages away. Using Find quickly moves you to the phrase and selects it so that you can make your change. Here's how to use Find:

1. Choose Edit, Find and Replace (or simply press Ctrl+F). The Find and Replace Text dialog box opens, as shown in Figure 3-9.

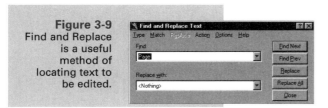

Figure 3-9
Find and Replace is a useful method of locating text to be edited.

2. Type the word or phrase in the Find text box, then choose Find Next. The insertion point quickly jumps to and selects the next occurrence of the word you've designated.
3. If the selection found is the incorrect one, choose Find Next or Find Prev to move to the next or previous occurrence of the word.
4. When the selection found is the one you want, click Close to close the Find and Replace Text dialog box.
5. Now type your correction, or press Del or ←Backspace if you want to erase the selection.

Of course, the Find and Replace feature can be used for far more powerful actions than just locating text. For example, you might want to locate and change every occurrence of a word or phrase throughout a document. Find and Replace not only can modify text, but also can locate and change formatting codes or merge codes. Rather than selecting text, a find-and-replace action can just position the insertion point in front of or after the located item. And, of course, it can search both forward and backward in a document.

By far, one of the most powerful (and fun!) uses for Find and Replace is to search and replace for Word Forms. The Word Form option is accessed through the Type menu on the Find and Replace dialog box. When this is checked, WordPerfect searches for all instances and forms of the word or phrase which exist in the Find text box, with the correct forms for the word or phrase typed in the Replace With text box. For example, suppose you want to replace the word spend (which appears in the document also as spending and spent) with buy. With Word Forms checked, replace pauses when it encounters spent and asks if you want to replace the word with bought.

CHAPTER 3 • SO HOW DOES WORDPERFECT WORK? 65

Hands On: Using Find and Replace to Change Text

The most common use for Find and Replace is to change one repetitive text phrase to a different phrase throughout a document. Suppose, for example, you have a form letter where the name of a client, Jessica Smith, appears throughout the form. Here's how to change Jessica's name to a new client name, Harrison Higgins:

1. Open the form letter in which you want to make the changes. You might want to open a *copy* of the file so that you don't accidentally save changes over the original file.
2. Press `Ctrl`+`F` to quickly open the Find and Replace dialog box.
3. Click in the Find text box, then type the text to be replaced, **Jessica Smith**.
4. Click in the Replace With text box, then type the new text, **Harrison Higgins**.

For a replacement to occur, WordPerfect must identify the text to be replaced, which it does by selecting the text. If your Replace With control is disabled, verify that Select Match is checked in the Action menu.

5. Click Replace. WordPerfect searches through the file, looking for `Jessica Smith`. When found, the text is selected and WordPerfect pauses.

While you can click Replace All immediately after entering your Find and Replace criteria, it's wise to check an individual entry at least once to avoid making critical editing mistakes in your document.

6. If your Find and Replace criteria are correct, click Replace All. WordPerfect finishes searching the document, making all replacements. When complete, a status box reports the number of replacements made. Click OK to close the status box, then Close to close the Find and Replace dialog box.

Hands On: Using Find and Replace to Change a Font Face Throughout a Document

Here's an example using Find and Replace to make some extensive changes to a document. Suppose that you import a report which was created in another word processing program and then find that all the fonts used in the document have been changed to the wrong one, Times New Roman. You need to change the fonts used back to Century Schoolbook, 12 point. Use these steps:

1. Press Ctrl+F to easily open the Find and Replace dialog box.
2. Choose Type, Specific Codes. The Specific Codes dialog box opens.
3. From the Find Codes list, select Font and click OK. The Find and Replace dialog box changes to the Find and Replace Font dialog box.
4. From the Find Font drop-down list, select Times New Roman.
5. From the Replace With drop-down list, select CentSchbook BT.
6. If desired, choose the appropriate Font Style to find/replace (bold, italic, and so on).
7. Click Find Next to double-check your entries. If Find has stopped at the correct location, click Replace.
8. The next time WordPerfect locates a Times New Roman font code and pauses for your input, click Replace All. Find and Replace then continues through the document, changing all Times New Roman font codes to Century Schoolbook.
9. When Find and Replace is complete, an informational dialog box reports the number of replacements made (or that the specific code is not found). Click OK and then click Close to close the Find and Replace dialog box.

For the Love of a Mouse

Some years ago I was asked by a client to write some documentation for the new WordPerfect for Windows 5.1. I'd managed to avoid Windows programs up until then, but their request forced me to take the great step. Not only would I have to learn a new WordPerfect product, but I'd have to learn something about Windows. And, horror of horrors, I'd have to learn to use a mouse! I thought it would be the end of word processing.

Of course, everything works out over time, and these days I'm pretty lost without my new best friend. I'm still a heavy keyboard user, but the mouse and I have a very charmed relationship. I've found that there are many things that can be done faster with a mouse than with a keyboard. (That's something I thought I'd never admit!)

Possibly the fastest thing to use your mouse for is selecting text, as previously mentioned in Table 3-2. And, of course, it's great for removing codes from the Reveal Codes window (just drag any unwanted codes off the window). But where a mouse really shines in WordPerfect 8 is its use with the ruler and guidelines.

Tip

Double-click almost any symbol or code anywhere on a WordPerfect window to open its associated dialog box.

Changing Tabs and Margins Using a Mouse

As you may remember, the ruler bar uses margin, tab, and paragraph symbols to illustrate the current settings of those items. You can use your mouse to drag those symbols around, thereby changing the settings.

Here's how to change margins:

1. Before you begin to use the ruler bar, you need to be sure that it's visible (by default, it is not). If it's not on your document window, choose View, Ruler.

2. Position the insertion point in the document where you want the new setting to begin. Alternatively you can select a portion of your document— in that case, the new settings will only affect the selected text.

3. Drag the left margin symbol to change the left margin, or the right margin symbol to change the right margin (see Figure 3-10).

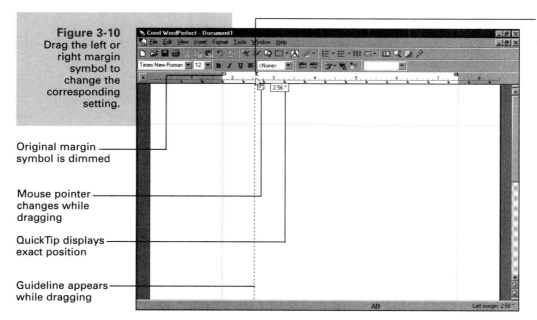

Figure 3-10 Drag the left or right margin symbol to change the corresponding setting.

Original margin symbol is dimmed

Mouse pointer changes while dragging

QuickTip displays exact position

Guideline appears while dragging

Margin symbol while moving

PART I • LET'S GET STARTED

Tip

If you change your mind while dragging a margin symbol, drag the mouse pointer to the top of the window (toward the menu bar, not the top of the document edit area) and release. The margin symbol snaps back to its original position.

4. Release the mouse button when the margin symbol is in the correct position.

Changing tabs works essentially the same way, although you can get a bit more sophisticated with tabs by changing tab types or dragging several tabs around at once. Table 3-3 lists the tab techniques possible with a mouse.

Whenever tab settings have been modified, a tab bar icon appears in the left margin as shown in Figure 3-12.

Table 3-3 Modifying Tabs Using the Mouse

To accomplish this	Use these steps
Add a tab	Click the ruler in the desired location
Delete a tab	Drag the tab symbol off the ruler. You'll see a little trash can like this:
Select several consecutive tabs	Point the mouse immediately to the left of the first tab to be deleted. While holding down Shift, drag through the remaining tabs, and then release both the mouse button and Shift. Selected tabs look like this:
Delete several consecutive tabs	Select the tabs to be deleted, then drag the selection off the ruler.
Move a tab	Drag the tab symbol to a new location and release.
Move several consecutive tabs	After selecting the tab symbols, point to the symbols and drag the tabs to their new location. Then release the mouse button.
Copy a set of tabs	Select the group of tabs to be copied. While holding down Ctrl, point to the selected tabs and drag them to their duplicate location on the ruler.
Change tab types for the next click	Point to an unused area on the ruler on the tab line, and then right-click to display the QuickMenu. Select an alternative tab type and then click the ruler wherever you want the new tab to appear. The tab QuickMenu choices can be seen in Figure 3-11; a sample ruler with several tab types is shown in Figure 3-12.

Chapter 3 • So How Does WordPerfect Work?

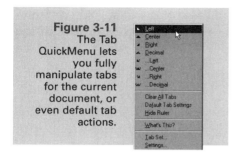

Figure 3-11
The Tab QuickMenu lets you fully manipulate tabs for the current document, or even default tab actions.

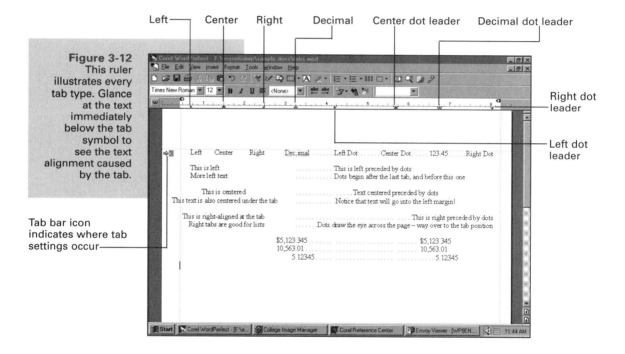

Figure 3-12
This ruler illustrates every tab type. Glance at the text immediately below the tab symbol to see the text alignment caused by the tab.

Tab bar icon indicates where tab settings occur

Tip

You can click the icon to view the current tab settings—this is especially useful if you've hidden the ruler bar.

Moving or Copying Using the Mouse

Drag 'n Drop, now generically called *drag and drop* and implemented in many applications, was a feature coined by WordPerfect with its earliest release of

WordPerfect for Windows. It's a perfect description of the easiest method of moving text from place to place in a document. Drag and drop *moves* selected text from one location in a document to another.

You can also use the mouse to *copy* text between locations. I like to use the term *copy and drop* to indicate that the text will be duplicated in the new location rather than moved.

MOVING OR COPYING TEXT USING THE MOUSE

Drag and drop works especially well when relocating text within the same screenful of text. But you can drag and drop text across several pages, or even between documents. Use these steps to drag and drop within a single document:

1. Select the text to be moved.
2. Point with the mouse anywhere within the selected text. (Don't click, or you'll deselect the text and have to start over!)
3. Drag the mouse pointer, watching the shadow cursor, to the location where you want the text to be inserted. As you drag, the mouse pointer changes, indicating that you're moving text:
4. Release the mouse button.

To copy and drop, use steps 1 and 2 of the drag and drop method. Hold down Ctrl while dragging the shadow cursor to the new location. As you drag, the mouse pointer changes, indicating that you're copying text:

Release the mouse button when the shadow cursor is in the correct position. The text appears in both places.

DRAGGING BETWEEN DOCUMENTS

Using either drag and drop or copy and drop between two documents requires a little more setup, but essentially you use the same technique:

1. Arrange the two documents on-screen so that you can see them at the same time. The easiest method is to open both documents, then choose <u>W</u>indow, <u>T</u>ile Top to Bottom or <u>W</u>indow, Tile <u>S</u>ide by Side. It's easiest to scroll though the destination document until you can see on-screen the location where you want to insert the text.
2. Now use the same steps described for drag and drop (or copy and drop), but point to the desired location in the other document window before you release the mouse button.

MOVING OR COPYING TEXT USING THE KEYBOARD METHODS

You can also copy and move text easily with the keyboard. Use these steps:

1. Select the text.
2. Press Ctrl+C (or choose Edit, Copy) to copy text to the Clipboard. Or press Ctrl+X (or choose Edit, Cut) to move text to the Clipboard.
3. Move the insertion point to the location where the text is to be inserted, and then press Ctrl+V (or choose Edit, Paste).

Getting Help When You Really Need It

There's nothing to be ashamed of when you just can't figure out how to make a feature work, or you don't remember the shortest method of accomplishing a task. WordPerfect 8 provides a number of different ways to obtain help.

Using the Windows 95-Style Help

Like all Windows 95 programs, WordPerfect 8 provides a fully searchable Help feature. You can locate the feature you're looking for by thumbing through Help books, searching through a complex Index, or by asking Help to find a specific term anywhere in the Help file.

Here's how to use the Windows 95-style Help feature:

1. From anywhere in WordPerfect, press F1 to move immediately to the Help Topics: WordPerfect Help dialog box shown in Figure 3-13.

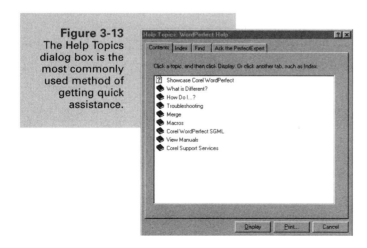

Figure 3-13 The Help Topics dialog box is the most commonly used method of getting quick assistance.

2. Select the tab you want to use to find your help topic.

   - The Contents tab allows you to open Help books, locate a Table of Contents item, and then open the subject text by choosing <u>D</u>isplay.
   - The Index tab displays a list of indexed items within the Help system. Begin typing the text you want to find in the <u>T</u>ype the First Few Letters of the Word You're Looking For text box. As you type, Help begins selecting a phrase or help item that matches your entry. When Help has found the correct entry, choose <u>D</u>isplay to read the corresponding help text.
   - The Find tab is your entry into a full database of all words within the Help file. The first time you use Find, Windows 95's Find Setup Wizard prompts you to create the database list. Select the list type you want, choose <u>N</u>ext, and choose <u>F</u>inish. Windows 95 creates the Word List and then redisplays the Find tab.

     Type the word or phrase you're researching into the <u>T</u>ype the Word(s) You Want to Find text box. Help displays matching words and associated phrases as you type. You can select from the matching word list to limit the topics found. When you see a topic you want to read, select it and choose <u>D</u>isplay.

While a fully maximized list takes slightly more space on a hard disk, it's probably best to create the full list so that you can be assured every possible word is available for your query.

3. While using Help, you can switch between all the Help tabs to more fully research your question. You also can print the displayed help text using the <u>O</u>ptions menu, or can <u>A</u>nnotate the entry, adding your own comments, so that you're able to quickly review any custom information you may need to track.
4. Wherever possible, click a link button or the Related Concepts button entries to move between related entries.
5. When you've finished reading your Help display, click Cancel or the Close button to close Help and return to your document window.

Using Ask the PerfectExpert

Ask the PerfectExpert is an easy, gentle, step-by-step help system that can hold your hand and demonstrate a particular WordPerfect feature that you want to see in action. It's especially useful when you really have no idea what a feature does

CHAPTER 3 • SO HOW DOES WORDPERFECT WORK? **73**

USING PROJECTS TO CREATE A DOCUMENT WAS DISCUSSED EARLIER IN THIS CHAPTER.

and you need help performing the steps. The term *PerfectExpert* is used by Corel WordPerfect Suite 8 to indicate some type of prompted response to a question or to assist you when performing tasks in any of the Suite programs. For example, when creating a project, the PerfectExpert appears in a panel down the left edge of the document window.

You can, however, ask a question of the PerfectExpert to open a series of help topics related to your question. To do so, use these steps:

1. From a document window, choose <u>H</u>elp, Ask the <u>P</u>erfectExpert. The Help Topics: WordPerfect Help window opens, with the Ask the PerfectExpert tab on top.

•••

Or, from the Help Topics: WordPerfect Help window, click the Ask the PerfectExpert tab.

•••

2. In the <u>W</u>hat Do You Want to Know? text box, type your query in the form of a question, then click the <u>S</u>earch button. A list of possible topics appears in the S<u>e</u>arch Results list. Figure 3-14 shows a completed query.

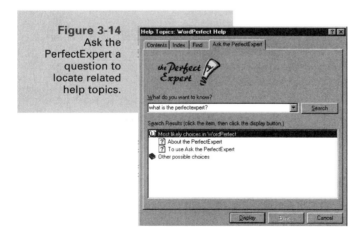

Figure 3-14
Ask the PerfectExpert a question to locate related help topics.

3. Select one of the resulting help topics, then click <u>D</u>isplay to open its help text.
4. When you've completed your Help session, click the application close button to return to your document window.

You can also use the PerfectExpert to prompt you through WordPerfect tasks you might perform while creating or editing a document. Use these steps:

 PART I • LET'S GET STARTED

1. Open the PerfectExpert by clicking the PerfectExpert toolbar button, or by choosing <u>H</u>elp, Perfect<u>E</u>xpert. The PerfectExpert panel opens at the left side of your document window, as shown in Figure 3-15.

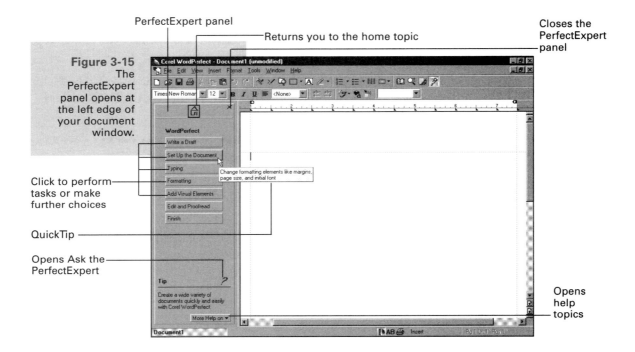

Figure 3-15
The PerfectExpert panel opens at the left edge of your document window.

2. Using the task buttons, thumb through the PerfectExpert to read tips about your task, or even get chances to perform the necessary steps.
3. To close the PerfectExpert panel, click the Close button.

Getting Online Help

Corel has an intricate Web site on the Internet from which you can learn about other Corel products, or access technical support directly. In addition, a number of independent Web sites and newsgroups focus on WordPerfect. Another very popular place to get outstanding, helpful responses to your WordPerfect questions is the WPUSERS forum on CompuServe.

Of course, the best place to start is with Corel itself. You can reach the Corel Web Site at **http://www.corel.com**. While the content of the site changes frequently (sometimes daily!), you'll generally be able to locate product support, read reviews, and see what's coming out soon (see Figure 3-16).

CHAPTER 3 • SO HOW DOES WORDPERFECT WORK? 75

Figure 3-16
The Corel home page is the best place to find out what's happening with Corel products.

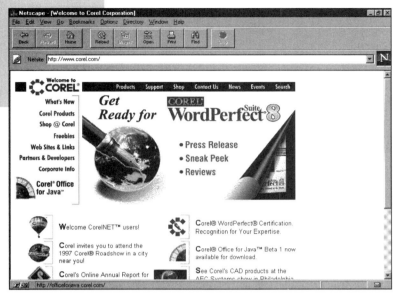

At the time this book was written, the electronic help locations listed below were all active and happily providing WordPerfect support:

Address	Description
http://www.corel.com	Corel Corporation home page
mailto:wptech@corel.com	E-mail address for technical support (you need to include your WordPerfect 8 serial number or support PIN)
http://www.corelmag.com	Home page for Corel Magazine
http://www.wpmag.com	WordPerfect Magazine Web site
http://www.i-us.com	Independent support group with several WordPerfect forums
ftp://ftp.corel.com/pub/ ↪wordperfect/wpwin	FTP site for document transfer and program patches
news://cnews.corel.com/ ↪corel.support.wordperfect7	Newsgroup
WPUSERS	CompuServe, GO WPUSERS
COREL	CompuServe, GO COREL

Part II
Daily Tasks

4 The Basic Business Letter. 79

5 Fine-Tuning and Enhancing Your Documents 119

6 Printing Your Document to Paper, E-mail,
or Fax 151

7 Same Letter to Lots of Different People! 171

4
The Basic Business Letter

In This Chapter

- **Working with Page Definitions**
- **Using Tabs, Indents, and Justification**
- **Adding Fonts and Attributes**
- **Including Special Symbols in Documents**
- **Using the Business Letter Project**

Basic business correspondence in the form of letters and memos probably occupies more time than any other single task in an office. While WordPerfect is a sophisticated, complex, word processing program, most of its daily use is in typing business correspondence. By learning the techniques used when creating letters and memos in WordPerfect, you'll be able to approach other document types with ease.

80 PART II • DAILY TASKS

This chapter will assist you in creating a basic business letter. You'll learn how to store and use addresses from the Corel Address Book in your letter, and how to use a project template to create your letter. In addition, you will modify page settings, use the tab and justification features to align text, create bulleted or numbered lists, create a header, and number pages.

Creating a Letter from Scratch

Nothing could be simpler. This section will walk you through the steps to create a typical business letter, complete with a header, page numbering, and some fancy fonts. This letter will be approached in two ways. Some of the steps will be presented in the order in which a document might be created, from the beginning to the end. A few steps will involve editing text you might have already typed into your document. The letter used as an example in this section is shown in Figure 4-1. Don't worry if you can't read the text right now—the text portion will be included in each of the hands-on sections later in this chapter. Glance at Figure 4-1 now just to get a general sense of the document itself.

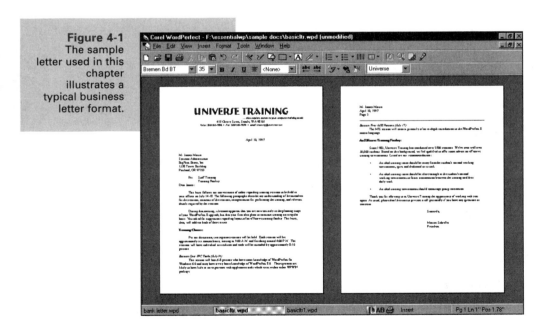

Figure 4-1
The sample letter used in this chapter illustrates a typical business letter format.

Some Basic Layout Thoughts

As discussed in Chapter 3, WordPerfect has already set up a typical business paper layout or *style* for you which has preset margins and tabs. If you use pre-printed letterhead, take a look at it before creating your first letter. You'll need to verify the size of the paper and how much room the letterhead logo might take, and to decide basically how you normally lay out or type a letter. Some letterheads require special margin settings so that the body of the letter does not print atop the logo.

Some businesses like to have all their text lined up on the left margin and right margin, termed *full block with full justification*. Others prefer a *modified block* style which typically tabs the first line of each paragraph and places the date and signature lines just to the right of center. Whatever your preference, you can use the default settings for WordPerfect, or change them accordingly.

It isn't necessary to make formatting changes before you type a document. You can easily change the appearance of a document as many times as you want after the text entry has been completed. In fact, it's often most effective to type your thoughts, and then later go back and format the document. Using this approach may result in getting your work done rather than exploring every new software feature!

Changing the Paper Size

In some offices where letterhead is printed commercially, the paper size actually measures 8 1/4 by 11 1/2 inches (referred to as A4 size) rather than 8 1/2 by 11 inches. If your letterhead does not match WordPerfect's defaults, your text will not align properly on your letterhead when printed. If your paper matches Word-Perfect's defaults, you don't need to select a paper size. You're ready to move to the next step.

Hands On: Selecting a Paper Size

Here's how to change the paper size to match your letterhead:

1. Position the insertion point anywhere within the page on which you want the new paper size to start.
2. Choose Format, Page, Page Setup. The Page Setup dialog box will open as displayed in Figure 4-2.

You can also open the Page Setup dialog box by choosing File, Page Setup.

Figure 4-2 Using the Page Setup dialog box, you can set different paper sizes for various pages of your document.

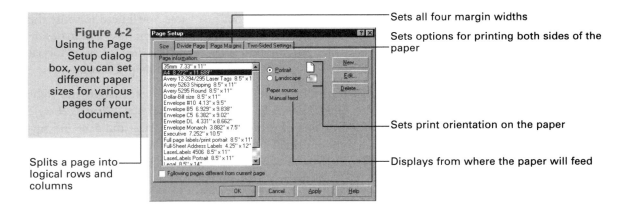

- Sets all four margin widths
- Sets options for printing both sides of the paper
- Sets print orientation on the paper
- Displays from where the paper will feed
- Splits a page into logical rows and columns

3. Select the A4 paper definition from the Page Information list. Notice that when selecting a paper definition you can also choose to have the text printed on your paper in either Portrait or Landscape mode. As you click a definition, the *paper source* setting for the definition appears to the right of the list. The paper source indicates the paper feed location for the selected printer.

4. If you typically load your letterhead from a paper tray, you need to change the location for the A4 paper size. To do so, click the Edit button. The Edit Page Size dialog box opens, as shown in Figure 4-3.

Figure 4-3 All settings for a defined paper size can be modified.

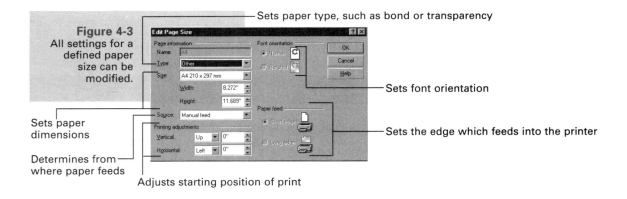

- Sets paper type, such as bond or transparency
- Sets font orientation
- Sets the edge which feeds into the printer
- Sets paper dimensions
- Determines from where paper feeds
- Adjusts starting position of print

5. Select the paper source from the Source drop-down list, then review the Edit Page Size dialog box for any other changes you need. When finished, click OK. You'll be returned to the Page Setup dialog box.

6. Click OK to return to your document window, assigning the selected page definition to your document. Click Cancel to abandon your choice.

Clicking New from the Page Setup dialog box allows you to create your own, custom paper definition, patterned after the currently selected paper definition. Be aware, however, that any custom page definitions you create are saved with the current printer and are available only when that printer is selected. Also, if you work on a network or share a printer, you might not have sufficient network rights to create page definitions. Talk to your system administrator if the New button is inactive.

Setting Page Margins

Like virtually all WordPerfect formatting instructions, you can change the margins in your document as often as you want. It can be beneficial to set up a page completely before starting to type.

Hands On: Changing Page Margins

While you can change the top and bottom margin settings as many times as you like, only the last change made for each page is kept. Therefore, changing a top or bottom margin results in only one setting for the page. Left and right margins, however, can be changed multiple times within the same page, and each change remains in effect until the margins are set again. Use these steps:

1. If the Page Setup dialog box is no longer on-screen, choose File, Page Setup to reopen the box.
2. Click the Page Margins tab to select it. Figure 4-4 displays the Page Margins tab as it will appear following step 3.

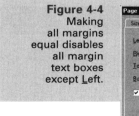

Figure 4-4 Making all margins equal disables all margin text boxes except Left.

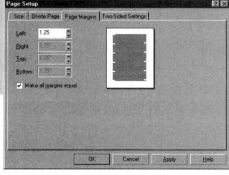

PART II • DAILY TASKS

3. In each of the four margin fields, type the measurement for the area to be kept blank around all four sides of the document. In this example, change the margins to 1 1/4" for each side by typing 1.25 in the Left field. Then check Make All Margins Equal. WordPerfect then sets each margin to the width in the first field. It's not necessary to include the inch marks (quotation marks); WordPerfect supplies those for you. As you make margin changes, the page preview displays your margin settings.

In most dialog box controls that require an exact measurement, you can type the measurement in a fraction form (1 1/3). WordPerfect automatically converts the fraction to a decimal.

4. Click OK to return to the document window.

Starting Your Letter

Now that you've verified the page settings for your document, it's time to get to work and actually type some text.

Be aware that this sample document proceeds rather methodically in an attempt to present as many features as possible. In the real world, you'd likely not type your letterhead manually on each letter. See Chapters 15 and 16 for thoughts about creating macros or projects to automatically insert this type of information.

Hands On: Adding a Letterhead

In this letterhead example, the text will be typed and then later modified to add appropriate fonts and text alignment formatting. Follow these steps:

1. As you type the text in the letterhead, press [Enter] at the end of each line. The text will automatically be placed at the left margin. Type the following:

   Universe Training
   ... the complete answer to your computer training needs
   415 Cherry Street, Seattle, WA 98101
   Voice: 206/555-7898 * Fax: 206/555-7899 * e-mail: training@universe.com

Note

Did you notice that the e-mail address automatically converted to a hypertext link? A *hypertext link* allows you to quickly jump to another document, a location within the current document, or a document stored elsewhere (perhaps on the Internet or an intranet).

Check Reveal Codes for the Hypertext codes. WordPerfect automatically converts text that looks like an Internet address to hypertext—the clue here being the combination of the @ symbol and the `.com` suffix in the e-mail address. If you ultimately send this letter via e-mail to James Martin, he'll be able to double-click the link and have his e-mail program start, with the Mail To field already filled out with the Universe Training e-mail address.

> CHAPTER 13 DISCUSSES HYPERTEXT LINKS IN GREATER DEPTH.

2. Press [Enter] three times to complete the letterhead.

Adding a Date

WordPerfect includes a powerful date feature which can be used to automatically insert today's date into any document. WordPerfect reads the date and time from your computer's clock and then arranges the date according to the currently selected format. The default date format is Month DD, YYYY (as in `April 14, 1997`). WordPerfect provides a number of different date formats; you also can design your own format.

Two different types of dates can be automatically added. The first, *date text,* simply inserts today's date in your document as normal text. As with any other text, date text does not change once it's typed. The second type, *date code,* on the other hand, adds a code to your document—this code changes to match the current date and time from the computer clock each time the document is opened, saved, or printed.

Hands On: Adding Today's Date to Your Letter

To add a date to your document, use these steps:

1. For modified block style, press [Tab] seven times to move the insertion point to 4.5". Watch the location of the insertion point in the Position indicator displayed on the application bar at the bottom of the document window.

PART II • DAILY TASKS

Tip

You can also just position the shadow cursor in the document where you want the date to appear, then click. All necessary tabs and returns will be added to the document automatically.

2. Choose Insert, Date/Time. The Date/Time dialog box opens, displaying a list of predefined date and time formats (see Figure 4-5).

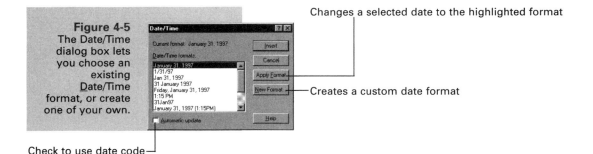

Figure 4-5
The Date/Time dialog box lets you choose an existing Date/Time format, or create one of your own.

Changes a selected date to the highlighted format

Creates a custom date format

Check to use date code

3. From the Date/Time Formats list, select the default format illustrated as `January 31, 1997`.
4. To have WordPerfect automatically update the date in the document each time your letter is printed, saved, or opened, check the Automatic Update check box.
5. Click Insert to add the date to the document.
6. Press [Enter] three times to move the insertion point to the address area.

Tip

The shortcut keys to insert the date in your document are [Ctrl]+[D] for date text and [Ctrl]+[Shift]+[D] for date code.

Addresses, Addresses, Addresses Everywhere!

Have you ever noticed how many different places you store and attempt to maintain addresses? Up until very recently in my office, I maintained a Rolodex, a Day-Timer with written addresses, a file with various business cards, and three different electronic address lists on my computer! Needless to say, things were never up-to-date anywhere.

With the emergence of Windows 95, I began rolling more and more of my multiple address lists into one place—the Exchange/Windows Messaging Address Book. Now, combined with a little electronic notebook, I maintain only one address list and update my computer list from my notebook periodically. This system isn't perfect, but it sure helps. The Address Book system within Corel WordPerfect Suite 8 is an important link in effectively managing my addresses without duplication of effort.

If your Windows 95 Microsoft Exchange program is still named Exchange, you might want to download and apply the program update, EXUPDUSA.EXE, from the Microsoft FTP site:

```
ftp://ftp.microsoft.com/softlib/MSLFILES/
```

Using the Address Book

The Address Book is a small but very useful application within Corel WordPerfect Suite 8 that stores names and addresses. Addresses can be physical addresses, e-mail addresses, and phone numbers. Entries in the Address Book can be inserted into any document. You can use addresses one at a time, or select several to include in a document. Another option is to select multiple addresses to use as a data source for a merge file. If you have a modem available to your system, and have the Microsoft Phone Dialer utility, you can ask Address Book to dial the selected number for you.

You can find more information about the Phone Dialer utility by searching the Windows 95 Help file accessed through Start, Help.

You can open the Address Book in two ways—by choosing Tools, Address Book; or by clicking the Address Book button in any dialog box that displays it, such as when creating an envelope. The Address Book button looks like this:

Unfortunately, the Address Book button does not appear on the default WordPerfect 8 Toolbar. Add it to the toolbar using the steps outlined in the Chapter 2 section titled, "Editing a Bar." You'll find the Address Book button in the Tools feature category in the Toolbar Editor.

PART II • DAILY TASKS

The first time you open the Address Book, you'll see the My Addresses Book when you choose Tools, Address Book or click the Address Book button. Then, by default, WordPerfect displays the last book opened each time you reopen the Address Book. Figure 4-6 shows how entries might appear in the My Addresses Book.

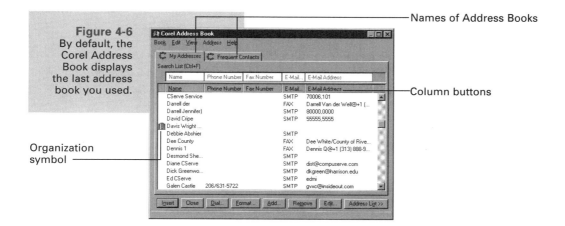

Figure 4-6 By default, the Corel Address Book displays the last address book you used.

Two types of addresses can be entered in your Address Book—a Person or an Organization. Figure 4-6 displays several Person entries and one Organization entry. You can tell that an entry is an organization by the appearance of the Organization symbol in the first column of the address list.

A Person entry holds information such as first and last name, personal street address, the name of any business with which this entry should be cross-referenced, and several phone numbers. A completed entry form for Person is displayed in Figure 4-7. If you've included a business name in your Person entry, an Organization entry is also created. It stores the name of the organization, along with its street address and phone numbers. Figure 4-8 displays an entry dialog box for an Organization entry.

> CHAPTER 7 HAS MORE INFORMATION ABOUT MERGING USING THE ADDRESS BOOK.

Hands On: Adding Names to Your Address Book

Because James Martin is a person to whom letters are frequently written, his name should be added to the Address Book prior to using it in the sample letter. You can add names and addresses to the Address Book at any time. To add James Martin to the Address Book, use these steps:

1. Open the Address Book by choosing Tools, Address Book. Select the Address Book to which you want to add the entry by clicking its tab—in this case, My Addresses.

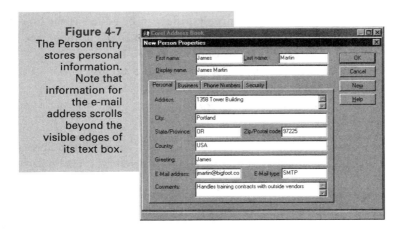

Figure 4-7
The Person entry stores personal information. Note that information for the e-mail address scrolls beyond the visible edges of its text box.

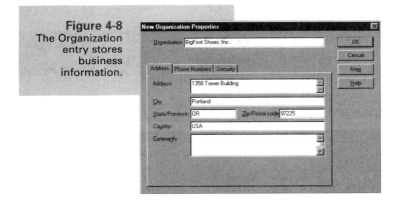

Figure 4-8
The Organization entry stores business information.

2. Choose <u>A</u>dd. The New Entry dialog box appears, as shown in Figure 4-9.
3. Select Person as the entry type, then click OK. The New Person Properties dialog box opens (refer to Figure 4-7).
4. Referring to Figure 4-7, complete the Personal tab for James Martin.

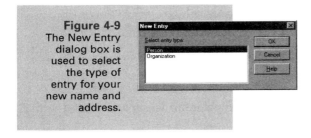

Figure 4-9
The New Entry dialog box is used to select the type of entry for your new name and address.

5. Click the Business tab so that BigFoot Shoes, Inc. can be added as the link between the person James Martin and the organization BigFoot Shoes, Inc. Complete the Business fields by typing **BigFoot Shoes, Inc.** in the Organization field, **MIS** in the Department field and **Systems Administrator** in the Title field.
6. Click the Phone Numbers tab and type **206/888-1234** in the Business phone field.
7. When you are satisfied with the entry, click OK. Both James Martin and BigFoot Shoes, Inc. are added as new entries in the current address book.

You can continue to add entries, one after another, by clicking the Ne*w* button (rather than OK) while still in the New Person Properties dialog box. You need to verify each entry by responding Yes when asked if you want to save your changes.

Hands On: Inserting an Address Book Entry in a Document

With a name stored in the Address Book, it's a simple task to use it in a document. Here are the steps:

1. Verify that the insertion point is at the beginning of the line where you want to insert the address for James Martin, then open the Address Book.
2. Select `James Martin` from the address list.

If your list is large, search for the name by pressing [Ctrl]+[F]. The first time you use the Name Search function, you'll see a brief informational message with instructions on how to search. After clicking OK to close the message box, you can type a name in the Name Search field to efficiently select a name. You can select multiple names by holding down [Ctrl] while clicking each name you want to use.

3. Choose *F*ormat to verify the layout for the address to be used in the document. The Format Address dialog box appears.
4. Select `Name, Title, and Company` as the *F*ormat to be used. As you select a *F*ormat, the preview window displays its appearance (see Figure 4-10).
5. Click OK to return to the Address Book.
6. Click *I*nsert. James Martin and his address information are inserted in the sample letter at the insertion point.
7. Press [Enter] twice to move the insertion point to the Re: line.

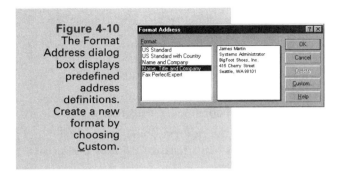

Figure 4-10
The Format Address dialog box displays predefined address definitions. Create a new format by choosing Custom.

Whenever the Address Book is open, you can make changes to an entry by selecting it and then choosing the Edit button. The Properties dialog box for that entry opens.

Make any desired changes, then click OK to store your changes. If you click Cancel, your edits are abandoned. Either way, you're returned to the Address Book dialog box.

Using the Microsoft Windows Messaging Address Book

Addresses stored in the Windows Messaging/Exchange Address Book can also be used in WordPerfect documents. Similarly, the Corel Address Book can be used as the Personal Address Book in Windows Messaging/Exchange. The Corel Address Book has a significant advantage over the Windows Messaging Address Book in how it handles multiple addresses that share the same organization. For example, suppose you want to store individual e-mail and phone numbers for several people who all work for the same company at the same physical address. With Windows Messaging, you need to create a separate address for each person, including typing the company name and address for each entry. The Corel Address Book stores the company information only once, then sensibly links it to each person within the organization.

Hands On: Using the Windows Messaging/Exchange Address Book in WordPerfect Suite 8

If you've already developed an extensive address list using the Exchange Address Book, you would no doubt prefer not to re-enter all that information. Here's how to use your existing address book in WordPerfect Suite 8:

1. From within WordPerfect, open the Address Book by choosing <u>T</u>ools, <u>A</u>ddress.
2. Choose <u>E</u>dit, <u>S</u>ettings. The Address Book Settings dialog box is displayed.
3. Select `MS Exchange Settings` as your <u>P</u>referred Profile, then click OK.
4. Close the Corel Address Book by clicking the Close button. Then close WordPerfect. Be sure to save any open documents if necessary.
5. Restart WordPerfect 8 and then open the Address Book. Your Corel Address Book dialog box should display tabs for each Address Book that existed in Windows Messaging/Exchange.

Adding a new entry to an Address Book that is jointly used by Corel and Windows Messaging requires you to choose an entry type, exactly the way you entered names in the Exchange Address Book.

If you want, you also can designate Corel Settings to be your default profile for Exchange. Within Exchange, choose <u>T</u>ools, <u>O</u>ptions, When Starting Windows Messaging. You also need to open the Corel Settings profile by selecting Mail within the Control Panel. Then add your other services to the Corel Settings profile so that your personal folders (or other services such as Internet Mail) are available.

Typing the Body of the Letter

With the address in place, you're now ready to type the body of the letter. There are two possible methods to properly format the text as you type. They're both mentioned here, because, while the first method is more common, the second allows for more consistency.

The text used in the sample letter follows this paragraph in bold. While the body of the letter is rather long, it will be used to illustrate the remaining features in this chapter. If you're working through this chapter step-by-step, use the first method to type the sample letter. Then you'll be able to continue without confusion for the rest of the chapter.

As with a real-life document, be sure to periodically save the example document to safeguard your work.

Re: Staff Training
Training Facility

Dear James:

This letter follows our conversation of today regarding training sessions to be held in your offices on July 14-18. The following paragraphs describe my understanding of the attendees for the sessions, contents of the sessions, compensation for performing the training, and relevant details required by the sessions.

During that meeting, it became apparent that you are now not only in the planning stage of your WordPerfect 8 upgrade, but that your firm also plans to continue training on a regular basis. You asked for suggestions regarding layout of an effective training facility. This letter, then, will address both issues.

Training Classes:

Per our discussion, two separate sessions will be held. Each session will be approximately six contact hours, starting at 9:00 A.M. and finishing around 4:00 P.M. The sessions will have individual outlines and each will be attended by approximately 8-10 persons.

Session One: IPC Techs (July 14)

This session will host 6-8 persons who have some knowledge of WordPerfect for Windows 6.0 and may have a very basic knowledge of WordPerfect 8.0. These persons are likely to have little or no experience with application tools which exist in either WPWIN package.

Session Two: MIS Persons (July 17)

The MIS session will consist primarily of an in-depth introduction to the WordPerfect 8 macro language.

An Effective Training Facility:

Since 1983, Universe Training has conducted over 2500 seminars. We've seen well over 30,000 students. Based on this background, we feel qualified to offer some advice on effective training environments. Listed are our recommendations:

Using [Enter] and [Tab] to Format Paragraphs

The most common method of typing paragraph text is to press [Tab] (if desired) to move the first line of text to the right one-half inch. Press [Enter] at the end of each paragraph and again to create blank lines between paragraphs. Be sure not to press Enter at the end of each line of text within the paragraph. Let text within a paragraph automatically wrap to the next line whenever the right margin position is reached.

Each time you press Enter, WordPerfect considers that you've finished a paragraph. Therefore, even a short line such as the Re: line is an individual paragraph.

Most fonts used in today's word processing systems (such as Times Roman, Arial, or ShelleyAllegro) are *proportional fonts.* This means, essentially, that every letter and character has its own inherent size or width. Characters in these fonts actually differ character by character. The obvious example is that the letter "w" is wider than the letter "i." It is difficult, if not impossible, therefore, to accurately align columns of characters using the space bar.

Some fonts, such as Courier, measure the size of the font by the number of characters that fit in a one-inch space. These fonts are called *monospace fonts.* You can use the space bar to align columns typed with monospace fonts, but be careful. If you later decide to change fonts, your text may be misaligned.

Hands On: Using Tabs to Align Text

Tabs are used to force text to align at precise locations. Because WordPerfect has provided default tabs every one-half inch, it's unnecessary to modify any settings. Use these steps to type and align the Re: lines:

1. Press Tab, then type **Re:**
2. Press Tab again, then type **Staff Training**. By including a tab after the Re: prefix, you'll be able to accurately align the next line of text. Press Enter to complete the paragraph.
3. Press Tab twice, then type **Training Facility**. Notice that the two subject lines align perfectly.
4. Press Enter twice to move to the salutation line.
5. Type **Dear James:** and press Enter twice.
6. Continue to type the remaining text of the document. WordPerfect automatically creates a new page as you cross the bottom margin, wrapping text to the beginning of the next page.
7. Be sure to save your document, naming it **training letter,** if you haven't already done so.

•••

You can start a new page manually at any time by pressing Ctrl+Enter. This key combination creates a *hard page break* in the document and inserts an [HPg] code in Reveal Codes. A *soft page break* ([SPg]) is automatically inserted by WordPerfect when it creates new pages for you. The soft page break location changes as you add or edit text. A hard page break, on the other hand, remains in exactly the same location.

•••

Using Paragraph Formatting

STYLES ARE DISCUSSED MORE FULLY IN CHAPTER 5.

The second method automatically formats paragraph text using the paragraph format feature. This method is probably more technically correct; however, over 90 percent of WordPerfect users never refer to this feature, considering it to be more work. It can become important when you exchange documents between users of Corel WordPerfect and Microsoft Word. Word heavily uses paragraph styles, while WordPerfect does not. You might find that documents convert more cleanly between the two programs if you use paragraph formatting in WordPerfect documents.

Note

One drawback to using paragraph formatting is that you must use heading styles to format headings for which you do not want to apply the paragraph formatting. Or, you can manually modify the format for each heading. For example, suppose that you have paragraph formatting in place which indents the first line of a paragraph 1/2", and you want to type a heading that should be aligned with the page left margin. You need to use a heading style, or change paragraph formatting for the heading, and then change it back to resume your paragraph typing.

Paragraph formatting adds codes to the document at the point where paragraph formatting is defined. These codes are listed below:

Code	What it does
[Para Spacing]	Stores number of lines, or points, that occur between paragraphs
[First Ln Ind]	Sets the distance the first line of each paragraph is indented

[Lft Mar Adj]   Adjusts the left margin for each paragraph based on the current page left margin (for example, if you type a left margin adjustment of .5″, and the page left margin is 1″, the paragraph begins 1.5″ from the left edge of the paper)

[Rgt Mar Adj]   Adjusts the right margin for each paragraph based on the current page right margin

Although the sample document created in this chapter does not use paragraph formatting, here are the steps you'll need to use paragraph formatting in other documents:

1. With the insertion point in your document where you want the paragraph style to begin, choose Format, Paragraph, Format. The Paragraph Format dialog box opens, as shown in Figure 4-11.

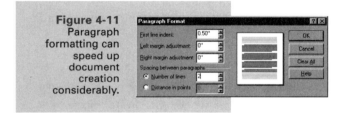

Figure 4-11 Paragraph formatting can speed up document creation considerably.

2. Type the paragraph settings you want to use in each field of the dialog box. Figure 4-11 suggests settings that are useful for most standard letters. As you type the settings to be used, notice that the preview window is updated to display the effect.

3. Click OK to store your settings and return to the document window. The insertion point now resides at the position where you'll begin typing your text.

4. Type the first paragraph and then press Enter. Paragraph formatting automatically inserts the correct distance after the text and positions the insertion point where the next paragraph should begin.

When you've completed the section in your document and want to stop using paragraph formatting, return to the Paragraph Format dialog box, as described in the previous steps, and click the Clear All button. This returns to the default settings. Then click OK to return to your document window.

Refining the Document

With the document text completed, you can now easily revise the file, adding fancy fonts or changing the general text format as you desire. Remember that formatting of any type can be included as you create a document from beginning to end, or can be added after the document has been typed.

Creating Bulleted or Numbered Lists

Bulleted lists contain paragraphs that each begin with a *bullet*, typically a round symbol used to indicate a special point of interest in a document. A bullet can be any symbol or character in WordPerfect's character sets. See the section titled "Using Special Characters," later in this chapter, for help in selecting other bullet characters.

Numbered lists are paragraphs that each begin with a number. Each subsequent paragraph in the list begins with the next higher number. Using the paragraph numbering feature allows you to move, delete, or add paragraphs and have the numbers stay in sequence.

Hands On: Creating Simple Bulleted or Numbered Lists

Use these steps to create a bulleted or numbered list:

1. Position the insertion point in the document where you want the first list item to begin. In the sample training letter, press Ctrl+End to move the insertion point to the very end of the document.
2. Click either the Bullets or Numbering button in the toolbar (see Figure 4-12). Then select the Bullet style or Numbering style you want to use from the drop-down palette of choices. A bullet or number is inserted when you make your selection. For the sample letter, select a small bullet from the Bullets palette.

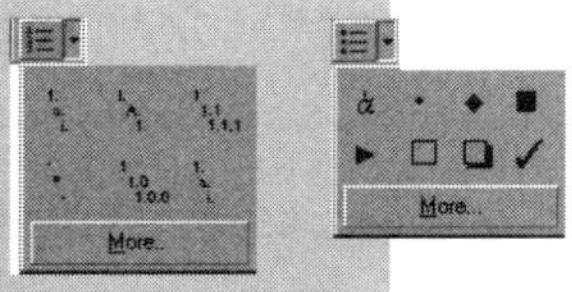

Figure 4-12 Use the Bullets and Numbering buttons to create simple, organized lists.

3. Type the following paragraph:

   An ideal training room should be away from the student's normal working environment, quiet and dedicated to its task.

   Notice that the text automatically wraps to the tabbed or *indented* position after the bullet. See the next section, "Understanding Tabs and Indents," for a fuller explanation.

4. Press [Enter]. The next number or bullet appears. Press [Enter] again to double-space between the paragraphs. The bullet or number also moves.

5. Type the following two bulleted paragraphs, pressing [Enter] twice at the end of each paragraph:

   An ideal training room should be close enough to the student's normal working environment to foster a connection between the training and their daily work.

   An ideal training environment should encourage group interaction.

6. When all the bulleted paragraphs are typed, and you've pressed [Enter] to end the last paragraph, a bullet will again be inserted. Press [←Backspace] to delete the bullet. You then can continue to type the remainder of the document, pressing [Tab] (or clicking the shadow cursor) where appropriate to align the signature lines with the date. Type the following:

   Thank you for allowing us at Universe Training the opportunity of working with you again. As usual, please don't hesitate to give me a call personally if you have any questions or concerns.

                                                              Sincerely,

                                                        Maxine Schiefler
                                                        President

Tip

If you've turned off bullets, you can begin adding bullets again by positioning the insertion point where you want a bullet to appear, and then pressing [Ctrl]+[Shift]+[B].

Caution

If you're using numbered paragraphs, pressing [Tab] increments the number to the next level, similar to how an outline works. If you accidentally do so, press [Shift]+[Tab] to move back one level. (See Chapter 8 for more help on outline levels.)

CHAPTER 4 • THE BASIC BUSINESS LETTER 99

Understanding Tabs and Indents

The combination of tabs and indents provides you with the ability to format text instantly. You'll be able to create lists with exactly the layout you have in mind without any fancy format requirements. Consider the examples illustrated in Figure 4-13 for a better understanding of how tabs, indents, and hanging indents differ.

First, a clarification of terms:

- A *tab* is used to position the first line of a paragraph only. Remember, however, that sometimes a paragraph is a single line. Tab codes are displayed in Reveal Codes as `[Left Tab]`, `[Right Tab]`, `[Dec Tab]`, or `[Center Tab]` (or, where dot leaders are used, `[...Left Tab]`, `[...Right Tab]`, `[...Dec Tab]`, or `[...Center Tab]`). Refer to Sections 1 and 2 in Figure 4-13 for examples of tabbed paragraphs.

- An *indent* (`F7`) moves the first line—and all remaining lines in the paragraph that wrap—to the tab setting where the indent placed the first line of text. You can use several indents in sequence, but the last indent in the series controls positioning and wrapping of the text. It can be more convenient to indent a paragraph or two rather than change a left margin. In Reveal Codes, an indent code reads `[Hd Left Ind]`. Sections 3, 5, and 6 in Figure 4-13 display indent examples.

- A *double-indent* (`Ctrl`+`Shift`+`F7`) sets the text to tab settings on both the left and right edges of the paragraph. Suppose, for example, you have tab settings at 1.5", 2", 6", and 7". If you use one double-indent, the text begins at 1.5" and wraps at 7". If you use two double-indents, the text begins at 2" and wraps at 6". A double-indent code in Reveal Codes says `[Hd Left\/Right Ind]`. Refer to Section 4 in Figure 4-13 for an example of a double-indent.

- A *hanging indent* (`Ctrl`+`F7` or `F7`, `Shift`+`Tab`) aligns the first line of text to the left of the remaining lines of text. A hanging indent is formed by using two formatting instructions. The placement of these two instructions determines exactly how the text wraps. First, you use indent (`F7`) to set the location where text will wrap on all lines except the first line. Then, you use a hard back tab (`Shift`+`Tab`) to move the first line of text back to the position where you want the first line to begin. In Reveal Codes, you'll see two codes: `[Hd Left Ind][Hd Back Tab]`.

• •

Pressing `Ctrl`+`F7` assigns a single-level hanging indent to the beginning of the current paragraph. Pressing `F7`, `Shift`+`Tab` allows you to design the hanging indent exactly the way you want it to look.

• •

> **Using a hanging indent requires that a tab is set where the back tab aligns. Without a tab setting, the first line of a hanging indent is positioned at the left edge of the paper.**

Here's an example. Suppose that you have tabs set at 1", 2", 4", and 5". The first line of text must begin at the left margin, also set at 1", while the text must wrap to 2". To create this example, first press F7, then press Shift+Tab. The insertion point first moves to 2", the location of the first tab setting. When a back tab is added, the insertion point jumps back to 1" where the first tab setting is located. As you type, text starts at 1" continues to the right margin, and then wraps to 2", the location of the indent. Sections 7 and 8 of Figure 4-13 show paragraphs created with hanging indents.

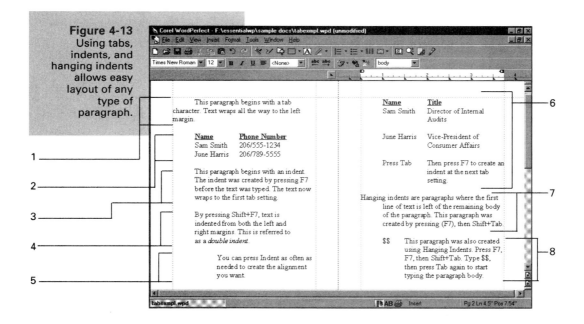

Figure 4-13 Using tabs, indents, and hanging indents allows easy layout of any type of paragraph.

Changing Fonts and Adding Attributes

Technically, the term *font* describes a typeface and all its associated sizes and styles. You can see a list of typefaces (called *font faces* in WordPerfect) by clicking the Font Face button on the property bar (see Figure 4-14). For example, Times New Roman is a typeface. A font is the combination of Times New Roman, 12

Chapter 4 • The Basic Business Letter 101

point, italic, black. We tend to use the term *font* loosely when discussing the appearance of the characters on-screen and at the printer.

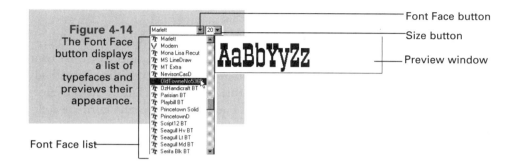

Figure 4-14 The Font Face button displays a list of typefaces and previews their appearance.

The fonts you use in a document often set its tone and emphasis. Using a font effectively can make a document appear warm and friendly, or formal and stuffy. Figure 4-15 suggests a few font groupings for your consideration.

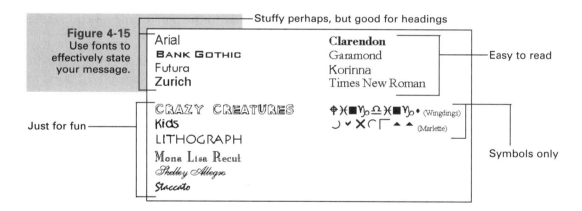

Figure 4-15 Use fonts to effectively state your message.

One hundred fonts are automatically copied to your system when you use the Typical installation of Corel WordPerfect Suite 8. The Corel WordPerfect Suite 8 CD, however, contains the files for 1,000 fonts so that you can freely set the mood for your writing.

Tip

You can easily add additional fonts to your system through the Corel WordPerfect Suite 8 setup program. If you've also installed the Bitstream Font Navigator from the Corel WordPerfect Suite 8 CD, you can further manage your fonts, adding, organizing, and printing font samples.

Fonts can be manipulated in a number of ways. You can change the size of a font or change its attributes (for example, by adding bold, italic, or redlining).

To quickly change a font size, click the Size button (refer to Figure 4-14) and select a size from the resulting drop-down list.

There are four methods you can use to access font changes and/or add attributes—the Font Face and Size buttons on the toolbar, the keyboard quick keys, the Font dialog box, and the QuickFonts toolbar button. You'll use different methods depending on particular situations. The first three methods are illustrated in the sections that follow. The fourth, QuickFonts, is one route to fonts and attribute combinations you have used recently.

THE FONT FACE AND SIZE TOOLBAR BUTTONS

Clicking either the Font Face or Size toolbar button opens a drop-down list of choices. The Font Face button displays a list of all typefaces available in WordPerfect. At the top of the list, separated by a line, are the last four font choices you've made. This is a quick method of repeating font selections without scrolling through the lengthy list of choices. As you move through the list of fonts, a preview of the selected font appears immediately to the right of the selection (refer to Figure 4-14).

The Size button displays a list of type sizes, measured in points, available for the currently selected typeface. The font sizes available usually range from 1 point to 72 points. A point size is measured from the top of the tallest capital letter to the bottom of the lowest descender in the typeface. For example, 10-point type in Times New Roman may not measure exactly the same as 10-point type in Arial. 72 points is roughly one-inch high.

Hands On: Changing Font Faces and Font Sizes for Existing Text

The Universe Training logo and letterhead lines are nothing more than fancy font faces and sizes. Here's how to dress up the logo by changing the fonts:

1. Select the first line of the letter, `Universe Training`, by triple-clicking anywhere in the line, or by clicking once in the left-margin opposite that text.
2. Click the Font Face button on the toolbar and select an alternative font. I selected `Bremen Bd Bt`, but you can use any decorative font face you like. `Universe Training` should now reflect the selected font face.

CHAPTER 4 • THE BASIC BUSINESS LETTER   **103**

3. With the `Universe Training` line still selected, click the Size button on the toolbar.
4. Select an appropriate font size. I used 36 points.
5. Click anywhere outside of the selected line to deselect it.
6. All remaining text in the logo is Times New Roman, 12 point. When you've finished adjusting the logo, it should resemble Figure 4-16.

Figure 4-16
The Universe Training logo looks different once you've applied new font faces and sizes.

KEYBOARD QUICK KEYS

Three key combinations exist in all the predefined keyboards except the Equation Editor keyboard. These key combinations provide a very easy method of adding common attributes either to selected text or to new text you're about to type. Here are the keyboard quick keys:

Keystroke	Attribute
Ctrl+U	Underline
Ctrl+B	Bold
Ctrl+I	Italic

To use these quick keys as you type, press the key combination once to turn on the attribute, type the text, and then press the key combination again to turn off the attribute.

PART II • DAILY TASKS

To use the quick keys with existing text, first select the text, then press the key combination. Click outside the selected text or press `F8` to deselect it.

Hands On: Using Keyboard Quick Keys to Add Common Attributes

The Universe Training letterhead uses italic to emphasize portions of its logo and address lines. Use these steps to add italic:

1. Select the line that reads `...the complete answer to your computer training needs.`
2. Press `Ctrl`+`I` (or click the Italics button on the toolbar) to add italic.
3. Select each of the following words in the fourth line, one at a time, and add italic: `Voice`, `Fax`, and `e-mail`.

USING THE FONT DIALOG BOX

The Font dialog box presents all possible font faces, sizes, and attributes in one easy place. You can quickly open the Font dialog box by double-clicking any font face, font size, or attribute code in Reveal Codes, or by double-clicking the QuickFonts button on the toolbar. Alternatively, choose Format, Font (or press `F9`) to open the dialog box.

The Font dialog box is shown in Figure 4-17. The various choices possible for fonts are listed in Table 4-1.

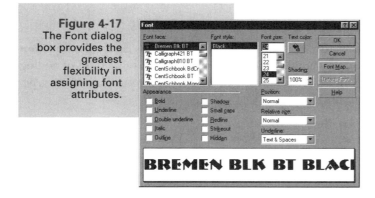

Figure 4-17 The Font dialog box provides the greatest flexibility in assigning font attributes.

CHAPTER 4 • THE BASIC BUSINESS LETTER

Table 4-1 Font Dialog Box Choices

Dialog Box Category	Choices	Use/Result
Font Face	varies	Lists the typefaces installed and available to WordPerfect 8
Font Style	varies	Lists the possible styles—such as Roman, Black, Regular—available to the font face
Font Size	1-72 points	Determines how big or small a font will print
Text Color	varies	Opens a color palette from which text color can be selected
Shading	1-100%	Assigns the percentage of color to be applied
Appearance	Bold	**Bold**
	Underline	<u>Underline</u>
	Double Underline	<u>Double Underline</u>
	Italic	*Italic*
	Outline	Outline
	Shadow	Shadow
	Small Caps	SMALL CAPS
	Redline	Redline
	Strikeout	~~Strikeout~~
	Hidden	
Position	Normal	Text aligns on the baseline
	Superscript	Super^{script} (size is 60% of normal)
	Subscript	Sub$_{script}$ (size is 60% of normal)
Relative Size	Fine	60% of normal
	Small	80% of normal
	Normal	100%
	Large	120% of normal
	Very Large	150% of normal
	Extra Large	200% of normal
Underline	Text Only	<u>Underlines text only, not spaces between words</u>
	Text & Spaces	<u>Underlines both text and spaces</u>
	Text & Tabs	Underlines text and also areas crossed by tabs, centers, flush right, or indents
	All	Underlines everything—text, spaces, tabs, centers, flush right, and indents
Font Map		Allows modification of font display, assignment of attributes, font substitution, and code pages
Default Font		Sets the default font used for the current document, or for all new documents

PART II • DAILY TASKS

Hands On: Using the Font Dialog Box

One option in the Font dialog box allows you to assign a relative size, rather than a specific font size, to text. For example, suppose you have a block of text which requires several font size changes. Most of the text is 12 point, but some text is larger, at 15 point, and other text is smaller, at 8 point. You want to retain the same percentage of change to the text that is larger or smaller as what you now have. Therefore, if you change the normal-sized text from 12 point to 11 point, you want the larger text to be about 13 point with the smaller text about 7 point. Selecting Relative Size in the Font dialog box automatically adjusts point sizes based on a percentage of normal, as listed in Table 4-1.

The words `Voice`, `Fax`, and `e-mail` all need relative sizing. Here's how to do it:

1. Select the first word by double-clicking it.
2. Open the Font dialog box using one of the methods previously described.
3. From the Relative Size pop-up control, select Small.
4. Click OK to close the Font dialog box, and then repeat these steps for the remaining words.

Using Special Characters

In addition to fonts, WordPerfect contains over 1,500 special characters, such as stars, happy faces, math symbols, Japanese Katakana characters, and other international characters. To open the WordPerfect symbols, click the Insert Symbol button (or press Ctrl+W).

When you click the Insert Symbol button, the Symbols dialog box opens (see Figure 4-18).

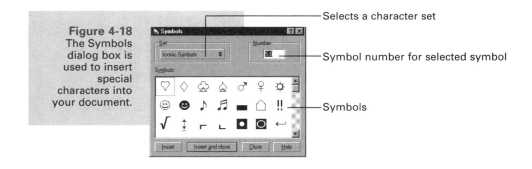

Figure 4-18 The Symbols dialog box is used to insert special characters into your document.

Symbols are grouped into 15 character sets. Each character set contains symbols related to that group. You can select and browse the character sets by opening the Set pop-up list (see Figure 4-19).

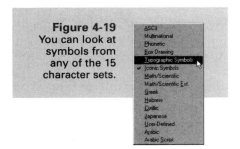

Figure 4-19
You can look at symbols from any of the 15 character sets.

When you select a symbol from the Symbols dialog box, the symbol's number is displayed in the Number text box. You can access a symbol in three different ways. You'll choose a particular method depending on whether you can remember the symbol number, whether there is a shortcut method to access the symbol, or whether you need to find the symbol in its character set and then locate it from the Symbols dialog box.

There are shortcuts you can use to insert symbols into your document without locating them in the Symbols dialog box or knowing their symbol numbers. Essentially, what you are trying to do is think of the combination of standard characters that might form your special character when put together. Here's an example. Suppose you want to insert an accented e (é). That symbol is a combination of the lowercase letter e and an apostrophe or accent character ('). Therefore, press Ctrl+W, then type **e** '. The accented e (é) appears.

Hands On: Including WordPerfect Characters

The letterhead for Universe Training would benefit from including some special symbols, rather than asterisks, as separators in the phone number and e-mail line. Here's how:

1. In the letterhead, select an asterisk (*).
2. Press Ctrl+W. The Symbols dialog box opens.
3. From the Iconic Symbols Set, select symbol 5,70.
4. Click Insert. The symbol replaces the selected asterisk and the Symbols dialog box remains open.

5. Select the remaining asterisk in the letterhead.
6. Click Insert *a*nd Close from the Symbols dialog box. The selected symbol replaces the asterisk and the Symbols dialog box closes.

You can find a list of possible keyboard shortcuts for symbols by searching for **Composing Characters** in WordPerfect Help.

To insert a symbol into your document using keyboard shortcuts, use these steps:

1. Position the insertion point in the document where you want the new character to appear.
2. Press Ctrl+W. The Symbols dialog box opens.
3. Type the keys used to form the symbol, then press Enter. The Symbols dialog box closes and the symbol appears in your document.

Center, Flush Right, and Justification

As you learned earlier in this chapter, tabs can be used to line up columns of text, or to position text at exact locations across a line. Indents are used to line up text that wraps from line to line. Three additional methods of aligning text can be used effectively in WordPerfect—center, flush right, and justification.

The center code (achieved by pressing Shift+F7) moves the text that follows the insertion point to the middle of the current line, equidistant from the left and right margins. The flush right code (achieved by pressing Alt+F7) aligns the text that follows the insertion point so that the right edge of the text is flush with the right margin. Each of these codes works on a single line of text only. More than one of these alignment instructions can appear on a single line. This gives you great flexibility, therefore, when you want to type text at the left margin, in the center, and at the right margin on the same line.

Justification, on the other hand, aligns text on every line that follows the code. Justification can align text at the left margin, centered between the margins, at the right margin, or at both the left and right margins. It can even be set to stretch short lines of text from the left margin to the right margin, adding significant space between words and characters where necessary. Figure 4-20 illustrates the difference between the center, flush right, and justification settings.

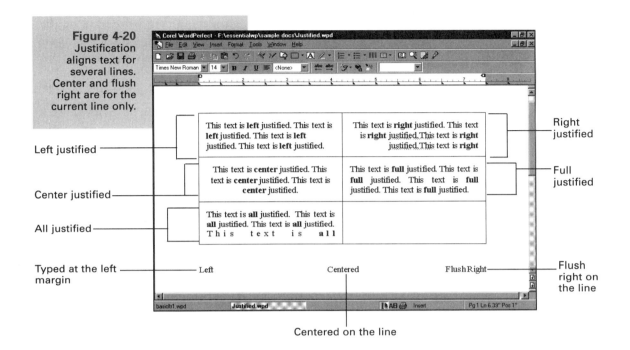

Figure 4-20 Justification aligns text for several lines. Center and flush right are for the current line only.

Hands On: Using Center, Flush Right, and Justification

Using each of these text alignment techniques is easy. Experiment with them on the sample letter typed earlier in this chapter. Here's how:

1. The Universe Training logo should be centered from left to right. Because the next line will be flush right, use the center feature. To do so, be sure that the insertion point is placed just before the U in Universe Training.

2. Press [Shift]+[F7] (or choose Format, Line, Center) to add a center code prior to the logo. In Reveal Codes, the center code appears as [Hd Center on Marg].

   The next line, beginning with ...the complete answer, should be right-aligned. Position the insertion point prior to the ellipsis.

3. Press [Alt]+[F7] (or choose Format, Line, Flush Right) to add a flush right code at the beginning of the line. The code [Hd Flush Right] can be seen in Reveal Codes.

4. The remaining two lines should both be centered. It would be an easy task to use the center line code at the beginning of each of them. For the purpose of learning, however, select and add a center justify code.

Select both lines quickly by first clicking the mouse just before `415` on the address line, and then, while holding down Shift, clicking the mouse again immediately after `universe.com` on the next line. When the justification code is added, it will properly start immediately before the text and end immediately after the text.

5. Click the Justification property bar button to display the drop-down list.
6. Select `Center`. Center justification is added to the text. Click in the document to deselect the text. A pair of [Just→] [←Just] codes is added to the document. When you move the insertion point just prior to one of the codes to expand it, you can observe the on/off action of these codes: [Just: Center→] and [←Just: Left].

Numbering the Pages

It is helpful to the readers of your letter (or any other document) if you number pages when the document is longer than one page. Letters typically display the page number in a header. *Headers* are text sections that appear at the top of each page, immediately below the top margin. They can contain as much information as you want them to, including graphics, tables, figures, and text. *Footers* are similar to headers, but they appear at the bottom of each page, immediately above the bottom margin. Headers and footers actually reside in floating codes that remain out of the way as edits are made to document text. You can insert, move, or delete text as you need to, without concern that a header or footer will be misplaced on the page.

Using Page Numbering

Page numbering appears at the top or bottom of a page, but typically includes very little text. You might precede the actual page number with the word **Page**, or might surround the page number with dashes (as in - # -), but generally the text in a page number is limited. Both page numbers and a header or footer occupy the same physical space on the paper. If you choose to use both, therefore, you must be sure that they do not overlap each other.

Page numbers can also include counters for chapters, volumes, or even secondary pages. You can include the maximum page count in the numbering sequence (as in **page 2 of 12 pages**). Counters can be Arabic numerals (1, 2, 3, …), alpha characters (a, b, c, …), or Roman numerals (i, ii, iii, …). You also can custom-design your page numbering sequence, adding text or other characters as you need them.

Chapter 4 • The Basic Business Letter

The steps to include page numbers on any document are the same. As with many other formatting instructions, remember that the formatting begins at the location of the insertion point and continues from that point forward in the document until a countermanding instruction is reached. For example, you might want to start numbering the pages of a document on page two, and then stop numbering on page four, so that pages five and six are unnumbered. Here's how to do so:

1. Position the insertion point on the page where numbering should begin.
2. Choose Format, Page, Numbering. The Select Page Numbering Format dialog box opens, as shown in Figure 4-21.

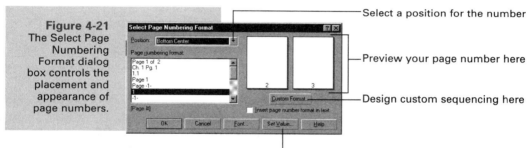

Figure 4-21 The Select Page Numbering Format dialog box controls the placement and appearance of page numbers.

3. From the Position drop-down list (see Figure 4-22), select the page location where you want the number to appear.

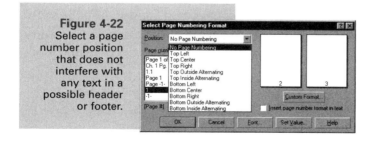

Figure 4-22 Select a page number position that does not interfere with any text in a possible header or footer.

4. Select the appearance for the number from the Page Numbering Format list, or click Custom Format to design your own format.
5. If desired, click Set Value to add numbering for volumes, chapters, or secondary numbers.

PART II • DAILY TASKS

6. When your page number choices are complete, click OK to return to your document. Check Reveal Codes to familiarize yourself with the appearance of the page numbering code. It appears at the top of the current page.

Creating Headers and Footers with Page Numbering

WordPerfect allows you to use as many as two separate headers and two separate footers at the same time in your document. Each is separately defined, and therefore can contain unique text and other objects. Of course, you must be careful not to overlap their contents, and not to place any text so that it might interfere with the appearance of a page numbering instruction. To avoid this problem, you can include page numbering within a header or footer.

While not strictly necessary, it's typically easiest to create a header or footer while you are in Page view so that you can observe the header or footer as it will appear in the actual document. To be sure that you're in Page view, choose View, Page.

Hands On: Creating Headers or Footers

Here's how to create a header for the sample letter in this chapter:

1. Move the insertion point to the beginning of the document by pressing Ctrl+Home.
2. Choose Insert, Header/Footer. The Headers/Footers dialog box appears.
3. Select Header A and click Create. WordPerfect places you in the area where a header will appear on the first page of the document. Don't worry about the fact that the header is on the first page of the document—in a later step, you'll suppress the header from this first page.
4. Type **Mr. James Martin** and press Enter.
5. Add today's date to the header by pressing Ctrl+D. Then press Enter.
6. Type **Page** and press the space bar once.
7. Click the Page Numbering button on the property bar to open its drop-down list. Select Page Number. The number 1 is inserted in the header.
8. Press Enter twice to add two blank lines after the page number.
9. It's also very easy to add graphic lines to a header. Click the Horizontal Line button on the property bar. A line is added to the header at the insertion point position.

CHAPTER 4 • THE BASIC BUSINESS LETTER 113

10. WordPerfect automatically includes one blank line between a header and text on a page. Press Enter twice to include two extra blank lines; this sets the header text a little farther away from the page text. Figure 4-23 displays the header as it now appears in the document, and identifies each of the header buttons on the property bar.

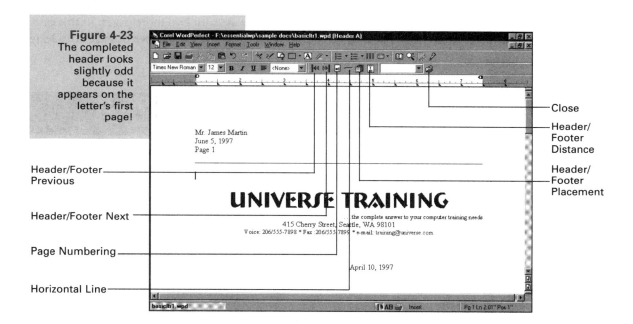

Figure 4-23
The completed header looks slightly odd because it appears on the letter's first page!

11. Click the Close button on the property bar to close the header and return to the top of the document. As you scroll through the document text, you can see the header you've just created.

You can easily edit a header or footer by clicking it. Make any desired changes, then click the Close button on the property bar (or press Ctrl+F4) to return to your document text.

I prefer to always define a header, footer, page number, or watermark at the very beginning of a document even if I might not want it to print on the first page. Using this technique forces all document formatting instructions to appear together in one easy-to-find location. You then can choose Format, Page, Suppress to prevent the appearance of the defined header, footer, page number, or watermark on the current page. Suppress interrupts the consecutive appearance of the function, but does not actually skip a number in the counting sequence.

One additional technique is Delay Codes (choose Fo_r_mat, _P_age, _D_elay Codes), which suppresses any code from appearing for a specified number of pages. Delay Codes is useful when, for example, you want to define codes at one location in the document, but do not want the codes to start for two more pages. In this case, you define the codes inside the delay code, with the _N_umber of Pages to Delay set to **2**.

Hands On: Supp_r_essing the Header from Page 1 of the Letter

To prevent the header from appearing on the first page of the letter, use these steps:

1. With the document open and the header created as previously described, choose Fo_r_mat, _P_age, S_u_ppress. The Suppress dialog box opens.
2. Click H_e_ader A (assuming that's the one you've created in the letter), then click OK. The header disappears from the first page of the letter. Don't panic, though. Scroll through the document. When you reach page two, the header appears with the page number automatically incremented to 2.

Using a Project to Create a Letter

You've now learned how to create a letter from scratch, and how to format and manipulate the text in any number of ways. You're now able to approach many different types of documents.

As you've learned, a number of projects are included with WordPerfect 8 to simplify some of your daily work activities; one of them is the business letter project. Similar to the memo project you used in Chapter 3, the business letter project guides you through several of the most commonly used business letter creation techniques.

Hands On: Using the Business Letter Project

WordPerfect 8 includes two possible letter projects, one for business letters and another for personal letters. Not only do they assist you with creating and formatting letters, they also include prewritten text! Here's how to create a letter about donating funds to your favorite organization:

Chapter 4 • The Basic Business Letter

1. Choose File, New (or press Ctrl+Shift+N). The New dialog box opens.
2. Select Corel WordPerfect 8 from the category drop-down list, if it's not already selected.
3. Scroll through the list of projects until you see Letter, Business. Click to select it, then click Create. WordPerfect loads the PerfectExpert, and opens a business letter template associated with the project.

   The first time you use a project or template, you may need to add yourself to, and select yourself from, the Address Book. This information is used to fill in certain information areas on the document you're creating. For example, in the letter, your personal information will appear in the letterhead. In a fax, however, your personal information might only be used to complete the return phone numbers.
4. If prompted, click OK to open the Address Book. Using the steps previously discussed, add yourself (or the person or organization for whom you're writing the letter) to the Address Book. When complete, click Insert to mark the entry for use by the project. The Letter PerfectExpert opens, as shown in Figure 4-24.

If you later want to select a different entry from the Address Book to be used on the letter, the Letter PerfectExpert enables you to do so easily.

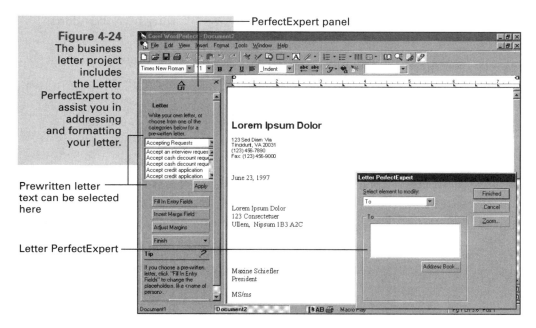

Figure 4-24 The business letter project includes the Letter PerfectExpert to assist you in addressing and formatting your letter.

Prewritten letter text can be selected here

Letter PerfectExpert

5. Start by addressing the letter. To appears as the default element in Select Element to Modify. For accuracy, it's usually best to use an entry from the Address Book (even if you need to add the entry first).

6. Click the Address Book button to open the Address Book, then locate and select the entry you previously created for James Martin. Click the Select button to add this entry to the Letter PerfectExpert.

If you use the scroll box on the vertical scroll bar in the Address Book, a QuickTip appears, displaying entries so that you know approximately where you are in the list.

7. Now, one at a time, select elements from the Select Element to Modify drop-down list. With each element, the Letter PerfectExpert is updated, displaying appropriate controls and text boxes for your input. For example, when you select Subject and Reference as the element, the Letter PerfectExpert displays controls that allow you to type the **Re:** line. Further, as you select each element, the letter itself (seen behind the Letter PerfectExpert) is updated to display your changes. Edit the following elements:

Element	**Control**	**Type this text, or make this choice**
From	From	If necessary, click Change and then select an alternate entry from the Address Book
Subject and Reference	Reference Line	**Donations**
Appearance	Letterhead Style	Traditional
	Text Format	Simplified
Closing	Writer's Initials	Type your initials
	Typist's Initials	Type your initials
	Enclosure(s)	Not checked
Courtesy Copies	Courtesy Copies	Not checked
Options	Date Format	January 31, 1997
	Punctuation	After Greeting :
		After Closing ,
	Center First Page Top to Bottom	Not checked

CHAPTER 4 • THE BASIC BUSINESS LETTER **117**

8. When you are satisfied with the elements, click Finished. The Letter PerfectExpert closes and the letter itself updates, reflecting all your modifications. The insertion point appears in the letter at the location where you now can type the body of the letter.

9. To add the prewritten donation letter text, scroll through the list of prewritten letters, then select Accept Donation Request. Click Apply to add the text to your letter. Notice, however, that two fields appear which must be completed: the name of the agency, and the amount. The letter now should look similar to Figure 4-25.

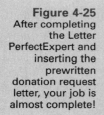

Figure 4-25
After completing the Letter PerfectExpert and inserting the prewritten donation request letter, your job is almost complete!

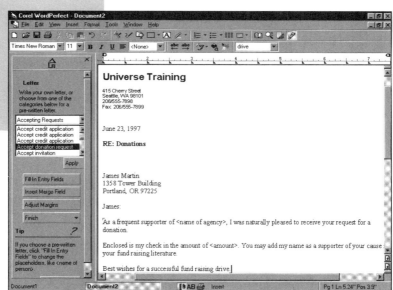

10. Click Fill In Entry Fields on the PerfectExpert. The first entry field, <name of agency>, is selected, so you can type the agency name.

11. Type **Center for the Preservation of Circus Clowns.** As you begin to type, the selected field name is replaced with your typing.

12. Click the Fill In Entry Fields button again to select the <amount> field. Type **$100.00**.

13. Because your letter is now finished, click the Finish button, then select Save. The Save As dialog box opens. Name your document **Circus Donation**, then click Save.

14. Now, click the Finish button again and select Close Without Saving. You'll see a prompt box which says `Are you sure you want to close without saving?`—click <u>Y</u>es. Your document closes, but the PerfectExpert panel remains open. Click the Close button on the panel to remove it from the document window.

As you can see, using a project allows you to create a letter, or any other document, quickly. However, since a project is limited by the imagination of the programmer(s) who designed it, you'll find that you typically have very little control over the appearance and formatting choices for the resulting document. It's therefore best to use a project to create the basics for the document, but then rely on your own superb skills to complete it!

5
Fine-Tuning and Enhancing Your Documents

IN THIS CHAPTER
- **Checking Spelling and Grammar in a Document**
- **Exploring the Thesaurus**
- **Using Styles for Consistency**

I can't spell very well, and the editors of this book will chime in and tell you that my grammar's none too good, either. It's fortunate that WordPerfect 8 has outstanding spell check, grammar check, and thesaurus features. When these are combined with typing assistance tools such as QuickCorrect, QuickWords, and Format-As-You-Go, I actually can get some work done without too much embarrassment!

This chapter will introduce you to these superb tools. You also will explore WordPerfect's Style feature, learning how to use its predefined styles and how to create your own styles. Using styles will enhance your documents by formatting the documents consistently and easily.

Using Spell Checker, Thesaurus, and Grammatik Features for Accuracy

The combination of WordPerfect's Spell Checker, Thesaurus, and Grammatik features offers you a method of creating flawless documents. These features work closely together so that you not only can verify the spelling of a word, but can check its definition, and can make sure that you've used it correctly in a sentence.

One additional feature, Prompt-As-You-Go, is a combination of Spell Checker, Thesaurus, and Grammatik, suggesting corrections or alternatives for the word in which the insertion point resides. First, it suggests correct spellings for a word that is possibly misspelled. Secondly, it suggests corrections for possible grammatical errors. And finally, if the word does not contain any spelling or grammatical errors, it suggests alternative words (similar to a thesaurus).

A couple of quick notes are important here, however. No proofreading tool is foolproof, including, probably, your own eyes. At least I can't catch everything! For example, Spell Checker can't necessarily tell if a word is misspelled, or is perhaps an acronym or proper name. Nor will Grammatik correct your thoughts or interpret what it is you're trying to say. And Thesaurus won't necessarily suggest words that are appropriate. Therefore, you should still manually proofread your document looking for errors or inconsistencies that were not caught by WordPerfect.

Hands On: Creating the Sample Document

You should begin by typing the example text for this section into a document. I realize that it's difficult to type something wrong on purpose. If you type the document exactly as it's presented here, however, you'll be able to follow along through each of the Hands-On exercises in this section. Complete these steps:

1. Type the following text on a new document window, exactly as it appears here:

I have a rathr garrulous chauffer. While he rarely leaves me lacking for conversation, he occasionaly leaves me speechles.

The other day my garrulous friend managed to run a red light which had the misfortune, quite by accident, to occur in the middle of a a sentence. We were immediately pulled over by an afishl representative of the law. The officer inquired why my chauffer did not akseed to the stlplight in the 1st place. My friend replied that he thought it an odd place for a stop sign, and hadn't see it.

My chauffer noticed the officer's accent and inquired if they might both be from Puyallup. When it turned out that they were, a twenty-minute conversation ensued. it began to fateeg me after awhile, but I just kept looking at the still blank ticket book and kept quiet like some egstinkt, mute ape.

Finally the two newfound friends said fairewell, and my chauffer drove off. I looked back in time to see the officer staring at his ticket book. He had forgotten to fill it out.

2. Save this file with the name `MISSPELL.WPD` so that you can refer to it throughout the rest of this section.

Checking for Correct Spelling

WordPerfect 8 has four methods of checking spelling: Spell Checker, QuickCorrect, Spell-As-You-Go, and Prompt-As-You-Go. As you typed the text of the `MISSPELL.WPD` document, you might have noticed that some words were automatically corrected as you typed, and that a series of little red marks appeared under some other words to flag them as possible misspellings. Words that are instantly corrected are a function of QuickCorrect. The red marks under other words are a function of a proofreading tool named Spell-As-You-Go. The Spell Checker feature is usually reserved for reviewing an entire document for correctness.

Spell-As-You-Go and Prompt-As-You-Go for Instant Error-Checking

Spell-As-You-Go flags possible misspellings as you type a document. When you open an existing document, it also flags possible misspellings in that document.

Prompt-As-You-Go displays possible replacement spellings for a word that might be misspelled. If, for some reason, you're not seeing flag marks under words you *know* are misspelled, or if nothing appears in the Prompt-As-You-Go button on the property bar, you should check to be sure that Spell-As-You-Go and Prompt-As-You-Go are active. Here's how:

1. Choose Tools, Proofread.
2. When enabled, a round bullet appears to the left of the Spell-As-You-Go menu item. If the bullet does not appear, click Spell-As-You-Go.
3. A checkmark appears to the left of Prompt-As-You-Go when enabled. If the checkmark does not appear, click Prompt-As-You-Go (see Figure 5-1).

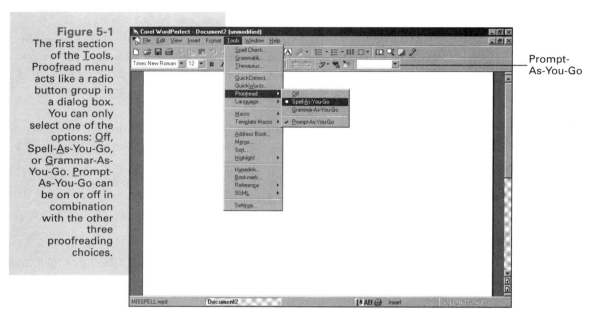

Figure 5-1 The first section of the Tools, Proofread menu acts like a radio button group in a dialog box. You can only select one of the options: Off, Spell-As-You-Go, or Grammar-As-You-Go. Prompt-As-You-Go can be on or off in combination with the other three proofreading choices.

Hands On: Using Spell-As-You-Go and Prompt-As-You-Go to Correct Misspellings

Spell-As-You-Go and Prompt-As-You-Go allow you to look up words from the spelling dictionary if they are unrecognized. Use these steps:

1. Open MISSPELL.WPD if it is not already open.
2. Click anywhere in the possibly misspelled word rathr. The Prompt-As-You-Go button displays a possible correction, rather.
3. Click the drop-down button on Prompt-As-You-Go to open a list of possible replacement words, similar to Figure 5-2.
4. Click the correctly spelled word, rather. This word replaces rathr in the document text.
5. Now place the insertion point in the next flagged word, chauffer.

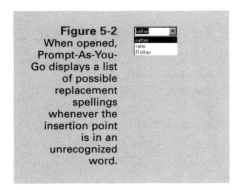

Figure 5-2
When opened, Prompt-As-You-Go displays a list of possible replacement spellings whenever the insertion point is in an unrecognized word.

6. This time, use Spell-As-You-Go to suggest replacements for the word. Right-click to open the QuickMenu. You see a list of possible replacement words, similar to Figure 5-3, which also is opened to display the additional words listed under More.

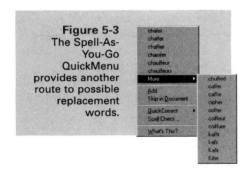

Figure 5-3
The Spell-As-You-Go QuickMenu provides another route to possible replacement words.

7. Click the correct spelling for the word, chauffeur, from the QuickMenu.

8. Usually, you'd go on to complete spell checking your whole document using one of the spell check methods. So that you can continue to use this silly document throughout the remainder of this chapter, however, close the document without saving any of your editing changes.

While in this example the correct spelling appeared, you'll find that many times the correctly spelled word you need does not appear on either the first or extended list of words in the Spell-As-You-Go QuickMenu. There are a number of other QuickMenu options:

Option	What it does
A̲dd	Adds the flagged word to the User Word List. The User Word List can be edited through the Spell Checker feature. It contains a list of all words you've added during spell check operations. The name of the User Word List file is WT80xx.UWL, where xx is the code for your language. The United States English version, therefore, stores the User Word List in a file named WT80US.UWL. This file typically resides in your Windows 95 folder.
Skip in D̲ocument	Ignores the word for this spell check operation and all future spell checks of this document.

Note

Skipping a word adds it to the Document Word List, marking it as <skip>. This means that the word will not be picked up as misspelled in any future spell check operations done on this file. If your intention was to not make a decision at this time, you're better off canceling the QuickMenu operation by clicking anywhere in the document.

You can force Spell Checker to look at all words, even if they were previously skipped, by starting Spell Checker, clicking the Op̲tions button, and selecting R̲echeck all text.

QuickCorrect	Offers another list of possible replacement words.
Spe̲ll Check	Opens the full version of Spell Checker and begins spell check operations on the current word. Spell Checker then proceeds to the end of the document (unless you cancel the spell check before the end).
W̲hat's This?	Displays help text for the Spell-As-You-Go feature.

QuickCorrect for Typos

QuickCorrect is a user-maintained list of words or characters that are commonly mistyped (see Figure 5-4). For each incorrect entry in QuickCorrect, a correct version is stored. When enabled, QuickCorrect scans as you type, looking for incorrectly spelled words or characters. When it can, it then instantly replaces each matched "mistake" with the correct word or phrase. A word is defined by WordPerfect as a string of characters ending with a space, a hard or soft return, or a symbol.

QuickCorrect is not limited to misspelled words. It's especially useful for instantly expanding abbreviations or acronyms into full phrases.

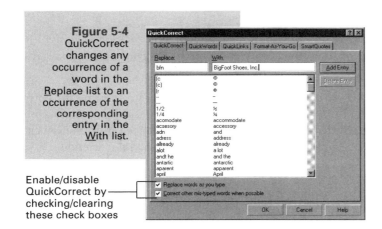

Figure 5-4 QuickCorrect changes any occurrence of a word in the Replace list to an occurrence of the corresponding entry in the With list.

Enable/disable QuickCorrect by checking/clearing these check boxes

QuickCorrect is enabled by default, so it begins checking and correcting words as soon as you start your first WordPerfect session. Also by default, QuickCorrect will look for, and automatically correct, any obvious misspellings wherever possible. Refer to Figure 5-4 for the controls that disable these actions. If you disable QuickCorrect, it remains disabled until you enable it again.

Hands On: Adding a QuickCorrect Entry

Approximately 150 entries are in the QuickCorrect list when WordPerfect 8 is installed. You can add as many additional entries as you need, and can delete entries for things that you do not want automatically corrected. Here's how to add a word or phrase to QuickCorrect:

1. Choose Tools, QuickCorrect. The QuickCorrect dialog box opens as you saw in Figure 5-4, although your list of words and entries may look different from those displayed in the figure.
2. In the Replace text box, type the misspelled word. As an example, type the abbreviation **bfs**.

3. In the With text box, type the correct word. You can include several words as replacement text, but you cannot include any formatting (such as a tab or indent) or attributes (such as underline or bold). Type **BigFoot Shoes, Inc.** as the replacement text for this example.
4. Click Add Entry.
5. Repeat steps 2 and 3 for any additional entries, then click OK to return to your document text.
6. Test your entry by typing **bfs** on your document, and then pressing the space bar. The entry is automatically corrected to **BigFoot Shoes, Inc.** (at least, it should be).

Delete any unwanted entry in the QuickCorrect dialog box by selecting the entry and clicking the Delete Entry button. As a safeguard, you're asked to confirm your decision to delete the selected entry before it is actually removed from the QuickCorrect list. Click Yes to perform the deletion, or No to cancel the deletion.

If you create outlines and use headings such as (a), (b), (c), be sure to delete the QuickCorrect entries for the copyright symbol.

Spell Checker Checks Everything!

Spell Checker is a full-fledged spell checker backed by a huge main word list. You can add other word lists, such as specialty lists of medical or legal terms. As you spell check a document, you can also add words to a User Word List so that they are included during spell check operations.

As Spell Checker proceeds through a document, all text—including headers, footers, and watermarks—is checked. You can choose not to check text in these locations if you want.

As you spell check a file, you can also use Grammatik and Thesaurus. These additional tools can be helpful in determining exactly which word is the correct word in a given situation!

Hands On: Spell Checking a Document

Probably the best way to explain how to use Spell Checker is to actually work through the sample file, MISSPELL.WPD, created earlier in this chapter. Open the file, then use these steps:

CHAPTER 5 • FINE-TUNING AND ENHANCING YOUR DOCUMENTS

1. Start Spell Checker by clicking its toolbar button (or pressing Ctrl+F1 or choosing Tools, Spell Check). Spell Checker starts immediately, looking up the word `rathr`. With `rathr` flagged, your screen should resemble Figure 5-5.

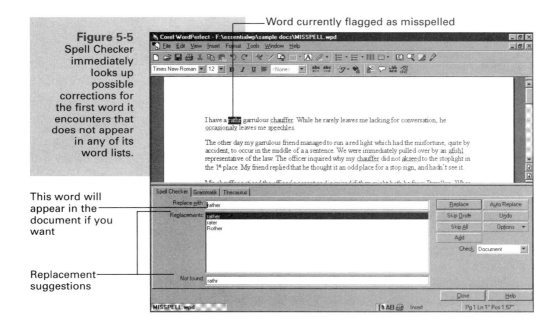

Figure 5-5 Spell Checker immediately looks up possible corrections for the first word it encounters that does not appear in any of its word lists.

This word will appear in the document if you want

Replacement suggestions

2. Review the Replace With choice. This is the word WordPerfect assumes is the best match for the misspelled word in the text. If that one's also incorrect, you can select the correct spelling from the Replacements list. In this example, select the word `rather`.

3. Click Replace to correct the word in the text with the word appearing in the Replace With field. WordPerfect then moves to the next suspected error—the word `chauffer`.

4. Using the same techniques, make these corrections:

Misspelled Word	Correctly Spelled Word
chauffer	chauffeur
occasionaly	occasionally
speechles	speechless

5. WordPerfect then moves to the next suspected error—the duplicate words a a. Spell Checker automatically looks for duplicate words and words with irregular capitalization, such as the word I when typed as i. To correct this duplicate word instance, click Replace.

6. Correct the word afishl with official. Then, notice that the word chauffer is corrected to chauffeur as it is passed by Spell Checker, because the correction was already made in step 4.

7. Next, make the correction to akseed, choosing accede from the replacement list.

Note

At this point, WordPerfect makes another *magical* correction, changing stlplight to stoplight. Why? Because QuickCorrect is defaulted to Correct Other Mis-Typed Words When Possible. If the stoplight correction is not made for you automatically, you need to make the correction using the normal steps. But then be sure to go back to QuickCorrect and check this important control. Refer to the earlier section "QuickCorrect for Typos" for more information.

8. Spell Checker next flags the word Puyallup as a possible misspelling. But this time, Spell Checker is wrong! Puyallup is correctly spelled. (It's the name of a small city midway between Seattle and Tacoma in Washington.) Either add Puyallup to the User Word List by clicking Add, or choose Skip Once to pass the word this time only. You also can ignore the word throughout this document by choosing Skip All.

9. The word fateeg is now flagged, and fatigue appears correctly as the choice in the Replace With field. Click Replace to correct the text.

10. The word egstinkt is flagged next, but Spell Checker can't find it in any of its word lists, as evidenced by the Not Found control. Unfortunately, Spell Checker does not recognize the word by any of its phonetic or lookup rules. You have to use Spell Checker's capability to look up words using *wild cards*—characters that substitute for missing letters. In the Replace With field, type **e*t**.

This indicates to Spell Checker that you know the first letter of the word is an e, and the last letter is a t, but you have no idea what letters might come between the two. Nor do you know how many letters are missing. As you begin to type, Spell Checker displays words which meet the pattern of letters you're typing.

11. Scroll through the list. The word extinct is so far down the list of possible replacements that WordPerfect reaches the maximum number of entries it can display before the correct word can be reached. One method you can use to shorten the list of possible replacement words is to include more known letters in the word pattern. Change the Replace With field to read **e?t*t**. Spell Checker now knows to look up words where e is the first letter, t is the third letter, and another t appears within the word or as the last letter of the word. A much smaller list of replacement words now appears.

12. Select extinct and click Replace. The replacement is made and the word fairewell is flagged; possible replacement words are listed.

You can also manually edit text or make a correction to a word when Spell Checker stops on a word. To do so, click in your document and make any changes you desire, then click the Resume button to continue using Spell Checker.

One additional method to manually correct a word is to type the correction in the Replace With box, then click Replace.

13. Select farewell from the list. Spell Checker displays a dialog box indicating that it has completed the spell check of the document. Click Yes to close Spell Checker.

14. Of course, the last step in spell checking is to save the document, safeguarding your changes. Be sure to save the MISSPELL.WPD document.

In addition to replacing words, looking them up, and adding words to a user list, a number of other options are available to you through Spell Checker. Table 5-1 contains a list of other Spell Checker options.

Using Thesaurus for Alternative Words and Word Meanings

Because I tend to compose as I type, I find WordPerfect's Thesaurus invaluable. I can look for synonyms (words that have the same or similar meanings) or antonyms (words that have opposite meanings). Although not installed by default, WordPerfect provides a full set of definitions for words in the Thesaurus. I highly recommend that if you've not installed these definitions, you do so by re-running Setup on the Corel WordPerfect Suite 8 CD. Then choose a Custom setup and select Definitions (and other Thesaurus options) from the list of Word-Perfect 8 components. When using the definitions you can also look up just the meaning of words that you've read but don't fully understand.

Table 5-1 Spell Checker Options

Use this function or button	To do this
Replace With	A selected or typed word appears in this field. Accept it by clicking Replace.
Replace	Replaces the flagged word in the document with the word appearing in the Replace With field.
Auto Replace	Adds the flagged word, as it is currently spelled, to the QuickCorrect list for automatic replacement as it is typed.
Skip Once	Skips the flagged word one time.
Skip All	Skips the flagged word for the remainder of the document (adds it to the document word list).
Add	Adds the flagged word, as it is currently spelled, to the User Word List.
Undo	Returns the corrected word to its original spelling.
Options	Opens a submenu of additional choices.

Tip: Rather than using the full-fledged Thesaurus, you can also open the Prompt-As-You-Go drop-down list to view a possible list of replacement words.

Thesaurus is an exceptionally easy tool to use. Here's how:

1. In a document window, type the word or phrase you want to look up.
2. Place the insertion point somewhere in the word, or select a word or phrase.
3. Choose Tools, Thesaurus (or press Alt+F1). Alternatively, click the Spell Check button on the toolbar, and then click the Thesaurus tab. The Thesaurus panel opens as shown in Figure 5-6.

The selected word or phrase is looked up in the Thesaurus. Synonyms and antonyms appear in the first pane of the Thesaurus panel. If you've also installed definitions, you'll see the word's meaning and part of speech displayed in the Definitions For list box (see Figure 5-7).

CHAPTER 5 • FINE-TUNING AND ENHANCING YOUR DOCUMENTS **131**

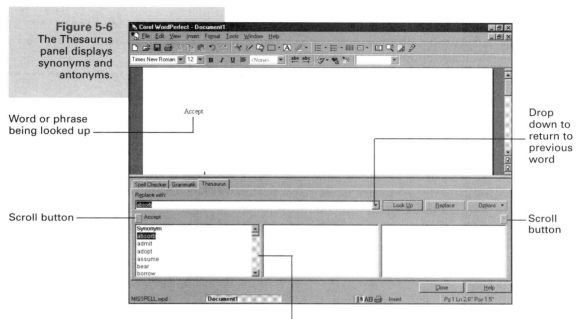

Figure 5-6 The Thesaurus panel displays synonyms and antonyms.

Word or phrase being looked up

Scroll button

Drop down to return to previous word

Scroll button

Scroll to view complete list of related words

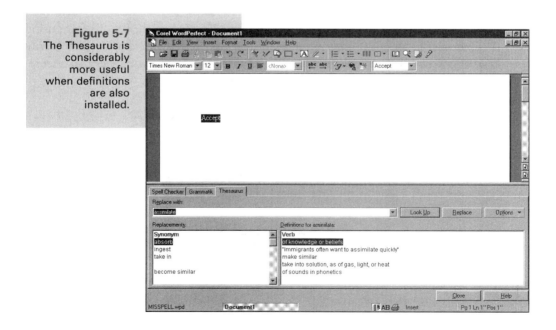

Figure 5-7 The Thesaurus is considerably more useful when definitions are also installed.

> **Tip**
> With definitions installed, click any of the possible replacement words to view the meaning associated with the word.

4. If a word or phrase you want to use appears in the Replacements list, select it and click Replace. The word then appears in the document, replacing the original word or phrase (and you can skip step 5). If an acceptable word does not appear in the Replacements list, go to step 5.

5. Select a word or phrase from the Replacements list, or type an entirely different word in the Replace With text box. Click Look Up. New replacement word lists appear in the next pane of the Thesaurus panel. You can go back to a previously reviewed word by opening the Replace With drop-down list.

6. Repeat steps 4 and 5 until you find an acceptable replacement for your original word. If you look up more than three words, you can scroll between the panes by clicking either of the pane scroll buttons (refer to Figure 5-6).

Checking for Grammatical Accuracy

Spell Checker alone won't find every wrong word. You might benefit from using Grammatik, an advanced grammar checker that reads your document to verify that correct parts of speech are used, and that phrases and sentences make sense. Grammar checking can be as strict or informal as you want.

Relying on Grammar-As-You-Go

Similar to Spell-As-You-Go, Grammar-As-You-Go reads through your document as you type it, or through existing text when you open a document, looking for grammatical or style errors. Phrases or words that break a grammatical rule are flagged with a slanted blue line under the word.

Hands On: Using Grammar-As-You-Go

Use the document MISSPELL.WPD to test the capabilities of Grammar-As-You-Go. Here's how:

1. Be sure that Grammar-As-You-Go is enabled by choosing Tools, Proofread, Grammar-As-You-Go.

CHAPTER 5 • FINE-TUNING AND ENHANCING YOUR DOCUMENTS 133

2. The word see is flagged, indicating that a grammatical error might have occurred.

3. With the mouse, point to the flagged word and right-click. Grammar-As-You-Go displays a QuickMenu of suggestions; the grammatical reason for the suggestion appears at the top of the list. You can accept one of the suggestions, or, if none of the suggestions appear to be correct, you can choose to skip the marked phrase or launch Grammatik.

4. In this case, select seen to correct the verb form. That's the only Grammar-As-You-Go correction you should make for now.

Full Grammar Checking with Grammatik

Grammatik proofreads a document, looking for grammatical errors. You can set an option which designates how rigid the checking rules should be, called a *checking style*. You can even create your own checking style, selecting those grammatical rules you want to apply to your own writing. The default checking style is Quick Check, which may miss several grammatical or style errors. You can change the checking style using the Options button any time after you start Grammatik.

Grammatik can be started while performing a spell check on a document, or as a separate task. While performing a spell check, click the Grammatik tab at the top of the pane to switch to grammar checking. Use the following steps to start Grammatik independently from your document window:

1. Choose Tools, Grammatik (or press Alt+Shift+F1). The Grammatik pane opens with the first error selected, similar to Figure 5-8.

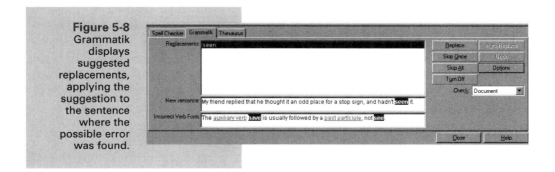

Figure 5-8 Grammatik displays suggested replacements, applying the suggestion to the sentence where the possible error was found.

2. If desired, select an alternative checking style by clicking the Options button and choosing Checking Styles. Highlight the checking style you want to use from the resulting list (see Figure 5-9), and click Select.

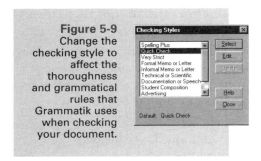

Figure 5-9
Change the checking style to affect the thoroughness and grammatical rules that Grammatik uses when checking your document.

3. Choose a corrected grammatical phrase from the possible list of replacements and click <u>R</u>eplace. Grammatik corrects the phrase in your document, and then continues to the next grammatical mistake.

4. You can click <u>C</u>lose at any time to exit Grammatik before you reach the end of the document; otherwise, Grammatik displays a dialog box prompting you to Close when it has finished checking the document for you. Click <u>Y</u>es in response to that prompt.

Easy Tools for Improving Speed and Consistency in Your Documents

Typing can be tedious. It requires a tremendous amount of repetition, and considerable attention must be paid to making everything look consistent and professional throughout a document. A sure indication of a professional document is technical accuracy, along with an orderly and aesthetically pleasing layout. Creating such a document can take far more time than is often allotted for the task. Word processing programs have attempted, for some time, to include features that help a user get beyond basic typing and into document creation. The typing tools discussed in this section can speed up document creation and enforce your formatting standards.

Automatic Typing Tools

Typing tools are designed to improve speed. Even the most proficient typist still stumbles over words and phrases that require finger-bending keystrokes, such as capitals that appear within a word, phrases that include punctuation, or names that include special characters such as umlauts or accents. Such complicated typing sometimes slows down text entry almost to a crawl. Three typing tools—

QuickWords, Format-As-You-Go, and SmartQuotes—are included in WordPerfect to handle these situations.

Using QuickWords for Automatic Phrase Entry

The QuickWords feature is similar to QuickCorrect. Abbreviations or acronyms are expanded to full words or phrases. With QuickWords, however, you also can include formatting such as tabs, indents, and centering. You can include font attributes such as font faces, and print attributes such as bold or redline. You even can include columns, borders, or graphics!

The QuickWords feature copies phrases from your document into the current template (see the following tip). You then assign an abbreviation to the entry; you'll use this abbreviation when typing. You can instruct QuickWords to expand each abbreviation immediately after it's typed, or to wait and expand all abbreviations in the document at once.

All WordPerfect documents are based on a template, usually the `WP8US.WPT` file that's stored in your `Corel\Suite8\Template\Custom WordPerfect Templates` folder. In addition to QuickWords, a template can store keyboards, menus, toolbars, styles, and macros. A template is an important tool when you're concerned about consistency and uniformity! You can learn more about templates in Chapter 16, "Understanding Templates and Projects."

Hands On: Creating a QuickWords Entry

A QuickWords entry is created from selected document text. This means that your entry must exist in the document before you can add it as a QuickWords entry. Here's a simple example for you to try:

1. In a new, blank document, type your full name, bold and centered on a line. Be sure to turn off bold immediately after you type your name. Finish the line by pressing Enter.
2. Select your name and assign an important font face with a larger font size. I used Arial in 25 point.
3. Open Reveal Codes, then select the complete line that contains your name, including the [HRt] code which finishes the line (see Figure 5-10).
4. Choose Tools, QuickWords. The QuickCorrect dialog box opens.

PART II • DAILY TASKS

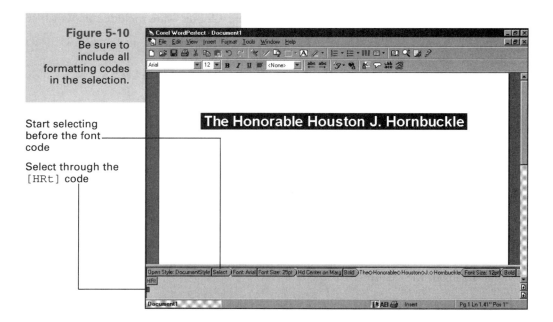

Figure 5-10
Be sure to include all formatting codes in the selection.

Start selecting before the font code

Select through the [HRt] code

5. With the QuickWords tab selected, type an abbreviation for your entry in the Abbreviated Form (Type This QuickWord in Document) field. Each abbreviated form is case-sensitive, so you'll need to remember the exact presentation you've entered. For this example, use **hhh** (for *Honorable Houston Hornbuckle*).

6. Click the Options button, and be sure that Expand as Text With Formatting is checked.

7. Verify that Expand QuickWords When You Type Them is checked.

8. Click Add Entry. The QuickWords entry and its associated abbreviation are added to the QuickWord list, and you're returned to your document.

You can preview your QuickWords entry after it has been added. To do so, choose Tools, QuickWords. The QuickCorrect dialog box opens with the QuickWords tab on top. Click the Abbreviated form in the Abbreviated Form list. The full, expanded form appears in the Preview of Expanded Form control.

9. Verify that your QuickWord entry works by typing the abbreviation, followed by a space or any symbol. It should immediately expand.

> To expand all QuickWords in the document at the same time, an optionally installed macro, EXPNDALL.WCM, can be played. You might need to add it to your installation using the Setup program on the Corel WordPerfect Suite 8 CD. Then choose Tools, Macro, Play, and double-click the macro EXPNDALL.WCM.

10. If you have any errors in your QuickWord entry, re-create the pattern text and select it. Then edit the entry by opening the QuickWords tab and selecting the abbreviation. Next, choose Options, Replace Entry. You'll be prompted to verify the replacement. Click Yes, then OK to return to your document window. Be sure to test the entry again!

Format-As-You-Go for Layout as You Type

The Format-As-You-Go feature corrects typing inconsistencies which occur as you type. It aids you by interpreting what you are trying to do, and adds any necessary formatting to make your document look professionally typeset. The Format-As-You-Go feature does not allow for customization; it is merely a list of on/off instructions.

CHAPTER 4 HAS MORE INFORMATION ON NUMBERED AND BULLETED LISTS.

You configure Format-As-You-Go through the QuickCorrect dialog box; choose Tools, QuickCorrect and select the Format-As-You-Go tab (see Figure 5-11). Most of the options for Format-As-You-Go are easily understandable; Table 5-2 describes a few of the less obvious choices.

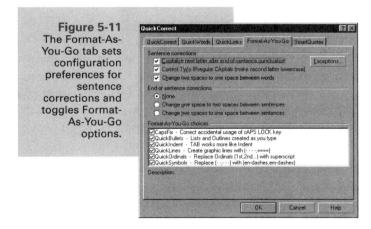

Figure 5-11 The Format-As-You-Go tab sets configuration preferences for sentence corrections and toggles Format-As-You-Go options.

Table 5-2 A Few of the Format-As-You-Go Configuration Options

Option	Description
Capitalize Next Letter After End-Of-Sentence Punctuation	WordPerfect considers the end of a sentence to be a period, question mark, or exclamation mark followed by a space or hard return. This choice capitalizes the next character after the end of a sentence if it is typed in lowercase. Exceptions are usually abbreviations that break the capitalization rule. If you type abbreviations or acronyms which end in a period in your text, you very likely will not want the next word in the sentence to start with a capital letter. Click the Exceptions button to enter those abbreviations in the exception list if they are not already included.
QuickBullets	QuickBullets senses the incidence of a bulleted or numbered list created by typing an asterisk or a number followed by a tab. It then assumes you are trying to create a bulleted or numbered list and starts the Bullets and Numbers function automatically.
QuickIndent	QuickIndent forces a tab to change to an indent where a bulleted or numbered list is begun. If, after a bullet or number, you really want to use a tab rather than an indent, be sure to remove the check from this option.
QuickLines	QuickLines interprets text typed as ======= or ------ as the intent to type a line and will substitute a horizontal graphic line.
QuickOrdinals	Ordinals designate the position of a number in a sequence, such as the st in 1st or the nd in 2nd. This choice forces the ordinal suffix to appear in superscript.

SmartQuotes

The last choice in the QuickCorrect suite of typing enhancements is SmartQuotes. SmartQuotes are the curly quotes that appear in professionally produced documents, rather than the inch-mark quotes commonly produced on a typewriter. Three types of quotation marks are possible: double-quotation marks for quoted text, single-quotation marks for quotes within quotes, and inch-marks which appear after a number. You can designate the appropriate usage for each of these quote types through the SmartQuotes QuickCorrect tab.

Not every font face includes a set of curly quotes, so SmartQuotes allows you to pick and choose characters from its WordPerfect character sets as substitute quotation marks. By default, double and single SmartQuotes are enabled, as are straight quotation marks after numbers.

To turn on or off SmartQuotes, or to specify the characters to be used, follow these steps:

1. Access SmartQuotes by choosing Tools, QuickCorrect and then clicking the SmartQuotes tab. Figure 5-12 displays this tab.

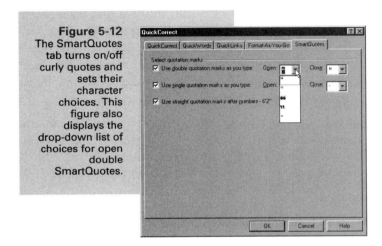

Figure 5-12
The SmartQuotes tab turns on/off curly quotes and sets their character choices. This figure also displays the drop-down list of choices for open double SmartQuotes.

2. To turn on or off SmartQuotes, check or clear the double and single quotation mark options.
3. Select a SmartQuote character style from the drop-down lists associated with each open and close SmartQuote.

Tip

If none of these choices is appropriate, you can select from any of WordPerfect's symbols by pressing Ctrl+W while in the Open or Close quote field. After you've selected your custom symbol, be sure to Close the Symbols dialog box.

4. When your selections are complete, click OK to return to the document window.

Caution

Although the WordPerfect Macro facility should automatically disable SmartQuotes, occasionally they remain enabled, causing a macro error. Be sure not to turn them on while editing a macro or while copying text into a macro file or macro command. For more information about macros, refer to Chapter 15, "Automating Daily Work with Simple Macros."

Using Styles for Consistency

Styles are used to add consistent formatting to similar types of text such as headings or paragraphs. A style definition stores multiple formatting codes in its own style code. That style definition is then applied to text, which in turn takes on the attributes stored in the style. For example, suppose you create a heading in a document that is originally centered, bold, and 12 point. After you print the document, you decide that the heading needs to be larger with a different font face. Modifying the style definition to include these changes dynamically updates all headings in the document to which the style was originally applied.

Style definitions are automatically saved with the current document. You can save styles to a separate file and then retrieve that style file into another document so that it can also use the style definitions. Style definitions can even be copied to a template so that they are available to all documents based on that template.

> **CHAPTER 16 OFFERS DETAILED INFORMATION ON TEMPLATES.**

Five types of styles can be defined:

- **Character styles** store codes which affect text within a paragraph. As an example, they can be especially useful when typing a technical document where new, not previously defined, words appear in italic, and perhaps in a different font face. Creating a character style named NewWords and then applying it to each new word will force a consistent appearance to these words.

- **Automatic character styles** also store codes which affect text within a paragraph. They are usually created from selected text in a document. When formatting is altered within one text area that uses the automatic character style, all other text areas to which the style has been applied immediately reflect the update.

- **Paragraph styles** affect an entire paragraph. Remember that a paragraph is any line, or group of lines, ending with a hard return. Headings are defined as paragraph styles.

- **Automatic paragraph styles** also affect entire paragraphs, but they do not require editing of the style definition itself. Editing any paragraph that used the style automatically updates all other paragraphs to which the style was applied. This is useful when typing a document where paragraph styles are used in the document body.

- **Document styles** contain formatting instructions that will affect a document from the position of the style code to the end of the document. Codes such as margin settings, default fonts, headers, footers, and page numbering instructions are often included in a document style.

CHAPTER 5 • FINE-TUNING AND ENHANCING YOUR DOCUMENTS 141

Of the five style types, four styles are considered to be *paired styles*. Only the Document Style is an *open style*. Similar to paired codes, paired styles have the ability to use format actions while the style is on, then can perform additional formatting when the style is turned off. (A *paired code* is one that has an on and off position, such as a font attribute code. The underline and bold codes are good examples.) Paired styles also have on and off positions. Figure 5-13 illustrates paired codes and paired style codes. They perform formatting instructions between their on and off positions.

An open style, on the other hand, affects a document's formatting from the point in the document where the style is added to the end of the document. A good comparison for an open style is to the actions of a header or footer. Once they're created in a document, they run from that point to the end of the document. Of course, a header or footer can be discontinued where necessary in a document. Not so with an open style. Once turned on, or *applied*, an open style remains active through the remainder of the document.

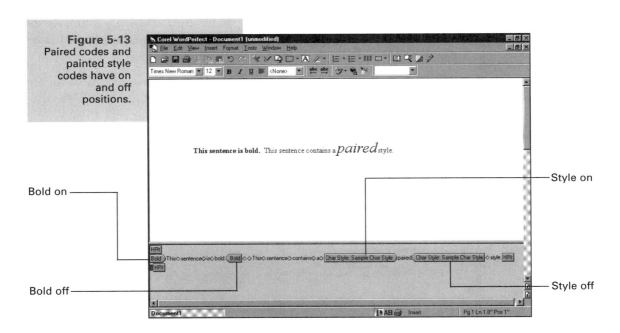

Figure 5-13 Paired codes and painted style codes have on and off positions.

A style definition is named. You can have as many style definitions in a style file as you need. Then you can have multiple style files. This provides the opportunity to update styles in a document as you retrieve new style files. For example, assume that you are creating a report. The first draft of the report must appear double-spaced for editing, with a footer displaying the draft number and draft date. The final version of the report must be single-spaced, double-spaced between paragraphs, and the footer must display the report date and page number. Now assume that you've defined and used a draft style definition named Paragraphs that sets spacing as double. You've saved that style definition in a file named DRAFT.STY. In a style file named FINAL.STY is another style definition, also named Paragraphs, that sets spacing as single. When the report is ready for final printing, you merely retrieve the FINAL.STY file into the report, replacing all existing definitions with the ones in the FINAL.STY file. The report automatically takes on single-spacing, double-spacing between paragraphs, and the updated footer—the Paragraphs style definition from the FINAL.STY file.

Including a Predefined Style in Your Document

WordPerfect 8 is full of predefined style definitions. Each time you create an outline, work with graphics, use an address, create a Web page, or use a header or footer, you're working with styles. These types of styles, called *system styles,* are automatically added to your document as you use their assigned features. As you create a header, for example, a style code is inserted at the beginning of the header. That header style includes the format settings used for headers.

In addition to system styles, five predefined heading styles are available for any document you create. Figure 5-14 illustrates the five predefined heading styles.

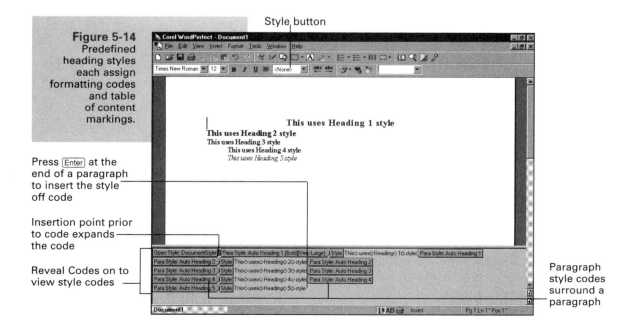

Figure 5-14 Predefined heading styles each assign formatting codes and table of content markings.

Press Enter at the end of a paragraph to insert the style off code

Insertion point prior to code expands the code

Reveal Codes on to view style codes

Paragraph style codes surround a paragraph

Hands On: Creating a Sample Document for Style Practice

Any document that uses headings can benefit from the WordPerfect predefined styles. Later in this chapter you'll learn how to create and edit styles, but for now try using these styles as they exist:

1. On a new document window, type the following text (be sure to finish each heading line by pressing [Enter]):

   This is a major heading, using the Heading 1 style

   This is a 2nd level heading, using Heading 2 style

   This is a 3rd level heading, using Heading 3 style

   This is a 4th level heading, using Heading 4 style

   This is a 5th level heading, using Heading 5 style

2. Position the insertion point at the end of the first line of text, press [Enter], and then type this text:

   This is text after a heading. It is normal text and will wrap as a standard paragraph from line to line.

3. Select the text you typed in step 2, and then copy ([Ctrl]+[C]) and paste ([Ctrl]+[V]) the text several times after each heading. When finished, your document should look similar to Figure 5-15.

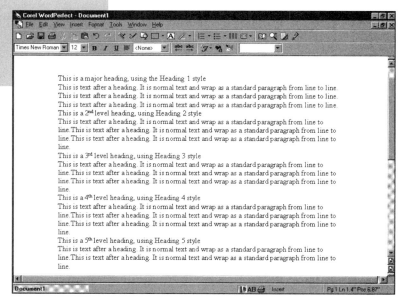

Figure 5-15
The sample styles document should start out looking like this.

4. Save the sample document, naming it `Sample Styles.wpd` or something similar.

Hands On: Using the Predefined Heading Styles

With the sample styles document created and saved, you can begin experimenting with the predefined heading styles. Here's how:

1. Select the first heading text by triple-clicking anywhere in the paragraph.
2. Select `Heading 1` from the Styles drop-down list in the property bar (see Figure 5-16).

Figure 5-16 Select `Heading 1` from the Styles drop-down list.

3. The heading is reformatted with the characteristics of the Heading 1 style.
4. Repeat steps 1 and 2 for each of the remaining headings, selecting `Heading 2` through `Heading 5` in turn.

Editing a Style

Any style, including the predefined styles, can be edited. The edits remain with the current document only, unless they are specifically saved to a style file or to a template.

Hands On: Editing the Predefined Styles

The formatting for Heading 1 in the predefined styles lacks the spacing instructions that usually appear after a heading to separate the heading from its supporting text. It also would emphasize the heading's importance if it used another, more impressive font face. Here's how to modify the Heading 1 style to include additional spacing and a new font code:

1. With the sample style document open, open the Reveal Codes pane by pressing [Alt]+[F3].

CHAPTER 5 • FINE-TUNING AND ENHANCING YOUR DOCUMENTS **145**

2. Press [Ctrl]+[Home] to position the insertion point at the beginning of the first heading. In Reveal Codes you should notice that the insertion point is immediately after the [Para Style: Auto Heading 1] and [Style] codes.

3. Double-click the first code, [Para Style: Auto Heading 1]. The Styles Editor dialog box opens, as shown in Figure 5-17. The Styles Editor dialog box similarly appears whenever you create or edit a style definition. Table 5-3, which appears at the end of this procedure, lists the dialog box elements and their purposes.

As an alternative, you can choose Fo_r_mat, _S_tyles (or press [Alt]+[F8]) to open the Style List dialog box. Then select the style to be edited from the Available _s_tyles list, and click _E_dit to open the Styles Editor dialog box.

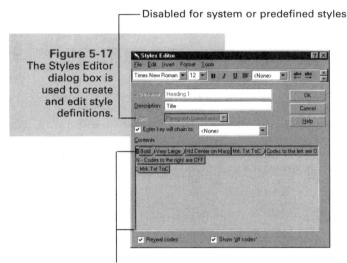

Figure 5-17
The Styles Editor dialog box is used to create and edit style definitions.

4. Click in the _C_ontents box immediately prior to the first code.

5. Select an alternative font face from the Font Face drop-down list. (I selected `Arial`.)

6. Verify that Show '_O_ff Codes' is checked, then click in the _C_ontents box immediately after the last code.

7. Press [Enter] twice to add two [HRt] codes. These two hard returns occur after the Heading 1 style is turned off.

Part II • Daily Tasks

8. Click OK to store your style changes, then click <u>C</u>lose to return to the document text. The document updates the text associated with Heading 1, displaying the extra space immediately below the heading.

Table 5-3 Components of the Style Editor Dialog Box

Item	Purpose
Menu bar	The menu bar for the Styles Editor is abbreviated from the normal WordPerfect 8 menu, containing only those features which can be included in a style.
Property bar	The Styles Editor property bar scrolls to display additional button choices.
Style Name	Style Name is assigned when you create a new style. System or predefined style names cannot be changed.
Description	The Description appears in the Style List dialog box. Use it to describe what the style will do and how you intend to use it. I like to also include the date the style was created or last edited.
Type	Sets the style Type. Select from the pop-up list of types.
Enter Key Will Chain To	Marks the style that will start when the [Enter] key is pressed, thus forming a *chain* of style definitions. The style can chain to `<None>`, the `<Same Style>`, or any other existing style in the document.
Reveal Codes	When checked, the Contents area will display Reveal Codes rather than a visual representation of the style definition. Since creating a style can sometimes be exacting, it's often easiest to work on a style definition with Reveal Codes checked.
Show 'Off' Codes	Show 'Off Codes' works together with Reveal Codes, displaying the Style Off code in the Contents box. By clicking after a Style Off code, you can include instructions to take place after the style is turned off.

It is not necessary to turn off the font face code at the end of a paired style. Formatting codes in effect prior to a paired style automatically continue after the paired style ends.

Creating Your Own Styles

Think of all the times you've reformatted a document based on someone's change of mind. Or, think of the number of different menus and buttons you've had to select to properly format each section of text in a report. With a little creativity, you can easily create your own styles based on the type of work *you* produce.

There are actually three different methods of creating styles. The easiest is to mimic a style based on formatting that already exists in a document. For example, if you've already typed a report with heading formatting from which you want to create a style, use the QuickFormat button to assign the formatting to other headings in the same document.

The second method is similar in that you'll copy from an existing paragraph and create a QuickStyle based on that paragraph's formatting. A QuickStyle is saved with a name and description, just like a style you create from scratch.

The third method requires you to create the style from scratch. These styles sometimes are more complex than either QuickFormat or QuickStyle. It's often easiest to start with a QuickFormat or QuickStyle and then edit the style to add other codes.

Hands On: Creating a QuickFormat Style

This example uses the sample letter created in Chapter 4. If you did not create that letter, just quickly create another document that contains at least four headings. The headings can be typed without any special formatting instructions.

The sample letter to James Martin contains four paragraph headings. Two of the headings, `Training Classes:` and `An Effective Training Facility:`, should be similarly formatted. The other two headings, `Session One` and `Session Two`, should also have similar formatting. Here's how to use QuickFormat to add styles:

1. Select the first heading, `Training Classes`.
2. Change the point size for the selected text to 14 point, then add bold and italic.
3. With the text still selected, click the QuickFormat button on the toolbar. The QuickFormat dialog box appears, as shown in Figure 5-18.
4. Choose H_eadings and click OK. A H_eading QuickFormat assigns a style to a complete paragraph. The mouse pointer then changes to a paint roller.
5. Using the scroll bar or your cursor arrows, locate the next heading, `An Effective Training Facility`. Click the mouse pointer anywhere in this heading, and the heading is reformatted to match the previous heading. If you have any additional paragraphs to which you want to apply the same QuickFormat, click the mouse pointer within each paragraph.
6. Open Reveal Codes to view the code assigned to a QuickFormat. It reads `[Para Style: Auto QuickFormat1]` for the first QuickFormat style. Any subsequent QuickFormat styles are numbered sequentially.

PART II • DAILY TASKS

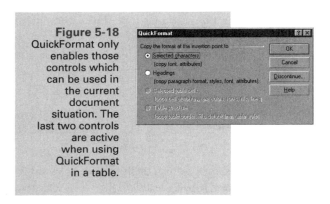

Figure 5-18 QuickFormat only enables those controls which can be used in the current document situation. The last two controls are active when using QuickFormat in a table.

7. When you have finished applying the QuickFormat, click the QuickFormat button on the toolbar to stop. The mouse pointer returns to its normal appearance.

If you begin typing while QuickFormat is active (that is, when the paint roller mouse pointer is active), QuickFormat is automatically turned off.

Double-click any QuickFormat code to open the Styles Editor, similar to any other style definition. You then can name the QuickFormat style definition, adding a description or other formatting. The style is then named and assigned a style type as either Character (paired-auto) or Paragraph (paired-auto), depending on the type of QuickFormat style you originally created.

Hands On: Creating a QuickStyle

QuickStyles are a shortcut method of creating a style from scratch. They are based on formatting in effect for selected text or the current paragraph. A QuickStyle can be an automatic paragraph style or an automatic character style.

The word `WordPerfect` exists several times in the letter to James Martin. Because Mr. Martin's company hasn't completely decided what software version to use, creating a character QuickStyle that contains the name of the software is efficient. Complete these steps:

CHAPTER 5 • FINE-TUNING AND ENHANCING YOUR DOCUMENTS

1. Select the words `WordPerfect 8` in the document text.
2. Apply bold and italic attributes to the selected text, and then, using the Font dialog box, change the text color to Red.
3. With the text still selected, click the Styles drop-down button and select `QuickStyle`. The QuickStyle dialog box opens.
4. Type **Program Name** in the Style Name field.
5. Type a descriptive phrase in the Description field to alert you to the purpose of the style, such as **WordP, bold, ital, red**.
6. Click Character with Automatic Update as the style type, and click OK. The character style is added to the style list and you are returned to your document.
7. With Reveal Codes open, double-click the `[Char Style: Auto Program Name]` code.
8. Click at the end of all codes in the Contents box.
9. Type **WordPerfect** and click OK to store the change and return to the document window. You now see both the text `WordPerfect 8` and the contents of the style code.
10. With Reveal Codes open, delete the text `WordPerfect 8`. Do not delete the `[Char Style: Auto Program Name]` code.
11. Throughout the remainder of the document, delete the text that reads `WordPerfect 8` or `WordPerfect`. At each location, select `Program Name` from the drop-down list on the Style button.
12. To see the power of styles, edit the style now by double-clicking its code. The Style Editor dialog box opens. In the Contents box, add the version number by clicking after the word `WordPerfect`. Type a space and the number **8**. Then click OK to return to the document. The text throughout the document now reads `WordPerfect 8`.

Creating a style from scratch is very much the same as creating any other style. You need to have a formatting plan in mind, however, since the style is created with no existing formatting in place. Here's how:

1. From a document window, select Format, Styles, or press Alt+F8. The Style List dialog box opens.

Use the Options button in the Style List dialog box to save styles to a file, or to Retrieve an existing style file.

2. Click C<u>r</u>eate. The Style Editor dialog box opens.

3. Type the name and description for your style in the <u>S</u>tyle Name and <u>D</u>escription text boxes, respectively.

4. Select the style type from the T<u>y</u>pe drop-down list. Determine whether you want to *chain* styles (that is, have this style automatically start another style when [Enter] is pressed in a paragraph formatted with the first style). If you choose to chain styles, open the drop-down list of styles for E<u>n</u>ter Key Will Chain To and select a style name.

   A good example of having one style chain to another occurs when you create an outline. The first level in a traditional outline often starts with something like the roman numeral I. The next level starts with the capital letter A. When you type the text for the first level, then press [Enter], the second level can automatically start (be chained) from the first level. Similarly, the third level can start when you press [Enter] after the second level, forming a third link in the chain.

5. In the <u>C</u>ontents box, include any text and formatting codes for your new style. Use the Re<u>v</u>eal Codes and Show '<u>O</u>ff Codes' check boxes to view the codes for your new style as you create it.

6. When finished, click OK to return to the Style List. You can immediately <u>A</u>pply your new style to text in the document, or <u>C</u>lose the Style List dialog box and return to the document text.

6

Printing Your Document to Paper, E-Mail, or Fax

In This Chapter

- **Printing a Document**
- **Printing Envelopes and Labels**
- **Solving Common Printing Problems**

With most home and business computers fully equipped with modems and Internet or other network access, the world is progressing beyond paper images and is rapidly moving totally into the world of electronic communications. But it's not quite there yet. Printing to paper and using stamps and envelopes still dominates the world of business communications, with e-mail communications and true electronic fax at a distant second and third.

This chapter will tell you how to use your printer with WordPerfect 8 documents, and will introduce you to the steps required to send your documents to someone by e-mail, or by fax through your fax/modem. You'll also learn how to create and print envelopes and labels.

Printing a Document

Printing a document to your default printer sometimes can be as easy as a simple keystroke combination. Other times, it can be as complex as selecting an alternate printer, designating the actual page or pages to be printed, instructing the printer to print on both sides of the paper, and maybe even allowing for extra binding width on the top or side of the paper! There are a lot of choices. But each choice has a specific function and impact on the actual outcome of the printout you'll receive.

> ### Hands On: Printing the Current Document to the Default Printer

In the previous two chapters you carefully created and edited a business letter for Universe Training. To print that letter, use these steps:

1. Open the sample training letter document you created in Chapter 3 and edited in Chapter 4. If you do not have that letter, just open any document you want to print.

2. To print the document, press [Ctrl]+[Shift]+[P]. The document is sent to the printer.

Tip

Several useful print-related buttons can be added to the toolbar. Using the Toolbar Editor (right-click the toolbar, then choose Edit) consider adding the buttons for Print Document, Print Page, and Printer Status. Refer to Chapter 2 for more help on editing toolbars.

If you need to print less than a full document, print a document which is not open in a document window, or make other printing choices, you need to work with WordPerfect's Print dialog box.

You can open the Print dialog box by clicking the Print toolbar button or choosing File, Print (or pressing [Ctrl]+[P]). Figure 6-1 shows this dialog box.

Chapter 6 • Printing Your Document to Paper, E-Mail, or Fax

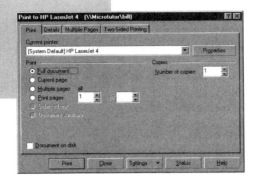

Figure 6-1
The Print dialog box is the route to more complex printing assignments.

Note

The title bar of the Print dialog box includes the name and printer port for the currently selected printer, so your Print dialog box will most likely display a different printer and port than Figure 6-1 displays.

While the Print dialog box contains several controls to help you print exactly what you want, it's not very complicated. Almost all controls are straightforward and easy to understand. Table 6-1 lists the controls found on the Print tab.

Tip

When printing more than one copy, it's much faster to *group* them, printing all copies of page 1, then all copies of page 2, and so on.

Tip

If you constantly make the same changes in the Print dialog box, such as always using two-sided printing, consider saving your print settings as WordPerfect's default print settings by choosing S̲ettings, S̲ave as Application Default and then clicking OK.

A few additional controls you should get to know appear on the Details tab. For example, to add a new printer for use within WordPerfect, you must first add it to Windows 95's printer selection. You can do so, including modifying the Windows 95's printer defaults, through the Details tab. In addition, you can modify the methods used by WordPerfect to feed paper into the printer, and select a default font for use by the printer, along with configuring several other controls for printing the current job. Most of these controls are fairly easy to understand, and won't be discussed in depth here.

Table 6-1   Print Tab Controls in the Print Dialog Box

Control or group	What it does
Shift + ←	One character to the left of the insertion point—continue pressing the ← key to select additional characters.
Current Printer	The Current Printer displays the name of the printer to which the document will print. This drop-down control allows you to select an alternate printer. You also can click the Details tab and then click System Printers to choose a different printer.
Properties	This button opens the Windows 95 Properties dialog box for the printer listed in the Current Printer control. (You also can access these controls through the Windows 95 Printer Settings dialog box.) While Windows 95 sets default settings for each printer, WordPerfect 8 exerts control over the Windows 95 configuration, specifying the paper sizes and paper trays needed by a document. You should use the printer Properties dialog box to control graphic print settings, how your printer handles True Type fonts, and specific device options.
Print	Use these controls to tell WordPerfect which pages should be printed on the current document. The default choice is to print Full Document—all pages. You can specifically tell WordPerfect to print the current page (the page on which the insertion point resides), a Print Pages range (such as 1 through 4), or Multiple Pages (such as 3, 5-7, and 9). Multiple Pages works together with the Multiple Pages tab; see the discussion of Multiple Pages following step 3 on the next page.
Number of Copies	Defaulted to one copy; type or spin to the number of print copies you need. This opens the controls to Collate or Group copies.
Document on Disk	A very useful tool, Document on Disk lets you print a document that you've not opened and want to print directly from the file. You then need to select or name the file to be printed.

However, one control is especially important in that it is sometimes overlooked when troubleshooting a printing problem—Print Text Only. This control is used to determine whether or not any graphic elements in a document print. A graphic element might be a piece of clipart, but can also be a graphic line or even a table border. If, when you print, these types of elements do not appear, be sure the Print Text Only box is *not* checked.

CHAPTER 6 • PRINTING YOUR DOCUMENT TO PAPER, E-MAIL, OR FAX 155

Using the Multiple Pages tab in the Print dialog box allows you to send non-adjacent pages to print. In addition to a selection of pages from a simple document, you can print pages from various chapters or volumes in the same print job. Use these steps:

1. Click the Print toolbar button (or press Ctrl+P, or choose File, Print). The Print dialog box opens.
2. Select the desired options on the Print tab.
3. Click the Multiple Pages tab, then type the selection of pages you want to print in each of the controls on the tab. You can type a selection of pages, secondary pages (pages numbered independently in a chapter or volume), all pages from multiple chapters (all of chapters 1 and 3), or all pages from multiple volumes (all pages from volumes 2 and 4). Here are some sample entries:

When printing from chapters or volumes, note that the page number selection from volumes has precedence over all other settings. Therefore, if you type a volume number in the volume control (such as the number 4), only pages and chapters in volume 4 will print—even if you specified pages and chapters from other parts of the document.

Type this	To print this
5-6	5, 6
4-6	4, 5, 6
2, 6-8	2, 6, 7, 8
-4	All pages from the beginning of the document through Page 4
4-	All pages from Page 4 through the end of the document
2, 4-	Page 2, then Page 4 through the end of the document

4. Click Print to print the pages you've selected.

The Two-Sided Printing tab allows you to configure the method your printer uses when printing on both sides of the paper. Again, most of these are fairly easy to understand (WordPerfect's done a good job of illustrating the purpose of the various controls).

One control takes a bit of extra explanation, though—Print as Booklet. A booklet is arranged differently than are two-sided pages. Booklets are the result of subdivided pages (each single physical page divided logically into two pages). Then, when assembled, these pages are stacked one on top of another and perhaps sta-

THE "TYPING AND PRINTING LABELS" SECTION LATER IN THIS CHAPTER TALKS MORE ABOUT PHYSICAL AND LOGICAL PAGES.

pled down the middle. Pick up any booklet in your office that contains stapling down the middle and open it. Notice that the paper for the pages is just folded. But the text must be logically ordered and numbered as you flip each page. So the first piece of paper might actually have the text for page 1 and page 8 printed on the front side, with the text for pages 2 and 7 on the flip side. When you enable the Print as Booklet control, WordPerfect automatically prints the text for the correct page at the correct location on the paper.

You can send documents to print from any file management dialog box, even the Windows 95 Explorer or My Computer file lists. Select the file or files to be printed, then right-click any selected file to display the shortcut menu. Choose Print. If WordPerfect 8 is not open, it starts and the selected files are sent to print.

What About an Envelope?

WordPerfect 8 has an advanced system of creating envelopes, with plenty of options so that your envelope prints exactly to your specifications.

The envelope feature can automatically pick up a recognizable address from the current document, or you can select an address from the Address Book. You can assign specific fonts to the return and mailing addresses. You can opt to omit or print the return address. You can even print a bar code above or below the mailing address to represent the ZIP code.

Creating an Envelope

Before an envelope can be printed, it must be created in WordPerfect. Creating an envelope can be as simple as selecting the envelope feature from the Format menu. If you have a letter on the document window, WordPerfect attempts to locate the letter's inside address (*mailing address*) and insert it on the envelope.

Hands On: Creating an Envelope

Open the sample letter you created in Chapter 4, or any other WordPerfect letter. Use these steps to create an envelope for the letter:

1. Choose Format, Envelope. The Envelope dialog box opens, similar to Figure 6-2. The mailing address on the letter should appear in the To text box of the Envelope dialog box. If the address is incorrect, go to step 2. If the address is correct, go to step 3.

CHAPTER 6 • PRINTING YOUR DOCUMENT TO PAPER, E-MAIL, OR FAX

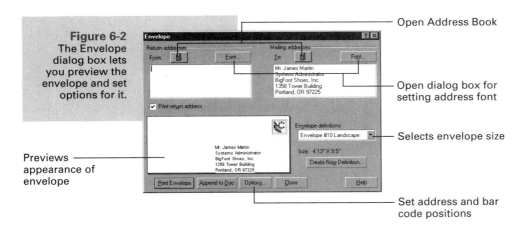

Figure 6-2
The Envelope dialog box lets you preview the envelope and set options for it.

2. Click Close to close the Envelope dialog box. Now select the complete mailing address and then choose Format, Envelope. The Envelope dialog box reopens with the correct address in the To text box.

3. If desired, click the Font button in the Mailing Addresses group to select an alternate font for the addressee. The Mailing Address Font dialog box opens. Set Font Face, Font Size, or any other appearance attributes you want, and then click OK to return to the Envelope dialog box.

4. Add the Universe Training return address by clicking the From Address Book button. (If the Address Book does not contain an address for Universe Training, click Add, then add the Universe Training organization using the steps you learned in Chapter 4.) Then select the address and click OK to include the address on your envelope.

5. Verify the Envelope Definition to be used for your printed envelope. You can select an alternate predefined envelope size from the definitions drop-down list, or use Create New Definition to define an envelope which exactly matches the paper envelopes you use.

6. To print a ZIP code or POSTNET bar code on your envelope, click Options. The Envelope Options dialog box opens, similar to Figure 6-3, from which you can exactly position the print locations for the return and mailing addresses, and choose an option for the United States Postal Service Bar Code.

7. Select either Position Bar Code Above Address to print the bar code above the mailing address, or Position Bar Code Below Address to print the bar code below the mailing address.

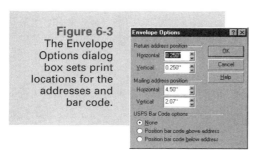

Figure 6-3 The Envelope Options dialog box sets print locations for the addresses and bar code.

8. When you are satisfied with the settings on the Envelope Options dialog box, click OK. You are returned to the Envelope dialog box. Because you've selected a position for the bar code, the POSTNET Bar Code control now appears immediately below the Mailing Addresses group of controls.

9. If the ZIP code does not automatically appear in the POSTNET Bar Code control, click the mouse in the text box—the ZIP code from the To text box appears.

10. Click Print Envelope to send the envelope directly to the printer, or click Append to Doc to add the envelope as a new page at the end of the current document.

Although it's tempting to quickly print the envelope directly to the printer, it's best to use Append to Doc. This way you can avoid the necessity of re-creating the envelope if you've made a mistake in your envelope layout—just edit the envelope page that was added to the end of your document.

Printing an Envelope

In the last section you created an envelope and either submitted it to print or appended it to an open document. Handling an envelope print job is unique to each printer, although there are some general guidelines that you should know. Almost all printers can print directly on an envelope. Some printers require that the narrow end of the envelope be inserted into the printer, adjusting the actual printing to landscape orientation, while others only print portrait orientation. You need to figure out your printer's idiosyncrasies before you feel that you've mastered printing envelopes (or even printing in general). The following list offers some troubleshooting suggestions for printing envelopes:

- *The address prints on the envelope, but in the wrong place.* The envelope paper definition controls whether WordPerfect thinks the envelope will feed short edge or long edge first into the printer. If you select the correct envelope definition based on the envelope size, you may find that the address does not print at the correct location. Edit the envelope definition by choosing File, Page Setup. Then select the envelope definition from the Page information list box and click Edit. Make any changes, then click OK to save your changes.

- *No matter how often you tell the envelope to print from the manual paper tray, the printer flashes a message telling you to put paper in another tray.* Double-check to be sure the paper source listed in File, Page Setup, Edit Page Size dialog box for envelopes is the same as it is in the Format, Envelope, Create New Definition dialog box. You may need to create a new envelope definition, even if the page size is the same, to tell WordPerfect where the envelope paper will be fed.

- *The envelope feeds correctly, but the print is rotated incorrectly.* Edit the envelope definition through File, Page Setup, correcting the font rotation choice.

- *The envelope feeds correctly, but nothing prints!* This is a common problem when you're feeding the short end of the envelope in first. Actually, something may be printing, but in the wrong place. Send the envelope to print again, but this time feed a full page of paper instead of an envelope. Does the address print on the opposite half of the paper? If so, edit the envelope definition, adding a Printing Adjustment to force the print to begin where it should.

- *The envelope prints correctly, but the flap is sealed when it comes out.* Laser printers are hot! Try using a different brand of envelopes the next time you purchase envelope stock. There are envelopes on the market designed especially for laser printers.

How About Labels?

As with envelopes, before you can print a label, you must create the label in WordPerfect. To make it easy, though, WordPerfect 8 includes over 250 Avery label definitions. All you need to do is select the label definition to match your label paper, type the data you want to print on the labels, and then send them to print.

Selecting a Label Definition

The Avery predefined label definitions were automatically installed when you installed WordPerfect. Definitions exist for address labels, diskette labels, round labels, file folder labels—the list seems almost endless. Moreover, you can create your own label definitions if none of the predefined ones meets your needs.

Hands On: Selecting a Label Definition

Before typing a label, you need to select a label definition. Here's how:

1. Choose Fo*r*mat, La*b*els. The Labels dialog box opens, similar to Figure 6-4. Your dialog box may look slightly different if you have not included both Lase*r* Printed and *T*ractor-Fed labels in your default label display, or if you have a different label selected.

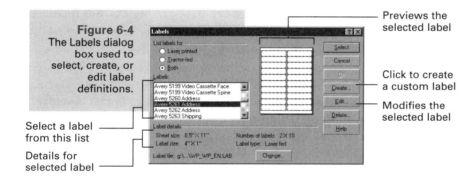

Figure 6-4
The Labels dialog box used to select, create, or edit label definitions.

Select a label from this list
Details for selected label

Previews the selected label
Click to create a custom label
Modifies the selected label

2. Scroll through the *L*abels list until you find the label definition you want to use. As you click each label definition, you see a preview of the label in the preview box.

3. Select the label definition you want to use—Avery 5261 for this example—and click *S*elect. The Label dialog box closes and you return to your document window. The document window displays a single label for the label definition you've selected, and, with Reveal Codes open, you can see [Labels Form] and [Paper Sz/Typ] codes.

CHAPTER 6 • PRINTING YOUR DOCUMENT TO PAPER, E-MAIL, OR FAX **161**

Typing and Printing Labels

A label page is made up of a *physical page* and a *logical page*. The physical page, stored in the [Paper Sz/Typ] code, consists of the dimensions for the actual paper which will be fed into the printer. The logical page, stored in the [Labels Form] code, controls the division of the individual labels on the paper. Each individual label, then, is a logical page; a number of logical pages fit together on a physical page. WordPerfect counts logical pages from left to right, then top to bottom. Figure 6-5 illustrates logical and physical pages.

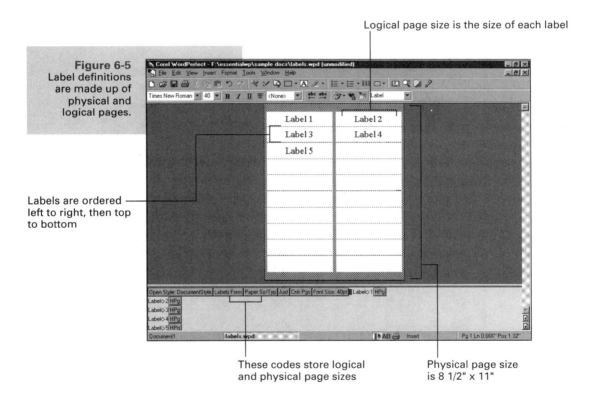

Figure 6-5 Label definitions are made up of physical and logical pages.

Typing a label is really no different than typing any other paper definition. Each label has four margins: top, bottom, left, and right. You can select formatting options, change font faces, and add graphics or lines.

PART II • DAILY TASKS

Hands On: Typing and Printing Address Labels

This example continues the Hands On topic, "Selecting a Label Definition." To demonstrate working with labels, the names and addresses will be centered vertically on each label:

1. Select Format, Page, Center. The Center Page(s) dialog box opens.
2. Click Current and Subsequent Pages to force each name and address label to be centered vertically. Click OK to return to the document window. The insertion point appears in the label, as shown in Figure 6-6.

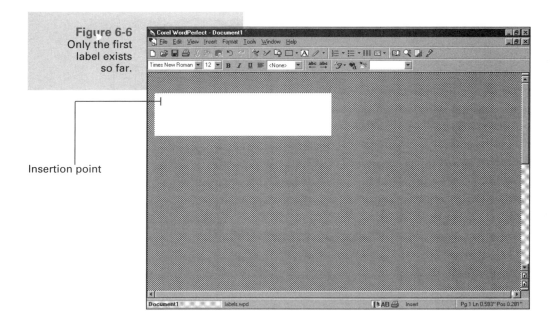

Figure 6-6
Only the first label exists so far.

Insertion point

SEE CHAPTER 7 ON MERGE OPERATIONS IF YOU WANT TO MERGE ADDRESSES TO LABELS.

3. For practice, type your own name and address on the first label, pressing Enter at the end of each line.
4. If your name and address fit on five or fewer lines, only one label exists. Press Ctrl+Enter to force a hard page break, thus creating the next label.
5. Entries in the Address Book can also be used on a label. To open the Address Book, choose Tools, Address Book.
6. Select an entry from the Address Book, then click Insert to add it to the current label. Press Ctrl+Enter to create the next label.

7. You can continue adding names and addresses to your labels, selecting them from the Address Book or typing them, one on each label. When ready, send the labels to print by clicking the Print a Document toolbar button.

You can select to print only specific labels, by label number, with the Print dialog box's Multiple Pages tab.

Troubleshooting Printing Problems

As you know, printers come in many flavors, each with its own idiosyncrasies. Because of this, you might find that some normal actions for WordPerfect and printers feel like problems with your particular setup. Understanding how Word-Perfect talks to the printer might help lessen the frustration you feel when things don't come out of the printer quite the way you intended.

The Printed Document Looks Different Than It Did On-Screen

All printers have a selection of built-in or *resident* fonts. Some older printer models only print with their own fonts—other fonts cannot be downloaded from another source. Most laser and ink-jet printers have an area around the perimeter of a page that cannot be printed on; this is the printer's *no-print zone*. Dot-matrix printers often have a form feeder that controls how far paper feeds into the printer when a print instruction is sent. These unique characteristics result in a document which looks different when it is opened on systems with differing printer selections.

> **You can find more information about fonts in Chapter 4.**

WordPerfect 8 and Windows 95 both include a number of True Type fonts. These fonts work in addition to any fonts that come with your printer. If you commonly print to a variety of different printer types, use True Type fonts rather than a particular printer's built-in fonts. When creating a document, WordPerfect formats each line based on the attributes of the font, wrapping text from line to line as required.

Here's a common scenario: You've created a document using built-in fonts from your laser printer. You've printed the document and it's beautiful. You now send the file by e-mail to another user who prints only to an ink-jet printer. It has a different selection of built-in fonts. That user opens the document and the pages are a different length! Why? There are a couple of possible reasons. WordPerfect has attempted to match the fonts originally used in the document with the fonts now available. Since each font has unique characteristics, the characters are of a slightly different size, resulting in different text wrapping positions. Carried through a complete page, those slight variations result in a different location when the text wraps to the next page. Consider also that the new printer may have an increased no-print zone at the top or bottom of the page, forcing WordPerfect's soft page breaks to occur at a slightly different location.

If you use several printers, you can tell WordPerfect not to reformat a document based on the default printer when the document is opened. Be careful, however. If you do not allow a document to be reformatted for the default printer when it is open, it reformats itself when sent to print on the default printer. Although the reformat occurs on the document window, it happens very quickly and then the document is sent to print. You might not notice the changes before the actual print occurs, resulting in a document at the printer looking different than it did when it was on-screen.

To tell WordPerfect not to reformat a document:

1. Choose Tools, Settings. The Settings dialog box opens.
2. Double-click Environment to open the Environment Settings dialog box.
3. Clear Reformat Documents for the WordPerfect Default Printer on Open.
4. Click OK and then click Close to return to the document window.

The default printer is automatically selected and used when you send a document to print. If you have only one printer available to you, it should already be checked as the default printer. Selecting a default printer sets it not only for WordPerfect 8, but for all Windows 95 programs. Therefore, you set the default printer through Windows 95 utilities.

Here's how to change the default printer:

1. Click the Start button on the Windows 95 taskbar.
2. Choose Settings, Printers. The Printers dialog box opens, displaying the list of printers installed for your system.
3. Right-click the printer you want to set as the default printer. A shortcut menu appears.
4. Verify that Set As Default is checked; if not, click to select it. The shortcut menu closes and you are returned to the Printers dialog box.
5. Click the Close button to return to WordPerfect 8.

CHAPTER 6 • PRINTING YOUR DOCUMENT TO PAPER, E-MAIL, OR FAX

I Sent It to Print, But Nothing Came Out!

This is by far the most common problem I hear when training new users. Of course, the tendency is to send a document to print over and over again, hoping that sooner or later one print submission will actually appear at the printer. Without some user intervention, however, no printout usually materializes. Here are a few areas you can check before assuming there is something faulty about your printer:

- Obviously, is the printer turned on, is the cable connected, and is it online? If it's offline, be sure that the printer isn't out of paper or requiring some other user intervention. Usually the printer is flashing some sort of code at you indicating that you need to do something at the printer itself before it can resume printing. It's helpful to tape a list of common printer error codes to the front of the printer (or somewhere close) so that you can quickly interpret what the printer wants you to do.

- If there are no codes flashing at the printer, but still no printout, there are two or three places you can check to see if the printer actually got the print job you submitted:

  From within WordPerfect, press Ctrl+P to return to the Print dialog box. Click the Status button at the bottom of the dialog box. The Print Status and History dialog box opens (see Figure 6-7) displaying the status of each print job currently waiting to be printed, a history of the jobs sent to each printer, and from where they were sent. The Status column lists the documents waiting to be printed, currently printing, canceled, completed, or in process. If you can see the document you sent to print in the Print Status list, you know that WordPerfect actually did send the document to print and some other problem prevented it from getting to the printer.

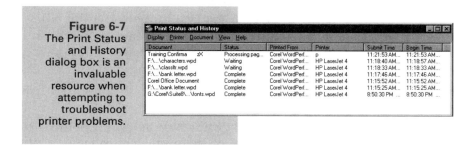

Figure 6-7
The Print Status and History dialog box is an invaluable resource when attempting to troubleshoot printer problems.

In the Windows 95 taskbar, a small icon representing the printer appears whenever a print job is pending. Double-click this icon to open the Windows 95 dialog box associated with the printer.

PART II • DAILY TASKS

If you are on a network, check the network print queue utility to determine whether the network received the print job. Usually, when a job is sent to print from WordPerfect, WordPerfect sends the job to the network, and the network actually submits the job to the printer.

You can delete a print job from either the WordPerfect Print Status and History dialog box or the Windows 95 dialog box for your printer. To do so in either dialog box, select the job to be deleted and then press Del.

Sending a Document via E-Mail or Fax

Most business systems now have hardware components in place to facilitate both electronic messaging and electronic faxing. All that's required is a modem either directly included in your own computer or available to you on your network. If you're networked, you can send e-mail across direct connections to other users on your network. Most modems can be used to send faxes directly from an application, using some sort of electronic fax software.

WordPerfect automatically reads your system configuration to determine what electronic or network services you have available — e-mail services, fax services, and even if the Windows 95 My Briefcase utility is available. These services enable you to use WordPerfect's electronic file transfer options. If you do not have e-mail services available to you, the Mail Recipient menu choice will not appear. Likewise, if you do not have a fax/modem configured for use with your Windows 95 system, WordPerfect will not display Fax Recipient in the File, Send To submenu.

Windows 95 includes programs for both of these services through Windows Messaging/Exchange. Windows Messaging can be used to send messages using a variety of communication services, including Microsoft Mail, CompuServe Mail, Internet Mail, and Microsoft Fax. In addition, Corel WordPerfect Suite 8 includes Netscape Navigator and Netscape Mail. Netscape Mail allows you to send messages across the Internet or an intranet.

CHAPTER 6 • PRINTING YOUR DOCUMENT TO PAPER, E-MAIL, OR FAX **167**

Using Your E-Mail Service

E-mail, short for *electronic mail*, is a direct method of sending a message to another user on some type of network, such as the Internet. An e-mail message may be anything from a simple "Want to have lunch?" to the full content of an extensive WordPerfect 8 document.

One method of sending a document by e-mail messaging is to create and save a file, open the e-mail new message window, address the message, and then locate and attach the file to the message. WordPerfect 8 simplifies these steps by launching your e-mail program for you, opening a new message window, and automatically including the currently opened document as an attachment.

Netscape Navigator is included with Corel WordPerfect Suite 8. It is not, however, automatically installed when you perform a Typical installation. To use Netscape, you need to restart the Corel WordPerfect Suite 8 Setup program, select Netscape Setup, and then proceed with the installation process.

With Netscape Mail or any other mail service installed that is MAPI- or CMC-compliant (such as Exchange/Windows Messaging, GroupWise, or Digital Teamlinks), sending a document using e-mail is a similar process.

Hands On: Sending an E-Mail Message

Use these steps to send a WordPerfect 8 document by e-mail:

1. Open the document you want to send. For this example, open the sample letter created in Chapter 4.
2. Choose File, Send To. From the submenu that appears, choose Mail Recipient. After a brief pause, the New Message dialog box appears with the currently open document attached to the message as an icon. Figure 6-8 shows how this looks (depending on the messaging service you use, your New Message dialog box may look different).

Note

Depending on your e-mail system configuration, you might now need to manually open your messaging service to actually send the mail over the network.

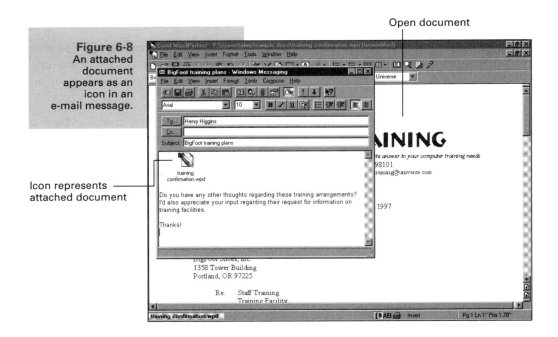

Figure 6-8
An attached document appears as an icon in an e-mail message.

Icon represents attached document

Note

If your messaging service is not currently open, you might see a Choose Profile dialog box prompting you to select the profile you use for Windows Messaging.

3. Address the message as you would any other e-mail message. Include a subject line, then add any other comments you want the recipient to see in the message text area. You can use the New Message toolbar buttons to format your comments.

4. Click the Send button on the message to submit the message for delivery. The New Message dialog box closes and you are returned to your document window.

Printing to Fax Services

Sending a fax involves little more than printing. Most fax software used with Windows 95 installs a print driver to your system. You then select that "printer" and print your document. On a simple computer configuration, the fax program handles the complete interface between the print driver and your phone line. Things can become a little more complicated when printing to fax on a network; however, Windows 95 also recognizes network fax printers.

Using this technology, WordPerfect 8 can be used to generate a document directly to fax. All formatting and features in the WordPerfect 8 document should appear unchanged in the fax document. As when printing to any alternate printer, be sure to use True Type fonts when faxing, to avoid the document being reformatted.

Refer to the section titled "Troubleshooting Printing Problems," earlier in this chapter, for more discussion of printer reformatting.

Hands On: Sending the Current Document as a Fax

Use these steps to fax a WordPerfect 8 document:

1. Open the WordPerfect document you want to fax. For this example, open the sample letter created in Chapter 4.
2. Choose File, Send To. From the submenu that appears, choose Fax Recipient. After a brief pause, your fax program is launched.
3. Follow any prompts, completing the fax address and cover sheet as you normally would when using your fax program.

You can optionally use one of the Fax Cover Sheet projects, found in the project list which appears when you choose File, New. Completing one of these projects is very similar to working with the projects described in Chapters 3 and 4 (and therefore won't be covered again here). These projects guide you through creation of a Fax Cover Sheet, optionally allowing you to use fax entries from the Address Book. When the Cover Sheet is complete, click the Finish button on the Perfect-Expert panel, then select Print/Fax. The Print dialog box opens. Select your fax printer from the Current Printer list, then click Print to submit the document to your fax program. Then use your fax program as you normally would.

7

Same Letter to Lots of Different Personnel

In This Chapter

- **Understanding Merge Processes**
- **Creating a Form Document**
- **Using Different Data Sources**
- **Including Envelopes in a Merge**

Has this ever happened to you? It's about 3:00 p.m. and your six year-old has an important soccer game at 6:30, yet you need to produce a mailing to 500 people before you can go home. It happened to me, and in those days the only way I knew how to accomplish the task was to create the letter once, then type the variable information by hand on each letter. Over and over again. Needless to say, I missed the soccer game. WordPerfect's merge feature would have been ideal, if I'd known how to use it.

Understanding Merge Terminology

The most common function of merge is to create a basic document, the *form*, and then combine that form document with data from another source, the *data file*. When properly created, the form document *merges* or combines with the data file to create a new document, starting each individual instance on a new page. For example, in a simple letter merge, the resulting letter for each entry from the data file starts on a new page in the output document.

Note

You'll find the terms *form document* and *form file*, as well as *data source* and *data file*, used interchangeably in both the WordPerfect Help text and this chapter.

Form documents can be as simple or as complex as you need them to be. They can use virtually every one of WordPerfect's formatting features, including graphics, tables, charts—whatever you need. The form document can evaluate circumstances that might arise and properly act on them. For example, you might send collection letters to only those people in a data file whose accounts are more than 30 days past due. A form document, therefore, contains all the text and formatting that remains constant for each data file entry. It includes special codes that are replaced by data file entries. And it includes instructions to evaluate certain conditions.

Data files can be created from several sources. These sources include:

- A file in WordPerfect, appropriately called a data file
- Your Corel Address Book
- A file from an ODBC-compliant database (*ODBC* stands for *Open Database Connectivity*)
- A database file from another application
- A spreadsheet file
- An ASCII or ANSI delimited file
- Your fingers on a keyboard filling in entries one at a time!

Both form documents and data files use the terms *records* and *fields* to delineate the information which will be merged. A *field* is an individual piece of information to be merged, such as a first name, address, or ZIP code. In a collection application, a field might be the amount owed, the date of the last payment, or the interest rate charged. Fields are usually referred to by a *field name,* although they can be numbered. You can name your fields with any user-friendly phrase, although it's a good idea to keep the field names short and to the point.

A *record* is the combination of fields which comprises an entire set of information. For example, the first name, last name, address, city, state, ZIP code, and phone number for one person combine to form *one record.* The same information for another person is another record and so on. As displayed in Figure 7-1, in an Address Book data file, each entry in the Address Book comprises a record, while each individual piece of information in the record is a field. Figure 7-2 displays a representation of records and fields in a table format.

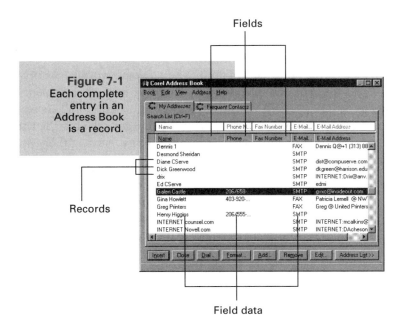

Figure 7-1 Each complete entry in an Address Book is a record.

To give you a feel for the differences in merging, the Hands On examples for the remainder of this chapter demonstrate merging a form sales letter with the Corel Address Book, with a database file, and then with an ASCII delimited file. Each of these examples uses the same form sales letter. One additional example uses a legal caption system to illustrate creating a WordPerfect data file.

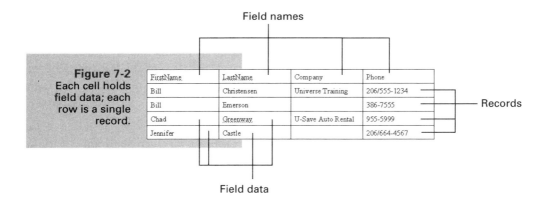

Figure 7-2
Each cell holds field data; each row is a single record.

Creating the Sales Letter Merge

The form and data sources for a merge can be created in any order. It doesn't matter whether you begin with the letter, or begin by manipulating your data source. You'll find that you work back and forth between the form document and your data source until you have everything just right.

Before you begin a merge task, however, you need to be sure that you have the necessary data available to you. For example, do you realistically have a list of names and addresses, including ZIP codes? Are the data reliable? While not totally necessary, in your name list can you isolate which is the first name and which is the last name? It's helpful to have these names separated so that you can say Mr. or Ms. Smith, Dear Gene, and so on. Also, remember that bulk mail to be handled by the U.S. Postal Service requires, at a minimum, a sort based on ZIP codes.

Before beginning to create the form letter, therefore, you must examine your data source to determine whether you have all the necessary data. You also need to know what the field names for the data are. If you plan to use the Address Book, you'll use its field names. If you plan to create the data file as a WordPerfect document, you can assign your own field names. Data which exist in a table or spreadsheet format use the first table row as field names.

Creating the Form Letter

With a good sense of the data to be included, you can now actually create a form letter. Remember that the form letter includes all the text and formatting which will exist on *every* letter, plus placeholders (field codes) for the field data.

Chapter 7 • Same Letter to Lots of Different Personnel

Hands On: Typing the Letter

It's typically easiest to type the text of a merge form document and then go back and insert the field codes as placeholders for your data. Figure 7-3 displays the text and layout for the sales letter.

Figure 7-3
The sample sales letter, without field codes inserted.

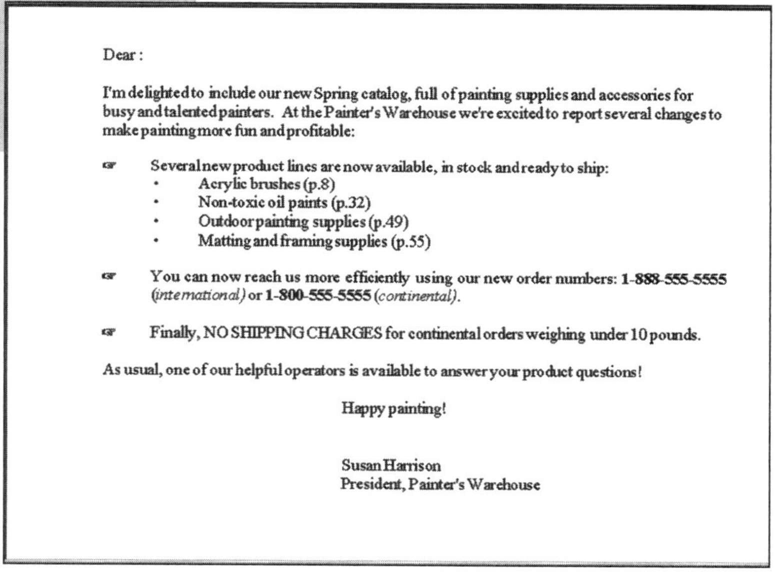

> Dear :
>
> I'm delighted to include our new Spring catalog, full of painting supplies and accessories for busy and talented painters. At the Painter's Warehouse we're excited to report several changes to make painting more fun and profitable:
>
> ☞ Several new product lines are now available, in stock and ready to ship:
> - Acrylic brushes (p.8)
> - Non-toxic oil paints (p.32)
> - Outdoor painting supplies (p.49)
> - Matting and framing supplies (p.55)
>
> ☞ You can now reach us more efficiently using our new order numbers: **1-888-555-5555** (*international*) or **1-800-555-5555** (*continental*).
>
> ☞ Finally, NO SHIPPING CHARGES for continental orders weighing under 10 pounds.
>
> As usual, one of our helpful operators is available to answer your product questions!
>
> Happy painting!
>
> Susan Harrison
> President, Painter's Warehouse

Follow these steps to create the letter:

CHAPTER 4 DISCUSSES BULLETED LISTS AND WORDPERFECT SPECIAL CHARACTERS.

1. Using Figure 7-3 as a guide, type the sales letter. The bulleted list was created using a combination of the Toolbar Bullet button and WordPerfect special characters.
2. When your typing is complete, save the letter using the name `Sample Sales.frm`. With the text of the document saved, you can now tell WordPerfect that the document will be used as a merge form document.

Hands On: Creating a Merge Form from the Letter

At any time, either before or after typing a document, you can designate it to be used as a merge form document. Here's how:

1. Choose <u>T</u>ools, M<u>e</u>rge. The Merge dialog box appears as shown in Figure 7-4.

Figure 7-4
Use the Merge dialog box to create form or data files, or to perform a merge.

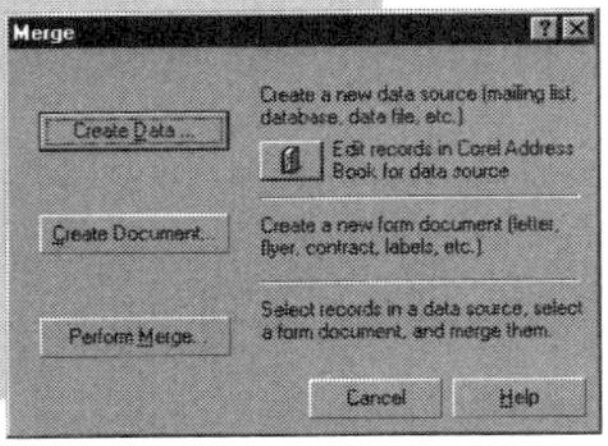

2. Click the <u>C</u>reate Document button. The Create Merge File dialog box appears.
3. Click the <u>U</u>se File in Active Window choice, then click OK. The Associate Form and Data dialog box opens. This dialog box is used to select the type of data source to be used with the form document being created.

This hands-on activity will be continued in the next section.

Associating an Address Book as the Data Source

As you know, a number of different file types can be used as a data source for a merge function. Of them all, however, an Address Book is the easiest to use and work with. You can merge all entries in an Address Book, or you can select specific records, optionally saving the selected records to a group. If you regularly merge to the same selection of people, or if you want to include custom fields, you can create an Address Book just for that group.

Hands On: Associating the Address Book with the Form Letter

The first step in using an Address Book with a merge is to associate the Address Book with the form letter. This Hands On example is a continuation of the previous example; if you did not complete the previous example, be sure to do so.

1. With the Associate Form and Data dialog box open, choose Associate an Address <u>B</u>ook, then open the pop-up list of available Address Books (see Figure 7-5).

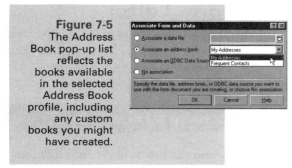

Figure 7-5
The Address Book pop-up list reflects the books available in the selected Address Book profile, including any custom books you might have created.

2. For this example, select the default Corel My Addresses Address Book (assuming you've actually included some entries in that book). If you've not added any entries to My Addresses, select an alternate Address Book which contains several entries. Before actually merging the sales letter with the Address Book, you'll be able to pick and choose which entries you want to include.

3. Click OK. You are returned to the document window. The Merge feature bar appears below the property bar.

Note

If you accidentally choose the incorrect Address Book, or you decide later to associate an alternate data source, there are a number of methods you can use to form that association. One of the easiest, in my opinion, is to first remove the merge feature bar, then re-designate the file as a merge file, forcing the association to again be created. This method more permanently binds the form and data files together so that you can easily move between the two files using the Merge Feature Bar Go To buttons.

To remove the merge bar, click the Options button on the feature bar, then click Remove Merge Bar. You are prompted that the Data File Association will be lost. Click OK. Now step back through designating the file as a merge form and choosing a data file source, selecting the new data source you want to use.

You also can select a new data source at any time through either the Insert Field or Merge feature bar button.

Adding Fields to the Form Letter

As with all feature bars, you can use either the mouse or the keyboard to open the dialog box associated with each button. To select a feature bar button, either click the button, or press [Shift]+[Alt]+ the access character shown on the button.

Hands On: Adding Field Locations to a Form Letter

With the letter recognized as a merge form, you can now add the field locations. When the fields are complete, your letter should resemble Figure 7-6. Note, however, that if you have chosen an Address Book other than Corel's default My Addresses, your field name selection may differ from those used in this example.

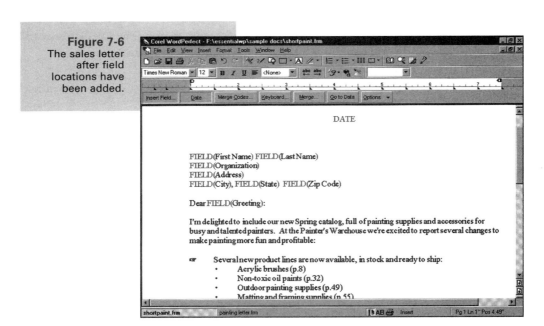

Figure 7-6
The sales letter after field locations have been added.

Use these steps:

1. Click the insertion point at the very beginning of the document, or press [Ctrl]+[Home].
2. Press [Enter] to open a blank line at the top of the document, then press [↑] to move back to the first line.
3. Click the shadow cursor at about 4 inches.

4. Click the Date button to insert the merge date code. Press Enter three times to place the insertion point at the correct location for the inside address.
 5. Click the Insert Field button to open the Insert Field Name or Number dialog box, as shown in Figure 7-7.

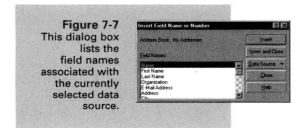

Figure 7-7
This dialog box lists the field names associated with the currently selected data source.

 6. Double-click the listing for First Name from the Field Names list. FIELD(First Name) is added to the document and the insertion point appears immediately after the field.

Tip

It's helpful to turn on Reveal Codes as you are learning to familiarize yourself with the appearance of the various codes as you create your document. By doing so, you'll be more comfortable with Reveal Codes when you need to edit a document that contains complex formatting.

 7. Press the space bar so that a space appears between the first name and last name.
 8. Double-click Last Name in the Field Names list. It is also added to the document.
 9. Press Enter to complete the name line of the inside address.
 10. In the order needed, continue double-clicking each field from the Field Names list to add them to the sales form. Be sure to include spaces, hard returns, and the comma between city and state.
 11. When you have finished adding the fields for the inside address, add any additional hard returns you need, then add the Greeting field in the salutation line.
 12. Click Close to remove the Insert Field Name or Number dialog box from the document window.

PART II • DAILY TASKS

When inserting the last field name for the document, you can click Insert and Close. If you find that you need additional fields later, just click the Insert Field button on the feature bar again to reopen the Insert Field Name or Number dialog box.

13. Press Ctrl+S to update the saved file.

Selecting Address Book Entries and Performing the Merge

With the form document completed and saved, you can now easily complete the merge by choosing the entries you want to use from the Address Book and then performing the merge.

Hands On: Selecting Address Book Entries and Performing the Merge

Selecting records from the address book is the first step to performing a merge. Use these steps:

1. Click the Merge button on the feature bar. The Perform Merge dialog box opens, as shown in Figure 7-8. The Perform Merge dialog box can be used to change the current merge configuration, allowing you to choose a different form document or data source. You can also choose the location for the new document that will be created as a result of the merge, or select a different data source file.

Changing the data source in the Perform Merge dialog box does not change the association between a form document and data file. It only instructs WordPerfect to use a particular file combination during the merge operation.

Typically, as displayed in Figure 7-8, the Perform Merge dialog box is already complete with the correct form document and data source. The default output location for the merge is a new document.

2. Click the Select Records button to open the Address Book. The Address Book opens with an Address List control on the right edge of the dialog box.

CHAPTER 7 • SAME LETTER TO LOTS OF DIFFERENT PERSONNEL **181**

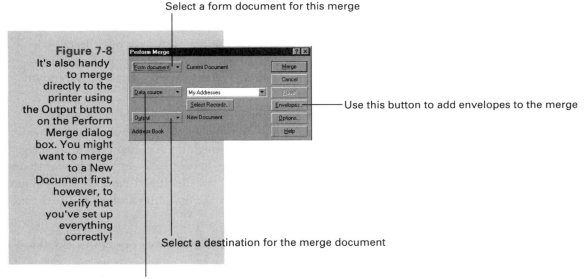

Figure 7-8
It's also handy to merge directly to the printer using the Output button on the Perform Merge dialog box. You might want to merge to a New Document first, however, to verify that you've set up everything correctly!

3. Browse through the Address Book, double-clicking each entry that you want to include in the merge. Each entry is added to the Select Address list. If you select an entry by mistake, double-click the entry in the Select Address list and it is removed from the list. Don't worry—it won't be deleted from the Address Book.

• •
Avoid selecting any Organization entries from your Address Book. They won't merge correctly to this document since entries of this type don't contain any name fields.
• •

4. When your list is complete, click OK to return to the Perform Merge dialog box.

• •
If you regularly merge to the same group of selected entries, click the Save Group button to save your entries to a named group, before clicking OK to return to the merge document. The next time you want to send e-mail, use the group in a merge, or work with these entries as a single unit, you can just select the group name from the list of entries.
• •

5. Click the Output drop-down list to select an alternate location for the resulting merge. A merge can be directed to the current document window,

a new document window, the printer, a file on disk, or even e-mail. For this example, select <u>N</u>ew Document.

6. Click the <u>M</u>erge button to perform the merge. After a brief delay, individual letters—one for each of your chosen Address Book entries—appear in a new document window. The insertion point is at the end of the last letter.

7. Press [Ctrl]+[Home] to move to the beginning of the merged documents. Browse through the document, pressing [Alt]+[Pg Dn] or clicking the Next Page button to move page by page through the file. Did everything merge correctly? Do you properly have spaces between the entry fields, and so on? If so, you can now print or save your new file. If not, close the file without saving, edit the form document and make corrections where required, and merge the file again.

To prevent blank lines where no data exists for a particular field, click the <u>O</u>ptions button in the Perform Merge dialog box before performing the merge. In the <u>I</u>f Field is Empty in Data Source control, select `Remove Blank Line`.

Adding Envelopes to the Merge

Similar to WordPerfect's Envelope feature, envelopes can be added to a merge. The envelopes can include any field from the data source, the POSTNET bar code, and a return address. Including envelopes with the sales letter merge instructs WordPerfect to first merge all the letters, then merge all the envelopes. When printing, all the letters will print first, then all the envelopes.

Hands On: Adding Envelopes to the Sales Letter Merge

Adding an envelope to the sales letter merge is as simple as completing one more dialog box. Here's how:

1. If you've not already done so, complete the steps to create the sales letter, associate it with the data source, and add all the necessary fields to the letter.

2. Click the <u>M</u>erge button on the Merge feature bar to open the Perform Merge dialog box.

3. Verify the <u>F</u>orm File, <u>D</u>ata Source, and O<u>u</u>tput areas as discussed earlier.

CHAPTER 7 • SAME LETTER TO LOTS OF DIFFERENT PERSONNEL **183**

4. Click the Envelopes button in the Perform Merge dialog box. Refer to Figure 7-8 to locate the button, if necessary. The Envelope dialog box opens.

5. Click in the Mailing Addresses text box, then click Field to open the Insert Field Name or Number dialog box.

6. If necessary, drag the Insert Field Name or Number dialog box out of the way of the Mailing Addresses text box (see Figure 7-9).

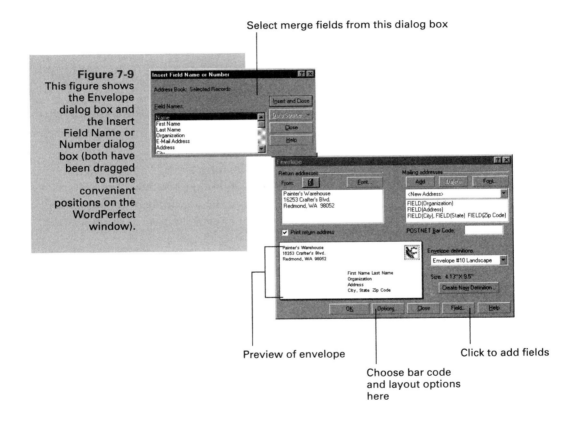

Figure 7-9 This figure shows the Envelope dialog box and the Insert Field Name or Number dialog box (both have been dragged to more convenient positions on the WordPerfect window).

7. Similar to adding fields to the sales letter, double-click each needed field in the Field Names list to add it to the Mailing Addresses text box. The insertion point remains immediately after each field when that field is inserted.

8. Repeat steps 5-7 for each field, formatting the address correctly by adding spaces and hard returns as required between fields.

If you regularly use the same layout for merged mailing addresses, click the Add button in the Mailing Addresses group. This adds the merge layout to a list of stored addresses, unique to envelopes. The next time you need to merge a letter, you can simply select the merge layout from the Mailing Addresses drop-down list.

9. To include the POSTNET Bar Code to the envelope, click the Options button at the bottom of the dialog box. The Envelope Options dialog box opens.

10. Click the desired location for the bar code from the USPS Bar Code Options group, then click OK.

11. Click in the POSTNET Bar Code text box, click the Field button, and double-click the ZIP code field to insert it.

12. If desired, select or type a return address in the Return Addresses text box.

13. Click OK to add the envelope definition to the merge and return to the Perform Merge dialog box.

14. Click Merge to perform the merge. The form letter and data source combine at the output location. Browse through the newly formed document to verify that the letters are at the beginning of the new document, and that each envelope is on a separate page at the end of the new document.

Merges Using Other Data Sources

Using an Address Book as a data source is the most straightforward (and by far the easiest) method in a merge. Because you can easily modify an Address Book to create custom fields, you may want to create custom Address Books and custom fields for almost all your merge forms. To a point, however, you are still limited by the amount and type of information you can realistically store in the Address Book.

To add custom fields to an Address Book, open the Address Book, then choose Edit, Custom Fields, New. Name the new field, then click OK. Continue adding fields as necessary, then click OK again to return to the Address Book. As you add or edit Address Book entries, open the Custom tab to complete the new fields.

For example, you can easily use an Address Book when the data represented works well with names and addresses, such as storing credit limits, or perhaps the names of other family members. But what if you work in a law firm and want to store client information that will merge repeatedly to different forms, such as family law or litigation forms? It's not uncommon in a legal application to even store a complete client caption in a merge field. These types of fields just aren't appropriate for an Address Book. Because this application for a merge presents some unique formatting challenges, it will be the focus of the example for a WordPerfect data file in the "Creating a WordPerfect Data File from Scratch" section, later in this chapter.

Another common use for merge is to combine a WordPerfect document of some sort with entries in a database or spreadsheet. It makes little sense to retype all the information from the database into *any* other data source. Therefore WordPerfect can merge with either a database or spreadsheet without forcing you to retype the data. The upcoming Hands On example for merging with a database uses a Paradox database.

Merging with a Database

Databases usually store information in a logical, straightforward manner. Almost every piece of information exists in some type of table file; within the table are the field names and field data. WordPerfect instantly recognizes most common databases, such as Paradox, dBASE, Clipper, an ODBC-compliant database, or even a SQL database that is ODBC-compliant. It also recognizes most common spreadsheets, such as Quattro Pro, Excel, and Lotus 1-2-3. If your database or spreadsheet is not recognized by WordPerfect, you usually can produce a recognizable ASCII or ANSI delimited file directly from that program, and then merge the resulting file with WordPerfect.

Search for **Import** in the WordPerfect Help index for more information about linking and importing data to and from a database or spreadsheet.

Using a Paradox Database as a Data Source

Paradox is included with the Professional version of Corel WordPerfect Suite 8. With that version are a few sample databases used in the Paradox documentation and help files. The following Hands On example uses the Paradox sample named CUSTOMER.DB which is copied to your system even if you have the Standard version of Corel WordPerfect Suite 8.

PART II • DAILY TASKS

Hands On: Using a Paradox Database as a Data Source

1. Open the sample Sales Letter form, `Sample Sales.frm`, created earlier in this chapter.
2. Click the Insert Field button, then click Data Source.
3. From the resulting drop-down list, select Data File. The Select Data File to Associate dialog box opens. Drop down the For Type list and select `All Files (*.*)` so that you can view all file types in the file list box.
4. Locate and double-click the sample file used in this example, `CUSTOMER.DB` (usually found in the `\Corel\Suite8\Samples` folder), or select another database. WordPerfect instantly creates a temporary document in another document window that contains all the data and field names contained in the database you've selected. The Insert Field Name or Number dialog box opens, displaying the database field names.
5. In the Sales Letter document, delete the address fields since they were created using field names from the Address Book. (You may need to drag the Insert Field Name or Number dialog box out of the way first!)
6. Insert each field onto your form as you would normally, including any necessary spaces or other formatting. Refer to Figure 7-10 as needed.

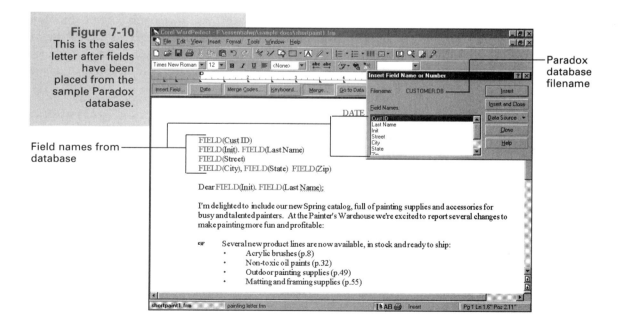

Figure 7-10 This is the sales letter after fields have been placed from the sample Paradox database.

Field names from database

Paradox database filename

CHAPTER 7 • SAME LETTER TO LOTS OF DIFFERENT PERSONNEL 187

7. When all fields are properly placed, click <u>M</u>erge. If desired, you can select specific records from the database (similar to selecting Address Book entries) or specify conditions for the merge. The Select Records dialog box is displayed in Figure 7-11.

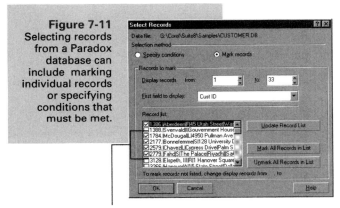

Figure 7-11
Selecting records from a Paradox database can include marking individual records or specifying conditions that must be met.

Checked records will merge

8. Click OK when you are satisfied with your conditions or record marking. Then click <u>M</u>erge to perform the merge. When the merge is complete, the output document contains one letter for each entry in the Paradox database.

Merging with an ASCII Delimited File

Virtually all databases and spreadsheets can export an ASCII or ANSI file with delimiters. Delimiters are characters which identify fields and records within the file. They can be characters such as quotes and commas, interpreted by Word-Perfect as tabs and hard returns. ASCII delimited files imported into WordPerfect usually appear similar to one of the examples pictured in Figure 7-12.

Merging with an ASCII file involves two steps. First you open the ASCII file, converting it to a WordPerfect data file. Then you merge the data file with the WordPerfect form file.

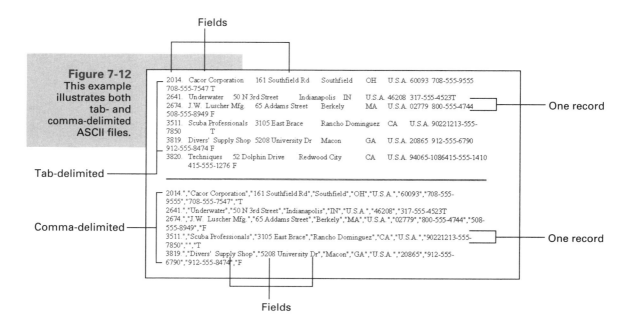

Figure 7-12 This example illustrates both tab- and comma-delimited ASCII files.

Hands On: Creating a WordPerfect Merge Data File from an ASCII Delimited File

To follow this example, you need an ASCII file containing name and address fields. Complete these steps to work with the file:

1. Open the ASCII file in WordPerfect. You'll see a dialog box asking you to confirm the current file format. Typically WordPerfect identifies all ASCII files as ASCII DOS Text files. While the delimited file is an ASCII text file, by forcing WordPerfect to examine the delimiters in the file, a WordPerfect merge data file can be created. From the Convert File Format From drop-down list, select ASCII (DOS) Delimited Text as the file format to use.
2. Click OK. The Import Data dialog box opens (see Figure 7-13).
3. From the Import As pop-up list, select Merge Data File as the file type to be created.
4. Verify that the delimiters are correct for your file. You can type any ASCII character in either the Field or Record text box, or select a Tab, Line Feed, Form Feed, or Carriage Return from the list boxes. Remember that delimiters separate fields and records.

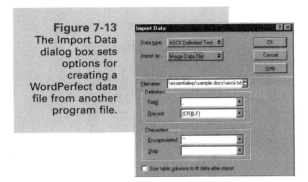

Figure 7-13
The Import Data dialog box sets options for creating a WordPerfect data file from another program file.

Note

A hard return at the end of a record is actually two characters—a carriage return and a line feed.

5. Verify that the Characters fields are also correct for your file. Encapsulated characters surround a field, identifying its start and end. Quotation marks are probably the most common characters for this purpose. If your file also contains one or more characters to be removed within the fields, identify the character(s) in the Strip text box.

6. Click OK. Figure 7-14 displays the resulting WordPerfect merge data file. Fields are numbered in a data file that has been automatically created by WordPerfect. Therefore, the first field in the record is field 1, the next is field 2, and so on. Each field is separated by an ENDFIELD code and a hard return. Each record is separated by an ENDRECORD code and a hard page break. Notice in the figure that the ENDRECORD code immediately follows the last field which holds the value T (maybe for *True*). Therefore, it looks like TENDRECORD, but this is not a single code; it's the value T followed by the ENDRECORD code.

7. Save the file so that it can be used when performing a merge. While not strictly necessary, you should use the extension **.DAT** when naming the file. WordPerfect automatically recognizes this extension as a merge data file.

8. If necessary, edit the form document to be used with the new data file so that the form document uses the correct field numbers.

9. Perform the merge using the converted ASCII data with your form document.

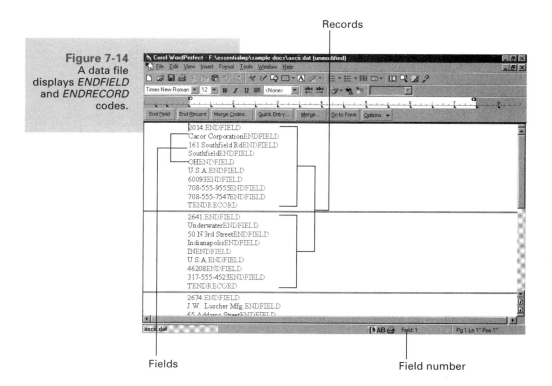

Figure 7-14
A data file displays *ENDFIELD* and *ENDRECORD* codes.

Creating a WordPerfect Data File from Scratch

Creating a WordPerfect data file requires that you think through the types of information you'll ultimately need when you're ready to merge with your form document. It might be easiest to actually begin with a list of the fields you anticipate using, then break down the list into the smallest fields possible. Think like the Address Book! The Address Book separates first name from last name, then adds a field for greeting. It separates street address from city, city from state, and state from ZIP code. Use small fields so that you can include them in any combination in your merge form document.

The Hands On example used in this section will break from the sales letter application, where lots of letters are created from a single form and single data file. This example will present the idea of using merge to create just one document at a time, but from an often-used form document. Form documents are not limited to letter-type applications. A form document can be a fill-in-the-blank form such as a delivery form, a legal form, even a data-entry form from which data is transferred to a database. Your imagination and ability to break down the needed data into manageable components are your only limitations in applying merge functionality to your repetitive daily tasks.

CHAPTER 7 • SAME LETTER TO LOTS OF DIFFERENT PERSONNEL

The following Hands On examples create a sample legal caption (the beginning of most legal documents, which may include names of plaintiffs/defendants, court name, case title, cause number, and so on) as the data file, and the beginning of a legal document as the form document.

Hands On: Creating a Legal Caption Data File and Defining Field Names

Creating a caption file assumes that four basic fields are necessary: the name of the client, the heading lines for the court system in which the client's matter is handled, the caption, and the cause or matter number. Other fields might be necessary for family law or estate-planning matter forms. At a minimum, you need to include names of each spouse, names and birthdates of children, names of guardians, and so on.

1. On a new document window, create the data file by choosing Tools, Merge. Then click the Create Data button from the resulting Merge dialog box. The Create Data File dialog box opens.

2. In the Name a Field text box, type the name of each merge field, pressing [Enter] or clicking Add after each field. The four fields are: **Client**, **Court**, **Caption**, and **Cause No**. If you make a mistake or need to reorder the fields, use the Delete, Move Up, or Move Down buttons until your fields are created as displayed in Figure 7-15.

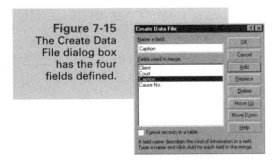

Figure 7-15
The Create Data File dialog box has the four fields defined.

3. When all fields are complete, click OK. A FIELDNAMES code is written to the document and the Quick Data Entry dialog box opens.

PART II • DAILY TASKS

Note

> The Quick Data Entry dialog box provides a method of adding record after record to your data file. It's a very useful, simple method of adding records without requiring you to manually include ENDFIELD and ENDRECORD codes after each field and record.
>
> The Quick Data Entry dialog box opens automatically when you create a data file from scratch. Alternatively, you can open the Quick Data Entry dialog box by clicking the Quick Entry button on the Merge feature bar.
>
> In the Quick Data Entry dialog box, each field defined is represented by a text box on the dialog box. You type in each field, then press Tab (or click Next Field or Previous Field). If you need to include a tab character in the field contents, press Ctrl+Tab. Likewise, press Ctrl+Enter to add a hard return character in a field. Pressing Enter from the last field in the data entry box forces the record to write to the data file.

4. Because creating court captions is a bit more complex than just straight data entry, the Quick Data Entry dialog box is inappropriate. Click Close to remove this box from the screen. A prompt appears, asking whether you want to save the changes to disk. Click Yes to save your development work on the new caption data file.

5. Name the caption file, using a name such as **CAPTION.DAT**, then click Save. The file is saved to disk and you are returned to the document window. Your document now resembles Figure 7-16.

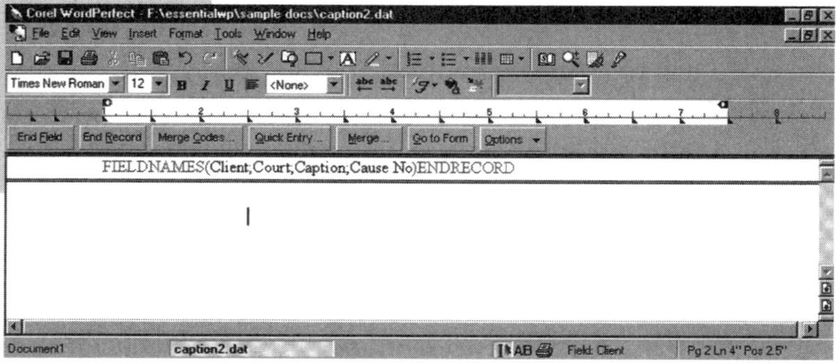

Figure 7-16
This is the Caption data file after creating the field names and saving the file.

The field names you created in step 3 appear between the left and right parentheses in the FIELDNAMES code. You can edit these field names as necessary, but be sure they remain within the parentheses and are separated from one another by a semicolon. If you accidentally delete the FIELDNAMES code, you can select it again by clicking the Merge Codes button.

The ENDRECORD code must be present after the field name list. It automatically includes both the code and the hard page break. If you accidentally delete an ENDRECORD code, press [Alt]+[Shift]+[Enter] to replace it, or click the End Record button.

Hands On: Creating a Legal Caption Data File and Adding the Data

In the State of Washington, legal captions typically include the name of the court centered between the left and right margins, with the names of the litigation participants, or *parties*, in a box which appears down the left margin. The box for the parties is typically bounded by right parentheses down the right edge, and a solid line at the bottom. The old-fashioned method of creating these boxes was to tab to the appropriate position on each line, then type the right parenthesis. The bottom line was typically "drawn" using an underline.

The caption also includes the cause number on the right side of the page, toward the top-third or so of the caption height. Figure 7-17 displays a sample finished caption. Most states use captions in a similar style.

This simple application uses two columns to properly align the party box and the cause number. The column definition resides in the form document. The caption formatting, using flush-right and underlined tabs to create the box boundaries, resides in the data file. Use the following steps to create the caption data:

1. Type the name for the client (**JJSmith** in this example). This will be used to select the caption for this client when you merge with the pleading form.

2. Click the End Field button (or press [Alt]+[Enter]) to add the ENDFIELD code. The code is written to the document, followed by a hard return.

3. Press [Shift]+[F7], or select Center Justification after clicking the Justification toolbar button. Type the name of the court for the caption: **IN THE SUPERIOR COURT OF THE STATE OF WASHINGTON FOR KING COUNTY**.

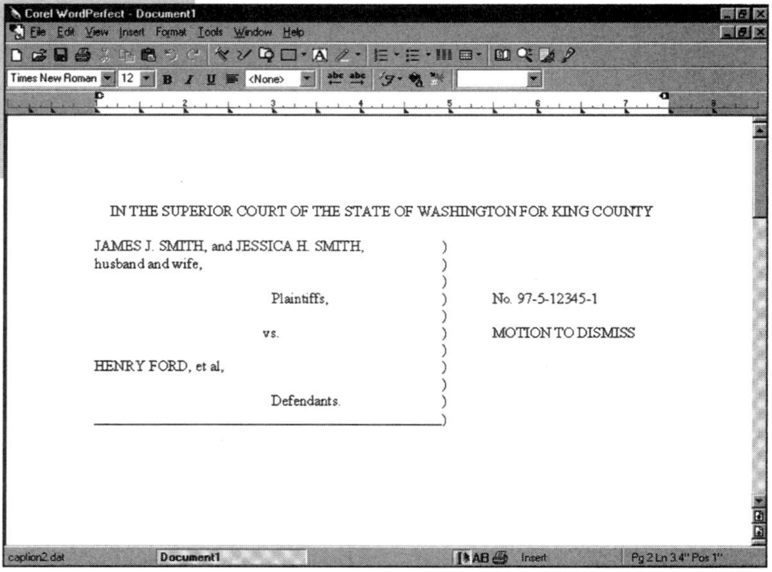

Figure 7-17
This is a sample court caption for the King County Superior Court in Washington.

4. Press Enter. If you used center justification in step 3, be sure to change to left justification. Complete the field by adding an ENDFIELD code.

5. Type the text for the first line of the caption, bearing in mind that it must fit within the width of the column you'll use for the party box. The complete party information for the caption reads like this:

JAMES J. SMITH, and JESSICA H. SMITH,	)
husband and wife,	)
	)
Plaintiffs,	)
	)
vs.	)
	)
HENRY FORD, et al,	)
	)
Defendants.	)
	)

CHAPTER 7 • SAME LETTER TO LOTS OF DIFFERENT PERSONNEL   195

• •
I usually try to limit the text so that it does not go beyond 4" on the ruler.
• •

6. Press [Alt]+[F7] to move the insertion point flush right, then type a right parenthesis.

7. Press [Enter] to complete the line, then continue typing the caption using flush right, tabs, and centering to properly align each line. Remember that the position of the right parenthesis will be controlled by the column definition in the form document. Use the remainder of the sample text following step 5.

8. Turn on Underline Tabs (this controls the bottom line for the box) by pressing [F9] (or choosing Format, Font). The Font dialog box opens. Drop down the Underline control, then select Text & Tabs. Click OK to close the Font dialog box.

• •
Underline Tabs is also an ideal method to use when creating signature lines. Using this method, press [Ctrl]+[U] to turn on the underline, press [Tab] until the line is the desired length, and press [Ctrl]+[U] to turn off the underline.
• •

9. Create the bottom box line by pressing [Ctrl]+[U] to turn on the underline, then [Alt]+[F7] for flush right. Press [Ctrl]+[U] again to turn off the underline, then type the right parenthesis. Press [Enter] to complete the line.

10. Add the ENDFIELD code to finish the caption field.

11. Press [Enter] three times (to force the cause number to appear three lines down from the top of the party box when merged), then type the cause number for the action, followed by ENDFIELD.

12. Click the End Record button. The ENDRECORD code is inserted, followed by a hard page break. Your caption data file should resemble Figure 7-18.

13. Repeat steps 1-7 and 9-12 for each caption you want to store in this data file. Step 8 only needs to be completed once in a file.

14. When all captions are complete, save the file.

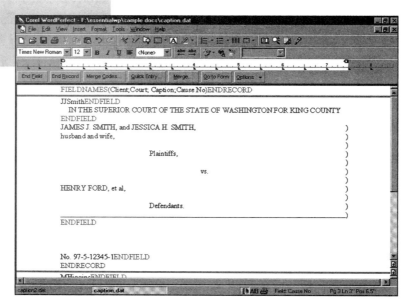

Figure 7-18
The caption file is complete.

Hands On: Creating a Legal Pleading Form

A pleading form usually contains custom pleading paper (perhaps numbered), with the firm's name and address often appearing in a footer. This example does not turn on or create pleading paper. Before creating a form similar to this one, you might consider using the Pleading Paper project, which assists you in creating custom pleading paper for your firm.

Follow these steps:

1. Open a new document window, then define the document as a merge form document. Associate the form with the caption data file as the data source.
2. Turn on Underline Tabs by pressing F9 (or choosing Format, Font). The Font dialog box opens. Drop down the Underline control, then select `Text & Tabs`. Click OK to close the Font dialog box.
3. Insert the first field, Court, using the Insert Field button, then press Enter twice to separate the Court field from the Caption field. You might find it helpful to refer to Figure 7-19 as you create this form document.
4. Define the columns by clicking the Columns toolbar button and selecting Format. The Columns dialog box opens.

SEE CHAPTER 11 FOR MORE INFORMATION ABOUT COLUMNS.

CHAPTER 7 • SAME LETTER TO LOTS OF DIFFERENT PERSONNEL 197

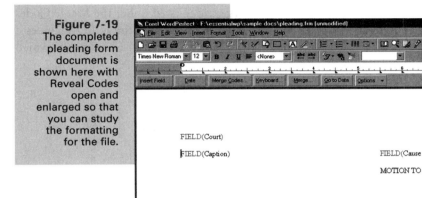

Figure 7-19
The completed pleading form document is shown here with Reveal Codes open and enlarged so that you can study the formatting for the file.

5. Verify that Number of Columns is set to 2, then click Parallel as the column type. Expand Width of Column 1 to 4", then click OK to close the Columns dialog box.

6. Insert the Caption field, then press Ctrl+Enter to force a hard column break. The insertion point moves to Column 2.

7. Insert the Cause No field, then press Enter twice. Click Close to remove the Insert Field Name or Number dialog box.

8. Type **MOTION TO DISMISS** as the name of the pleading.

9. Turn off columns by clicking the Columns toolbar button and selecting Discontinue. The insertion point returns to the left margin.

10. Type the remainder of your pleading text. Be sure to save the document periodically. Name the file `Pleading.frm` (or something even more descriptive, such as `Motion to Dismiss`). WordPerfect automatically suggests the extension `.frm` to identify it as a merge form document.

11. Merge your pleading form with the caption data file, selecting the individual caption to be merged from the select records list.

Merge contains many other powerful commands beyond those discussed in this chapter. Be sure to experiment with using the KEYBOARD command to prompt the user when a merge occurs; it's an excellent tool for fill-in-the-blank forms. In addition, experiment with the various merge codes listed under the Merge Codes button. The Reference Center on the Corel WordPerfect Suite 8 CD includes a "Merge Programming Commands" book that you can refer to (and print) which is devoted to advanced merge uses.

Part III
Reports and Presentations

8 An Organized Report Starts with an Outline..... 201

9 Using Tables for Powerful Data Presentation 223

10 Maintaining Your Report's Organization 265

8

An Organized Report Starts with an Outline

In This Chapter

- **Working with Outline Definitions**
- **Adding Items to an Outline**
- **Changing a Level Style**

A creative, well thought-out business report is usually highly structured. Topics build one upon another, covering each subject in a logical manner, with the most important topics introducing other subordinate subjects. Composing a report becomes much easier, therefore, when an outline is created that identifies and organizes each important category and subcategory.

Creating an outline is rarely a one time through, all-done matter. Often, as a report develops, additional topics appear of equal importance while other topics are pushed to a lesser role. Rearranging and editing an outline by hand can be a cumbersome, lengthy task.

Using WordPerfect 8 to create your outline offers several advantages over creating an outline by hand:

- WordPerfect automatically inserts each outline number, correctly identified by its place, or *level*, in the outline.
- You can rearrange the complete outline, or each section of the outline. WordPerfect maintains sequential numbering for you, based on the position of the text in the outline.
- You can type the complete, supporting text in the outline and then hide the text, displaying only the outline headings.
- You can customize the appearance of the outline at any time, forcing numbers to appear in just the correct location and using the correct characters or symbols.
- You can stop and restart an outline as often as you need in the same document; you can also use different outline definitions in the same document.

This chapter will introduce you to using WordPerfect 8's powerful outline features, while creating a business plan and a legal research brief. You will learn various techniques to assist you in creating an outline, as well as editing, rearranging, and modifying an outline. You'll also learn how to add supporting text to an outline, then print the outline with or without the text.

Choosing an Outline Definition

In an organized outline, each topic is typically numbered in some fashion, although not necessarily with numerals. Some outlines use bulleted or other special characters to delineate different headings. Different types of reports demand different outline layouts. Figure 8-1 displays three different outline definitions.

Each outline definition consists of eight outline *levels*. A level indicates the importance of the topic. Level 1, therefore, is the most important, with levels 2 through 8 being of lesser importance. See Figure 8-2.

Chapter 8 • An Organized Report Starts with an Outline

Figure 8-1
Different report types use different outline definitions.

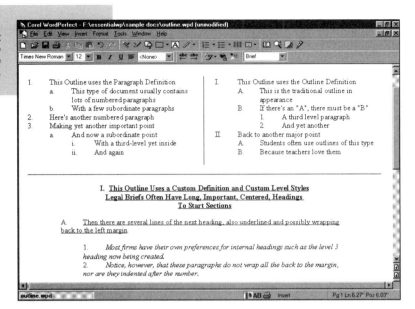

Figure 8-2
An outline can contain a maximum of eight levels; each level is governed by its own style.

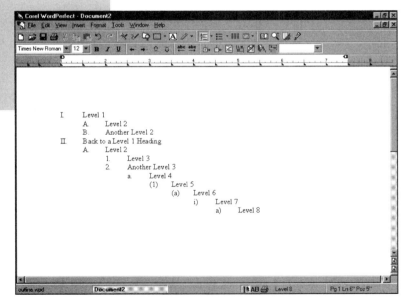

PART III • REPORTS AND PRESENTATIONS

Outlines differ from lists in that they contain sublevels.

SEE CHAPTER 4 FOR MORE INFORMATION ABOUT CREATING NUMBERED OR BULLETED LISTS.

In addition to a number, bullet, or some other character, each level contains its own formatting, or *style*. A number of outline definitions are predefined, using the predefined level styles. You can edit any of the predefined definitions, changing to other predefined level styles, or you can create new level styles. To make things more confusing, you might choose to create an outline definition totally from scratch, then use existing styles or create eight new level styles. The legal brief numbering definition you saw at the bottom of the screen in Figure 8-1 is a completely custom definition using eight custom level styles. The other two outlines represented are predefined in WordPerfect 8 and use the WordPerfect 8 level styles.

Hands On: Choosing an Outline Definition for a Business Plan

SEE CHAPTER 5 FOR MORE STYLE BASICS.

It's easiest to select an outline definition before you begin typing text for the outline, although it's not strictly required. If you wait to select the definition until you have already typed the text, you may need to do some heavy editing to be sure that everything is correctly numbered and formatted. Here's how to choose an outline definition:

1. Choose Insert, Outline/Bullets & Numbering. The Bullets and Numbering dialog box opens (see Figure 8-3).

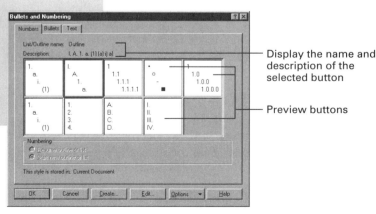

Figure 8-3 Select an outline definition from the Numbers tab of the Bullets and Numbering dialog box.

Chapter 8 • An Organized Report Starts with an Outline

2. With the Numbers tab on top, click the Outline preview button. (It's the second button.) A dark border appears around the button and the button name and a brief description of the selected definition can be seen above the preview buttons.

3. Click OK to accept the definition. The first level of the selected definition appears in the document and the property bar changes to display several buttons you will use to manipulate the outline. Figure 8-4 illustrates the updated property bar.

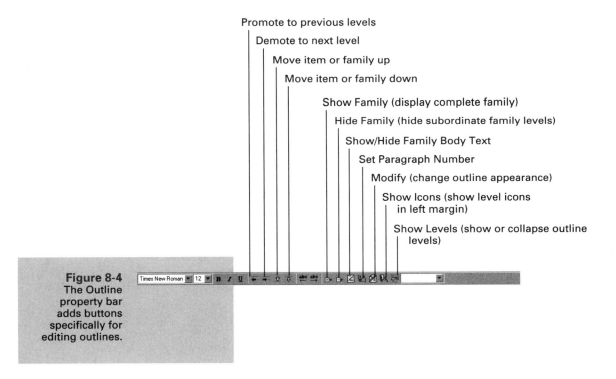

Figure 8-4
The Outline property bar adds buttons specifically for editing outlines.

Typing an Outline Definition

SEE CHAPTER 4 FOR MORE INFORMATION ON INDENTS.

Adding text to an outline is slightly different than typing on a document where you might manually number paragraphs. As you type, text wraps normally at the end of a line. But almost all of the predefined outline definitions use numbers in combination with indents. This means that as you type, text automatically wraps from line to line to the next tab position following the inserted number. Use these keys or buttons in an outline:

PART III • REPORTS AND PRESENTATIONS

Press or click	For this result
Enter	Finish the current line and start a new line by moving to the next number in the same outline level, or move the current level down by one line
Tab or Demote button	Demote, or go down one level
Shift+Tab or Promote button	Promote, or back up one level
Shift+Ctrl+L	Create a line break in the current level
Backspace	Delete the current level style

Hands On: Typing the Business Plan Outline

Figure 8-5 shows the text and layout for the sample business plan. Refer to it as you create the outline using the steps that follow.

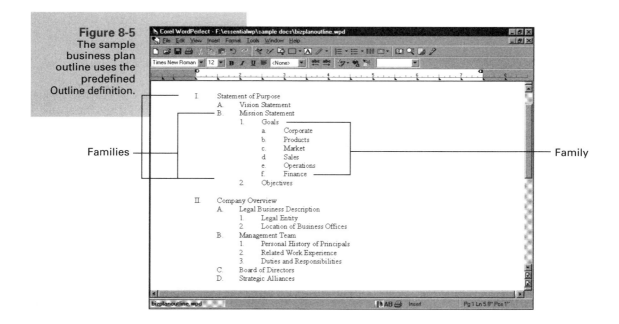

Figure 8-5 The sample business plan outline uses the predefined Outline definition.

Follow these steps:

1. With the Outline definition selected as described in the previous hands-on exercise, type the text **Statement of Purpose**.

CHAPTER 8 • AN ORGANIZED REPORT STARTS WITH AN OUTLINE 207

2. Press Enter. The insertion point moves to the next line and another level 1 number appears.
3. Press Tab. The insertion point moves to the next tab position and the level 2 number appears.
4. Type the text **Vision Statement**, then press Enter.
5. Type the remaining text for the major heading I. Statement of Purpose. Press Enter twice after the last line, **Objectives**, to force a blank line between the two major headings.
6. Press Shift+Tab to promote the number to a level 1 heading. Now type the remaining outline levels using these same keystrokes.
7. Save your sample outline using the filename **BizPlan.wpd**.

Understanding Outline Families

Outline levels create *families*. An outline family is an outline level plus any subordinate levels which may reside immediately beneath that level. Figure 8-5 displayed several families. For example, the entire set of levels from I. Statement of Purpose through 2. Objectives form a family. Another family can be formed starting with B. Mission Statement through 2. Objectives. Another family in the same group can be formed starting with 1. Goals and finishing with f. Finance.

Outline families can be manipulated as a single unit. For example, you can move a complete outline family to another position in the outline with a single move command. You can also hide or display outline levels.

Hands On: Rearranging the Business Plan Outline

After careful thought, you need to move the complete Mission Statement family to the first level after the Company Overview item. Here's how:

1. To facilitate moving and manipulating outline families, it's easiest to start by displaying the outline level icons. To do so, click the Show Icons button on the property bar. The icons are displayed in the left margin, as shown in Figure 8-6.
2. Select the complete family starting with B. Mission Statement by pointing to the outline level icon which appears to the left of the heading. Then click. Refer to Figure 8-6, where the mouse pointer is in the correct position to select the full Mission Statement family.

PART III • REPORTS AND PRESENTATIONS

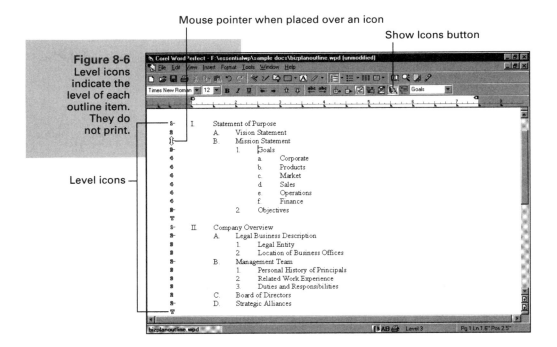

Figure 8-6 Level icons indicate the level of each outline item. They do not print.

Level icons

3. Drag the mouse pointer through the level icons. As you move the pointer through areas of the outline that are not currently selected, a horizontal line appears at the location the selected family will be inserted when you release the pointer. Drag the pointer until the underline appears immediately below II. Company Overview, and then release the mouse button (see Figure 8-7).

Hands On: Hiding and Displaying Outline Levels

In addition, you want to see an overall view of the major headings in the outline, displaying only levels 1 and 2. Use these steps to hide or display portions of your outline:

1. Click the insertion point anywhere in the outline.

Tip

If you click anywhere outside of the outline, the outline property bar disappears and is replaced by the property bar which affects the text at the insertion point. Click inside an outline itself to work with the property bar buttons.

CHAPTER 8 • AN ORGANIZED REPORT STARTS WITH AN OUTLINE **209**

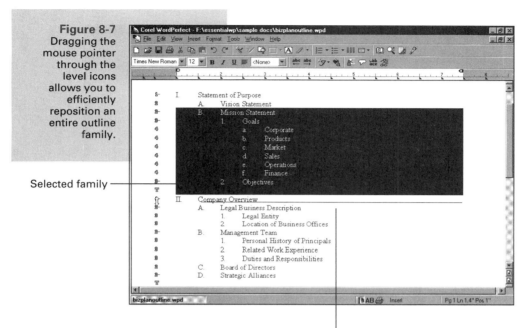

Figure 8-7
Dragging the mouse pointer through the level icons allows you to efficiently reposition an entire outline family.

Selected family

Line indicates position family will be inserted

2. Open the drop-down box for the Show Levels button, then select 2.
3. Click anywhere in the outline to update its display. Only level 1 and level 2 outline items are now visible, as shown in Figure 8-8.
4. Open the Show Levels button again and select 8, then click back in the outline. Now all levels are redisplayed.

You can also hide a single family's subordinate levels using these steps:

1. Click anywhere in the level you want to hide.
2. Click the Hide Family button. All subordinate entries to the current item are now hidden.
3. Click the Show Family button to redisplay the complete family.

Adding New Items to an Outline

Possibly more than any other type of document, an outline is subject to revision after revision. You'll want to rearrange the outline families, add text to an outline that isn't numbered, or delete or add new outline items.

PART III • REPORTS AND PRESENTATIONS

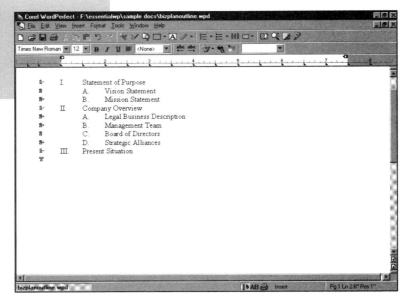

Figure 8.8
With only two levels displayed, the outline presents a more streamlined plan.

Hands On: Adding New Outline Items to the Business Plan

Adding new outline items to an existing outline is simple. Follow these steps:

1. Click at the end of the line which reads `A. Vision Statement`.
2. Press [Enter]. A new line appears, appropriately numbered `B.`. Notice that the following item is now renumbered `C.`.
3. Press [Tab] to demote the level to `1.`. The insertion point moves to the proper new text location and the following item number again is corrected—it now reads `B.`.
4. Type the new outline items using the text that follows as your example. Remember to press [Enter] to end the first two lines and create the next number in sequence.

    1. One Year
    2. Five Years
    3. Ten Years

> If you accidentally delete an outline level you need, press Ctrl+Z to quickly Undo your deletion. Alternately you can either press Backspace to move to the end of the previous level and press Enter again, or press Ctrl+Shift+F5 to open the Insert Paragraph Number dialog box. Then indicate the outline level, start value, and number type you need. Click OK to add the number to your outline.

Body text is text anywhere in the outline that does not contain an outline level style. You'll use body text to flesh out the actual outline and begin adding the *body* or content to your report. Just like hiding outline levels, you'll be able to hide or display all of the body text in your report. This allows you to switch back and forth between the report in its outline appearance and as a complete presentation.

Hands On: Adding Body Text to the Business Plan

Use this technique to add body text to the business plan:

1. Click the insertion point at the end of the Statement of Purpose line.
2. Press Enter to add a new line. A new level 1 number is added to the outline and the insertion point is at the position to add a new outline item.
3. Press Backspace to delete the outline level. Notice that the level icon now indicates a T and the property bar now displays buttons for use while typing text. Press Enter again to add a blank line after the heading and before the body text.
4. Now type the following text for your report (this text can be seen in Figure 8-9):

   ```
   Universe Training will specialize in providing hands-on,
   comprehensive, training to business personnel which
   specifically addresses the need for formal training to
   meet new job requirements.
   ```

Hands On: Hiding and Redisplaying Body Text

To hide or show body text in your business plan so that you can review the outline, then return to the full report, use these steps:

PART III • REPORTS AND PRESENTATIONS

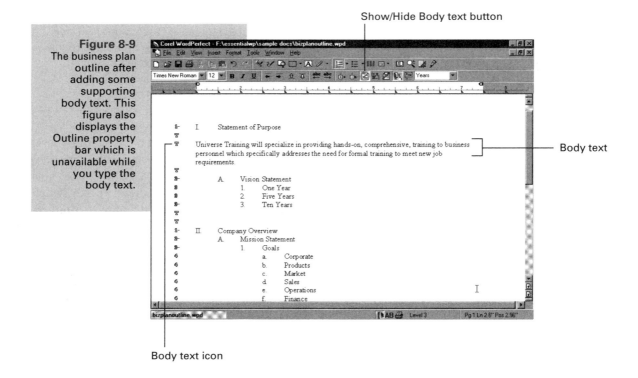

Figure 8-9 The business plan outline after adding some supporting body text. This figure also displays the Outline property bar which is unavailable while you type the body text.

1. Click in the business plan on any outline level item.
2. Click the Show/Hide Body Text button. The business plan contracts, temporarily hiding all text which does not appear in an outline level item.
3. Click the Show/Hide Body Text button again to expand the report, redisplaying all body text.

Modifying an Outline's Appearance

As you have discovered, creating and editing an outline is quite simple. WordPerfect 8 provides powerful predefined outline definitions which can be used for most outlines. But what if you really don't care for the numbering system used in any of the predefined outline definitions? Maybe you'd prefer to have the text appear in bold for each level 1 outline item. Or perhaps you've already created an outline and now want to use a completely different outline definition.

CHAPTER 8 • AN ORGANIZED REPORT STARTS WITH AN OUTLINE 213

Hands On: Selecting a Different Outline Definition

Changing to a different outline definition after an outline has been created is as simple as choosing one of the other definitions. Use these steps:

1. With your insertion point in any outline item except for body text, choose Insert, Outline/Bullets & Numbering. The Bullets and Numbering dialog box opens.
2. Click the preview button for the definition you want to use for your outline. Click the first button, Paragraph, to change the outline to a paragraph numbered outline definition.
3. Click Resume Outline or List in the Numbering group, then click OK. All outline levels update, displaying the numbering and styles for the selected definition.

You can start a new outline, effectively starting all numbering sequences over again, by making sure that the insertion point does not reside in an outline level. Then open the Bullets and Numbering dialog box and select Start New Outline or List from the Numbering group.

The Text tab in the Bullets and Numbering dialog box contains three additional outline definitions, named Headings, Quotations, and Definitions. Select the Headings definition to automatically dress-up your business plan outline items, effectively turning them into report headings, including adding table of content marks.

Sometimes, however, none of the predefined outline definitions will work for your document. WordPerfect 8 is a flexible program which lets you produce documents that reflect your own formatting tastes.

Creating a Custom Outline Definition

As a quick review, remember that an outline definition contains a maximum of eight levels, and each level consists of a number and a style. You can create a style from scratch, creating numbers and level styles for each level in your custom definition. Or you can change the appearance of the number and modify a level style for any of the predefined definitions.

This section will guide you in creating the first two levels of the custom legal brief definition displayed in Figure 8-8. Refer to Figure 8-8 as needed for visual guidance of the definition.

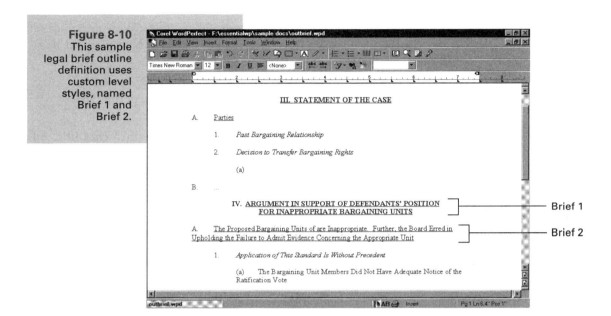

Figure 8-10 This sample legal brief outline definition uses custom level styles, named Brief 1 and Brief 2.

Creating and Naming the Legal Brief Definition

Creating your own definition involves planning the appearance of each level. You'll need to determine what the number for each level should look like, or even if you will use a number at all. Then you must identify what formatting features you want to include in the level styles.

For example, in Figure 8-10, outline level 1 displays a bold, capital Roman numeral followed by two spaces. Then underline is turned on and continues for the remainder of the outline item. Further, the complete outline level is centered and single-spaced.

Outline level 2 displays a capital letter, followed by a period and tab. Then underline is turned on.

CHAPTER 8 • AN ORGANIZED REPORT STARTS WITH AN OUTLINE **215**

> **Hands On: Creating and Naming a Custom Definition**

To create a custom outline definition similar to those shown in Figure 8-10, start with these steps:

1. Choose Insert, Outline/Bullets & Numbering. The Bullets and Numbering dialog box opens.

2. Click Create to open the Create Format dialog box. Figure 8-11 shows the Create Format dialog box with a suggested List/Outline Name and Description completed.

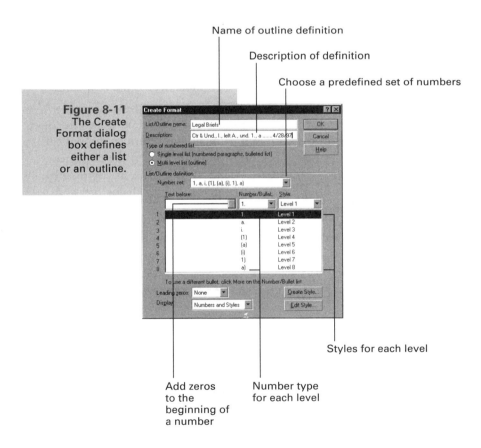

Figure 8-11
The Create Format dialog box defines either a list or an outline.

3. Type **Legal Briefs** in the List/Outline Name text box. The name you supply here will appear as the List/Outline Name in the Bullets and Numbering dialog box.

4. In the Description text box, type a description for the outline definition. It's helpful to include an abbreviated explanation of what the level styles look like and the date you created the definition. This description will appear in the Bullets and Numbering dialog box. The sample definition says **Ctr & Und., i., left A., und. 1., a** which describes the levels to be contained in the definition.

5. Select Multi Level List (Outline) from the Type of Numbered List group so that your outline definition will allow more than a single level and level style.

To create a custom list, select Single Level List (Numbered Paragraphs) from the Type of Numbered List group. You can then select any character, not just numbers, for your list by completing the number and style for a single level.

6. Click the drop-down button to open the Number Set for the List/Outline Definition. Then select the set which reads I, A, 1, a, (1), (a), i), a).

7. When you are finished with your outline or list definition, click OK to save the definition with the current document and return to the Bullets and Numbering dialog box. Click OK again to return to the document window. You can return to the Create Format dialog box at any time by selecting a definition from the Bullets and Numbering dialog box and clicking the Edit button.

If you use custom numbers in the level definitions, the Number Set automatically changes to User Defined.

Defining the Level Styles

The next step in creating a custom definition is to define the styles for each level to be included in the outline definition. Modifying an existing outline definition uses the same techniques. Three separate settings, as evidenced from the three columns in the List/Outline Definition group in the Create Format dialog box, are necessary for each outline level. These three settings define any text that should appear before a number (as in *Section* 1), define the appearance of the number for each level, and then determine how the level should look (bold, centered, and so on) in the document. You can further include leading zeros for each number (as in 0.01) from the Text Before drop-down list box.

CHAPTER 8 • AN ORGANIZED REPORT STARTS WITH AN OUTLINE **217**

> ### Hands On: Defining (or Modifying) Level Styles for a Legal Brief

FOR MORE INFORMATION ABOUT DOCUMENT STYLES, SEE CHAPTER 5.

Use the techniques which are listed below to edit or create numbering schemes and level styles for your outline definition.

1. Choose Insert, Outline/Bullets & Numbering to open the Bullets and Numbering dialog box. The Legal Briefs definition now appears in the last preview button.
2. Click the Legal Briefs button, then click Edit to open the Create Format dialog box.
3. In the Create Format dialog box, select Level 1 in the list box.
4. Click Create Style to define the style for the first brief numbering level. The Styles Editor dialog box opens.

Tip

••
Choose Edit Style to modify a level style you previously defined.
••

> **Editing a predefined level style can affect more than a single outline. The predefined Bullets, Outline, and Paragraph outline definitions all use the numbered level styles: Level 1, Level 2, and so on. If you change the level style in one definition, you'll also modify it for the other outline definitions used in the document. You won't change a level style permanently, however, unless you copy the style back to the default Template. To avoid accidentally changing another outline definition, it's best to create a new style with a new name.**

5. Type the name **Brief 1** in the Style Name text box.
6. Type a description for the level in the Description text box. Figure 8-12 displays the finished style for this example, including a sample description.
7. From the Type drop-down list, select Paragraph (paired) if it is not already selected. A paragraph style affects a complete paragraph—ideal for an outline where each item is contained in a single paragraph.

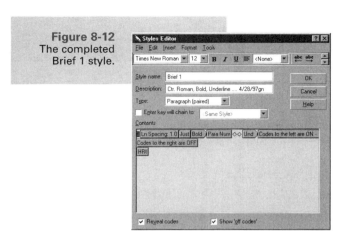

Figure 8-12
The completed Brief 1 style.

8. Remove the check from the E<u>n</u>ter Key Will Chain To check box. After the Brief 2 level style has been defined, you'll need to edit the Brief 1 style and chain it to Brief 2. This means that when Brief 1 is in use and you press (Enter), Brief 2 will automatically begin.
9. Verify that both Re<u>v</u>eal Codes and Show '<u>O</u>ff Codes' are checked.
10. Finally, click at the beginning of the codes in the <u>C</u>ontents box so that you can add format codes to the Brief 1 style. As you add formatting instructions, codes are written to the <u>C</u>ontents text box. As with any other code display, you can drag an unwanted code out of the box, or double-click the code to modify its settings.
11. Legal briefs are often typed using double-spacing. But the headings themselves must be single-spaced. Include a single-spacing code in your style by choosing Fo<u>r</u>mat, <u>L</u>ine, <u>S</u>pacing from the menu bar in the Styles Editor dialog box. The Line Spacing dialog box opens. Type **1** in the <u>S</u>pacing control, even if it is already displayed, then click OK. This forces WordPerfect to write the code to the style <u>C</u>ontents text box.
12. Click the Justification drop-down list button in the Styles Editor property bar. Choose Center. A [Just] code is added in the <u>C</u>ontents box.
13. Click the Bold button on the Styles Editor property bar or press (Ctrl)+(B) to add a [Bold→] code just prior to the [Para Num] code.

It's not necessary to turn off codes in a paired style. When the style itself is turned off, the codes in effect before the style was turned on will revert, just like any other paired code action.

CHAPTER 8 • AN ORGANIZED REPORT STARTS WITH AN OUTLINE **219**

14. Press → once, then delete the [Ignore Left Ind] code which appears immediately after the [Para Num] code by pressing Del or by dragging it out of the Contents box.

If you accidentally delete the [Para Num] code, press Ctrl+Z to undo your edit, or press Ctrl+Shift+F5 to open the Insert Paragraph Number dialog box. Then select the correct level number and number type. Click OK to insert the number code in the style.

15. Press the space bar twice to add two spaces immediately after the paragraph number.
16. Click the Underline button on the toolbar, or press Ctrl+U to add an [Und On] code.
17. Click after the [Codes to the Left are ON - Codes to the Right are OFF] code, then press Shift+Enter to add a [HRt] code. This forces one hard return to be included in the style itself. The additional hard return required to create a blank line between the first level and the next will be created when you press Enter as you finish the entry for the heading in the brief.

Because dialog boxes use Enter and Tab to make choices within the actual dialog box, you must use a few special key combinations to produce codes. Press Shift+Enter to add a hard return to a style, Ctrl+Tab to add a Left Tab, and Ctrl+Shift+Tab to add a Back Tab.

18. Click OK to save your level style to the outline definition and return to the Create Format dialog box. Brief 1 is named as the Style for the first level.
19. Repeat steps 3-10 for the second level. Name the style **Brief 2**. Figure 8-13 displays the completed Brief 2 level style.
20. With the Brief 2 style completed, edit the Brief 1 style by selecting it from the list of level styles. Then click Edit Style. With the Styles Editor dialog box open, check the Enter Key Will Chain To control and select Brief 2 from the drop-down list (you may need to scroll through the list to locate it). Then click OK to return to the Create Format dialog box.
21. Click OK to return to the Bullets and Numbering dialog box. Now select the Legal Briefs preview button (you'll need to watch the List/Outline Name field to verify your choice). Click OK to use the Legal Briefs outline definition in your document.

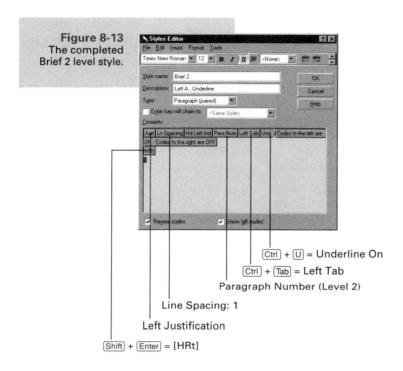

Figure 8-13
The completed Brief 2 level style.

[Shift] + [Enter] = [HRt]
Left Justification
Line Spacing: 1
Paragraph Number (Level 2)
[Ctrl] + [Tab] = Left Tab
[Ctrl] + [U] = Underline On

22. Verify that the outline definition works as you anticipated. If necessary, edit the outline definition and the level styles, making changes where required.

To create several short lines using the same paragraph style (as illustrated earlier in Figure 8-9), use the line break key combination, [Ctrl]+[Shift]+[L], where you want to end a line.

Saving a Custom Definition for Use with Other Documents

Creating custom outline definitions can be time-consuming, as you've seen. They can take a lot of trial and error, then editing until they work just right. If you've spent the time to create or modify any definitions or styles, be sure to save them so that you can retrieve them into another document.

Hands On: Saving the Legal Brief Definition

Saving the complete Legal Brief outline definition allows you to use the definition in other briefs. Use these steps:

1. Open the Bullets and Numbering dialog box using the same keystrokes you previously learned. Now click the Options button to display its drop-down list.
2. Select Save As. The Save Outline Definitions To dialog box opens.
3. Type the name you want to use for your style file. Use a name that's descriptive of the style itself, such as **BRIEF.STY**.

• •
WordPerfect 8 stores styles in the `Corel\Suite8\Template` folder unless you specify a different folder when naming your style.
• •

4. Click User Styles as the Style type to be saved, unless you've also made changes to the System styles. If you've modified any of the system styles, notice that you can save just the System Styles, just the User Styles, or Both.
5. Click OK to create the style file.

Hands On: Using a Saved Style File in Another Document

When you are ready to create another brief using your Legal Brief outline definition, you'll need to retrieve the definition into the new document. Here's how:

1. Choose Insert, Outline/Bullets & Numbering to open the Bullets and Numbering dialog box.
2. Click the Options drop-down button, then select Retrieve. The Retrieve Outline Definitions From dialog box opens.
3. Type the name of your stored style file (`BRIEFS.STY`) or select it using the folder button.
4. Click OK to add the styles to your current document.
5. Now select the outline definition as you normally would, and click OK.

Note

Although WordPerfect automatically stores styles in the `Corel\Suite8\Template` **folder, it doesn't seem to know where to go to locate the styles when you attempt to retrieve them into your document. You'll need to use the Browse button to select the style manually, or include the full path when typing the style filename.**

Additionally, the folder button does not display the default folder for saved styles. You'll need to open the specific folder, then specify that you want to see all files by entering *.* in the Filename text box.

9

Using Tables for Powerful Data Presentation

IN THIS CHAPTER

- Create, Format, and Edit Financial Tables
- Include Sums and Complex Formulas
- Use Floating Cells in Document Text
- Chart a Table for Visual Presentation
- Sort Table Entries

Almost all business reports, such as the basic business plan outline created in the previous chapter, contain financial tables, staffing charts, time lines and so on. This chapter will help you create a projected gross revenue table, and a simple payment calculation appropriate to basic financial planning. In addition, you'll experiment a bit with charting, another function of Corel WordPerfect Suite 8 which links WordPerfect 8 to the powerful charting tools of Presentations 8.

While creating the financial tables in this chapter, you'll be introduced to techniques you can use for *any* table, not just a table similar to the hands-on examples in this chapter. You'll become familiar with the most commonly used table features, including effective formatting, summing rows and columns, and how to work with the table formula bar. You'll learn how to add and delete rows and columns, how to automatically fill an area of your table with data, and how to sort your table entries. You'll also learn how to use floating cells—special areas of a table that are embedded in the text of your document.

A Simple Revenue Projection Table

Creating a table in WordPerfect is as easy as dragging the mouse pointer! Once created, you can immediately start typing in your new table or you can dress it up by formatting different areas. Before creating the financial table, however, you need some text introducing the subject. In a new document, type the text which follows this paragraph. In a business plan, this text might logically appear in a "Financial Projections" section, followed by the table you'll create in this chapter.

> **Universe Training**
>
> **Initial Revenue Projections**
>
> **Universe Training has performed a careful study based on historical data from each of our contracted trainers. This study has provided accurate data as to the average number of students we might expect at each seminar, and the trends for the number of sessions for each month. This data is represented in Table 1, Projected Gross Revenue from Scheduled Classes, based on the assumption that only one set of equipment is available for hands-on sessions.**

Center the two title lines, then add an impressive font face to the company name. Add italic to the section title. Be sure to save your report periodically so that you can easily return to this chapter if you've been interrupted. Use a name you'll remember, such as `Financial Tables.wpd`.

Creating the Projected Gross Revenue Table

Creating any table is easily accomplished using the mouse. You should have a basic idea of the number of columns and rows you might need. If your first guess at the table size is incorrect, however, you can easily add columns and rows at any location in an established table.

CHAPTER 9 • USING TABLES FOR POWERFUL DATA PRESENTATION **225**

Hands On: Creating a Table

To create the Revenue table, use these steps:

> REFER TO APPENDIX B TO IDENTIFY EACH TOOLBAR BUTTON.

1. Position the insertion point in your document at the location you want the new table to appear; for this example, two lines after the introductory paragraph you previously typed is a logical location.

2. With the mouse, point to the Table QuickCreate button on the toolbar. As you press and hold the mouse button, the table palette opens.

3. Drag the pointer through the palette to indicate the table size you want to use. The Projected Gross Revenue table starts with a table size of 6 columns by 5 rows (see Figure 9-1).

Figure 9-1 Drag the mouse pointer through the table palette to set the table size.

Place insertion point here before using Table QuickCreate button

Table palette

4. Release the mouse pointer when the table is the correct size. The table appears in the document and the insertion point appears in the first cell (see Figure 9-2).

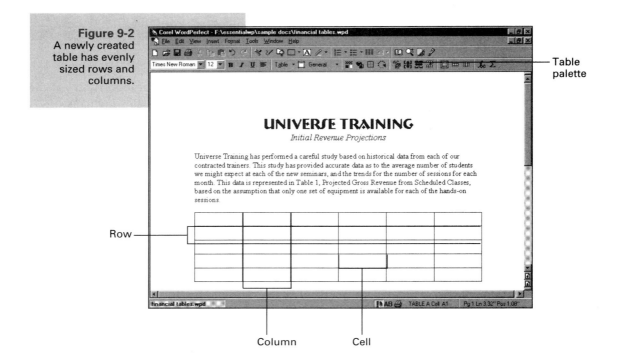

Figure 9-2 A newly created table has evenly sized rows and columns.

As with most features in WordPerfect 8, the context-sensitive property bar updates to display buttons useful in a table. Figures 9-3 and 9-4 identify these buttons for you. Additional buttons will appear while you're working in a table, depending on your current situation. Refer to Appendix B to identify any additional buttons. Remember also that you can rest the mouse pointer on a button to see its associated QuickTip.

Tables have logical names for each row and column, similar to most spreadsheet programs. For example, the first row in a table is row 1, the second is row 2, and so on. The first column is column A, the next is column B, and so on. The cell at the intersection of the two is referred to by both the row and column names. Therefore the first cell in a table is named A1, the next cell to the right is B1, then C1, and so on. The leftmost cell in the second row is A2. While in a table, you can turn on row and column *indicators* by right-clicking in the table to display the QuickMenu (or clicking the Table drop-down menu button on the property bar), then choosing Row/Column Indicators. The indicators appear on the left and top edges of the document text area.

With the table created in the document, you need to know a few basics about moving around, typing, and working with a table. Then you'll be ready to actually begin adding important data. Table 9-1 lists these useful keys and techniques.

Chapter 9 • Using Tables for Powerful Data Presentation

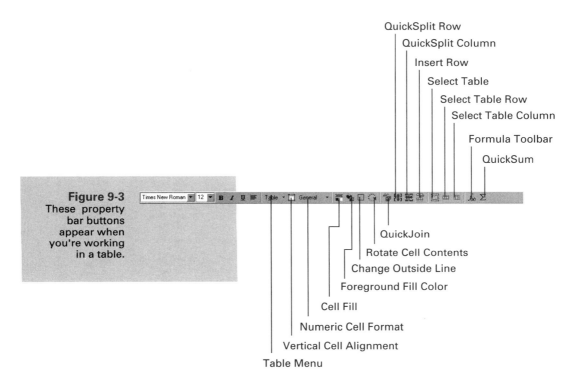

Figure 9-3 These property bar buttons appear when you're working in a table.

Labels: QuickSplit Row, QuickSplit Column, Insert Row, Select Table, Select Table Row, Select Table Column, Formula Toolbar, QuickSum, QuickJoin, Rotate Cell Contents, Change Outside Line, Foreground Fill Color, Cell Fill, Numeric Cell Format, Vertical Cell Alignment, Table Menu

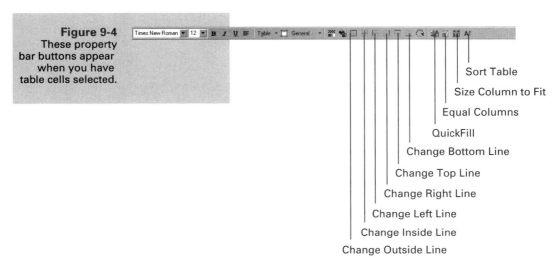

Figure 9-4 These property bar buttons appear when you have table cells selected.

Labels: Sort Table, Size Column to Fit, Equal Columns, QuickFill, Change Bottom Line, Change Top Line, Change Right Line, Change Left Line, Change Inside Line, Change Outside Line

PART III • REPORTS AND PRESENTATIONS

Table 9-1 Table Keys and Techniques

Key or mouse action	Action
Tab	Go to the next cell from an empty cell; add a new row from the last cell in a table
Shift+Tab	Go to the previous cell from an empty cell
Alt+→	Go to the next cell
Alt+←	Go to the previous cell
↑	Go up one cell
↓	Go down one cell
Alt+↑	Go to the beginning of the cell immediately above
Alt+↓	Go to the beginning of the cell immediately below
Alt+Shift+→	Select the current cell and the next cell
Alt+Shift+←	Select the current cell and the previous cell
Alt+Shift+↑	Select the current cell and the cell immediately above
Alt+Shift+↓	Select the current cell and the cell immediately below
Type in a cell	Add text to the cell; the text wraps at the edge of the cell, expanding it as necessary
Point to left or top edge of cell, then click	Select the cell
Point to left edge of cell, then double-click	Select the current row
Point to top edge of cell, then double-click	Select the current column
Point to left or top edge of cell, then triple-click	Select the complete table

Using QuickFill to Type a Series of Data

A Revenue Projection table often displays a series of months or years across the top of the table. WordPerfect can automatically fill a row or column with incrementing or decrementing numbers or dates. You can use standard numbers, Roman numerals, days of the week, months of the year, or even quarters of the year, once you set the pattern for WordPerfect to use. A series of incrementing or decrementing numbers must be based on a simple addition or subtraction formula. For example, a pattern that starts with 10, 15 will fill the remaining cells with a series continuing with 20, 25, 30, 35, and so on. A pattern of 15, 10 will continue as 5, 0, -5, -10.

CHAPTER 9 • USING TABLES FOR POWERFUL DATA PRESENTATION

Hands On: Using QuickFill to Complete a Series of Months

A series of data is established by supplying at least two adjacent cells with data. Here's how:

1. In cell A1, type **January.**
2. In cell B1, type **February.**
3. Click the Select Table Row button on the Table Property bar to select the complete Row 1.
4. Click the QuickFill button. The remaining months appear across row 1.
5. Click anywhere in the table to deselect the row. Your table should now resemble Figure 9-5.

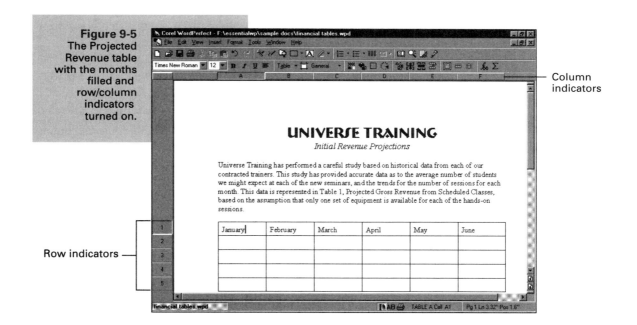

Figure 9-5 The Projected Revenue table with the months filled and row/column indicators turned on.

Rotating Text in a Table

Very often when you type headings in a table, they're too long to fit appropriately in the current column widths. For example, although the month names in the Revenue table fit nicely within the columns as the table now appears, as soon as any additional columns are added, they will not (they'll wrap within the width of the column). You could then size the columns, or even reduce the font size for the text, both appropriate solutions for this table. You know that this table will ultimately have two more columns, however, so for now it's helpful just to rotate the text so that the columns can stay the same size, or even smaller.

Hands On: Rotating Text

You can rotate text in 90-degree increments in either a clockwise or counter-clockwise direction. Because rotating text actually sends the text to a graphic text box, it's best to do as much formatting for the text as possible before you rotate it. WordPerfect retains the font face, font size, and font style attributes when text is rotated. If you want to add additional formatting, such as including double underlines or small caps, you need to edit the text box and add the desired attributes in the text box itself. Here's how to rotate the text for the Revenue table:

1. Select the complete row 1, then open the Font dialog box by choosing Format, Font, or pressing F9. From the resulting Font dialog box, select Arial as the font face for the headings. To draw extra attention to the headings, select Bold from the Font Style list. (Don't select Bold from the Appearance group! Appearance attributes are dropped when text is placed in a text box during rotation.) Finally, be sure that the Font Size is 12 point. When your selections are complete, click OK to return to the table.

2. With the row still selected, right-click to display the table QuickMenu, as shown in Figure 9-6.

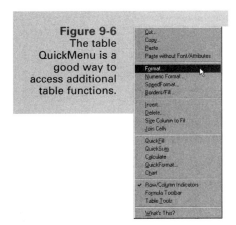

Figure 9-6
The table QuickMenu is a good way to access additional table functions.

3. Choose Format, then click the Cell tab in the resulting Properties for Table Format dialog box, as shown in Figure 9-7. An abbreviated list of

Chapter 9 • Using Tables for Powerful Data Presentation **231**

functions accessible through this dialog box appears in Table 9-2, following this hands-on example. Remember that you can right-click controls in a dialog box to see QuickTips for the controls.

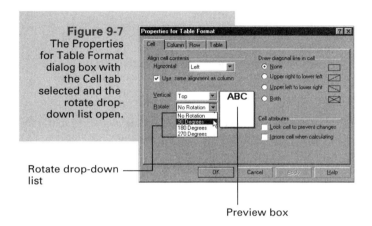

Figure 9-7
The Properties for Table Format dialog box with the Cell tab selected and the rotate drop-down list open.

Rotate drop-down list

Preview box

4. From the Rotate drop-down list, select 90 degrees. The cell preview updates to illustrate rotated text. Click Apply at the bottom of the dialog box. Behind the dialog box you can see the text rotate in the exposed portion of the table.

Tip

The Apply button in any dialog box lets you visualize the changes to your document while leaving the dialog box open.

Note

The Rotate button on the Table property bar rotates text in 90-degree increments clockwise, while the Properties for Table Format dialog box rotates text counter-clockwise.

5. From the Vertical drop-down list, select Bottom to align the text with the bottom of the cell.
6. Select Center from the Align Cell Contents, Horizontal drop-down list. This centers the text left-to-right within the cell.
7. Click OK to close the dialog box and return to the document window. Click in any cell of the table to deselect the row.

Table 9-2 Functions Accessed via the Properties for Table Format Dialog Box

Tab or feature	Performs this function
Cell Tab	
Align Cell Contents Group	Arranges entries in a cell
Draw Diagonal Line in Cell Group	Adds line(s) from corner to corner in a cell; if text resides in the cell, the line(s) will be placed over the text
Cell Attributes Group:	
Lock cell to prevent changes	Prevents user from editing a cell
Ignore cell when calculating	Use when a heading or other entry exists in an area that will be referenced by a formula, or summation action
Column Tab	
Align Contents in Cells Group:	
Horizontal	Aligns entries in all cells of the column left-to-right
Decimal Alignment	Sets the exact measurement the decimal should appear from the right margin in the column, or sets the number of digits for which space should be allotted in the column
Column Width Group:	
Width	Sets the exact width of a column
Always Keep Width the Same	Locks the width of the column so that it does not change if other columns in the table change width
Inside Margins in Column Group	Sets the left and right margins for the columns
Row Tab	
Row Attributes Group:	
Divide Row Across Pages	Allows a row to span a page break
Header Row	Marks a row or rows to appear at the top of each page when a table crosses a page break
Lines of Text Per Row Group	Sets the number of text lines that can appear in a row; the default is Multiple lines, which allows a row to expand as text is entered
Row Height Group	Sets the height of a row; the default is Automatic, which means that the row height expands automatically as multiple entry lines are typed into the row
Row Margins Group	Sets the Top and Bottom inside row margins

Chapter 9 • Using Tables for Powerful Data Presentation

	Table Tab
Align Contents in Cells Group	Sets the horizontal or decimal alignment for the table
Table Size Group	Provides an additional method of setting the size of a table, increasing or decreasing the table at the right and bottom edges
Column Width Group	Sets the default column width for all columns in the table; checking Always Keep Width the Same locks the column size for all columns
Inside Margins in all Columns Group	Sets default Left and Right margins for all columns in the table
Insert New Rows Automatically	When checked (the default), pressing Tab from the last cell in a table produces a new row at the bottom of the table
Disable Locks in All Cells	When checked, overrides any individual cell locks which may have been placed on the cells using the Cell tab

Adding Rows or Columns to the Table

It's a fairly common situation that once you have established your table size, you find you've forgotten an important column, or you need to insert a row. It would seem logical, in fact, to add a column at the left edge of the Revenue table to be used for each row heading.

Hands On: Adding Columns to a Table

A row or column can be added to the table at any position. Here's how:

1. Because the row headings should logically be in the first column, click in any cell of column A.
2. Right-click to display the QuickMenu, then select Insert. The Insert Columns/Rows dialog box opens.
3. Click Columns in the Insert group, then verify that you want to insert 1 column, to be placed Before the current column. Figure 9-8 displays the Insert Columns/Rows dialog box after your selections are complete.
4. Check Keep Column Widths the Same to resize all the existing table columns to the same width.
5. Click OK to return to the document window. The new column appears as column A.

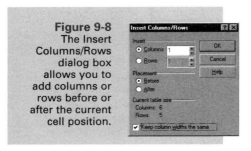

Figure 9-8
The Insert Columns/Rows dialog box allows you to add columns or rows before or after the current cell position.

6. Using the same technique, add a column for Totals after column G.
7. Type the heading **Totals** in cell H1, then select the cell, formatting and rotating the text to match the other column headings.

Type the remaining data for the table, using the data which follows this paragraph. Use QuickFill to type the data for the price per student. Then format column A, changing the font face to Arial. Now select all of rows 2 through 5, changing the font face to Arial (it's easiest to use the Font Face drop-down list). Finally, reselect all of column A and press Ctrl+B to add the bold attribute to the text. When your table is complete, it should resemble Figure 9-9.

# of Classes	4	5	5	4	4	4
# of Students	24	17	18	24	18	23
$ Per Student	749	749	749	749	749	749
Gross Revenue						

Sizing Table Columns

With the text in place it's easy to see that column A, the row headings column, really needs to be wider, while the data columns can be narrower. WordPerfect provides several methods of accomplishing this:

- Place the mouse pointer on any vertical line at the edge of a column, then drag the column edge to the desired width. As you drag the edge, a QuickTip appears, displaying the width of the columns on either side of the mouse pointer (see Figure 9-10). Release the mouse to set the column widths at the current pointer position.

- Drag the column marker in the ruler bar. A guideline appears along with the QuickTip displaying the exact width of the affected column (see Figure 9-11).

CHAPTER 9 • USING TABLES FOR POWERFUL DATA PRESENTATION **235**

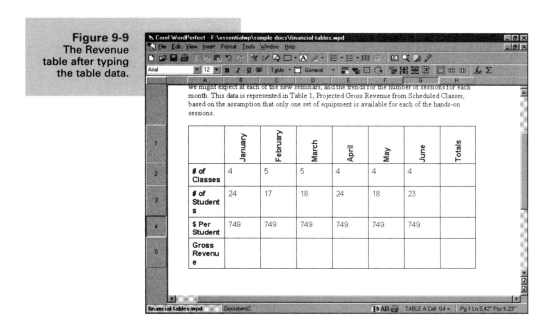

Figure 9-9
The Revenue table after typing the table data.

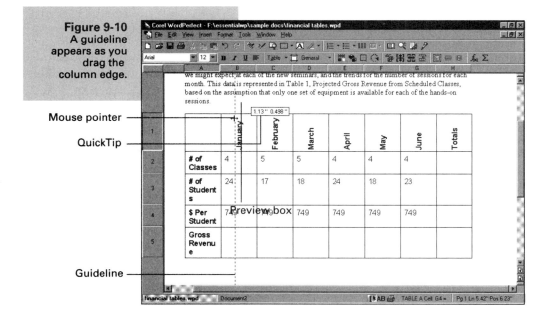

Figure 9-10
A guideline appears as you drag the column edge.

Mouse pointer
QuickTip
Guideline

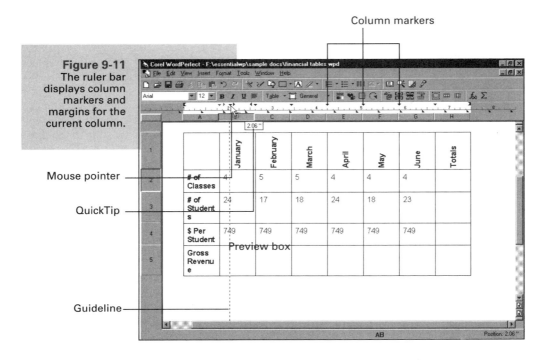

Figure 9-11 The ruler bar displays column markers and margins for the current column.

- With the insertion point in the column to be changed, right-click the table to display the QuickMenu, then choose Format. Click the Column tab, then type or select the desired width in the Column Width text box.
- Select any cell in the column, then click the Size Column to Fit button on the Table property bar.

Hands On: Sizing the Row Heading Column

The headings for each of the data rows wrap in inappropriate places. Once the row heading column is the correct size, the data columns also need to be sized. Use these steps:

1. Select any cell containing data in column A, then click the Size Column to Fit button on the Table property bar.
2. Select cells B1 through G1 (all the month cells in the first row). To select the cells, you can drag the mouse pointer through each cell, or select the first cell, then hold down Shift while you click in the last cell. Each cell in the range is then selected.
3. Right-click to display the QuickMenu, then choose Format.

CHAPTER 9 • USING TABLES FOR POWERFUL DATA PRESENTATION   237

4. Click to select the Column tab.
5. Click in the Width text box. The equal width measurement is automatically calculated and inserted in the text box.
6. Click OK to apply the selected width and return to the table.

Rather than using the QuickMenu, you can click the Equal Columns toolbar button to size the columns to equal widths.

7. Click anywhere in the table to deselect the row.

Joining and Splitting Cells

The general format of the table is almost complete, with one exception. The table doesn't have a title! Title rows, as you might expect, typically appear as the first row of the table. They usually span the width of all columns and are often set apart with special formatting to draw a reader's eye.

Hands On: Creating a Title Row

The title row for the Revenue table could have been added at any time. Adding it now, however, allows you to experience joining and splitting cells. Here's how:

1. Add a new row immediately above the current heading row by first placing the insertion point in any cell in the top row (it's easiest in this table to click in cell A1, to avoid selecting a rotated text box), then clicking the Insert Row button (or pressing Alt+Insert). The row containing the names of the months then becomes row 2, and the title row is the new row 1.
2. Click the QuickJoin button on the Table property bar. The mouse pointer displays two small arrows immediately under the main pointer arrow.
3. Drag the mouse pointer from cells B1 through H1. The cells join, becoming a single cell.

Occasionally it can be difficult to select cells for joining using the QuickJoin button. When you do so, WordPerfect assumes that you are attempting to drag to create a graphic box and displays a graphic box guideline. Wrong! If you're continually having this problem, deselect the QuickJoin button, then select the cells to be joined. Then right-click to display the QuickMenu and choose Join Cells.

4. In the Title bar cell (B1), type **Projected Gross Revenue from Scheduled Classes**.

5. Just for practice, split cell A1 into two rows. To do so, click the QuickSplit Row button on the Table property bar. The mouse pointer changes, showing a split column pointer. As you point to cell A1, a guideline appears showing you approximately where the split will occur.

6. Position the mouse pointer in cell A1, then click the mouse. The cell splits, forming new rows 1 and 2. Notice that cells which contain the table title (Projected Gross Revenue from Scheduled Classes) are now two rows high, maintaining the integrity of the table rows.

7. Now join cells A1 and A2. Next join cells A1 and B1. The row is updated, with the title text centered across the joined cells. Turn off the QuickJoin feature.

8. Finally, select both row 1 and row 2, then right-click and choose Format. From the Row tab, select Header Row to tell WordPerfect that these two rows must appear at the top of each new page if the table happens to span more than one page. Click OK.

The application bar at the bottom of the document window displays the current insertion point location. As you click in various cells, the table location updates, showing you the cell address. You can quickly notice a row marked as a header by observing the asterisked cell address in the application row.

Dressing Up the Table's Appearance

So far in this chapter, you've learned how to format a table by manipulating the text rotation and sizing the cells. Heading rows are often shaded to draw the reader's eye to their purpose. Rows, columns, individual cells or even the complete table can also contain various fills. Further, you can modify all the lines that surround each cell, or add a border to the table itself. You should also set the numeric format for the dollar values in the table, adding decimal points and possibly dollar signs.

Using WordPerfect's Predefined Table Formatting

WordPerfect 8 offers at least 40 predefined table formats which display many of the most common table appearance settings. You can choose one of these layouts by right-clicking within a table, then selecting SpeedFormat. The Table Speed-Format dialog box opens, as displayed in Figure 9-12.

Chapter 9 • Using Tables for Powerful Data Presentation   239

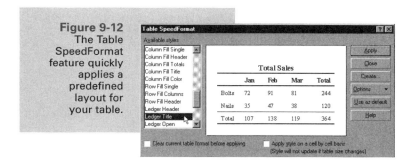

Figure 9-12 The Table SpeedFormat feature quickly applies a predefined layout for your table.

> **Chapters 5 and 8 discuss more about styles.**

As you select a SpeedFormat style from the Available Styles list, the preview box displays a representative table with the formatting in place. You can optionally create your own SpeedFormat style based on the format of the table currently active in the document window. As with any other style, it can be saved to the default template or to a style file for use in other documents.

Shading the Cells for Emphasis

Think of *fill* as the background shading or design of a cell. It sits behind the table text. A table can also have a default fill, with each cell then having its own fill, if desired. Similarly, each cell is surrounded on four sides by lines, plus the table can be surrounded by a border. If you print to a color printer, you can set colors or even gradient patterns for your fill and line values.

While each of these elements can definitely add pizzazz to your table, be careful not to get too carried away adding design elements to your table! To do so will take away the importance of the data you're trying to present.

Hands On: Adding Fills to the Title and Header Rows

The Revenue table actually has three different header or title areas: the table title row, the column headings displaying the name of each month, and the row headings identifying the purpose of each row's values. The steps in this exercise guide you through formatting the title row with a black background and white text. You'll also shade the heading rows with a 30% yellow shading, appropriate for color printing. Use these steps:

1. Select cell A1, then click the Cell Fill button. The Fill palette opens, as shown in Figure 9-13.

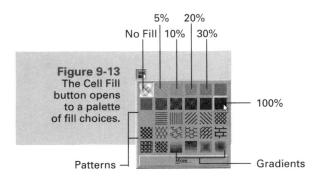

Figure 9-13
The Cell Fill button opens to a palette of fill choices.

2. Select 100% fill (second row, rightmost button). The row receives the fill, but because it is still selected, the row appears to be white. (It looks as though the text has disappeared because the text also is selected within the cell.)
3. Choose Format, Font (or press F9) to open the Font dialog box.
4. Click the Text Color button to open its palette. Click the white tile to select white text.
5. While you have the Font dialog box open, also select Arial, Bold, 14 point to draw yet a little more attention to the heading. When your selections are complete, click OK to return to the table.
6. With the heading cell still selected, apply center justification using the Justification button on the toolbar.
7. Click in another table cell to deselect the title row. When deselected, the row appears black with white text.
8. Select all cells in row 2, then click the Cell Fill button again. Click the 30% fill button (refer to Figure 9-13 to locate it).
9. Click the Foreground Fill Color button, then click one of the yellow tiles to add a light yellow background to the heading row. If you print to a black-and-white printer, you'll probably prefer to keep the Fill Color black, with a fill percentage of 20% or so.
10. Select cells A3 through A6, applying the same 30% fill and light yellow color.

Be careful when adding a background fill to text. If your fill color is black, keep the percentage to 30% or less. This still gives you a nice, even shade of gray behind the text. If you make it too dark, you won't be able to easily read the black text on the gray background.

You must select the fill percentage before selecting a fill color.

Adding and Hiding Lines to Separate Sections of the Table

Line styles are often used in a financial report to indicate the bottom of a column, or to break the addends from the total. For example, a column of numbers often ends with a double-line under the total, and a dashed line above the total. In a table, single lines usually appear between each cell, with a single line appearing around the outside of the table. But you can easily hide lines or select from a palette of other line styles to add emphasis to the table, or to even make the table not look like a table at all.

You can change lines of each cell separately, select groups of cells, or even change the lines for the entire table at the same time. It's important to remember, however, that each cell is surrounded by four lines—its top, bottom, left, and right lines. And the line when printed actually appears to take up space within the cell. This means that if you format the lines differently in cells that lie next to each other, the lines might not align correctly, as shown in Figure 9-14.

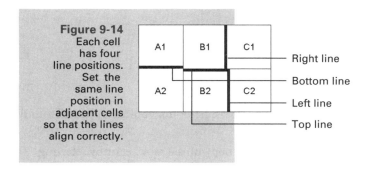

Figure 9-14 Each cell has four line positions. Set the same line position in adjacent cells so that the lines align correctly.

Hands On: Modifying Table Lines

The Revenue table would benefit by removing the lines for the inner cells, then changing the lines between the headings and text to double. For consistency, you'll add a double-line border. Here's how:

PART III • REPORTS AND PRESENTATIONS

1. First, set the table border to double. Start by positioning the insertion point anywhere in the table, then right-click to display the QuickMenu. Choose Borders/Fill. The Properties for Table Borders/Fill dialog box opens.
2. Click the Table tab to move it to the front.
3. Click the Border button to open the line palette, then click the double-line tile, or select Double from the drop-down list on the palette (see Figure 9-15). The preview box is updated to display the double border around the table.

An effective fill style is Alternating Fill, which shades every other row or column (or both). From the Table tab, you can also select a fill for the entire table, or set a default line style for the table.

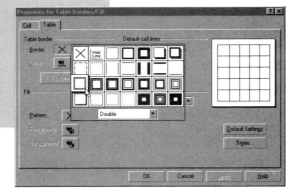

Figure 9-15 The Table tab with the Border palette open. From here you can select a border to appear on the perimeter of the table.

4. Finally, click OK to return to the table. The double border appears around the outside of the table.
5. To remove the lines from the number body of the table, start by selecting cells B3 through H6. Now right-click to display the QuickMenu and again choose Borders/Fill to open the Properties for Table Borders/Fill dialog box.
6. With the Cell tab on top, click the Inside button to open the line palette.
7. Click the X tile. Notice as you pass the mouse pointer over the tile that the name of the line style appears in the text area of the drop-down list at the bottom of the palette.

8. Click OK to return to the document window, then click in the table to deselect the area. The cells are now delineated by lightly-dotted lines. These serve as a representative line only—the table guidelines. (If you want, you can turn off these guidelines by choosing View, Guidelines and then removing the check from the Tables check box. When you click OK, the guidelines are hidden.)

9. To add a dotted line above the Gross Revenue row, select the Gross Revenue row, then click the Change Top Line property bar button. The line palette opens on the top of the document window.

10. Click the dotted-line tile (see Figure 9-16). The line is added to the table.

Figure 9-16
The property bar line buttons each open the line palette.

11. To complete the line changes, add a dotted line on the left side of the Totals column, and double lines around the inner perimeter of the data area. Figure 9-17 shows the table with all lines and formatting you've completed so far.

Setting Number Types to Align the Numbers

Although none of the totals and formulas for the table have yet been completed, you can format the cells so that they appear with dollar signs and properly aligned. The price per student row should also align with the totals, while the two rows which display the statistics can have right-aligned, decimal-aligned, or centered numbers.

Aligning numbers can actually take several steps. Setting a numeric format merely tells WordPerfect how to handle and display the numbers when calculating a sum or formula. Formatting number alignment sets their position within the cell. If your number format alignment is set to decimal align, two decimal places are reserved within the cell space. You might also, therefore, need to change the amount of space reserved for decimal places, even if no decimals appear with your number format.

PART III • REPORTS AND PRESENTATIONS

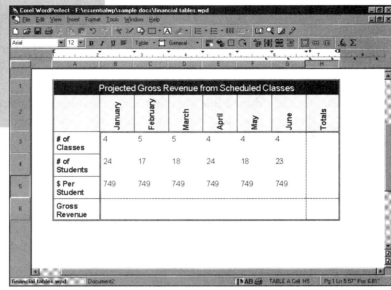

Figure 9-17
Adding simple lines to a table dramatically changes its appearance from very basic to something special!

Hands On: Setting Number Types and Aligning Text

Use these steps to tell WordPerfect how to format table cells with currency and no decimals:

1. Select the figures in row 5, the `$ Per Student` row. Be sure to also include the cell for the total.

2. Click the Numeric button on the property bar, then select `Accounting` from the drop-down list. Numbers formatted as the accounting type display a dollar sign, placing the dollar sign at the left edge of the cell. The numbers in the row now appear with dollar signs and two decimal places. You may find as I did using different printer selections, that the decimal places wrapped to the next line!

3. Right-click to display the QuickMenu, then choose Numeric Format. This is an alternate location to select number types. The Properties for Table Numeric Format dialog box opens with the Cell tab on top.

4. Experiment with different number types by selecting them from the Format for Numbers in Cells group. As you select each type, look at the preview box to view its appearance.

5. Select Accounting as the Number type for the numbers.

6. Type or select **0** in the Num<u>b</u>er of Decimal Places text box. Then click <u>A</u>pply.
7. Drag the Properties dialog box out of the way of the table to observe the format now displayed in the selected row. Make changes to the number type if you want, then click OK to close the Properties dialog box.
8. With the cells still selected, right-click to display the QuickMenu again. This time choose Table <u>T</u>ools. The Tools palette opens and remains open until you specifically close it or click somewhere outside of the table in your document. (This palette is especially useful when you want to make several changes to your table without needing to continually access the QuickMenu.) You might want to drag this palette out of the way of the table so that you can view the table as you work.
9. From the Tools palette, click the For<u>m</u>at button. The Properties for Table Format dialog box opens.
10. Select `Decimal Align` from the Align Cell Contents H<u>o</u>rizontal drop-down list, then click <u>A</u>pply to view the results. The numbers in each cell move slightly to the right, but not enough. This is because space for two decimals is still being held, by default, in the cell.

Since no decimals will be calculated, right-alignment is also appropriate. Be careful, however, when choosing an alignment style that might be used for negative numbers. The right parenthesis which is often used to display a negative number sometimes forces the number one too many digits to the left.

11. To remove the space set aside for displaying decimals, click the Column tab, then enter **0** in the Digits after Decimal text box. Click OK to write your changes to the table and return to the document window.
12. For consistency, decimal-align the rows for number of classes and number of students. Then center the row headings. Figure 9-18 displays the table with the formatting complete.

Using Table Math and Formulas

Like most popular word processing programs, WordPerfect 8 can quickly sum columns and rows. In addition, though, a set of almost 100 mathematical functions is available for use in a table. You can copy formulas from cell to cell, set absolute or relative cell references in a table, or even nest functions. Areas of a table can also be named for easy reference in a formula.

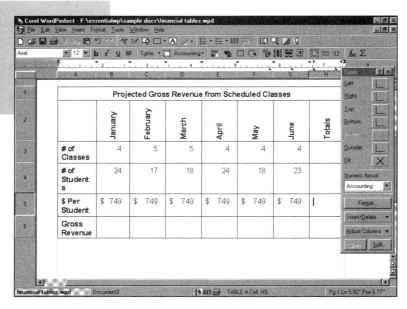

Figure 9-18
This is the formatted Projected Revenue table with the Tools palette open.

Summing Rows and Columns

At any time after entering figures into a table, you can quickly sum the columns and rows.

Hands On: Summing Rows

The total number of classes and students offered in the representative six-month period needs to be totaled in the table. Use these steps:

1. Click in cell H3, the cell that will display the total number of classes.
2. Click the QuickSum button on the property bar. The total, 26, appears in the cell. Notice also that the application bar at the bottom of the window displays the current cell (H3) and the value or formula represented in the cell.

Tip

You can enlarge the General Status button that displays the table information, by editing the application bar. To do so, right-click to display the QuickMenu, then choose Settings. Then, as with any other button on the application bar, drag the edge of the General Status button to a size large enough to display all the cell information.

3. Now sum the number of students, using the same technique. Notice, however, that the sum displayed is also 26. QuickSum always assumes first that you want to sum the numbers above the current cell.

Note

The QuickSum button totals either rows or columns. It first attempts to sum preceding numbers in the current column. If the column does not contain numbers, then QuickSum looks to the left in the current row, summing any numbers which appear there. You can also select a range of cells, then click QuickSum. You need to include a blank cell at the end of the selected row or column to receive the calculated total.

4. To correct the sum, first delete the incorrect total in cell H4. Then select cells B4 through H4. As soon as you attempt to select a cell, WordPerfect asks you to verify that you want to replace the existing formula in cell H4. This safeguard prevents you from accidentally overwriting a critical formula. In this instance, however, click Yes to replace the formula, then continue to select the cells, including cell H4.
5. Right-click to display the QuickMenu, then choose QuickSum. The total, 124, appears in cell H4. Click in cell H4 so that you can read the formula in the application bar and deselect the row. The application bar displays the formula +SUM(B4:G4).
6. Click the Formula Toolbar button to open that toolbar. The Formula toolbar appears in two rows immediately above the document text area. With the insertion point in cell H4, you can see the summation formula +SUM(B4:G4) in the formula text box. The colon between the two cell names is shorthand for naming a complete *range* of numbers. This formula could also be written SUM(B4,C4,D4,E4,F4,G4). However, WordPerfect understands that the cells are sequential, and uses the range character instead.

Table 9-3 lists the purpose for each button on the Formula toolbar.

Writing Formulas

Formulas can be written for almost any arithmetic, date, financial, logical, or string function you need to perform in WordPerfect. For example, you can write business formulas to calculate payment amounts on a loan, interest earned in an annuity, or logarithms, square roots, or cosines. Most formulas in a WordPerfect document, however, are fairly basic and are easily created by pointing to table values with your mouse. While you can create complex tables and formulas in WordPerfect, you may want to reserve extensive calculations for a spreadsheet program such as Quattro Pro which also ships with Corel WordPerfect Suite 8.

Look up **Sample Formulas** in the WordPerfect Help index for examples of different types of formulas. You can also find a detailed explanation of each formula in the Table Functions appendix in the printed Corel WordPerfect 8 user's guide.

Table 9-3 Items on the Formula Toolbar

Button/Element	Purpose
TABLE A.K4	Displays the table name and current cell
✗	Cancels formula changes
✓	Accepts a formula
+SUM(B4:J4)	Write or edit a formula here
Calculate	Appears at the end of the formula edit box, prompting when formulas should be recalculated
QuickSum	Sums numbers above or to the left of the current cell
Functions...	Opens the Functions dialog box
Names...	Opens the Names dialog box so that you can name the table (use the Edit button), a cell, a row, a column, or a range of cells
View Error...	Helps troubleshoot formula errors
Calculate	Recalculates a table
QuickFill	Fills cells based on a pattern
Copy Formula...	Duplicates a formula
(icon)	Displays/hides row/column indicators
Close	Closes the formula bar

CHAPTER 9 • USING TABLES FOR POWERFUL DATA PRESENTATION   249

Hands On: Creating the Gross Revenue Formula

The Projected Gross Revenue table presents an opportunity for a simple formula by requiring calculation of revenue based on the number of classes in a month, times the average number of students anticipated, times the class tuition charged for each student. Here's how to create the formula:

1. Click to place the insertion point in cell B6, the Gross Revenue cell for January.
2. If the Formula toolbar is not already visible, click the Formula Toolbar button.
3. Click the Functions button to open the Table Functions dialog box, shown in Figure 9-19.

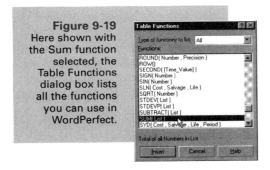

Figure 9-19 Here shown with the Sum function selected, the Table Functions dialog box lists all the functions you can use in WordPerfect.

4. Double-click SUM(List). The Table Functions dialog box closes and SUM(List) is inserted in the Formula Enter/Edit text box. List is selected, so you can immediately begin pointing to the correct cells in the table that will be used to complete the formula.

Tip

You can type a function name directly into the Formula Enter/Edit text box without using the Table Functions dialog box. You can also type a formula directly in a cell if you precede the initial symbols, functions, or numbers with either + or =.

5. Click cell B3 (number of classes for January). The cell name is placed in the formula.
6. Type * (the symbol for multiplication). The symbol is added to the end of the formula.

> You can use other arithmetic operators in a formula, including + (addition), – (subtraction), and / (division). For the complete set of arithmetic and logical operators that can be used for formulas, look up **table calculations: formula, about** in the WordPerfect Help index.

7. In turn, click cell B4, type *, and click cell B5.
8. Press [Enter] or click the Accept the Formula button. The result of the formula, $71,904, appears in cell B6, the cell where the insertion point appeared before beginning the formula. Be sure to review the result to assure yourself that it makes sense. If it doesn't, check your formula to be sure that you've entered each cell reference correctly.
9. The formula now needs to be copied to each cell in the Gross Revenue row, except the last cell, which will contain the total Gross Revenue for the period. Click the Copy Formula button to open the Copy Formula dialog box.
10. Click the radio button for Right, then press the increment arrow on the spin control until you hear a beep, signaling that you've reached the maximum number of cells available to the right of the current cell. Click the decrement arrow once so that the formula is not copied to cell H6, the intersection between the Totals column and Gross Revenue row.
11. Click OK to copy the formula to the right. The gross revenue for each month is calculated and inserted in the appropriate cell.
12. Review the totals to be sure they are correct. As you click in each Gross Revenue cell, notice that the formula is automatically updated to reflect the correct *relative cell references* for each column.

> You can force a formula to use an *absolute cell reference* by enclosing the cell name between brackets in the formula. For example, SUM(B3*[B4]*B5) would be updated to read SUM(C3*[B4]*C5) when copied one cell to the right. As you can see, an absolute cell reference stays the same, while a relative cell reference updates as it is copied.

13. Calculate the total gross revenue by summing the Gross Revenue row. You may need to reformat the table slightly to display the calculated revenue without wrapping. Also, if you've not already done so, you should now format the cells as numeric type accounting with zero decimal places. Figure 9-20 displays the finished table.

CHAPTER 9 • USING TABLES FOR POWERFUL DATA PRESENTATION

Figure 9-20
The completed Projected Gross Revenue table now has all formulas calculated.

Projected Gross Revenue from Scheduled Classes							
	January	February	March	April	May	June	Totals
# of Classes	4	5	5	4	4	4	26
# of Students	24	17	18	24	18	23	124
$ Per Student	$ 749	$ 749	$ 749	$ 749	$ 749	$ 749	
Gross Revenue	$ 71,904	$ 63,665	$ 67,410	$ 71,904	$ 53,928	$ 68,908	$ 397,719

Caution: Formulas do not automatically recalculate when the table is edited in any way. If you change numbers, rearrange anything, or add or delete table rows or columns, be sure to recalculate the table by clicking the Calcula<u>t</u>e button.

Using Floating Cells to Include Calculations in Text

Think of a *floating cell* as a one-cell mini-table which resides in the body of a document. This is an especially useful tool when you want to include a calculation in the document without creating a full table. You can also use a floating cell to link a number in the document to a calculation in a table that appears elsewhere in the document.

Computing Payments for a Financed Equipment Purchase

Universe Training sees a need for an additional set of computer equipment. However, they do not have sufficient resources to purchase the equipment outright. This example makes a very simple calculation based on the assumption that they can finance their purchase at an interest rate of 18% per year with a down payment of $5,000. (Of course, don't presume that this would be a *wise* business decision!)

Hands On: Creating a Floating Cell That Calculates Payments

The monthly payment calculation for Universe Training's new equipment is contained in a floating cell. Use these steps to create the cell and the calculation:

1. Add the text which follows to the bottom of your financial tables document. Be sure to include a space at the end of the last incomplete sentence so that the new figure will appear in the correct location in the text.

   The numbers represented in the Projected Gross Revenue table can be significantly impacted by purchasing another set of equipment for hands-on classes. An additional set of equipment is estimated to cost $28,700. Current cash only allows an outlay of $5,000, however. Using the $5,000 as a down payment, the equipment can be purchased on a two-year contract through Equipment Leasing & Loan Company for a monthly payment of

2. From the WordPerfect menu, choose Insert, Table. The Create Table dialog box opens.

3. Click Floating Cell, then click Create. The Table formula bar opens.

4. Click the Functions button to open the Table Functions dialog box, then double-click the PMT function to add it to the Enter/Edit Formula text box. The Rate% field is currently selected.

5. Rate is a calculation based on the interest rate divided by the number of periods. Type **18%/12**. This formula replaces the Rate portion of the function.

6. Now select PV in the formula, replacing it with the simple formula **(28700-5000)**, the amount of the purchase price for the equipment, minus the down payment. Be sure to include the parentheses around both sides of this subtraction formula to let WordPerfect know that an inner calculation must take place.

7. Type **24** as the number of periods. Be sure to delete the placeholder Periods.

8. Type **0** for the Future Value, then delete the remaining argument placeholders in the formula. Your completed formula should read: **PMT(18%/12,(28700-5000),24,0)**.

9. Click the Insert Formula button to insert the calculation in your document. The calculated payment reads 1183.20121668. You now need to format the cell to reflect the payment as currency with a two-decimal display.

CHAPTER 9 • USING TABLES FOR POWERFUL DATA PRESENTATION   253

10. Click anywhere in the calculated payment amount to display the Table toolbar. Click the Numeric button on the property bar and select Currency as the number type. The document is updated to display the payment with a dollar sign and two decimal places.

11. Finally, add a period after the total, completing the sentence. Figure 9-21 displays the completed document.

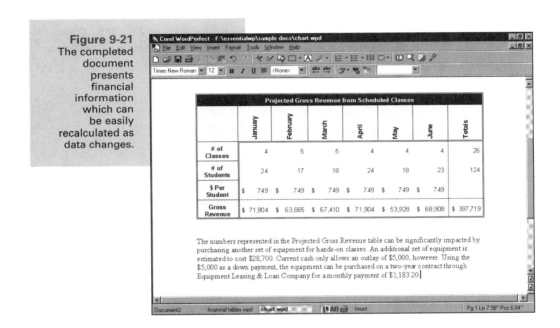

Figure 9-21
The completed document presents financial information which can be easily recalculated as data changes.

Using Table Data to Produce a Chart

Sometimes it's easiest to see a visual representation of data. A full table of numbers often masks trends, while viewing them in a chart can make relationships obvious. WordPerfect uses the capabilities of Corel Presentations to create sophisticated area, bar, bubble, high/low, line, pie, radar, surface, table, and scatter charts. Each of these chart types can be effectively used to present particular types of data.

Financial data similar to that presented in the Universe Training Gross Revenue Projection Table is ideally suited to both a bar chart and a line chart. Fortunately, Presentations has one additional chart type, mixed, which allows chart types to be combined. Pertinent data from the Projected Gross Revenue table can quickly be presented in a mixed bar and line chart. The charting abilities of Presentations are staggering. Consider this charting example to be a *teaser*—you'll want to spend time playing with the various chart types in addition to this example.

Depending on the layout of your table, you can click anywhere in the table, then choose Insert, Graphics, Chart to insert a chart in the document. WordPerfect copies the entire table, launches Presentations, and creates a bar chart in the current WordPerfect document based on the table data. You can then edit the appearance of the chart, changing the chart type and the appearance of each element in the chart. Unfortunately, because WordPerfect maintains the link between the table in the WordPerfect document and the chart in Presentations, you cannot select specific columns or rows for inclusion or exclusion from the chart. The entire table is placed in the chart. Using the Projected Gross Revenue table, a chart is created that looks similar to Figure 9-22, which is not terribly useful. By selecting only specific rows from the table, a much more useful chart can be created.

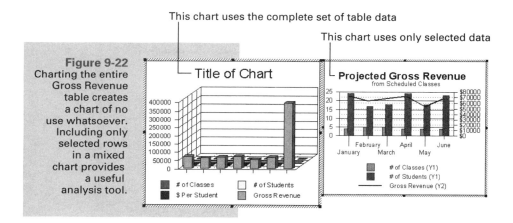

Figure 9-22 Charting the entire Gross Revenue table creates a chart of no use whatsoever. Including only selected rows in a mixed chart provides a useful analysis tool.

It's important, therefore, to be able to pick and choose the data to be included in a chart. The following hands-on activity steps you through one method of creating a chart based on existing table data. Because the charting capabilities of Presentations are extensive, be sure to review the Presentations 8 Help text relating to charts.

Hands On: Creating an Effective Chart Using Table Data

The chart presented in this hands-on activity is a mixed chart—a vertical bar chart and a line chart. Use these steps:

1. In the Projected Gross Revenue table, select cells A2 through G6. Be sure not to include the title row for the table; you can include the totals column and exclude the column in the chart, but it's easiest to only copy those rows and columns which should be included in the chart.

2. Copy the selection to the Clipboard by pressing Ctrl+C, clicking the Copy button on the toolbar, or choosing Edit, Copy. The Cut or Copy Table dialog box opens. Click Selection, indicating what portion of the table should be copied, then click OK.
3. Click in the document after the table, at the beginning of the paragraph you added when creating a floating cell.
4. Choose Insert, Graphics, Chart. After a brief pause, WordPerfect opens a Presentations window within the document-editing window. A chart, datasheet, and Range Highlighter appear, using sample data provided by Presentations. The Chart toolbar appears at the top of the document window and will be used for many of the steps in this activity. Figure 9-23 identifies its buttons for you.

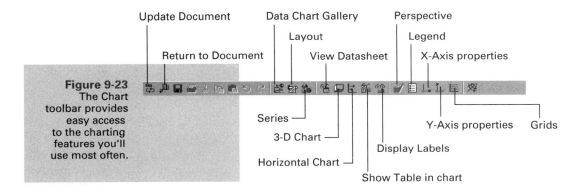

Figure 9-23
The Chart toolbar provides easy access to the charting features you'll use most often.

5. Click the Close button on the Range Highlighter to remove it from the document window and reduce a bit of the clutter. The Range Highlighter is used to help you identify different portions of a datasheet, but it won't be used in this activity.
6. Position the mouse pointer over the first cell in the datasheet (just to the left of the word Legend). The mouse pointer points to both the Legends row and the Labels column (see Figure 19-24). Click in the cell to select the complete datasheet.
7. With the mouse pointer still in the first cell, press Ctrl+V (or click the Paste button on the toolbar, or choose Edit, Paste) to paste from the Clipboard to the datasheet. The data from the Projected Gross Revenue table replaces the sample data and the chart reflects the new data (though not very well yet!). The insertion point appears after the last cell. Press Ctrl+Home to move to the first cell in the datasheet.

PART III • REPORTS AND PRESENTATIONS

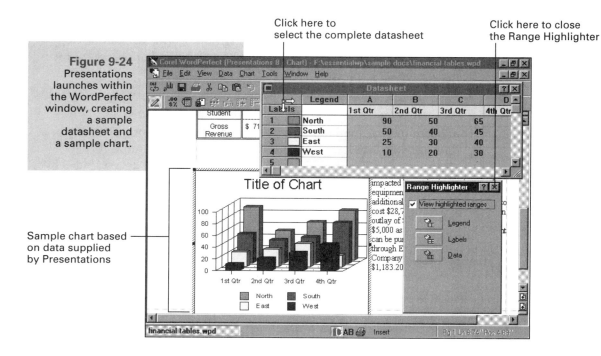

Figure 9-24 Presentations launches within the WordPerfect window, creating a sample datasheet and a sample chart.

Sample chart based on data supplied by Presentations

8. The data for row 3, $ Per Student, is not needed in the chart, and therefore should be excluded. Position the mouse pointer over the first cell in row 3, the cell which displays the row number and the color sample (see Figure 9-25). Click to select the row.

9. Right-click the row to display the QuickMenu, then choose E̲xclude Row. The chart is updated with the row removed.

10. Select row 4 by clicking its row number, right-click to display the QuickMenu again, then choose E̲dit Series. The Series Properties dialog box opens (see Figure 9-26).

11. Click L̲ine and Secondary (Y2̲) to change the data representation to a line based on a secondary Y axis. Then click OK. Figure 9-27 displays the appearance of the chart after these changes.

Any time you make changes to the appearance of the chart, you can click the Previe̲w button to see the effect of your change. A small Series Properties dialog box opens at the bottom of the window, allowing you to accept the change (by clicking OK), cancel the change altogether and return to the datasheet (by clicking Cancel), or return to the previous view (by clicking B̲ack).

CHAPTER 9 • USING TABLES FOR POWERFUL DATA PRESENTATION 257

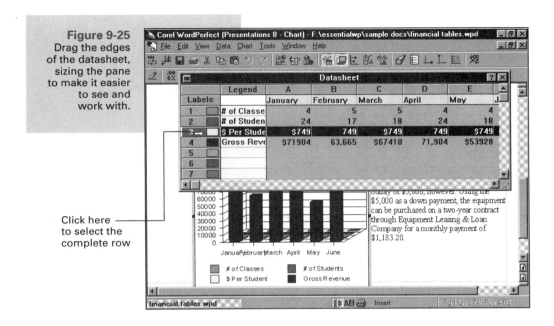

Figure 9-25
Drag the edges of the datasheet, sizing the pane to make it easier to see and work with.

Click here to select the complete row

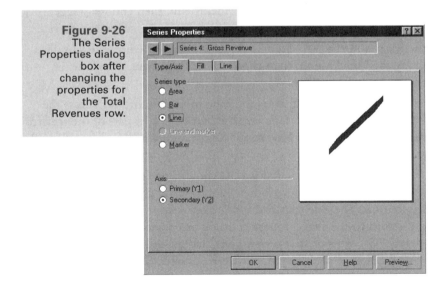

Figure 9-26
The Series Properties dialog box after changing the properties for the Total Revenues row.

12. All changes to the data that will be represented are now complete. Close the datasheet by clicking its close button in the upper-right corner. You can later open the datasheet, if necessary, by clicking the Datasheet button on the Chart toolbar.

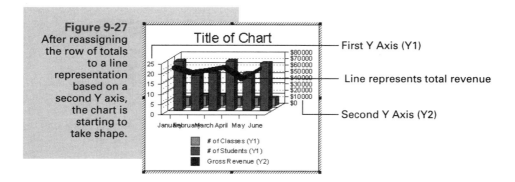

Figure 9-27
After reassigning the row of totals to a line representation based on a second Y axis, the chart is starting to take shape.

Hands On: Enhancing the Chart

Now it's time to dress up the chart by adding a title and making the labels more readable. Continue the activity with these steps:

1. In the chart itself, click the label `January`. Four handles appear, indicating that the label is selected.

2. Right-click to display the Axis Label QuickMenu, then choose Stagger Labels. The labels are staggered, one up and one down across the X Axis.

3. Next, click the `Title of Chart` text, selecting it for editing. Right-click to display the QuickMenu, then choose Title Properties. The Title Properties dialog box opens.

4. The complete title for the chart is too long to fit comfortably across the chart. In the Display Chart Title text box, type the first part of the title for the chart, **Projected Gross Revenue**. The remainder of the chart title will be created as a subtitle.

5. While in the Title Properties dialog box, you can optionally select a different font face and font attributes. Preview your changes by clicking the Preview button. The title font size appears to overpower the chart. Click Back to return to the Title Properties dialog box, then select a smaller font size, maybe 35 points or so. Preview your changes again. If you are satisfied with the appearance of the chart, click OK, or click Back to try again.

6. To create the subtitle, choose Chart, Subtitle. The Subtitle Properties dialog box opens. It looks and acts similar to the Title Properties dialog box. In the Display Chart Subtitle text box, type the subtitle **From Scheduled Classes**. Make any desired font attribute changes, previewing them if you want, and then click OK.

CHAPTER 9 • USING TABLES FOR POWERFUL DATA PRESENTATION

7. Finally, change the perspective of the chart slightly so that you can more clearly see the bars which represent the number of classes. Click the Perspective button on the toolbar. The Perspective dialog box opens (see Figure 9-28), from which you can change the angle the data is represented.

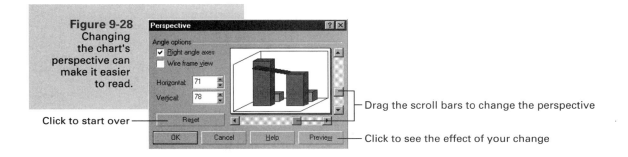

Figure 9-28 Changing the chart's perspective can make it easier to read.

8. Try dragging the scroll bars for both the vertical and horizontal perspective until you're satisfied with the appearance of the chart. Be sure to Preview the chart frequently to see the effect of your changes. When you are satisfied, click OK to return to the chart.

   Finally, you may decide that you can't see the data well enough using 3D charting. Changing the chart to 2D makes it easier to see all the data.

9. Click the Layout button on the Chart toolbar to open the Layout/Type Properties dialog box. Remove the check from the 3D Appearance control, then Preview the chart to view the effect. Like it? If so, click OK. If not, click Cancel to return to the 3D Layout.

Figure 9-29 displays the completed chart, using one possible layout and charting type. There are any number of modifications you can make to your chart so that it better reflects the message you are attempting to create with this visual tool. You might decide to change chart types, or to provide a completely different perspective of the financial data by charting the total number of classes rather than the classes by month. Learning to chart effectively takes practice and possibly input from others with more experience. Don't hesitate, however, to try the different charting capabilities in Presentations. Almost every chart type and formatting possibility you need are available to you through this powerful tool.

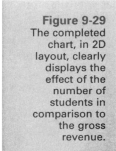

Figure 9-29
The completed chart, in 2D layout, clearly displays the effect of the number of students in comparison to the gross revenue.

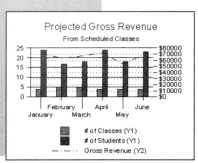

Sorting Table Entries

By their very nature, tables are the ideal tool for organizing, comparing, and analyzing data. Even the most powerful spreadsheet program on the market presents and organizes data in table format.

As an example, I use tables to create a quick-and-dirty cash flow report on a monthly basis. On that table I list the bills I need to pay, the date they're due, the dates I expect to get paid, and so on. Then I sort the table by date and recalculate to see whether I can spend money on anything frivolous, which rarely seems to happen! Somehow, to me, this is easier than dealing with my very full-featured accounting program.

Sorting can be also be a useful tool when analyzing data. You can ask sort to select, or *extract,* rows from your table which meet specific criteria.

Sorting in a table is similar to sorting any other document type. As you work with the sort function, notice that you can also sort a merge data file, lines, paragraphs, and columns.

Figure 9-30 displays a sample table which will be used as the example in this section. To follow along, create the table, then save your file with the name `Credit Limits.wpd`. Using the table QuickMenu, choose Format, then click the Row tab, and format the first row as a Header Row. Header rows repeat at the top of each page as a table expands to multiple pages.

Be sure to format any header rows you may have in your table. Doing so automatically excludes the header rows from any sort you perform.

CHAPTER 9 • USING TABLES FOR POWERFUL DATA PRESENTATION

Figure 9-30
This sample table will be used for sorting and extracting.

Name	Next Pmt Date	Amount	Credit
Alan Misher	03/15/97	599.00	7,000.00
Arthur Chesin	03/12/97	80.16	15,000.00
Barbara E. Coehn	03/01/97	1,609.12	12,000.00
Charles Gibley	03/15/97	541.09	12,000.00
Dick Kent	03/12/97	12.09	500.00
George Smith	03/27/97	2,534.00	7,000.00
Adam M. Chesin	03/02/97	654.19	15,000.00
Helen Nelburn	03/20/97	876.87	5,000.00
Martha Myers	03/04/97	1,501.34	5,000.00
Maven Myers	03/15/97	38,761.00	5,000.00
Nancy Smith	03/10/97	142.98	10,000.00
Ray Kohl	03/25/97	542.86	12,000.00
Scott Kaufman	03/10/97	2,000.00	5,000.00
Stanley C. Arkin	03/04/97	2.49	15,000.00
William Watson	03/30/97	32.09	10,000.00

Hands On: A Simple Alphabetic or Numeric Sort

Most sorts are relatively simple. You sort by the first word in the column in either ascending (A to Z) or descending (Z to A) order. Here's how:

1. To sort the table entries by each person's first name, first select the Name column. To do so, first click anywhere in the Name column, then click the Select Table Column button.

2. Click the Sort button on the Table toolbar. A list of four sort options appears.

3. Click `Alpha Ascending` to sort the entries by first name. The table rearranges each complete row, with the names now in alphabetical order by first name.

Don't like the results of a sort? Click the Undo button (or press Ctrl+Z) to return to the pre-sorted state.

However, Undo will only work if you have set Sort so that you can undo the operation if you've made a mistake. To do so, click Options on the Sort dialog box, then select Allow Undo After Sorting.

Sometimes it's more meaningful to sort by another word in a column. For example, the Next Payment Date column actually consists of three words: the month, the day, and the year. Words are defined as ending with a space, a slash, or a hyphen. Sorting by the first word is of no use at all because all the months are the same.

PART III • REPORTS AND PRESENTATIONS

Hands On: Sorting By the Second Word in a Column

Use these steps to sort the date column by the day of the month:

1. Select the date column.
2. Choose <u>T</u>ools, So<u>r</u>t (or press Alt+F9). The Sort dialog box opens. Notice that several sorts are predefined. None of the predefined sort definitions sorts by the second word in a table column, though, so you must create a new sort definition.
3. Click the <u>N</u>ew button to open the New Sort dialog box. Figure 9-31 displays both the Sort dialog box and the New Sort dialog box.

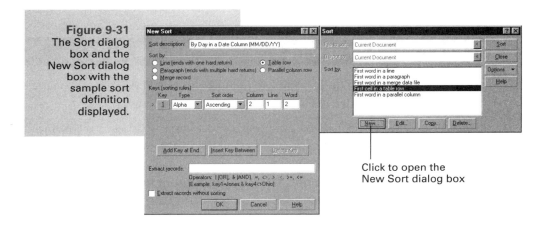

Figure 9-31 The Sort dialog box and the New Sort dialog box with the sample sort definition displayed.

Click to open the New Sort dialog box

4. In the <u>S</u>ort Description text box, type a brief description of the sort definition you are creating. The sample description is **By Day in a Date Column (MM/DD/YY)**.
5. Verify that <u>T</u>able Row is selected in the Sort By group.
6. Modify Key <u>1</u> by changing Type to Numeric, Column to **2**, and Word to **2**.

Note

Keys **are the rules by which the sort will operate. For example, the sort identifies each column in a table by number, then each word in the column. Key 1 is the most important sorting requirement, then Key 2, then Key 3, and so on. You can create a maximum of nine keys, each with its own sorting rules.**

> To sort by the last word in a column, set Word to **-1**. This is especially useful when sorting a list of names, such as the one presented in this hands-on activity.

7. When the key is complete, click OK to return to the Sort dialog box, then click <u>S</u>ort to perform the sort. The table rows are rearranged in date order.

Suppose that you want to determine which debtor owes you the most money. You can sort the columns by the Credit column, in descending order. Suppose, however, that you want to determine which debtors are over their credit limit. This involves extracting, or selecting, specific data based on the value of two columns.

Always save the document before extracting data! Extracting data displays only the resulting data on the document window. Data not meeting the extraction rules is deleted from the document window. A saved file allows you to start over if you've made a mistake in your sort keys or extract criteria.

Hands On: Using Sort to Extract Data

Use these steps to determine which debtors are over their credit limits:

1. Select all rows in the table.
2. Choose <u>T</u>ools, So<u>r</u>t (or press Alt+F9) to open the Sort dialog box. Click <u>N</u>ew to create a new sort definition, then describe the definition in the <u>S</u>ort Description text box: **Extract rows where amount is > credit limit**.
3. Extracting records based on values in two keys requires that both keys be defined. Define the first key, click Add Key at End, then define the second key. Define the keys using these values:

	Key 1	Key 2
Type:	Numeric	Numeric
Sort Order:	Ascending	Ascending
Column:	3	4
Line:	1	1
Word:	1	1

PART III • REPORTS AND PRESENTATIONS

4. Type **key1 > key2** in the Extract Records text box. This statement tells WordPerfect that you want to see all rows where the value represented in Key 1 (the Amount column) is greater than the value in Key 2 (the Credit column). See Figure 9-32.

In an extract statement, you can use the operators | (OR), & (AND), = (equal), <> (not equal), > (greater than), < (less than), >= (greater than or equal), and <= (less than or equal). Click the Help button on the New Sort dialog box for additional information about writing extract statements.

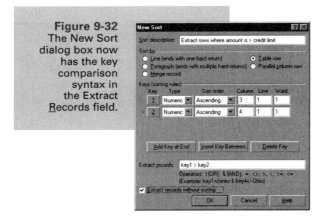

Figure 9-32 The New Sort dialog box now has the key comparison syntax in the Extract Records field.

5. Click OK to return to the Sort dialog box, then Sort to extract the record. You should see one row—Maven Myers owes $38,761, substantially more than her credit limit of $5,000!

10
Maintaining Your Report's Organization

IN THIS CHAPTER

- **Understanding WordPerfect's Document References**
- **Creating a Table of Contents**
- **Working with Lists**
- **Adding an Index and Table of Authorities**
- **Breaking a Document into Subdocuments**

Organization. "If you'd just get organized…" My mother used to get after me to organize my closet, and I did. But it never stayed organized for very long. Getting organized is easy. Staying organized is the difficult part!

PART III • REPORTS AND PRESENTATIONS

The same thing can be said about the written word. Every manuscript, every report, every book—everything written is controlled by some type of organizational structure. Chapter 8 began the discussion about organization by presenting WordPerfect 8's outline feature. Outlining is the *getting organized* part.

This chapter presents the *staying organized* discussion by helping you understand how to use WordPerfect 8's features to document and maintain the organization of your report. Once you've added the organization features covered in this chapter to your document, WordPerfect will keep your document organized!

You will learn how to create a table of contents, an index, and a list of tables. You will learn how to maintain cross-references, those statements throughout a manuscript which read "*see page 12*" or something similar. You will also learn how to create a table of authorities—a special index that gives credit to the sources you've quoted throughout your report. Finally, you will learn how to combine several small documents into a larger document, a technique which is useful when creating reports with several sections or *chapters*.

Including Document References in a Report

Five different document reference types can be automatically maintained by WordPerfect—lists of document items, an index, cross-references to other items in the document, a table of contents, and a table of authorities.

A *table of contents* is basically nothing more than a outline of the document, including page numbers where the outline items or headings appear. It's typically created at the beginning of a document. An *index* usually appears at the end of a document, listing words and phrases and their locations in the document. A *list* can appear anywhere in the document, although typically towards the front. It gathers the names and locations of like items in the file, such as all the tables, all the figures, or all the charts.

A *cross-reference* is a pointer to another item's location in the document. It's common to see phrases such as "*see Table 14 on page 22*" in a file. This phrase actually contains *two* cross references—one to the table and one to the page. Finally, while not exclusively so, a *table of authorities* is almost always used in a legal document to organize in one location all the citations that appear in the document.

WordPerfect loosely groups all these organizational structures, calling them *references*. Adding any of the reference types to your document involves the same three basic steps:

1. Mark the text to be included in the reference with the appropriate reference code.
2. Define the reference type at the document location where it should appear.
3. Generate the reference.

Marking text involves selecting the text to be included, such as a heading for a table of contents, then adding the table of content mark or code. Defining the reference means creating a page or area of the document where the reference will appear and telling WordPerfect how the reference is to look. Generating creates all of the references at the same time, actually creating the table of contents or the list.

Basically, all reference marks are added to the document using similar steps. Marks are codes created by the reference type you are creating. You might want to turn on Reveal Codes while you are marking the text so that you can view the resulting codes, and to make sure that any appropriate formatting is included between the codes.

Hands On: Creating a Sample Business Plan

Figure 10-1 displays the outline created in Chapter 8 for a beginning of a basic business plan. This outline will be used again throughout this chapter to demonstrate the references. If you saved the outline (it was named `bizplan.wpd`), open the file so that you can reuse it. If not, go ahead and create a document that looks similar to this one, or use another document that you've already created to which you want to add references.

Follow these steps:

1. To add some pages to the document so that the references appear in scattered locations, type some filler text beginning on an empty line after the first entry in your outline:

    This is filler text for a business plan report. This is filler text for a business plan report. This is filler text for a business plan report.

2. Now copy and paste your filler text repeatedly throughout the outline so that it builds up the document until it is about four or five pages long. You might even want to include a few extra returns to make your text look more like typical paragraph text.

    Figure 10-2 shows the outline with the filler text in place.

3. Be sure to save your new document, naming it `reference.wpd` so that you can use it repeatedly throughout this chapter.

PART III • REPORTS AND PRESENTATIONS

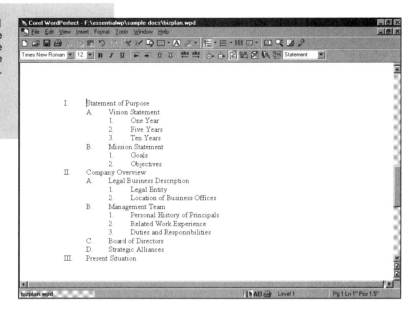

Figure 10-1
Create and save a simple outline document to use in this chapter.

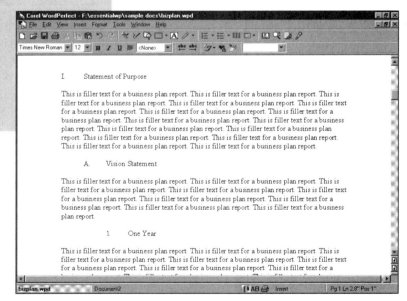

Figure 10-2
A report contains text, not just a bare outline.

Creating a Table of Contents

In Chapter 8 you created a simple outline for a business plan. You discovered that outline items are each dependent on an outline definition, and the numbers or

CHAPTER 10 • MAINTAINING YOUR REPORT'S ORGANIZATION

levels in the outline were controlled by *styles*. A table of contents is really nothing more than an outline documented by the page numbers on which the outline item or heading appears. If you include a table of contents instruction in each outline level style, it's very easy to actually create a table of contents for the document.

A table of contents can contain a maximum of five levels. This means that as you add marks to your document, you'll want to consider at which level the entry should appear. Figure 10-3 illustrates a table of contents with five levels.

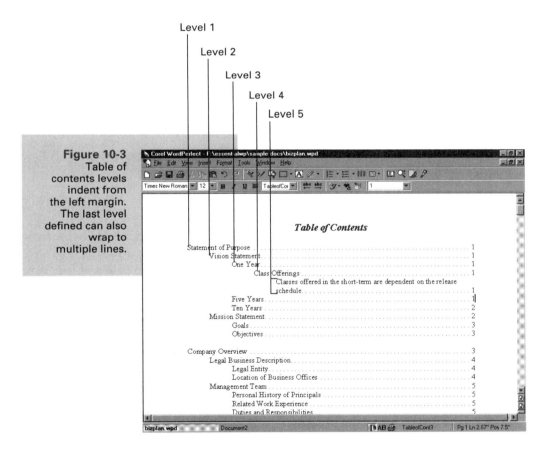

Figure 10-3
Table of contents levels indent from the left margin. The last level defined can also wrap to multiple lines.

Marking Table of Contents Entries

It's ideal to include table of content marks in a style, especially if a style was used to create headings in the document. But not all documents were created with styles. And sometimes it's just more work to create and apply styles throughout the document, than it is to just mark table of contents entries.

PART III • REPORTS AND PRESENTATIONS

MANUALLY MARKING ENTRIES FOR A TABLE OF CONTENTS

With a document that's already been fully created without styles, it's easiest to manually mark each heading to be included in the table of contents. To illustrate this procedure, I've stripped the style codes from the business plan outline then centered and numbered each of the headings by hand. If you follow along, be sure not to save your modified document since it will be used again in the next hands-on activity.

WordPerfect 8 automatically creates an outline and automatic paragraph numbering when it sees formatting in a document resembling an outline. For this hands-on example, you'll want to turn off Format-As-You-Go by choosing Tools, QuickCorrect, then click the Format-As-You-Go tab. Remove the checkmark from QuickBullets in the Format-As-You-Go Choices group.

Manually marking text for inclusion in the table of contents is simple. Follow these steps:

1. Turn on Reveal Codes so that you can see all formatting surrounding the heading.
2. Select the heading text and any formatting you want to include in the table of contents. For example, if your selection contains codes such as bold and italic, the table of contents entry for this heading is also bold and italicized. Similarly, if you include a center code or a paragraph number code, they appear in the table of contents (see Figure 10-4).
3. Choose Tools, Reference, Table of Contents. The Table of Contents property bar will open. The Table of Contents property bar will remain open until you click the Close button on the property bar.
4. Click Mark 1 to add the table of contents level 1 code to the document. See Figure 10-5.
5. Repeat steps 2, 3, and 4 to mark each heading in the document with the appropriate level.
6. While you'd normally save your document at this point, *don't* for this example. Close the document without saving the changes, then open the original `reference.wpd` file again for use in the next hands-on activity.

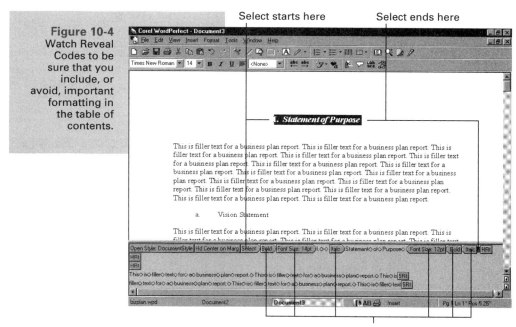

Figure 10-4 Watch Reveal Codes to be sure that you include, or avoid, important formatting in the table of contents.

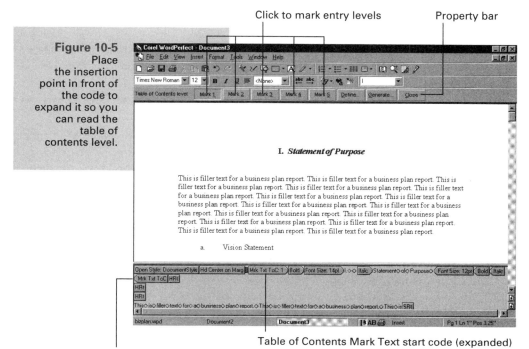

Figure 10-5 Place the insertion point in front of the code to expand it so you can read the table of contents level.

MARKING TABLE OF CONTENTS ENTRIES THROUGH A STYLE

Including your table of contents markings in a style code is far less time-consuming than marking each individual heading in a long report. It's also more accurate since placing the marking correctly once, in the style code, affects all entries which use the style.

Hands On: Including Table of Content Marks in a Style

The steps here add table of content marks to the default outline level styles:

> **REFER TO CHAPTERS 5 AND 8 FOR MORE INFORMATION ABOUT STYLES.**

1. Open `reference.wpd` if it's not already opened.
2. Turn on Reveal Codes, then double-click the [Para Style: Level 1] style code in the first line of the document, just at the beginning of the first outline level, Statement of Purpose. The Styles Editor dialog box opens. Figure 10-6 identifies each of the important elements which appear in the Styles Editor dialog box for this hands-on activity.
3. Check the Show 'Off Codes' check box at the bottom of the Styles Editor dialog box.
4. Press → twice to position the insertion point just to the left of the [Codes to the Left are ON - Codes to the Right are OFF] code.

•••

Include the [Para Num] and [Hd Left Ind] codes in the selection to include them in the table of contents.

•••

5. Press [Shift]+→ to select the [Codes to the Left are ON - Codes to the Right are OFF] code.
6. Choose Tools, Reference, Table of Contents from the Styles Editor menu. The Table of Contents property bar appears at the bottom of the document window.

> **REFER TO CHAPTER 9 FOR MORE INFORMATION ON OUTLINES.**

7. Click Mark 1 to add the [Mrk Txt ToC] code pair to the style Contents text box.
8. Click OK to record your changes and return to the document window. All entries in the document which use a Level 1 outline style are now also marked as a level 1 table of contents entry.
9. Position the insertion point immediately prior to the Style code to expand it and verify that the [Mrk Txt ToC] code is included in the style code.

CHAPTER 10 • MAINTAINING YOUR REPORT'S ORGANIZATION **273**

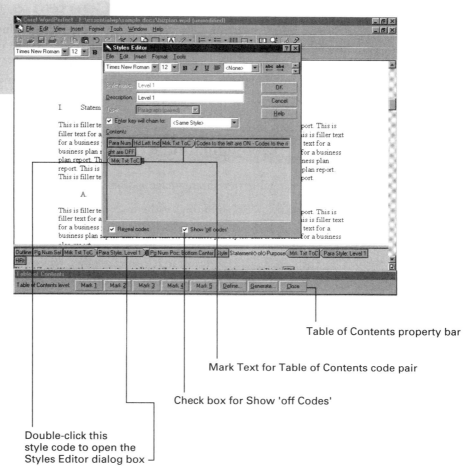

Figure 10-6 Double-clicking a code opens its associated dialog box.

Table of Contents property bar

Mark Text for Table of Contents code pair

Check box for Show 'off Codes'

Double-click this style code to open the Styles Editor dialog box

10. Now position the insertion point at the beginning of the next heading, `Vision Statement`. Locate the Style code for this level 2 heading, double-click the code and mark the style as a level 2 Table of Content entry. When finished, click OK to return to the document again.

11. Open the Styles Editor for each of the remaining outline levels 3 through 5 in your document, adding table of content mark codes for each level. Remember that you only need to edit one style code for each level. Doing so automatically updates all the remaining entries which use the same style.

12. Save your updated document so that you will retain your edits.

PART III • REPORTS AND PRESENTATIONS

Defining the Table of Contents

A table of contents almost always appears at the very beginning of the document, immediately after the title page, if there is one. Defining the page lets you set up the appearance to be used for the table of contents entries. You can include text such as a title for the page, or additional formatting instructions such as custom page numbering or a new header or footer.

Hands On: Defining the Table of Contents Location

Defining the table of contents page is simple. Use these steps:

1. Go to the very beginning of the document by pressing Ctrl+Home, Ctrl+Home. This places the insertion point prior to any formatting codes in the document.
2. Turn on Reveal Codes so that you can view precise placement of the table of contents page. Now place the insertion point after any title page you may have in the document, but before any codes which strictly govern the body of the document, such as a header or footer code.
3. With the insertion point positioned correctly, press Ctrl+Enter to add a hard page break to the document, creating a blank page.
4. Now press ↑ to move back to the new, empty page.
5. Type a title for the table of contents page, formatting it appropriately. Then press Enter three or four times to separate the title from the area where the actual table of contents entries will appear.
6. Choose Tools, Reference, Table of Contents. The Table of Contents property bar will appear.
7. Click Define to open the Define Table of Contents dialog box (see Figure 10-7).
8. Enter the maximum number of table of contents levels you marked in your document.

Even if you only think you marked three levels, you can set numbering for five levels to be sure that everything is included. However, if you *know* that you only marked three levels and you also know that the level three uses long headings, you might want to set the Number of Levels to 3, then check the Display Last Level in Wrapped Format check box.

CHAPTER 10 • MAINTAINING YOUR REPORT'S ORGANIZATION   275

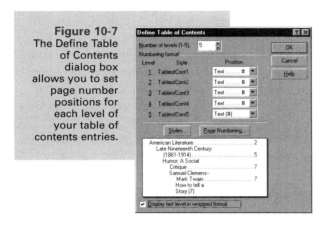

Figure 10-7
The Define Table of Contents dialog box allows you to set page number positions for each level of your table of contents entries.

9. For each level, open the Position drop-down list, then select the page number position and format you want to use for that level.

10. Check <u>D</u>isplay Last Level in Wrapped Format if your last level often contains long text that might not all fit on one line.

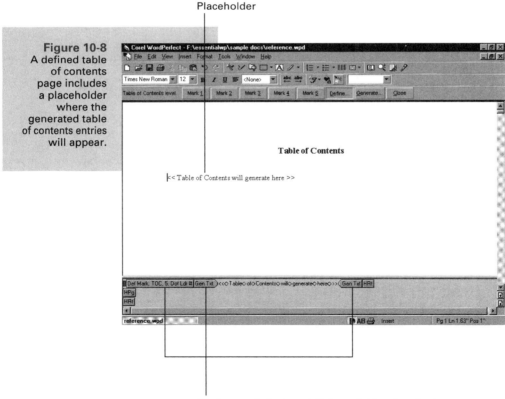

Placeholder

Figure 10-8
A defined table of contents page includes a placeholder where the generated table of contents entries will appear.

Codes created when defining a table of contents

PART III • REPORTS AND PRESENTATIONS

11. If you're comfortable with styles, you can also modify the default table of contents styles by clicking the Styles button.

12. Click the Page Numbering button to add page numbering to the bottom of each generated table of contents page. Now choose between including the page number in the Document Page Number Format or as a Custom Page Number Format. If you choose Custom, you can add additional text to be printed with the page number digit (such as `Page xx` or `-xx-`). When your page number choice is complete, click OK to accept your choice and close the Page Number Format dialog box. (Clicking Cancel abandons your choices.)

13. When all levels are complete, click OK to return to the document window. The text `<<Table of Contents will generate here>>` has been inserted in the document and the `[Def Mark]` codes appear in Reveal Codes. See Figure 10-8.

14. If all references are complete, you can now generate the table of contents, using the steps listed later in this chapter.

Note

If you accidentally delete one or both of the `[Def Mark]` or `[Gen Txt]` codes, the reference will not generate. You will then need to recreate the reference definition.

Creating a List of Report Items

A list is a grouping of the names of like objects, such as graphics, which appear throughout your document. This list notes for the reader on what page the item appears. A good example of a list exists in this book. Look near the front of the book to find the "Hands On Topics" list. Notice that each activity is named and referenced by page number. You can create as many different lists in your documents as you require.

SEE CHAPTER 9 FOR MORE INFORMATION ABOUT CREATING TABLES.

Hands On: Preparing a Document for a List of Tables

To prepare the `reference.wpd` document for a list of tables, edit the file and create several tables. Use these steps:

1. Position the insertion point somewhere in the paragraph following the

CHAPTER 10 • MAINTAINING YOUR REPORT'S ORGANIZATION 277

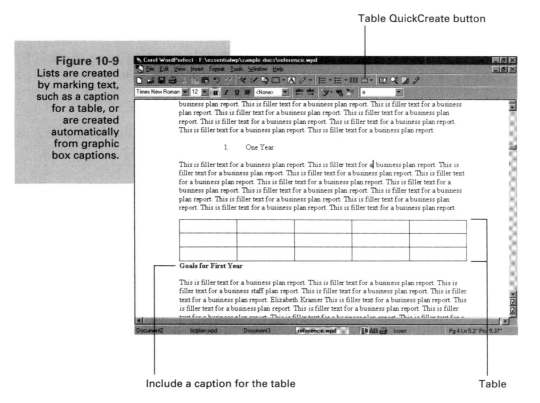

Figure 10-9
Lists are created by marking text, such as a caption for a table, or are created automatically from graphic box captions.

heading One Year. Create a quick table, 5 columns by 3 rows, using the Table QuickCreate button on the toolbar.

2. On the line immediately following the table, type a caption for the table: **Goals for First Year.**

You can also include a table in either a table or a text graphics box. By doing so, a caption can be created which is maintained as part of the table box itself. Graphic boxes are numbered so that you can include the box number in your list. Chapter 12 will help you understand more about graphic boxes and captions.

3. Create tables again immediately after the entries for Five Years and Ten Years, creating captions under each table which read **Goals for Five Years** and **Goals for Ten Years**. These three tables will appear in a list of tables. Figure 10-9 displays the first table.

4. When all tables are finished, be sure to save your file again.

Marking List Entries

Graphic boxes with captions are a special type of item that can automatically be included in a list without marking. Unfortunately, if you want to maintain a list of any other type of item, such as a list of tables, you'll need to manually mark the item text. Of course, you only need to mark the item once, then it remains marked through all subsequent edits and document changes.

Marking an item tells WordPerfect 8 what to include on which list. You can have as many different lists as you need to organize your document.

Hands On: Marking Text for a List

You can include as much, or as little, information in a listed item as you require. Here's how to include the table captions you created in a list:

1. With Reveal Codes turned on, select the complete text for the first table caption. In the selection include any formatting codes, such as <u>bold</u>, that you want to also include in the list.
2. Choose <u>T</u>ools, Referen<u>c</u>e, <u>L</u>ist. The List property bar will appear above the typing area of the document window.
3. Click in the <u>L</u>ist text box, and type a short name for your list such as **Tables**. This name will be used to identify on which list the marked item should appear. As you mark items throughout a lengthy document, you can create additional lists by naming them in the <u>L</u>ist text box.
4. Click the <u>M</u>ark button to surround the selected text with [Mrk Txt List] codes for the Tables list. The beginning and ending codes will appear in Reveal Codes and the text will be deselected.
5. Now locate the caption for the next table and select it.
6. From the <u>L</u>ist text box, verify that the Tables list is selected (it will be, because it's the only list created in the document). Now mark the caption by clicking the <u>M</u>ark button.
7. Finally, mark the last table caption in the same way. Be sure to save your document. After all, if this were a real report, you'd very likely have far more than three simple entries for your list!

Defining the List

Lists can appear at any location in a document. Sometimes a list appears at the beginning of each chapter, but most commonly they appear toward the front of a report since they identify and locate items for the report. Remember that you'll

CHAPTER 10 • MAINTAINING YOUR REPORT'S ORGANIZATION 279

need to define a page or location for each list for which you've marked items. If you have a list of figures and a list of tables you'll need to define two separate list pages.

Hands On: Defining the List

To place a list on the first page after the table of contents, use these steps:

1. Press Ctrl+Home to move to the beginning of the document, then click the Next Page button or press Alt+Pg Dn until you locate the table of contents page. Then go one more page.
2. Press Ctrl+Enter to insert a hard page break. This will add a new, blank, page immediately after the table of contents page. Now press ↑ to position the insertion point at the beginning of the blank page.
3. Type a title for the list, including any desired formatting. Press Enter three times to separate the title from the list entries.
4. Choose Tools, Reference, List to open the List property bar.
5. Now click the Define button to open the Define List dialog box.
6. When you marked your first list item a list definition was automatically created using the WordPerfect defaults. Click the Edit button to open the Edit List dialog box (see Figure 10-10).

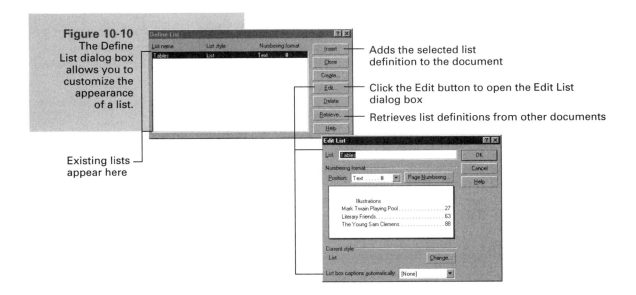

Figure 10-10 The Define List dialog box allows you to customize the appearance of a list.

Existing lists appear here

Adds the selected list definition to the document

Click the Edit button to open the Edit List dialog box

Retrieves list definitions from other documents

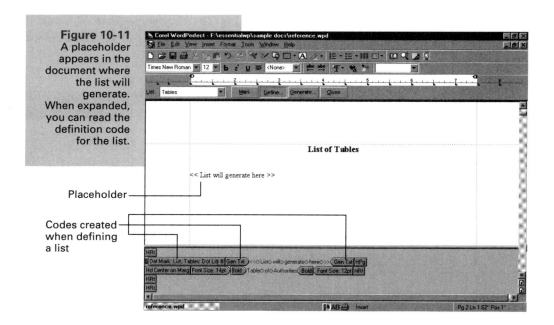

Figure 10-11 A placeholder appears in the document where the list will generate. When expanded, you can read the definition code for the list.

Placeholder

Codes created when defining a list

7. Open the Numbering Format Position drop-down list, then select the number style and position you want to use.

8. If desired, click the Page Numbering button to select a numbering option for this list page.

9. Click OK to return to the Define List dialog box, then Insert to add the definition code to your document. The phrase `<<List will generate here>>` appears in your document at the location where the list will appear. The [Def Mark] codes for a list definition can be viewed in Reveal Codes, as shown in Figure 10-11.

10. If all reference types are marked and defined, you can now generate the list.

Creating an Index

An index usually appears at the end of a book. It alphabetizes a list of major topics, with perhaps minor topics also included. For example, if you created a report about vacation activities in your area, you might have major topics such as Outdoor Activities, Indoor Activities, and Activities for Children. Then minor topics for Outdoor Activities might be Swimming, Boating, Hiking, and so on.

Marking index entries can take an incredible amount of time and effort. It's usually best accomplished after all edits are complete on your document since marking index items also produces a lot of extra codes which you must be careful not to delete.

To simplify marking each occurrence of a word in your document, you can create a list of major topics in another document, called the *concordance* file. The concordance can then be referenced for inclusion in the document. When the index generates, the concordance updates, listing the location of every word or phrase found in the document which appeared in the concordance. Any manually marked index items found in the document are then also added to the concordance.

You can get as detailed as you want in an index, creating multiple subheadings and major headings for all possible combinations of a phrase. For example, the phrases *previous credit history* and *line of credit* offer several indexing possibilities:

>Credit
>>Previous History
>>Line of
>
>History
>>Credit
>
>Line of Credit
>Previous Credit History

So that you'll have some items to actually generate in a index, edit the `reference.wpd` document, adding phrases throughout the document. You'll want to add each one of them at least a couple of times on various pages to get the full effect of a generated index. Remember, the sample document doesn't need to

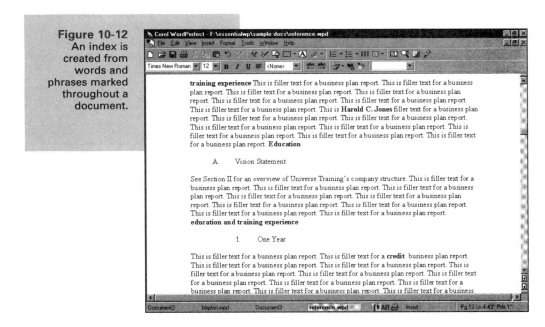

Figure 10-12 An index is created from words and phrases marked throughout a document.

make sense, it's just for illustration purposes. To give you the idea, Figure 10-12 includes a few of the phrases, typed in bold so they're easier for you to find. It's not necessary for you to use boldface. Here are the words and phrases:

training experience	**staff**
Harold C. Jones	**line of credit**
Elizabeth Kramer	**previous credit history**
Phyllis Martin	**technical**
degree	**education**

With the words inserted in the document, be sure to save your file.

Manually Marking Major and Minor Entries for an Index

Like marking any other reference item, you must locate and select words or phrases that you want to include in an index. And you must locate and mark *every* instance of the word or phrase so that it is included in the final index. Using WordPerfect's search and replace feature simplifies the task tremendously.

Hands On: Marking Words and Phrases for an Index

Marking words and phrases for inclusion in an index takes some effort, but it's not at all difficult. Here's how:

1. Locate and select the first word or phrase you want to include in the index. Using Figure 10-12 as the example, select the phrase `training experience`. If your phrase includes any formatting, it's a good idea not to include the formatting inside the selection, so refer to Reveal Codes frequently.
2. Choose Tools, Reference, Index. The Index property bar will appear immediately above the document area of the document window.
3. Click in the Heading text box. The phrase `training experience` will appear in the text box and will be added to the Heading list.
4. Click Mark to mark the complete phrase as a single entry for the index. Reveal Codes now displays a code which reads [Index: training experience] when expanded.

   Now, include `experience` as a major heading and `training` as a subheading. Continue, using these steps:

5. Select experience, then click in the Heading text box. The new selection will be added to the list, replacing whatever phrase already exists in the Heading text box. As you click in the Heading text box, each new entry is added to the list.

6. Double-click training and click in the Subheading text box. Now click Mark to add the major heading experience to the list with a subheading of training. Another index code can be found in Reveal Codes, which reads [Index: experience;training].

7. Now you must search through the document, marking every instance of experience and training experience. To do so, press Ctrl+F to open the Find and Replace dialog box. Type **experience** in the Find text box, then click Find Next. The next instance of the word experience will appear, selected, and the Find and Replace dialog box will remain open.

8. Select the full phrase training experience in the document, then open the Heading drop-down list and click training experience, then click Mark. Now mark the additional main heading and subheading entry as instructed in step 6.

9. Repeat steps 7 and 8 until no other instances of training experience, training, or experience can be found in the document.

10. Find will prompt when it finishes searching through the document that no additional instances of the word experience can be found. Click Yes to continue searching at the beginning of the document. This will position you back at the first instance of the word so that you can now begin marking another phrase.

11. Repeat these steps for these words and phrases: staff, line of credit, and previous credit history. Be sure to also index credit as a major heading, with line of and previous history as subheadings.

Creating a Concordance File for Index Entries

A *concordance file* is referenced by a document when an index is generated. It is, quite simply, a separate file containing a list of words or phrases, each on a separate line. When an index is created using a concordance file, WordPerfect searches for each instance of each entry in the concordance file as it generates the index. Much easier than marking every single entry in a document!

The capitalization of an entry in the concordance file takes precedence over capitalization in the document. This means that if an entry in the concordance file appears as "Degree" and in the document the word appears as "degree" and "Degree," it will be listed in the index as "Degree." A concordance file entry can

Part III • Reports and Presentations

also be used as a subheading. To do so, mark the entry in the concordance file as a subheading.

Hands On: Creating a Concordance File

Creating a concordance file is as easy as creating a new document. Here's how:

1. Open a new document window.
2. Type each of the following entries, pressing Enter after each entry so that it appears on a separate line:

   staff
   Harold C. Jones
   Elizabeth Kramer
   Phyllis Martin
   education
   technical
   degree

To retain lower-case capitalization in your concordance file, choose Tools, QuickCorrect. Click the Format-As-You-Go tab, then remove the checkmark from Capitalize Next Letter After End-of-Sentence Punctuation.

Although not required, you'll find that an index generates more quickly from a concordance file that has been sorted alphabetically. To sort a long concordance file, choose Tools, Sort. From the resulting Sort dialog box, select First Word In a Line from the Sort By list. Then click Sort.

3. Mark the three names each as subheadings under the heading for `staff`.

To include an entry as both a major and a subheading in a concordance file, you must list the entry twice. The mark one of the entries as a subheading. The unmarked entry will be generated as a major heading.

4. Save the concordance file, using an obvious name such as **concordance.wpd**.

CHAPTER 10 • MAINTAINING YOUR REPORT'S ORGANIZATION **285**

Defining an Index

Defining the index page is similar to defining any of the other reference types. You'll need to create a blank page for the index to generate, usually at the end of your document.

Hands On: Defining an Index

Use these steps to add an index definition to your document:

1. Press Ctrl+End to move to the end of the document, then press Ctrl+Enter to add a page break.
2. Type the title you want to use for your Index, including any formatting. Now press Enter three times to add space between the title and the generated index.
3. Choose Tools, Reference, Index to open the Index property bar.

If you already have a property bar open for another reference type, right-click on the existing property bar, then select the alternate property bar from the resulting QuickMenu.

4. Click Define to open the Define Index dialog box, displayed after completion in Figure 10-13.
5. Select the Numbering Format Position and Page Number choices for the Index from their respective drop-down lists.

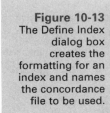
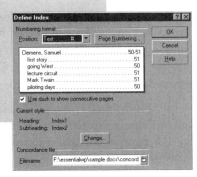

Figure 10-13
The Define Index dialog box creates the formatting for an index and names the concordance file to be used.

6. Verify the page preference in the Use Dash to Show Consecutive Pages control. If checked, consecutive pages will print as 5-10 rather than 5, 6, 7, 8, 9, 10.

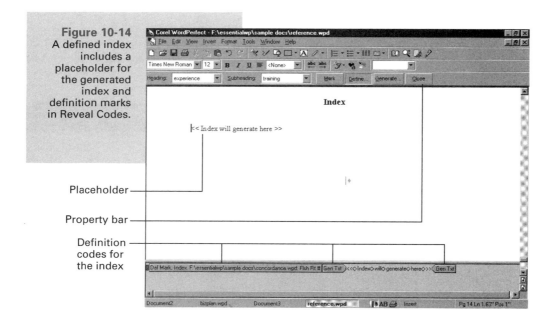

Figure 10-14
A defined index includes a placeholder for the generated index and definition marks in Reveal Codes.

Placeholder
Property bar
Definition codes for the index

7. Type the name for your Concordance File in the Filename text box, or click the folder button to select the file from a file management box.

8. Click OK to add the index definition mark to your document. The placeholder <<Index will generate here>> will appear in the text. Open Reveal Codes to view the inserted [Def Mark] code, shown in Figure 10-14.

Creating a Table of Authorities

A table of authorities most often appears in a legal document. Legal research papers or reports in support of a legal position, called *briefs,* heavily cite or quote other legal decisions and various types of regulations or laws. These are considered the *authorities*—the definitive source for the information. When gathered together in a list, the list is referred to as a table of authorities.

But a table of authorities certainly isn't limited to a legal document. Reports of all types sometimes refer to quotes which appear from other sources. Especially in a educational setting, reports or papers often contain citations from research materials. These citations, references, and quotes can also be gathered together in a table of authorities.

As with every other type of reference, the advantage is that the document can be edited without the necessity of manually recreating the table or list of citations. You can add or delete pages or sections prior to the occurrence of a citation.

When the document is generated, all reference locations are updated in the table of authorities.

Defining a Table of Authorities

A table of authorities can contain several sections. For example, in a legal brief you might have one section for Cases, another for Constitutional Provisions, and another for Rules and Regulations. A report for college might include sections for sources such as Magazines, Books, Encyclopedias, or even Internet Web Pages. Before beginning to mark any entries for inclusion in the table of authorities, you must, therefore, plan the section types to be included. As you mark entries for the table of authorities, you also include the section name in which the authority will be placed.

Because a table of authorities is so heavily used in law firms, the sample text used in this hands-on activity focuses on legal text. To follow along with this hands-on activity, create the text which appears in Figure 10-15 at the end of your `reference.wpd` document. It doesn't need to be letter perfect, of course.

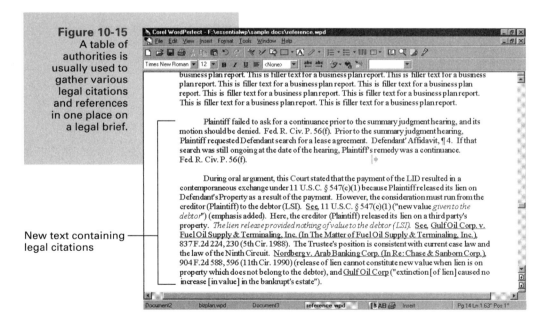

Figure 10-15 A table of authorities is usually used to gather various legal citations and references in one place on a legal brief.

New text containing legal citations

Hands On: Defining a Table of Authorities Page

A table of authorities can be placed either at the beginning of a legal brief, usually right after the table of contents, or at the end of the brief. This example will place the table of authorities at the front of the document. Use these steps to define the table of authorities:

1. Press Ctrl+Home to move to the beginning of the document.
2. If you've defined table of contents and list pages, click at the end of the list page. Press Ctrl+Enter to add a page break after the table of contents page. Then press ↑ to return to the blank page. The insertion point should now be at the top of a new, empty document page.
3. Center and format a title for the table of authorities page. Press Enter four times to separate the page title from the first section title. Now center and italicize title lines for each section: **Cases**, **Rules and Regulations**, and **Statutes**. Follow each title line with four hard returns. Figure 10-16 displays the page as it should now appear.

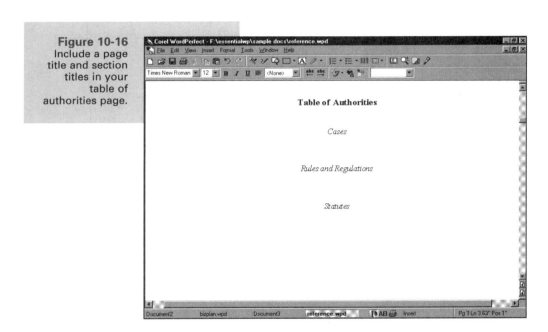

Figure 10-16
Include a page title and section titles in your table of authorities page.

4. Place the insertion point two lines below the section heading for **Cases**, then choose Tools, Reference, Table of Authorities to open the Table of Authorities property bar.
5. Click Define on the property bar. The Define Table of Authorities dialog box will open.
6. Click Create to name and format the first section for your table of authorities page.

CHAPTER 10 • MAINTAINING YOUR REPORT'S ORGANIZATION **289**

7. Type **Cases** in the Name text box to begin defining the first section.
8. The default appearance for numbering format is usually sufficient, although you should make any changes you need. Click the Position drop-down list, then select the location for the page number to be used in the Cases section.
9. If you want a page number to print at the bottom of the table of authorities page, click the Page Numbering button, then choose between including the page number in the Document Page Number Format or as a Custom Page Number Format. If you choose Custom, you can add additional text to be printed with the page number digit (such as `Page xx` or `-xx-`). When your page number choice is complete, click OK to close the Page Number Format dialog box.
10. Check the Include Underlining in Generated Table check box to retain any underlining you may have used in the document text authorities.
11. Check or clear the Use Dash to Show Consecutive Pages control. If checked, consecutive pages will print as 5-8. If cleared, consecutive pages will print as 5, 6, 7, 8.
12. Click OK to return to the Define Table of Authorities dialog box. With the newly defined section selected, click Insert to add the definition code to the table of authorities document page. The text `<<Table of Authorities will generate here>>` will appear in the document.

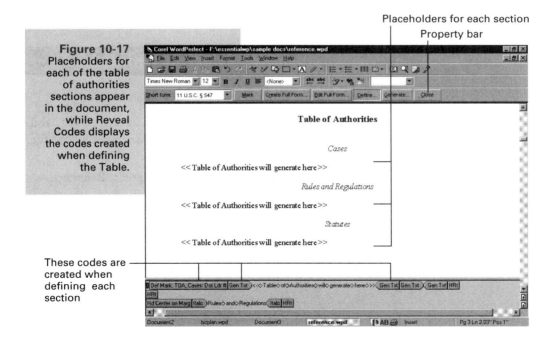

Figure 10-17 Placeholders for each of the table of authorities sections appear in the document, while Reveal Codes displays the codes created when defining the Table.

These codes are created when defining each section

When the document is generated the text will be replaced with the actual text for the authorities.

13. Now position the insertion point two blank lines below the Rules and Regulations section heading and define the section using steps 6-12 again. When complete, repeat the steps one more time for the Statutes definition. Figure 10-17 displays the page as it now appears.
14. With all sections defined, be sure to save your document.

Marking Table of Authorities Entries

Marking a table of authorities entry is slightly more complicated than marking any of the other reference types. An authority entry typically contains lengthy reference information, including the name of the source, its date of publication, its author, the pages being quoted or cited, and so on, but only the first time it is quoted. This first reference is called the *full form* by WordPerfect. The next time the same authority is referenced, it often appears in the document in some sort of abbreviated form, naming just enough information to make it clear that this is a repeat of a previously referenced authority. This abbreviated entry is referred to as the *short form*.

To keep things organized, you name both the full form and the short form when the full form is marked. The short form doesn't necessarily need to match the short form used in the document text, by the way. You'll just use the short form you named to mark every other reference to the original citation in the document.

Hands On: Marking Items for a Table of Authorities

Use these steps to mark long and short forms for a table of authorities:

1. Locate the first citation in the document, `Fed. R. Civ. P. 56(f)`. You can use Find and Replace to locate it quickly, or just skim through the file until you find it.
2. Select the complete text of the authority, then choose Tools, Reference, Table of Authorities. The Table of Authorities property bar will appear.
3. Click Create Full Form. The Create Full Form dialog box will open, displaying the first section name created when the table of authorities page was defined.
4. Click the drop-down button for the Section Name, then select Rules and Regulations.

CHAPTER 10 • MAINTAINING YOUR REPORT'S ORGANIZATION **291**

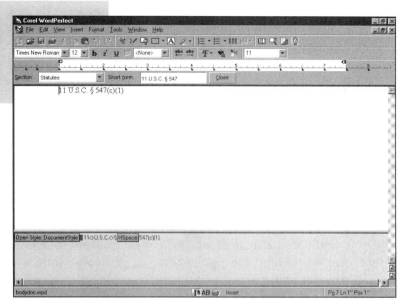

Figure 10-18 Abbreviations are often avoided in a table of authorities page.

5. In the Short Form text box, click at the end of the citation, then press ←Backspace to delete the text (f). While preferences vary from attorney to attorney, a Rules and Regulation short form is often limited to Fed. R. Civ. P. 56.

6. Click OK to open the Full Form formatting page.

7. Format or type the full citation name here as you want it to appear on the generated table of authorities (see Figure 10-18).

8. When the authority is complete, click Close to return to the document text. A [ToA] code appears in Reveal Codes which, when expanded, displays the full form for the authority.

9. Now search for additional instances of the same authority. If found, verify that the correct short form is selected in the Short Form drop-down list, selecting it from the list if necessary. Then click the Mark button. A [ToA] short form code is added to the document, visible in Reveal Codes.

Be sure to save your file periodically to safeguard your work!

10. Continue searching and marking all instances of the same short form. When all are marked, search one more time to position the insertion point

at the first location for the form. Now move to the next authority, marking its full form and then all short form instances. Following are the list of sections for each authority:

Authority	Suggested Short Form	Section
11 U.S.C. § 547(c)(1)	11 U.S.C. § 574	Statutes
Gulf Oil Corp. v. Fuel Oil Supply...	Gulf Oil Corp. v. Fuel Oil	Cases
Nordberg v. Arab Banking Corp...	Nordberg	Cases

Using Cross-References to Point to Other Locations

Cross-references provide a method of referring to another location in a document. This book contains several cross-references. For example, in the margin you periodically see a statement such as "For more information on...see Chapter 4." You also see references in regular text to a particular figure number. These are both cross-references.

The WordPerfect cross-reference feature provides a method of being even more specific. You can include statements such as "See Figure 12 on page 20." Then if the figure changes location or if figures are added or deleted, the cross-reference updates to reflect the new figure and page number the next time you generate the document.

A cross-reference contains two parts, the *reference* and the *target*. The *reference* is the statement in the document that directs your attention—the place where you say "*See page 12.*" The *target* is the item to which you are referring (page 12). Targets can be pages, secondary pages, chapters, volumes, paragraph or outline numbers, footnotes, endnotes, a caption number, or any other counter such as a figure number. When creating a target, you assign it a name. The target name is then used to link the reference and the target together.

The business plan document, now named `reference.wpd`, will again be used in this hands-on example. Since it was originally created using an outline, each of the headings are complete with an outline number. We can use these outline numbers, in combination with page numbers to create some sophisticated cross-references.

Hands On: Including a Cross-Reference in a Report

This example will create two cross-references, one to the heading *Company Overview* and another which references the Ten-Year Goals table created in the hands-on example for lists. Use these steps:

1. Position the insertion point on the first text line following the heading A. Vision Statement. Now type **See Section x for an overview of Universe Training's company structure.** The *x* will be replaced, when marked and generated, with the outline number for the Company Overview section. Now delete the *x* placeholder in the line you just typed, leaving the insertion point at that same location.

2. To open the Cross-Reference property bar, choose Tools, Reference, Cross-Reference. The property bar will appear above the text area of the document window.

3. Click in the text area of the Target text box and type a name for the target such as **Company Overview Section**.

4. Now click the Reference drop-down list button. Select Paragraph/Outline to indicate the type of reference you are creating.

You can use the same target name with different reference types. This allows you to create a statement such as *See Section I on Page 12*. To do so, name the target, then select the first reference type from the Reference drop-down list. Now click Mark Reference. Now select the second reference type from the Reference drop-down list and click Mark Reference again. When generated, both reference types will appear.

5. Click Mark Reference. A question mark (?) will appear in the text. By viewing Reveal Codes, however, you will note that a [Ref Para] code has been added to the document. When generated, the question mark will be replaced with the section number.

You can mark either the reference or the target first. If the target has been already marked, the actual target value will appear when you mark the Reference. If, however, you later delete the target, the reference will again display a question mark. You'll need to mark the target again, then generate the document, to update the reference text correctly.

6. Now locate the target. The easiest method in a long document is to use WordPerfect's Find and Replace feature. To do so, press Ctrl+F, then type **Company Overview** in the Find text box. Click Find Next. WordPerfect will locate and select the text. Click Close to close the Find and Replace dialog box, then click in the document or press F8 to deselect the text.

7. With Reveal Codes open, be sure the insertion point resides between the [Para Style] codes. It's not strictly necessary, but neatest to place the insertion point at the beginning of the first word. This will avoid placing the reference code in the middle of a word.
8. Verify that the correct target name is visible in the Target text box of the property bar. If it isn't, click the drop-down list button and select Company Overview from the list.
9. Click Mark Target. A [Target] code will be added to the document, visible in Reveal Codes.
10. Now position the insertion point at the end of the document and type **See the list of ten year goals on page**.
11. This time mark the target before marking the reference. Locate the table named Goals for Ten Years, placing the insertion point immediately before the caption text.
12. Click in the Target text box and type **10-year table** as the target name.
13. Click Mark Target to add the [Target] code to the document.
14. Return to the end of the document. If necessary, add a space after the word page then select Page from the Reference drop-down list.
15. Now click Mark Reference. A [Ref Pg] code will be added to the document and a question mark will again appear in the text.
16. If you've created all of your references for the document, you can now generate the references.

Generating the References

Generating references creates or updates all of the reference codes in the document. If you've previously generated the references then edited them, generating the references again will delete your edits while creating updated references. You can prevent any reference from being regenerated by deleting its definition codes.

Before you generate, you should:

- Save your document! Generating a long, complicated, document can take several minutes. WordPerfect makes several passes through the file, writing temporary files while sorting through the various reference codes it finds. Saving your document prior to generating also ensures that you can return to the document's *before* status if you've made a serious error.
- Review the document to be sure that page numbering values are appropriate. Remember that the table of contents page, for example, actually adds a page to the beginning of the document, possibly forcing

Chapter 10 • Maintaining Your Report's Organization

page one of your text to be page two. Reassign a new page value to the text and various portions of the document. Think about assigning custom page numbering styles to the reference pages, such as numbering them with lower-case roman numerals.

Hands On: Renumbering the Document Page

> **See Chapter 4 for more information about Page Numbering.**

To tell WordPerfect that the first page of text should be numbered as Page 1, rather than the page number appearing in the application bar, use these steps:

1. Position the insertion point at the beginning of the first page of your report text.
2. Choose Fo_r_mat, _P_age, _N_umbering. The Select Page Numbering Format dialog box will open.
3. Click the Set _V_alue button, then type **1** in the _S_et Page Number control.
4. Click OK twice to add the [Pg Num Set] code to the document. You can verify the new page number in the Combined Position display button on the application bar.

Hands On: Generating the References

With all references, definition codes, page numbering correctly entered, and the document saved, it's time to see the results! Use these steps:

1. If you still have a property bar open for any of the reference types, click the _G_enerate button. If not, choose _T_ools, Referen_c_e, Ge_n_erate. The Generate dialog box will open.
2. If your document was created using the master and subdocument feature, check _S_ave Subdocuments to write all updated references to the subdocuments. If your document also contains hypertext links you can update the links by clicking _B_uild Hypertext Links.
3. Click OK to generate the document. After a pause, your document will reappear, displaying all updated references.
4. Skim through the document, reviewing each reference. Did they generate correctly? If not, edit the reference marks, then generate the document again.

Breaking Up Your Report into Manageable Sections

Working on a very long document is cumbersome and slow. There's really no limit to the length of a document in WordPerfect 8, but I've found that documents which are more than 75 pages or so are difficult to maintain and edit. Documents of this length usually contain sections or chapters, making them ideal candidates for subdocuments.

In addition, you may find that preparing a report such as a business plan requires input from many other people, resulting in many documents which should be *rolled together* to form one, neatly assembled, document.

Both of these examples would benefit from WordPerfect's master and subdocument feature. In fact, any document which requires collaborating with other users, or that can be formatted logically into sections, can use the master document feature effectively.

A *master document* is a standard WordPerfect document that creates links to other files, called the subdocuments. *Subdocuments* are complete files that are handled as you would any other WordPerfect file. You can edit them, print them, include reference marks in them, and so on. You can include cross-references from one subdocument to another subdocument.

The master document usually contains all of the definition marks for references, such as the definition for the table of contents and the index. The subdocuments can then contain references such as index marks or even cross-references to other subdocuments. When you generate the master document, it then updates all of the subdocuments.

Styles in the master document override any styles in the subdocuments, including the initial styles of the subdocuments. You can, and should, however, include in the subdocument any specific formatting such as a header or footer.

Before adding a new header or footer code in the subdocument, be sure to precede the instruction with a Discontinue code. This will prevent the header or footer from a previous subdocument from continuing on through the next subdocument in sequence when the master document is expanded.

To gather all of the subdocuments together, you open or *expand* the master document. This adds all of the subdocuments to the master document. When you are finished using the expanded master document, you can then close or *condense*

CHAPTER 10 • MAINTAINING YOUR REPORT'S ORGANIZATION 297

the subdocuments, optionally saving any changes to the subdocuments as they are removed from the master.

Creating a Master Document

A master document is exactly the same as any other document except that it contains subdocument codes. A master document can contain text, it can contain definition marks, formatting, or simply the links to the subdocuments.

> ### Hands On: Creating a Master Document and Subdocuments

To prepare an example for creating a sample master document and subdocuments, all text from the existing `reference.wpd` document will be moved to a new file, leaving the definition codes for the table of contents, list, table of authorities, and an Index for use in the master document. The text will be saved to a new file and two additional subdocuments will be created.

First, create the two new subdocuments. The first document should resemble Figure 10-19; the second document should resemble Figure 10-20. With the documents created, mark the title line in each subdocument as a Level 1 table of contents entry. Name the first subdocument **FinStmts.wpd**; name the second document **Resumes.wpd**. Close both documents.

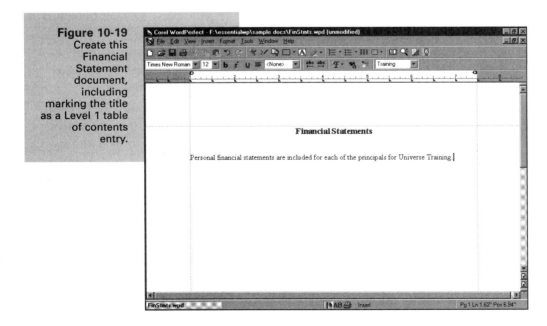

Figure 10-19 Create this Financial Statement document, including marking the title as a Level 1 table of contents entry.

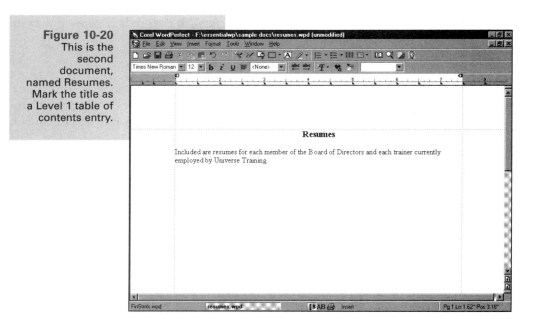

Figure 10-20
This is the second document, named Resumes. Mark the title as a Level 1 table of contents entry.

Now, move just the text and its reference markings from the business plan document created throughout this chapter to a new document window:

1. Open the document `reference.wpd` if it's not already open.
2. Position the document on the first page of text, starting with the first line, `I. Statement of Purpose`. Double-check in Reveal Codes to be sure the insertion point is prior to the `[Outline]` code.
3. Select the remainder of the document by pressing Ctrl+Shift+End. Now press Shift+↑, then Shift+← until the Index page is no longer selected and you can see the selected last line of the document text.
4. Press Ctrl+X, or click the Cut button, to cut the selected text. Click the New Blank Document button on the toolbar to open a new document window, then press Ctrl+V, or click the Paste button, to paste the text to the new document.
5. Save the new document, naming it **bodydoc.wpd**.
6. Return to the `reference.wpd` document window by choosing Window, then selecting the appropriate document number. This document still contains all of the definition marks for each of the references. You should

Chapter 10 • Maintaining Your Report's Organization 299

be returned to the same location you were before cutting the text of the document, a blank page just before the Index definition. Add a page break if necessary so that you are on a blank page.

7. The remaining shell of the `reference.wpd` document will be used as a master document. Save the file to record your changes.

Hands On: Creating a Master Document

Remember that it's not necessary to create a master document using an existing file. You can create a new document which just contains subdocument codes—a simple way of assembling forms together. A master document can be *any* document that contains subdocument codes. For this example, however, it was easier to just move the existing text out of a fully referenced and defined document rather than starting completely over. Now use these steps to add subdocument references to the `reference.wpd` document, thus creating it as a master document:

1. If not already in the correct location, place the insertion point on a blank page following the table of contents, list, and table of authorities pages.
2. Choose File, Document, Subdocument. The Include Subdocument file management dialog box will open.
3. Select the first subdocument, `bodydoc.wpd`, then click Include. The dialog box will close. The [Subdoc] code is added to the document, visible in Reveal Codes, and a subdocument icon appears in the left margin. Click the icon to read the comment naming the subdocument (see Figure 10-21).

Subdocuments appear as icons when the view mode is either is either Page or Two Pages. In Draft mode, subdocuments appear as comments.

4. Insert a hard page break after the first subdocument code, then repeat steps 1 through 3, adding `FinStmts.wpd` and `Resumes.wpd` each as a subdocument. Be sure to add a hard page break between the documents. Figure 10-22 displays the appearance of the master document when viewed in Draft mode.
5. Save the `reference.wpd` document.

300 Part III • Reports and Presentations

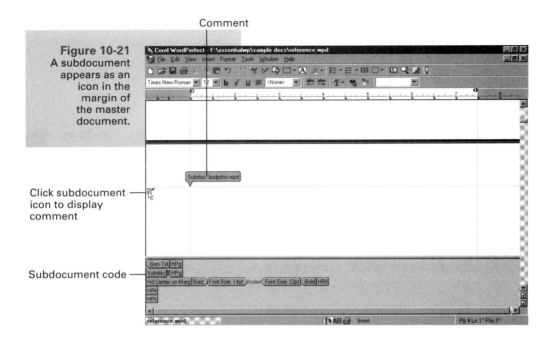

Figure 10-21 A subdocument appears as an icon in the margin of the master document.

Comment

Click subdocument icon to display comment

Subdocument code

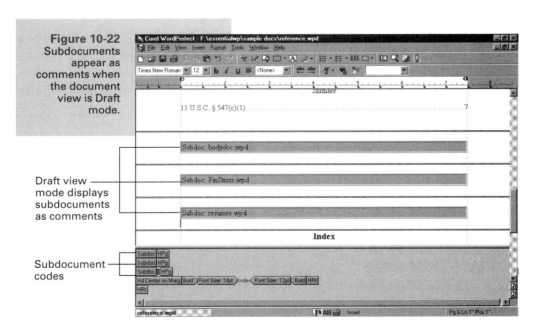

Figure 10-22 Subdocuments appear as comments when the document view is Draft mode.

Draft view mode displays subdocuments as comments

Subdocument codes

Generating References from a Master Document

Reference definition codes which exist in a master document are generated from reference marks which may exist in the master document and in all subdocuments. A table of contents definition code in the master document, for example, will gather items from all table of content marks which are found in the master document and in each subdocument. You can generate references even if the master document is condensed.

Hands On: Generating References from a Condensed Master Document

Generating references through a master document is almost identical to generating references in a single document. Use these steps:

1. Choose Tools, Reference, Generate. The Generate dialog box will open.
2. To save any cross-references which might exist in the subdocuments, check the Save Subdocuments check box.
3. If you know that any of your subdocuments, or the master document, contains hypertext links, check the Build Hypertext Links check box to update the links.
4. Click OK to generate the references. WordPerfect will first expand each of the subdocuments in the master document, generate each reference, and then condense the master document. If the Save Subdocuments check box was marked, all references will be updated and saved in the subdocuments. The master document now contains all generated reference pages.

Rolling the Whole Report Back Together Again

Expanding a master document adds the selected subdocuments to the master document. This is especially useful where you want to check the formatting for each of the subdocuments. It can be tricky to assure exact formatting, especially if several different people created subdocuments. At the very least, you should expand the master document, make any necessary changes, then condense the master document again, saving the changes to the subdocument.

Remember that you can distribute styles to each person who will create documents for your report. Styles will make formatting consistent in each subdocument.

PART III • REPORTS AND PRESENTATIONS

Not all subdocuments must be expanded at the same time. You can select each subdocument, expand the master and edit the resulting master document. When your edits are complete, you then contract only those subdocuments you are finished with, leaving the remaining subdocuments open for further editing.

Hands On: Expanding and Contracting the Master Document

Use these steps to expand the master document:

1. Open the master document, `reference.wpd`.
2. Choose File, Document, Expand Master. The Expand Master Document dialog box opens, as displayed in Figure 10-23. The checkmarks in front of the subdocument names indicate that they will be expanded.

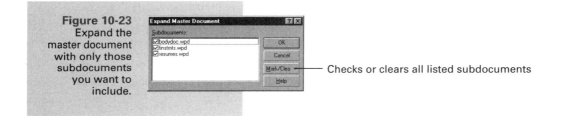

Figure 10-23 Expand the master document with only those subdocuments you want to include.

Checks or clears all listed subdocuments

3. With all subdocuments checked, click OK to expand the master document. After a brief pause you will be returned to the document window. [Subdoc Begin] and [Subdoc End] codes appear in Reveal Codes for each expanded subdocument. In Draft View mode, the starting and ending positions for the subdocuments appear as comments. In Page or Two Page View mode, the positions appear as icons in the left margin (see Figure 10-24).

Be sure not to delete the starting or ending subdocument code. If you do, you won't be able to condense the master document.

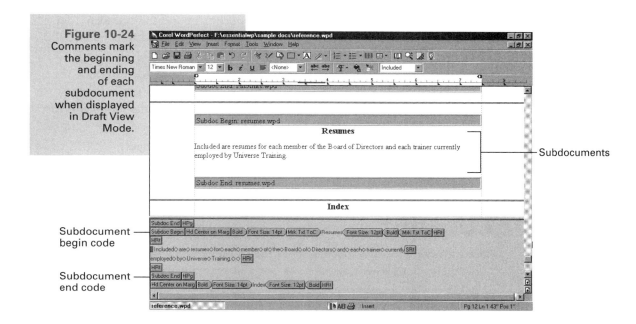

Figure 10-24 Comments mark the beginning and ending of each subdocument when displayed in Draft View Mode.

Subdocument begin code

Subdocument end code

4. Scroll through the document, reviewing the placement and formatting for each subdocument.

   When you've completed your document edits, condense the master document. Condensing removes the subdocument from the master document. It's not necessary to save changes to condense it, but if you have made edits of any kind between a subdocument start or subdocument end code you'll want to be sure to save your changes.

5. Choose File, Document, Condense Master Document. The Condense/Save Subdocuments dialog box will open, as shown in Figure 10-25.

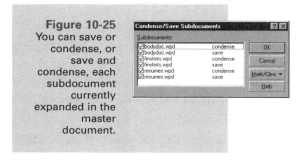

Figure 10-25 You can save or condense, or save and condense, each subdocument currently expanded in the master document.

6. To save the changes made to each subdocument and fully condense the master document, be sure each subdocument is checked to condense and save.
7. Click OK to condense the master document and save edits to the subdocuments. After a brief pause you will be returned to the master document. Scan through the document to notice that the subdocuments have been removed from the master document.
8. Close the `reference.wpd` document, saving your changes.

Connecting Other Items to a Document

Sometimes it's just not practical to include all other documents or items as a subdocument in a master document. A business plan typically includes voluminous financial data created in a spreadsheet program such as Quattro Pro or Excel. You can easily insert or *embed,* a spreadsheet from those programs in your WordPerfect document, but what if the data is still being manipulated? You'd certainly want your business plan to contain the most recent, up-to-date, numbers! Linking the spreadsheet to WordPerfect makes far more sense using *Object Linking and Embedding* (OLE).

> CHAPTER 13 TELLS YOU MORE ABOUT HYPERTEXT LINKS AND WEB SITES.

Further, in a very lengthy business plan, you might want the reader to be able to quickly move to other, related, portions of the same document such as the CEO's resume, or even to another document such as a personal letter from the CEO to all stockholders. By including Hypertext Links in your business plan, the reader can quickly jump to the linked location.

With the importance of the Internet and now an intranet in most businesses, you can also include a direct link to a Web site by including a Web address in your WordPerfect document. WordPerfect refers to this feature as *QuickLinks*.

Linking Objects Using OLE

The term *object* is used in this chapter to refer to other items such as text, a graphic, a chart, or any other type of information that is usually created and edited in a program other than WordPerfect. An object can either be *linked* or *embedded* using OLE technology. A few important terms need to be defined here so that you'll understand what happens when you use OLE.

A copy of an *embedded object* is actually added to the document. If you double-click the embedded object, the program used to create the object usually launches from inside WordPerfect, so that you can edit the object. This is called *in-place editing*. But the object itself still stays within WordPerfect. For example, suppose you create a spreadsheet in Quattro Pro, then embed it in WordPerfect. A *copy* of the spreadsheet appears in your WordPerfect document. If you double-click the spreadsheet in WordPerfect, a small Quattro Pro editing window appears in the WordPerfect document. You can make changes to the spreadsheet and then close the editing window. But the changes you made only appear in the WordPerfect document copy. The original Quattro Pro spreadsheet remains unchanged.

A *linked object* is visible from within WordPerfect, but the file itself continues to be maintained from the program used to create the object, the *source application*, or *OLE server*. For example, suppose you create a graphic in Corel Draw, then link the graphic file to WordPerfect. The image appears in WordPerfect. As you print the WordPerfect file, the graphic prints and appears to be part of the document. However, suppose you now edit the graphic in Corel Draw. When you update the link in the WordPerfect document the graphic appears in its edited form.

The Corel WordPerfect Suite 8 uses OLE technology to connect graphics in WordPerfect to either Presentations or WordPerfect Draw, if Presentations was not installed. Choosing to edit a WordPerfect graphic in a document opens either a Presentations or WordPerfect Draw editing window in WordPerfect. WordPerfect Draw and TextArt are two examples of small programs, called *applets,* which can only be launched from within another application.

Hands On: Adding an Object to the Business Plan

Within WordPerfect, a graphic is probably the most common object to use OLE technology. Graphics will be discussed in depth in Chapter 12, but follow these steps to include a graphic as an OLE object to a file:

1. Open the document `resumes.wpd` created as a subdocument earlier in this chapter. Then go to the end of the document by pressing Ctrl+End.
2. Choose Insert, Object. The Insert Object dialog box will open as displayed in Figure 10-26. From the Insert Object dialog box you can create a new OLE object using one of the OLE server applications listed in the Object Type list box. You can alternately select an existing file, including the file contents as an OLE object in your document.
3. Click Create from File. The Insert Object dialog box changes to display a file control.

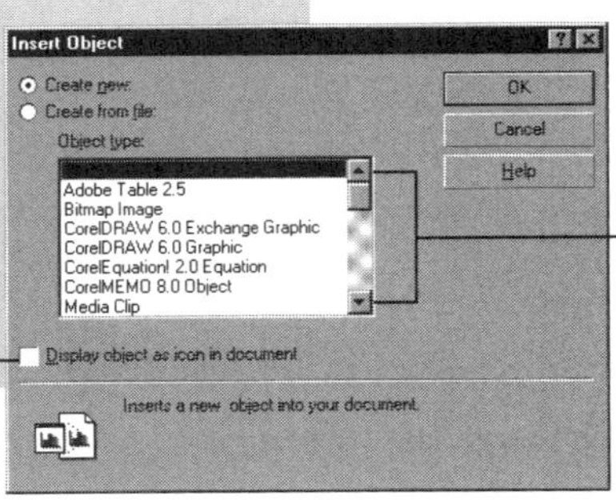

PART III • REPORTS AND PRESENTATIONS

Figure 10-26
You can create a new object or select an existing file to be added to your document as an object.

This list is created from registered OLE Server applications

Displays the newly created object as an icon in your document

4. Click the Folder icon. The Insert as Object dialog box opens to the ClipArt folder.
5. Select the filename `Rose2.wpg`, then click <u>I</u>nsert. You'll be returned to the Insert Object dialog box.
6. Check the <u>L</u>ink check box to insert a picture of the graphic into your document. Notice as you check or uncheck the <u>L</u>ink check box that a brief description of the action appears at the bottom of the dialog box.

• •

Linking an object usually results in a smaller document.

• •

Once you've included linked objects in your document, be sure not to move the object's location. If you do, WordPerfect will no longer be able to locate the object and you'll need to insert the object again.

7. Click OK. After a brief pause, the object will be inserted into your document. Small black squares, called *handles*, appear around the object indicating that it's currently selected.
8. To prove OLE, double-click the graphic. After a brief pause, either Presentations 8 or WordPerfect Draw will open in a window on the WordPerfect document window. See Figure 10-27.

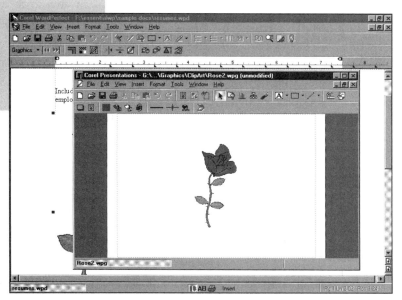

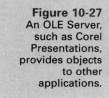

Figure 10-27 An OLE Server, such as Corel Presentations, provides objects to other applications.

9. Click the Application Close button (the x button in the upper right-corner of the title bar). The OLE Server will close and you will be returned to the document.
10. Click anywhere outside of the graphic to deselect it. Then save your file.

Hypertext Links to Other Documents

A hypertext link *jumps* the reader to another location in either the current document or another document. They're commonly found in Web documents, but certainly aren't limited only to them. Suppose, for example, that you were creating a list of personnel policies. You might have sections for bonuses, sick leave, vacations, stock options, and so on. Providing hypertext links to each section would allow the reader to quickly jump to the section they wanted to review without having to read through the entire file to find the correct text. In fact, in a very long document, it's helpful to include a hypertext link at the end of the file that jumps the reader back up to the top of the document. Or include a link at the end of each section which jumps to a menu of other hypertext links from where the reader can make a jump to the next location.

In a similar example, each of the sections might be separate files. Including hypertext links would enable the reader to jump to the required document. The document would automatically open and place the reader at the linked location. You should also create a link in the second document so the reader can return to the first document.

A hypertext link can also link to a Web site. See a later section in this chapter, "QuickLinks to the World Wide Web," for more information.

Creating Hypertext Links to Other Documents

With the `resumes.wpd` document still open, adding a link to a personal resume file for the CEO of Universe Training is appropriate. First, however, a resume document for the CEO must be created. Therefore, open a new document window and create a simple resume similar to the one displayed in Figure 10-28. Save and close the file using a filename similar to **wilsonresume.wpd**.

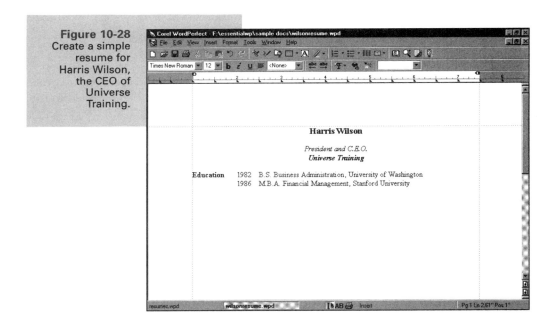

Figure 10-28 Create a simple resume for Harris Wilson, the CEO of Universe Training.

Hands On: Adding a Hypertext Link to the Business Plan

Add a link to the resume document to the personal resume of Harris Wilson. Use these steps:

CHAPTER 10 • MAINTAINING YOUR REPORT'S ORGANIZATION 309

1. Position the insertion point at the end of resumes.wpd. If you've included the rose graphic from the previous hands-on activity, the end of the document may appear to be to the right side of the graphic.
2. Type the link text: **Resume for Harris Wilson**.
3. Now select the link text and choose Tools, Hyperlink. The Hyperlink Properties dialog box will open as displayed in Figure 10-29.

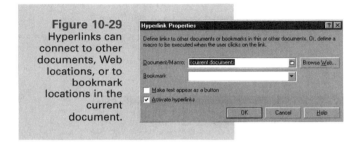

Figure 10-29
Hyperlinks can connect to other documents, Web locations, or to bookmark locations in the current document.

4. Click the Folder icon on the Document/Macro control to open the Select File dialog box.
5. Locate and select the resume document, wilsonresume.wpd. Then click the Select button. The filename will added to the Document/Macro text box.
6. Click OK to create the link. You will be returned to the document and the link text will appear underlined and in blue. A [Hypertext] code can be seen in Reveal Codes.
7. The mouse pointer changes to a pointing hand as you point to the link text. Click the link text to open the resume file. The resumes.wpd file will close (prompting you to save changes if you've not done so already), and the resume for Harris Wilson will open.

• •

When you open a document that contains Hypertext links, you'll be prompted to update the links. Click Yes to perform the update. If you're sure nothing has changed in the linked object, you can choose No to more quickly open the file.

• •

8. Now, include a hypertext link from the wilsonresume.wpd file back to the resumes.wpd file. Type the link text **Back to the Business Plan**. Then select the text and open the hyperlink dialog box again. Select the resumes.wpd file using the Document/Macro folder icon. When the file

PART III • REPORTS AND PRESENTATIONS

selection is complete, click the check box <u>M</u>ake Text Appear as a Button. Then click OK to add the hypertext link to the resume. Figure 10-30 displays the hypertext link in button form.

9. Test the link by clicking the button. Be sure to save the `wilsonresume.wpd` file when prompted.

Although you can include hypertext links in both button and text format, try to be consistent with your selection so that the reader doesn't get confused.

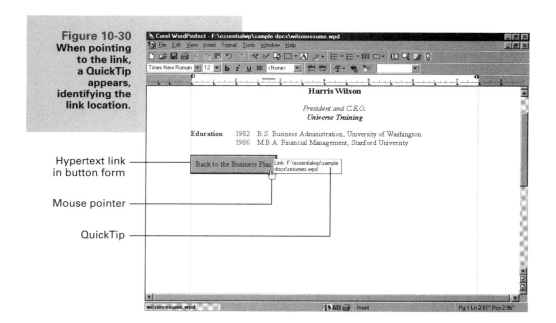

Figure 10-30
When pointing to the link, a QuickTip appears, identifying the link location.

Hypertext link in button form

Mouse pointer

QuickTip

Using Bookmarks for Hypertext Links in the Same Document

WordPerfect's bookmark feature is used to create hypertext links within a single document. A bookmark is a special code that you create and place in a document to store a particular location. To go to a bookmark in a document, you open either the Bookmark or the GoTo dialog box, select the desired bookmark and click <u>G</u>oTo or OK.

Creating a hypertext link to move to a named bookmark in the file is less cumbersome for the reader, however. As with any other hypertext link, the user can now just click the link to move to the bookmark. A linked bookmark is especially useful in forms where the fill-in locations are widespread. Click the link to quickly move you from place to place in the form so that needed data can be entered!

A special type of bookmark called a QuickMark can be automatically inserted in a document each time you save file. This is especially handy when you want to return to the same edit location over and over again each time you open a document. You can set the preference for adding a QuickMark to the document on file save by choosing Tools, Bookmark. The Bookmark dialog box will open. Now check the Set QuickMark on File Save control at the bottom of the dialog box. To automatically place the insertion point at a QuickMark location when you open a document, also check the Go to QuickMark on File Open check box. When your choices are complete, click Close to return to your document.

Hands On: Adding a Bookmark-Based Hypertext Link to a Document

The `bodydoc.wpd` document created earlier in this chapter is of sufficient length to explore hyperlinks using bookmarks. A bookmark must be created in the document before the hypertext link can use the bookmark as a link. Here's how:

1. Open the `bodydoc.wpd` file. Now position the insertion point at the first subheading: A. Vision Statement.

2. Create a bookmark named Vision Statement by choosing Tools, Bookmark. The Bookmark dialog box will open.

3. Click Create to open the Create Bookmark dialog box. The full text of the heading will appear automatically in the Bookmark Name text box (see Figure 10-31). You can change the bookmark name if you want, but Vision Statement is sufficient for this example. The choice Selected Bookmark is not appropriate for hypertext links. It instructs WordPerfect to select the bookmark text when you go to the bookmark from another location in the document.

4. Click OK to close the Create Bookmark dialog box and return to the document. Open Reveal Codes to view the bookmark code.

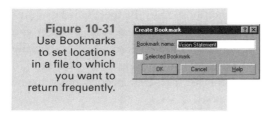

Figure 10-31
Use Bookmarks to set locations in a file to which you want to return frequently.

5. For the purpose of this activity, the hypertext link will be created at the end of the document. Position the insertion point at the end of the document by pressing Ctrl+End.
6. Press Enter twice to open a blank area at the end of the document. Now type the text for the link: **Go to Vision Statement.**
7. Now create the hypertext link. Select the link text, then choose Tools, Hyperlink. The Hyperlink Properties dialog box will open.
8. Click the drop-down control in the Bookmark control, then select Vision Statement.
9. Check Make Text Appear as a Button, if desired, then click OK to add the Hypertext Link to the document.
10. Save the document, thus preserving the link. Now test the link by clicking it. You should be immediately returned to the Vision Statement section of the document.

QuickLinks to the World Wide Web

FOR INFORMATION ABOUT CREATING WEB DOCUMENTS IN WORDPERFECT, SEE CHAPTER 13.

If your computer system has access to the Internet, or to an intranet, you can include hypertext links, called QuickLinks, in a WordPerfect document.

WordPerfect automatically recognizes Internet phrases that begin with text such as `http://www`, `ftp://ftp`, or e-mail addresses such as `hwilson@utrain.com`. When it encounters such a phrase, it automatically creates a QuickLink in the document to that Web location.

Several QuickLinks are already included in WordPerfect's QuickCorrect, QuickLinks tab (see Figure 10-32). Open the QuickLinks list by choosing Tools, QuickCorrect, then click the QuickLinks tab. You can add your own Web locations to the stored QuickLinks list. To do so, type the word or phrase you want to use as your link in the Link Word text box. Then type the Web location in the Location To Link To text box. Click Insert Entry to add your entry to the list of links. At the bottom of the QuickLinks tab, a checkmark appears beside Format

CHAPTER 10 • MAINTAINING YOUR REPORT'S ORGANIZATION **313**

Words as Hyperlinks When You Type Them. Removing this checkmark causes WordPerfect to ignore any of the link words in the document, treating them as regular text rather than as a hyperlink.

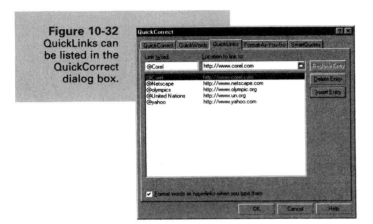

Figure 10-32 QuickLinks can be listed in the QuickCorrect dialog box.

Hands On: Adding a QuickLink to your Document

To include a Web QuickLink in your document, use these steps:

1. Open a new document window.
2. To create an automatic QuickLink, type:
   http://www.corel.com/products/wordperfect
   (This is the location for WordPerfect information at the Corel Web site.) Press [Enter]. WordPerfect recognizes the address as a Web address and formats it as a QuickLink.
3. Now, insert a QuickLink from QuickCorrect by typing **@netscape**. WordPerfect recognizes the entry and creates a QuickLink code for **http://www.netscape.com**.

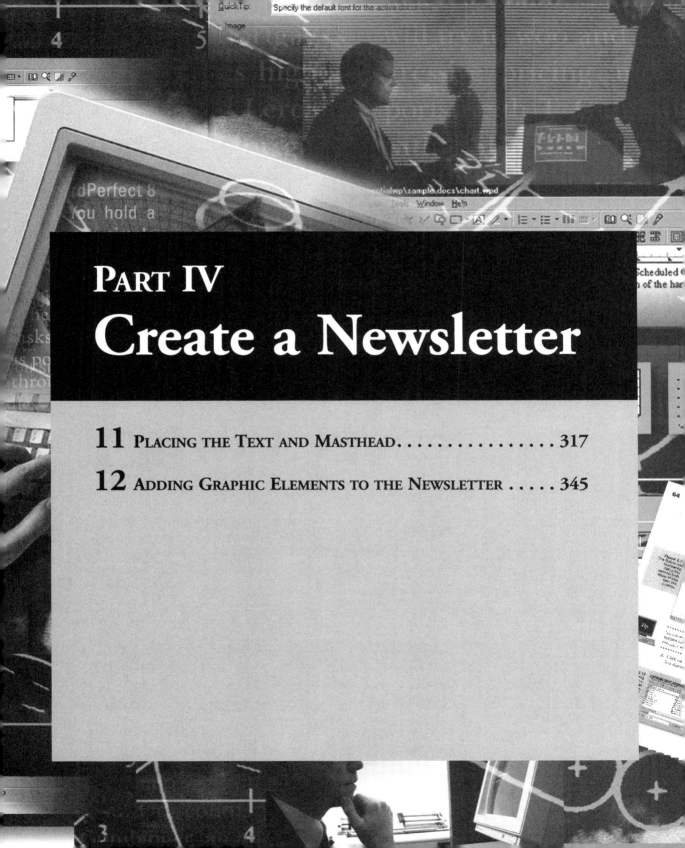

Part IV
Create a Newsletter

11 Placing the Text and Masthead.................317

12 Adding Graphic Elements to the Newsletter.....345

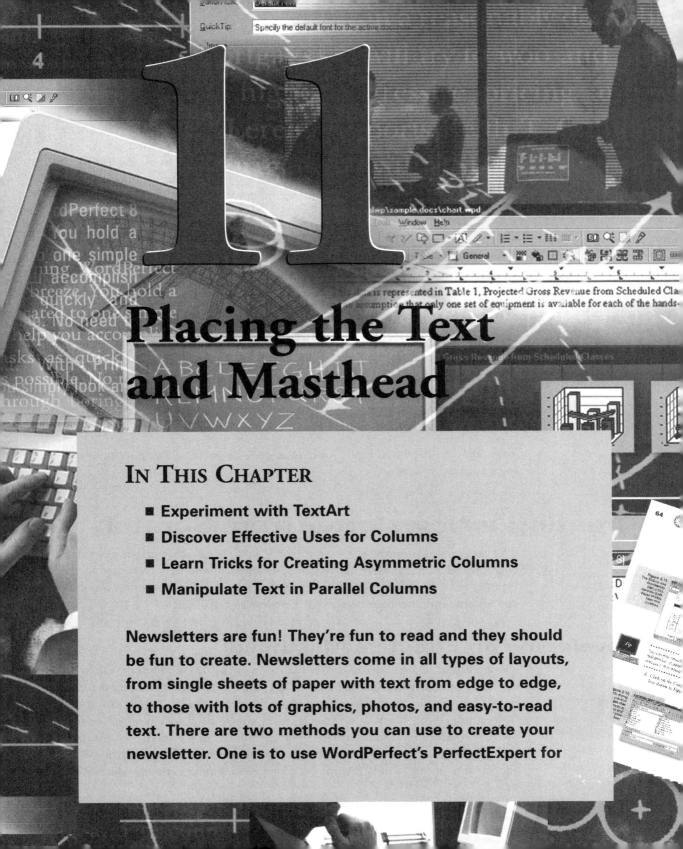

11

Placing the Text and Masthead

IN THIS CHAPTER

- Experiment with TextArt
- Discover Effective Uses for Columns
- Learn Tricks for Creating Asymmetric Columns
- Manipulate Text in Parallel Columns

Newsletters are fun! They're fun to read and they should be fun to create. Newsletters come in all types of layouts, from single sheets of paper with text from edge to edge, to those with lots of graphics, photos, and easy-to-read text. There are two methods you can use to create your newsletter. One is to use WordPerfect's PerfectExpert for newsletters. The other is to create the newsletter completely from scratch. You experimented with the PerfectExpert in Chapter 3 and again in Chapter 4. Creating a newsletter using the PerfectExpert is every bit as simple and easy to use. You just need to start by selecting the Newsletter project from the list which appears when you choose File, New. Then follow the familiar prompts, selecting choices from the drop-down lists and various controls presented by the Newsletter PerfectExpert.

This chapter, therefore, will introduce you to techniques you can use when creating a newsletter from scratch. This will allow you to further enhance a newsletter you create using the Newsletter PerfectExpert, or to create a newsletter using your own ideas.

A newsletter can be as unique as you are. There are no hard and fast rules about how a newsletter should look. You can use a large title (usually called the *masthead*) across the top of the page, or run it down the side. You can use columns to organize your text, and graphics or charts to illustrate important concepts. You can include a table of contents on the first page, page numbers, or volume numbers. This chapter will suggest some accepted conventions, but you should rely on your own good taste and experience when creating any document, including a newsletter.

You'll also be introduced to one technique you can use for creating scripts—typing in parallel columns.

Creating a Newsletter from Scratch

This section will introduce you to methods you can use to create a newsletter which looks different than the types of newsletters you can create using the Newsletter PerfectExpert. You'll learn how to create columns of various numbers and widths, and how to dress up your newsletter's masthead.

Developing an Effective Masthead

The masthead of a newsletter carries the name of the newsletter itself. Often it's the name of your company, although many times a newsletter has become such an important ritual that it has its own identity and personality. A law firm might, for example, create a newsletter that it distributes to its clients as an advertising piece. It could contain short articles about each of the new associates to the firm, perhaps discuss a new legal decision that could have an effect on many of its clients, and so on. In this example, the masthead should certainly identify the

Chapter 11 • Placing the Text and Masthead

name of the firm, but should also give the reader a reason to continue reading the newsletter. This is done by creating an effective, eye-pleasing masthead.

You probably receive all kinds of newspapers and newsletters every day. (If you're like me, you receive more than just a few!) Review a few of them, paying specific attention to the appearance of the masthead. Is it eye-catching? Does it adequately display the reason and purpose for the newsletter? I'm a firm believer that imitation is the best form of flattery—and the best source for learning new techniques. Find a few of the mastheads you like, then use them as guidelines for your own newsletter.

Included in the masthead are often additional pieces of information, such as the date for the publication, and perhaps a volume or issue number. Sometimes there's a subheading, which clarifies the purpose for the newsletter.

Using Tables and Text to Create a Masthead

You learned about using tables for financial data presentation in Chapter 9. Tables can also be used effectively to control placement of information. Figure 11-1 displays a before and after masthead using table formatting.

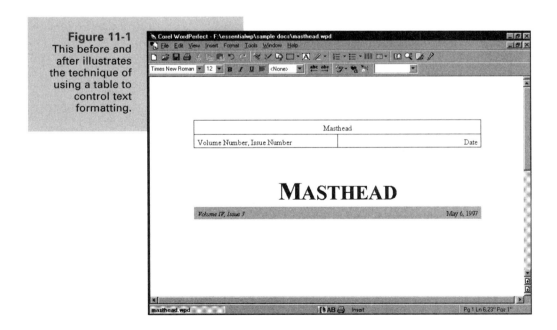

Figure 11-1
This before and after illustrates the technique of using a table to control text formatting.

PART IV • CREATE A NEWSLETTER

> FOR ADDITIONAL HELP ON CREATING TABLES AND TABLE FORMATTING, SEE CHAPTER 9.

Hands On: Creating a Masthead Using a Table for Layout

A simple masthead such as the one displayed in Figure 11-1 can be easily created using WordPerfect's table feature. Here's how:

1. On a blank document, use the Table button to create a two-row, two-column table.
2. Now join both cells in the first row. Format the joined cell to use center row alignment.
3. Press F9 (or choose Format, Font) to open the Font dialog box. Select an appropriate font face from the Font Face drop-down list. Figure 11-1 used the traditional Times New Roman, although you can use any font you like. Then select a Font Size for your text (I used 40 points), check Bold, Outline, and Small Caps from the Appearance group, then click OK to return to the document. Now type the text **Masthead**.
4. In cell A2, select an appropriate font face and size (Times New Roman, 10 point, italic, was used in the sample), then type the Volume Number and Issue Number: **Volume IV, Issue 3**.
5. Format cell B2 as right-aligned, then type the date. All of the text for the masthead is now in place.
6. Select the entire table. Then, using Borders/Fill, set all inside and outside lines to `None`.
7. Finally, select row 2 and, again using Borders/Fill, set the fill level to 20%.
8. Click outside the table and press Enter two or three times to add some space between the masthead and the first text.

Using TextArt to Create an Effective Masthead

TextArt allows you to squish, squeeze, bend, and stretch text into predefined shapes. You can rotate text in any direction, and add textures, colors, and patterns, creating both two-dimensional (2D) and three-dimensional (3D) images. TextArt enables you to create an effective, one-of-a-kind masthead for your newsletter.

Although TextArt itself is included in a Typical WordPerfect 8 installation, it only includes the 2D options. To follow along with all of the Hands On activities in this chapter, you'll need to add the Advanced 3D options using the Corel WordPerfect Suite 8 Setup application.

Note

TextArt creates a graphic image from text. The image is stored in a WordPerfect graphic box. This section will discuss the methods used to work with TextArt. You can learn more about manipulating graphic boxes in Chapter 12.

Hands On: Creating a Masthead with TextArt

Like most WordPerfect features, TextArt is powerful, but easy to use. Here's how:

1. Open a new document, then type the text you want to use for your masthead. Keep the text short, no more than two or three words. You can type the text on a single line, or you can stack the text, one word on a line. The text **The Busy Painter** will be used throughout this activity.

2. Now select the text, then choose Insert, Graphics, TextArt. After a brief pause, the TextArt application starts. If you've previously used TextArt, the settings you worked with the last time are used to display your masthead text. Figure 11-2 shows the masthead text as it might appear on your system.

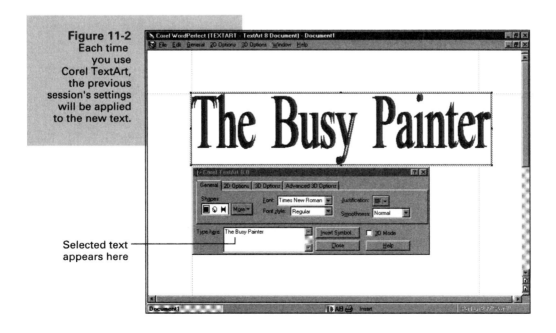

Figure 11-2 Each time you use Corel TextArt, the previous session's settings will be applied to the new text.

Selected text appears here

Note

You can use any number of TextArt's controls to change the appearance of your text. The next few steps introduce you to a few of them, but you should take some time to explore the various controls and options so that you'll become familiar with them.

The next few steps assume that you are working in 2D (height and width) Mode; be sure the 3D Mode (height, width, and depth) check box is not checked for now.

3. To change the shape of your text, select one of the last three shapes used from the Shapes display box, or click More to open the shape palette (see Figure 11-3). Each time you select a shape, the shape palette closes and the text is rendered in the shape you selected.

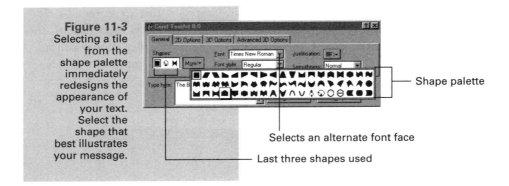

Figure 11-3 Selecting a tile from the shape palette immediately redesigns the appearance of your text. Select the shape that best illustrates your message.

4. Before deciding on a shape, try modifying the shape by changing the font face used for your masthead. To do so, open the Font drop-down list, then select a font you'd like to try. Some font faces are also available in more than one font style, such as italic or bold. Use these two controls together to change the appearance of your masthead.

5. Some font faces only display in uppercase letters. If that's the case with your font, click in the Type Here text box, changing your original text to either all uppercase letters or all lowercase letters. If your masthead is more than one word, also try stacking the text. Each time you make a change to the text, the graphic box updates, displaying the effect on your text (see Figure 11-4).

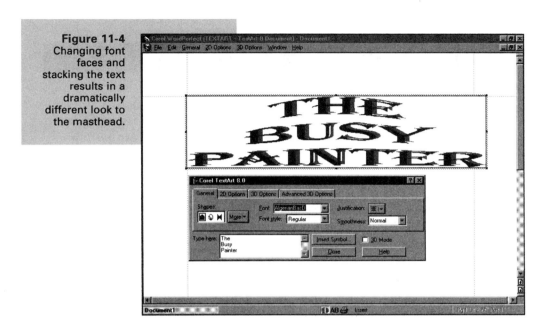

Figure 11-4 Changing font faces and stacking the text results in a dramatically different look to the masthead.

6. Click the 2D Options tab to display additional controls (see Figure 11-5). Table 11-1 identifies these controls for you.

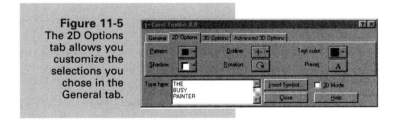

Figure 11-5 The 2D Options tab allows you customize the selections you chose in the General tab.

7. For practice, select one of the cross-hatched patterns from the Pattern control, changing the Pattern color to a yellow. Add a thin black outline to the text. Finally, test one of the Preset 2D shapes. Your masthead is redrawn using all of the settings for the shape you've selected. Don't like it? You can view and modify each individual setting for the preset shapes using the General and 2D Controls.

The two 3D tabs allow you to add depth to your masthead. You're able to set the direction and color of two light sources, add a *bevel* (edge shapes), and rotate the text in three dimensions.

PART IV • CREATE A NEWSLETTER

Table 11-1 2D Controls for TextArt

Control	Affects TextArt in this fashion
Pattern	Opens a palette of designs which can be added to the face of the text, including colors for the text and the pattern. Click the None tile to set the pattern to a solid color. Click No Fill to make the text transparent.
Shadow	A shadow appears behind the text by default. Use the shadow palette to change the color, position, and width of the shadow. Click the center-most tile on the palette to hide the shadow.
Outline	Think of the outline as a line that goes around the perimeter of each letter, similar to what you might do with a pencil if you were to trace the letters. The outline palette is used to set both the color and width for the outline.
Rotation	When clicked once, rotation handles are added to the text within the graphic box. Point to one of the handles with the mouse, then drag in the direction you want the text to turn. As you drag, an outline appears illustrating the shape your text will assume as it rotates. If you double-click the rotation control, a dialog box opens allowing you to specific exact rotation settings.
Text Color	The text color palette can be found in several locations. Select the color you want to apply to your text by clicking any of the color tiles.
Preset	Select any of the five present shapes to apply the settings to your text.

Tip

The more attributes and manipulation you add to your text, the busier it becomes. Keep your font face, patterns, and fill simple to effectively use rotation.

REFER TO CHAPTER 12 FOR MORE DETAILS ON MANIPULATING GRAPHICS.

8. On any of the TextArt tabs, check the 3D Mode control to enable the 3D controls. Your TextArt image is immediately updated, displaying the 3D settings used in your previous TextArt session, or the default TextArt settings.

9. Click the 3D Options tab to view and experiment with the 3D controls (see Figure 11-6). Table 11-2 briefly explains these controls.

10. When your image looks just right, click the Close button or click anywhere outside the TextArt box to add the image to your document. TextArt closes and your image appears in your document. Graphic handles appear around the image, indicating that the image is selected.

Figure 11-6
3D Options will start out based on the shape settings you selected using the General and 2D Options tabs.

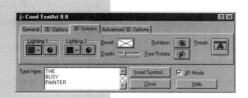

Table 11-2 3D Controls for TextArt

Control		Affects TextArt in this fashion
Lighting 1 Lighting 2		These two controls are used to select a color and light direction for the main and secondary sources of light. To get a sense of how these controls work, imagine two lamps, each with a different color bulb shining from various locations on your 3D text. The combination of the Lighting 1 and Lighting 2 color palettes affects the final color in the TextArt image. You'll need to experiment to find effective color choice and light source combinations.
Bevel Depth		Bevel adds a shape to the edge of the text, making it appear as though it has a ridge, cove, or cup shape. In combination, Depth sets the pitch of the bevel.
Rotation		Rotation displays a palette of 3D rotation points. Click the tile which represents the spherical rotation image you want to apply to your text. With careful selection of shape, shading, lighting, and rotation, your masthead can appear to come forward or recede.
Free Rotate		Free Rotation is fun! A rotation circle, illustrating a 3D rotation *ball*, will be added to your TextArt image. Drag the mouse through the image to rotate the image through the rotation ball. When finished, click the Free Rotate control again to stop.
Preset		3D presets allow you to apply a complete set of TextArt choices. Click any of the tiles on the Preset palette to make your selection. After applying one of the choices, you can edit the selection using other 3D controls.
Advanced 3D Options tab		This tab allows you to add textures to the face and bevel of your image. You can change the size, lighting, and print quality for your TextArt image.

With the TextArt image added to your document, you can now treat it as you would any other graphic box. It can be sized, dragged around the page, have wrap options set, and so on.

PART IV • CREATE A NEWSLETTER

Hands On: Sizing and Placing the Masthead

You may find that when the masthead was drawn onto the page by TextArt it was inappropriately sized. Perhaps it extends into the margins, or perhaps it's just too large. Use these steps to size and place the masthead so that it looks just right:

1. Position the mouse pointer over any of the corner handles. The pointer changes to a slanted, double-headed arrow. Click and drag to size the masthead proportionally, either larger or smaller, until it fits nicely into the space you want to use for the masthead. Try making the masthead smaller, so that it's no larger than about one-half the width of the page.

2. While the image is selected, you can also drag the masthead to a new location on the page. To do so, point to a center position of the image (the mouse pointer appears as a four-sided arrow). Then drag the image to the desired location, in this case roughly centered between the margins. When complete, click outside the image to deselect it.

3. Complete your masthead by adding any subheadings you might require, such as the volume and date. You can use a table to format your text, or just use standard text formatting, such as flush right, to position the text at the desired location. Be sure to save your masthead so that you can use it in your newsletter. Figure 11-7 displays two mastheads, both displaying layouts using TextArt and tables in combination.

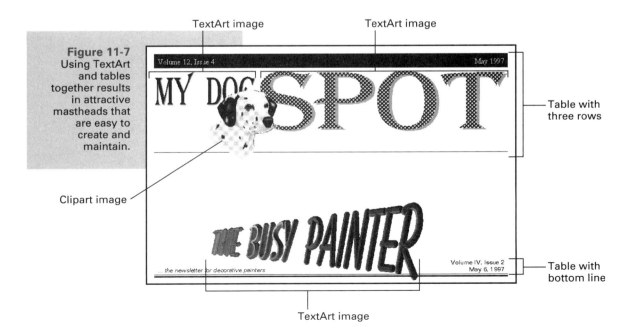

Figure 11-7 Using TextArt and tables together results in attractive mastheads that are easy to create and maintain.

CHAPTER 11 • PLACING THE TEXT AND MASTHEAD   **327**

To force your TextArt image to appear over the top of a table, as shown in both mastheads in Figure 11-7, select the TextArt image to see the image handles, then right-click while pointing to the image. Choose W_r_ap from the QuickMenu, then select In _F_ront of Text to force the image to lay over the top of the table.

Using Columns to Control Text Flow

WordPerfect 8 offers four column types that can be used in a newsletter; each has its own strengths and ideal purposes.

- *Newspaper columns*, probably the most commonly used column type, flow text down each column until the bottom margin is reached. Then the text wraps to the top of the next column.
- *Balanced newspaper columns* work in a similar fashion with one exception. Text is evenly spaced between the columns so that each column remains approximately the same length. Figure 11-8 displays an example of both newspaper and balanced newspaper columns.

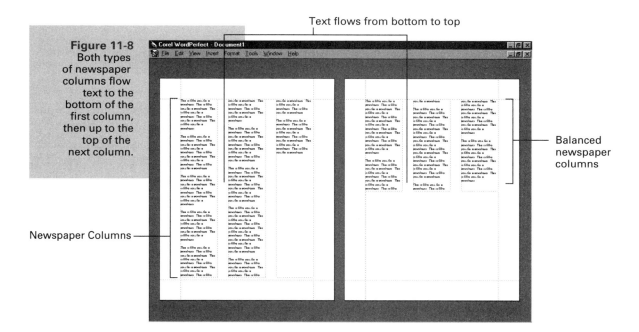

Figure 11-8 Both types of newspaper columns flow text to the bottom of the first column, then up to the top of the next column.

Newspaper Columns

Text flows from bottom to top

Balanced newspaper columns

PART IV • CREATE A NEWSLETTER

- *Parallel columns* look very similar to tables, organizing columnar text into rows or *sets* across the page as shown in Figure 11-9. Text in any of the parallel columns can span a page break. When the last column is complete, a new set begins.

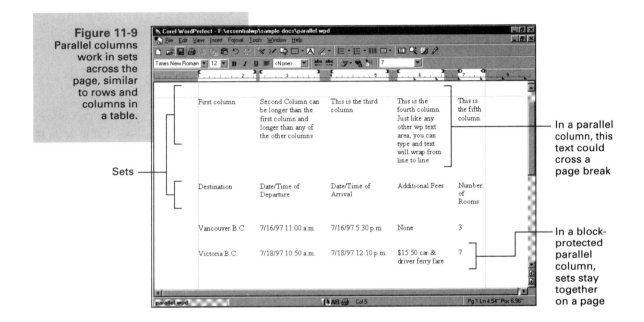

Figure 11-9
Parallel columns work in sets across the page, similar to rows and columns in a table.

- *Parallel with block protect columns* are similar to parallel columns with one exception: they cannot cross a page break. Each column set is *block protected* and must stay together on a page. If the text in any of the columns extends to a new page, the entire set moves to the new page. The set is *protected* and therefore stays together as a unit. Figure 11-9 displays an example of parallel columns.

Parallel and parallel with block protected columns are not necessarily appropriate for use in managing text flow in a newsletter, but they are appropriate for presenting data in a tabular format. They're discussed in more depth later in this chapter to present you with a full understanding of how columns work and so that you feel comfortable with column names and terminology. In almost every instance, however, tables can present the same data with far less effort, especially during an editing process.

WordPerfect enables you to create up to 24 columns (too many for pages $8^1/_2$" wide!). By default, each column will be exactly the same width with an empty space between the columns (referred to as the *gutter space*) of one-half inch. Of

> **CHAPTER 4 EXPLAINS SELECTING OR DEFINING OTHER PAPER SIZES.**

course, you probably wouldn't want to create more than about three columns for most newsletters. In fact, one rule of thumb is that, for ease of reading, most text lines should be no longer than about 20 words or so, at about a maximum of three inches. That matches almost exactly with the line length you'll achieve using either two or three columns on a page.

Creating Columns

Newspaper columns are the easiest column type to create. You can type your text first; in fact it's easiest to do so. Then turn on columns. The text will instantly be reformatted to the column definition you've selected.

Hands On: Creating an Article for Your Newsletter in Columnar Format

Creating and using columns for organizing articles in your newsletter is a simple task. Use these steps:

1. Click in the document after the masthead where you want the text of the first article to begin. You should begin at the left margin.

2. Decide on the font face you want to use for your article headings, then type and format **A New Oil Paint Standard?** as the title for the first article. Use a font size of about 24 points so that the title is large enough to establish its importance. Press (Enter) to complete the line.

Tip

It's an accepted practice to use the same font face for all titles in a newsletter. Most designers will encourage you to use a sans serif font, although it's not a hard and fast rule. You do, however, want to keep your text and heading fonts simple. It's generally best to use no more than one serif font face and one sans serif font face if at all possible. You can add bold or italic attributes and change the font size to add a little variety to the page where necessary.

3. Now type the text for the article, beginning with:

   The release of the new non-toxic vegetable oil paints are taking the oil painting industry to a higher level of safety.

   Be sure to include a space or two after the end of the sentence. Then copy and paste the text repeatedly until you've filled about two-thirds of the page or more. Include a few paragraph breaks so that the text more closely resembles an actual article.

4. Click back in the text at the very beginning of the title for the article, so that you are in the correct position to create the columns.

5. Now click the Columns button on the toolbar (see Figure 11-10) and select `3 Columns`. When you release the mouse button, the text flows into three evenly-spaced newspaper columns.

6. Don't like three columns? Change the number of columns to two by again clicking the Columns button and selecting `2 Columns`. The text instantly changes shape again.

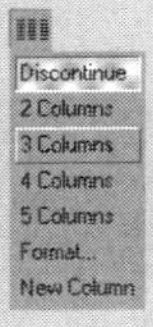

Figure 11-10
The Columns button quickly defines newspaper columns.

Full Justified or Left Justified

On a personal level, I prefer left justified text in columns. Left justification adds more white space to the document, making it more pleasing and restful to the eye.

Full justification spreads the text from column edge to column edge, adding space between the words so that they align evenly. While beautiful to look at, some designers feel that the additional space between the words makes the text hard for the eye to follow as you read. Full justified text is, therefore, often used for publications where you might not want to encourage the reader to actually *read* the text, such as in a complicated contract.

I noticed during the last tax season, however, that the tax guidelines I received formatted text in two columns, each about 3 inches in width, with text left justified!

Typing Text in Columns

Typing text in columns really is no different than typing in any other document. Text wraps automatically as you reach the right edge of the column just as it does as you reach the right margin on a full page. In fact, each column has its own left and right margins within the column layout itself. View the ruler bar while in a column to notice the left, paragraph, and right margin markers inside the column markers.

There are two extra keystrokes you can use, however, to quickly move between columns without using the mouse:

Press	To move to
Alt+→	The column immediately to the right
Alt+←	The column immediately to the left

The column to which you want to move must actually exist, however. If you press Alt+→ and nothing happens, check to be sure that you've already included text (even a code or space) in the next column. If nothing exists in the column, you can't go there, just like you can't go to a page in a document that doesn't exist.

You can also move to the top and bottom of columns, or to the first or last column, using the Go To feature. Double-click the page number in the application bar, or press Ctrl+G, to open the Go To dialog box. In the Position list, double-click the position to which you want to move.

You can also force a column to break just where you want, rather than where it normally would based on the column's definition. For example, when creating newspaper columns, the text normally extends to the bottom of the page and then wraps to the top of the next column. You can force the column to break at an earlier position by pressing Ctrl+Enter, or by choosing New Column from the Columns button drop-down list. A hard column break inserts a [HCol] code in Reveal Codes.

Changing the Appearance of Your Columns

You might find that, after viewing the result of using newspaper columns in either two or three columns, your text just doesn't look the way you envisioned. Perhaps you would rather have a larger space between the columns, or perhaps you need to balance the columns so that the text flows evenly between them.

With columns already created, you can easily change the width of the columns, the gutter space, and the number of columns. You can also size the existing

PART IV • CREATE A NEWSLETTER

columns by using your mouse to drag column markers until they look right to you. If you want to change to a new column type, you need to work with the Column Format dialog box.

DRAGGING COLUMN MARKERS OR GUIDELINES TO SIZE COLUMNS

Figure 11-11 displays the three-column layout for the newsletter as it now exists. All guidelines are visible and the ruler bar is also open. Using these two tools will make changing the width of the columns and gutter space much simpler.

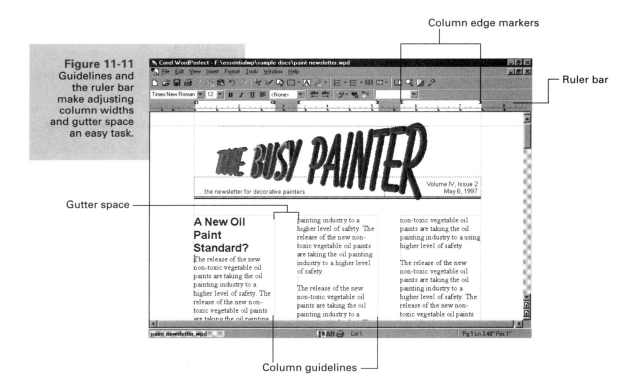

Figure 11-11 Guidelines and the ruler bar make adjusting column widths and gutter space an easy task.

The easiest method to size columns is to drag the column marker in the ruler, drag a guideline marking the edge of a column, or drag the gutter space. Each of these tasks is accomplished the same way.

Hands On: Sizing the Columns and Gutter Widths

To size your columns or change the amount of space between columns, use these steps:

1. Position the mouse pointer over the column marker or guideline.
2. Now click and drag the mouse pointer to the position you want the column edge to assume. As you drag the various markers, the mouse pointer changes appearance depending on the marker type you are using. As you drag a column marker in the ruler, the mouse pointer looks like ▯; when dragging a guideline, it looks like ↔; when dragging the gutter space it looks like ↔. In each instance, a guideline and QuickTip appear to assist you in accurately placing the column.
3. With the column edge in the desired location, release the mouse. The column text is adjusted, flowing into the new column dimensions.

SIZING COLUMNS USING THE COLUMN DIALOG BOX

Changing the widths of columns by dragging the column markers is efficient, but it can also be frustrating. Just when you think you've set everything up the way you want it, make one more change and the columns change widths! WordPerfect carefully controls the width of all columns and gutter spaces so that total width remains within the left and right margins of the paper.

The Columns dialog box allows you to change the type of columns you have defined, or explicitly set the widths for each column. You can use the Columns dialog box as you create your columns, making all settings as the columns are actually created. Or you can edit the current column definition.

Hands On: Locking in Column Settings

Use these steps to change column settings using the Columns dialog box:

1. Position the insertion point anywhere in the current column set. Click the Columns button, then select Format from the resulting drop-down list. (You can alternately choose Format, Columns.) The Columns dialog box opens, as displayed in Figure 11-12.

PART IV • CREATE A NEWSLETTER

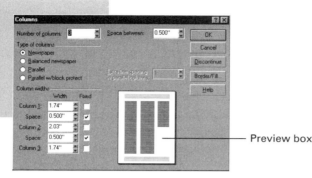

Figure 11-12
You can create new columns or change existing settings using the Columns dialog box.

Preview box

Tip

With columns already defined, you can double-click the Column button in the application bar to quickly open the Columns dialog box.

2. Change Number Of <u>C</u>olumns to **5**, then click in the <u>S</u>pace Between control and change the setting to **.25**. As you make changes, the Preview box is updated, displaying a projected image for your document.

3. The Column Widths group allows you to type the exact width you want to use for each column. In the Column <u>1</u> box, change the width to **2"**. Press [Tab] to move to the Space control. As you move from the width control, the Preview box displays the effect of your change. All remaining column widths are adjusted so that the total width of all columns still remains within the left and right margin settings for the page.

4. Click the Fixed check box for the Column <u>1</u> width. This locks in the width setting for column 1 so that it will not be adjusted as other column widths are modified.

5. Using the Column Widths scroll bar, scroll to column 4, then change its width to **2"**. Notice that the widths of columns 2, 3, and 5 adjust, while column 1, whose width is fixed, remains the same.

Tip

The Column Widths scroll bar appears when more than three columns are defined, enabling you to edit column width settings for additional columns.

6. Click OK to apply your changes to your newsletter. Whew! Ugly!

CHAPTER 11 • PLACING THE TEXT AND MASTHEAD   335

7. Return to the Columns dialog box, changing the layout to a two-column balanced newspaper layout. Click OK to return to your newsletter. Notice that the column text is now evenly spaced across both columns.

Dressing Up Columns with Borders and Fills

Borders and fills can add eye-appeal, or special emphasis to a column or group of columns. Including a line between columns helps separate one column from another and also helps draw the reader's attention down a column. Borders and fills can also be added to individual paragraphs or to a page; you may want to experiment with different border groupings to find an effective layout.

To add a border or fill to your column, first open the Columns dialog box, then click the Border/Fill button. The Column Border/Fill dialog box opens, displaying three tabs as shown in Figure 11-13. As you make choices, the effect of your selection can be seen in the Preview box on each tab. The Apply Border to Current Column Group Only check box determines whether your selection will also apply to subsequent column groupings in your document, or whether they should stay with the current column definition only.

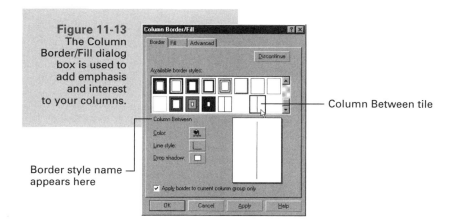

Figure 11-13
The Column Border/Fill dialog box is used to add emphasis and interest to your columns.

Border style name appears here

Column Between tile

Select the border you want to apply to your column grouping from the Border tab, Available Border Styles palette. All of the borders will appear around the perimeter of the complete column group with the exception of the Column Between tile. As you click a tile, the name of the border style appears immediately below the Available Border Styles palette (refer to Figure 11-13).

Some types of newsletters benefit greatly when you add color to the borders. Changing the Line Style and adding a Drop Shadow are also effective methods of customizing the border you select. Figure 11-14 displays the palettes you will see when you select the Color, Line Style, and Drop Shadow controls from the Border tab.

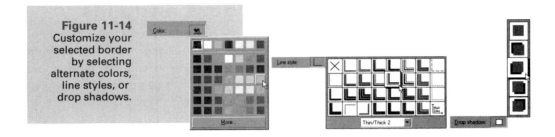

Figure 11-14 Customize your selected border by selecting alternate colors, line styles, or drop shadows.

Clicking the Fill tab enables you to add interest to columns by shading the area of the page used by the column group. You can select from solid fills based on a percentage of color, patterned fills, and gradient fills. Either solid fills or gradient fills can typically be effective behind text. Selecting a pattern fill can make text almost impossible to read. If you select a pattern or gradient fill, you can also select both foreground and background colors for the fill. A sample fill choice is shown in Figure 11-15.

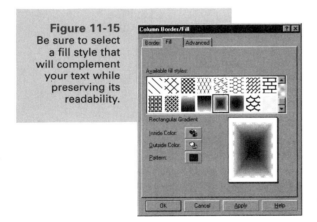

Figure 11-15 Be sure to select a fill style that will complement your text while preserving its readability.

The Advanced tab is used to customize the appearance of a gradient fill. You can change the shape of the gradient fill to a linear, circular, or rectangular pattern, and then also set the offset positions to specify where the gradient begins within the fill. The controls in the Spacing group will determine the relationship between the border and the text. Setting the Inside spacing controls how close the text will come to the inside of the border you selected; Outside spacing controls how close text will come to the outside of the border. A border selection, with customized gradient and spacing can be viewed in Figure 11-16.

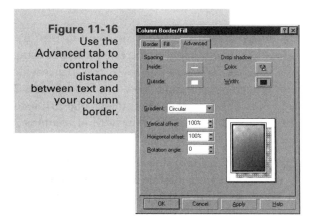

Figure 11-16 Use the Advanced tab to control the distance between text and your column border.

Hands On: Adding Lines Between the Columns

To add a vertical line between the columns of your newsletter, use these steps:

1. Position the insertion point within the column group, then click the Columns button, and select Format. Now click the Border/Fill button to open the Column Border/Fill dialog box.

2. From the Available Border Styles palette, scroll to the last line of tiles, then click the Inside Border tile.

3. Click OK to return to the Columns dialog box, then click OK again to return to your newsletter. A vertical line now extends from the top to the bottom of the columns.

When using newspaper columns, the vertical line only extends as far as the text of your columns. As you add more text, the line extends further. In parallel columns, the line is broken between each set of rows.

To force a line to extend the full length of the page, use a graphic line. You learn more about graphic lines in Chapter 12.

Creating Asymmetric Columns

Even though WordPerfect automatically assists you by creating sized and spaced columns, not all applications look best with a symmetrical layout. In fact, many designers prefer to use an asymmetrical layout based on the premise that it's more interesting and draws the reader's attention better.

One of my favorite methods of creating attractive asymmetric columns is to use the rule of three or five. For example, imagine that you've created a layout using three columns. Each column on a standard layout will be about two inches wide with about a one-half inch gutter between the columns. Now you *join* columns 2 and 3 together leaving one column of two inches on the left, then a one-half inch gutter, followed by a wide column of about $4^{1}/_{2}$ inches (the width of columns 2 and 3 plus the gutter space between them).

Similarly, you can work with a layout of five columns, creating one column that's a combination of columns 1, 2, and 3 and another column that's a combination of columns 4 and 5. Figure 11-17 displays a simple newsletter using the five-column layout.

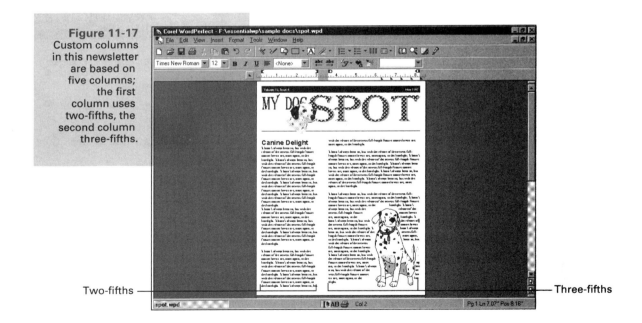

Figure 11-17 Custom columns in this newsletter are based on five columns; the first column uses two-fifths, the second column three-fifths.

CHAPTER 11 • PLACING THE TEXT AND MASTHEAD 339

Hands On: Creating Asymmetric Columns

To create an asymmetric column layout in your Busy Painter newsletter, use these steps:

1. Open the newsletter file, then position the insertion point anywhere in the current column definition for your newsletter. If necessary, change the definition to reflect two evenly-spaced newspaper or balanced newspaper columns.

2. Position the insertion point at the top of the document by pressing Ctrl+Home.

3. Choose Insert, Watermark. The Watermark dialog box opens. Click Create to open the watermark page. A watermark page is a handy, out-of-the-way place to create visual guidelines that will be used to size and place asymmetric columns.

> FOR MORE INFORMATION ABOUT WATERMARKS, SEE CHAPTER 12.

Tip

A *watermark* is a special page that displays text or graphics behind the document page. Once created, it acts similarly to a header or footer, in that it appears on every page that follows.

4. If you've changed your margin settings for your newsletter, you must also change the margin settings in the watermark page so that they match exactly. For example, if your newsletter has left and right margins of one-half inch, change the left and right margins in the Watermark page to one-half inch.

5. Now define five evenly-spaced columns. To do so, click the Columns button, then click 5 Columns. Five column guidelines can be seen in the watermark page if guidelines are turned on.

6. Press Enter until the insertion point moves from column 1 to column 2.

7. Add a vertical line between each column by double-clicking the Column button in the application bar to quickly open the Columns dialog box. Finally, click the Border/Fill button.

8. From the Available Border Styles palette, click the Column Between tile, then click OK to add a line between each column set. Click OK to return to the Watermark page, then click the Close button on the Watermark property bar to return to your newsletter. The lines from the watermark page are visible in your newsletter. Don't panic! The watermark page is only used as a guideline and will be deleted when the asymmetric columns are created.

PART IV • CREATE A NEWSLETTER

9. Now drag the gutter between your two newsletter columns until it spans either the second or third column lines visible from the watermark page (see Figure 11-18). The text of your newsletter flows into the new asymmetric columns.

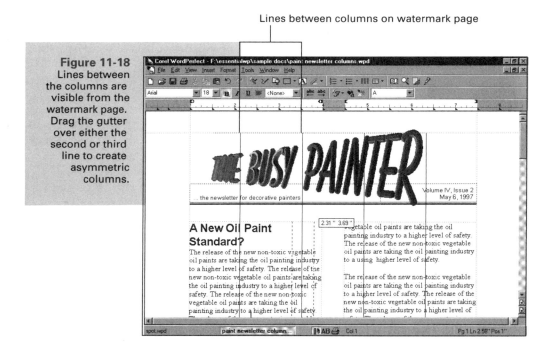

Figure 11-18 Lines between the columns are visible from the watermark page. Drag the gutter over either the second or third line to create asymmetric columns.

10. To delete the watermark, press Ctrl+Home to return to the top of the page. Choose Insert, Watermark, Discontinue. The watermark code is removed from your newsletter.

Using Parallel Columns to Type a Script

Parallel columns are an ideal method of easily formatting text such as a script. Scripts are typically formatted with one set of text in the left column which controls what should be happening while the other column displays the dialogue for the same moment. As a script is developed, the activity must stay in synch with the dialogue. Parallel columns work in just such a fashion. Each column in a column set or column row stays in synch with all of the other columns in the set.

CHAPTER 11 • PLACING THE TEXT AND MASTHEAD   341

> **Tip**
>
> You can now use tables to create the same type of appearance and action. After creating your table, edit the Row format by choosing F̲ormat from the QuickMenu. Then, from the Row tab check D̲ivide Row Across Pages.

While actually creating parallel columns is very simple, typing and editing in them can be tricky.

Hands On: Creating a Script Using Parallel Columns

Figure 11-19 displays a sample script. Follow these steps to duplicate it:

1. Open a new document window, then open the Columns dialog box (click the Columns button, then select Format).

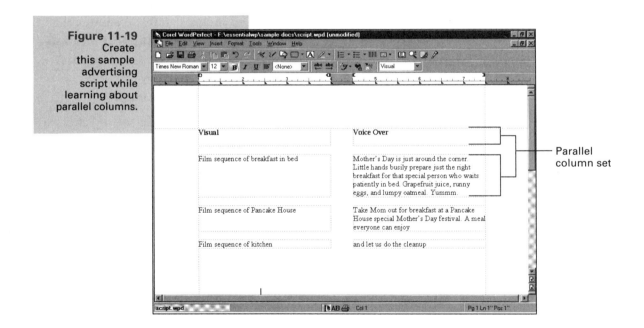

Figure 11-19 Create this sample advertising script while learning about parallel columns.

2. Set Number of C̲olumns to **2**, then click P̲arallel as the column type. Verify that the E̲xtra Line Spacing in Parallel Columns is set to 1. Extra line spacing controls the blank line that appears between each column set.

3. Click OK to return to the document window. With guidelines on, you see one delineated parallel column set.

4. Now type **Visual** as the heading for the first column. Be sure to boldface the title so that it has a little more emphasis than the text.

5. Press Ctrl+Enter to complete the first column and move to the second column. Turn on Reveal Codes to notice that a [HCol] code appears.

6. Now type **Voice Over** as the heading for the second column, also in bold. Press Ctrl+Enter again to complete the first column set. The insertion point now appears at the beginning of the second column set.

7. Type the text for each of the column sets, pressing Ctrl+Enter between each column and at the end of each set, using the text which follows this paragraph. If you make a mistake, move back to the previous column in a set by pressing Alt+←. You can return to the next column in a set by pressing Alt+→.

Film sequence of breakfast in bed	Mother's Day is just around the corner. Little hands busily prepare just the right breakfast for the special person who waits patiently in bed. Grapefruit juice, runny eggs, and lumpy oatmeal. Yummmm!
Film sequence of Pancake House	Take Mom out for breakfast at a Pancake House special Mother's Day festival. A meal everyone can enjoy...
Film sequence of kitchen	... and let us do the cleanup.

As you can see, creating parallel columns is easy. Pressing Ctrl+Enter after each column entry in a set automatically moves the insertion point forward to the next set; and then completes a set and starts the next.

Editing is similar, as long as you keep in mind that each column ends with a [HCol] code. Add one additional set to your script using these steps:

8. Position the insertion point at the beginning of the second set, the `Film sequence of Pancake House`.

9. Press Ctrl+Enter. The `Visual` text moves to the Voice Over column and the `Voice Over` text moves forward to the next set (see Figure 11-20). Press Ctrl+Enter again to force the entire set to the next row.

10. Press ↑ once to move to the beginning of the blank set, then type the new text (remember that you can press Alt+→ to move to the second column since it already exists!):

Film pans to Dad making pancakes on the BBQ	The master chef is in his element...

CHAPTER 11 • PLACING THE TEXT AND MASTHEAD **343**

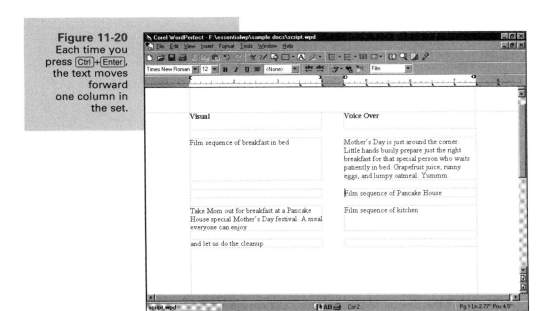

Figure 11-20
Each time you press Ctrl+Enter, the text moves forward one column in the set.

12

Adding Graphics to a Newsletter

IN THIS CHAPTER

- **Working with Clipart**
- **Manipulating an Image**
- **Wrapping Text around Graphic Boxes**

Possibly no other elements get as much attention in a newsletter, or any other document type for that matter, as do well placed, appropriate, graphics. This chapter will introduce you to a few of the graphic features in WordPerfect 8, all designed to help you add effective graphic elements to your documents. You already discovered how much impact fun and powerful TextArt images can have on your newsletter's masthead. Now you will learn a little about including clipart images, photos, or graphics from other programs in a WordPerfect document. This chapter will help you become comfortable with sizing images and then placing them precisely on the page where you want them to be—and keeping them there! While this chapter won't make you into a computer artist, you will also be introduced to a few of the drawing tools available to you in WordPerfect, along with learning how to make some basic edits to a clipart image.

A Few Design Thoughts

Each chapter in this book has offered suggestions for creating attractive documents. It's easy to get a little carried away when adding graphic elements to a document, however, so listed below are a few thoughts about working with graphics. Very loosely defined, graphic elements in a WordPerfect document include clipart, photographs, pictures of any type, line art, lines, borders, fills, and font faces. Font faces? Well, yes. Font faces affect the look and feel of your document. Especially in titles and headlines where they tend to be large and fancy. Fonts are, therefore, a visual, graphic, element which affect the overall appearance of your document. Further, although you can't manipulate a font face when text is merely typed, the text itself can be manipulated similarly to a graphic when placed in a text box.

- Keep graphic elements simple. A total combination of about five elements or so is plenty for a single page. Therefore, you might include your masthead as one graphic, maybe a border around a page, and two additional images or so.

- Make sure that the graphic elements don't overwhelm the text. Graphic elements should *enhance* your message, but not detract from it.

- To avoid clutter on a single page, make one graphic a main focal point, with other graphics taking subordinate roles. In many newsletters, the masthead might be considered the main graphic. However, you should consider whether the lead article in your newsletter should typically receive greater attention than the masthead. If so, the masthead should be designed so as not to draw attention from that article's attention-grabbing graphic.

- Along the same line, be sure that your graphics have some relationship to the subject at hand. Adding tropical fish to an article introducing the newest associate might not be appropriate.

- Be sure to use the Zoom button frequently, selecting Full Page so that you can get a complete view of the layout for the entire page.

- Similarly, when creating documents that will have two pages side by side, frequently change your View to Two Pages so that you can see both pages at once. Remember that a two-page spread can all be seen at the same time. Both pages need to compliment each other.

- Pay special attention to the amount of white space you include. White space is the area of the document where nothing appears. It's used to help balance the various elements of your document while giving the reader's eye a comfortable resting place. It's probably better to err on the side of too much white space rather than too little. But be careful not to include a large block of white space in the center of a page. This creates a hole in the middle of your document.
- An excellent place to gain white space is around a headline. Doing so provides a *frame* which calls attention to the headline.
- Some designers feel that a page should still be in balance when it's rotated 180 degrees so that you are viewing the document upside down. Is it still in balance and comfortable to look at?
- Other designers prefer an asymmetric look, without perfectly balanced columns, text, and graphics which can lead to boredom.
- Print your document often. Things often look different on paper than they do on screen. Sometimes it's a good idea to walk away from the printed document, then come back and look at it later. You'll find that a break will lend fresh perspective.
- Finally, remember that there are really no hard and fast rules. Only suggestions.

Adding Images to Your Newsletter

The Standard edition of Corel WordPerfect Suite 8 contains over 10,000 clipart images and 200 photos! Not all of the images are copied to your computer during a Typical installation, but you can copy the entire contents of the \Corel\Suite8\Graphics folder to your hard drive if you feel you'll need instant access to every possible image. Of course, if you choose to do so, be prepared. Copying all of the clipart and photo images will require over 225 MB of disk space!

WordPerfect clipart is in WordPerfect's native .WPG format. You can also use images from screen shots, scanners, bitmaps in .JPG, .BMP, EPS, .PCX, and .TIF formats, along with many other types. Once you've added a graphic image to your document, you can save the image to a separate file in .WPG format. Using Presentations, you can convert almost any image to another image type, making Corel WordPerfect Suite 8 a truly versatile graphics conversion tool.

The vast majority of the clipart collection is organized into scrapbooks, a method used by Corel to organize the images and shrink the amount of space required by graphic files. From the scrapbooks, you drag or copy the image you want to your document window. The photo collection can be found as separate files on your CD, in the \Photos folder.

You can view the photos by clicking the Toggle Preview On/Off button in any WordPerfect file management dialog box. With Preview enabled, right-click to change the viewer option from Cont<u>e</u>nt to Page Vie<u>w</u>. You might also find it helpful to increase the size of the file management dialog box (thus increasing the size of the preview window) by clicking the Maximize button, or by dragging a corner of the dialog box to the size you want to use. You can also size the preview window by dragging the separator bar which divides the list window from the preview windows.

In addition to using the images supplied with Corel WordPerfect Suite 8, you can also add virtually any other image you may want to your document, such as images you may have scanned or images from clipart collections from other programs.

Using the Scrapbook to Locate a Corel Clipart Image

The Corel Scrapbook is a unique organizational tool which gathers images together into special files, called scrapbooks. If you view a file list of the Corel WordPerfect Suite 8 CD, you'll see that each clipart folder contains a file with the extension .SCP. That scrapbook file contains the clipart images in .WPG format. To use a scrapbook, you must first find the image you want to use, then copy or drag the image to your document.

Hands On: Adding a Clipart Image to a Newsletter

The hands-on activities used in this section are based on The Busy Painter newsletter created in the last chapter. You can add images to that newsletter, or to any other document you want. Use the steps that follow to locate and add a Clipart image to your document:

1. Open the newsletter `paint newsletter.wpd`.
2. Click the Clipart button on the toolbar, or choose <u>I</u>nsert, <u>G</u>raphics, <u>C</u>lipart. The Scrapbook will start with the Clipart tab in front as shown in Figure 12-1. The images you see in the Clipart tab exist in the small

Chapter 12 • Adding Graphics to a Newsletter **349**

Scrapbook file, named `compact.scb`, copied to your system during installation. They represent only a very small fraction of the complete Clipart collection.

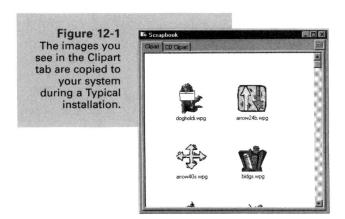

Figure 12-1
The images you see in the Clipart tab are copied to your system during a Typical installation.

3. Scroll through the scrapbook until you see an image you like. Click the image to select it. The image `call0010.wpg` was chosen since it looks a little like a splash of paint. (Throughout the rest of this chapter, this image will be referred to as the *paint splash* image.)

4. Drag the image from the Scrapbook dialog box to the newsletter. As you drag, a dashed guideline will appear, indicating the perimeter of the clipart image. See Figure 12-2. (You also could copy the graphic to the Clipboard, and then paste it in the document.)

   The image will appear in the newsletter at the location to which it was dragged or pasted and the text will automatically wrap around the image.

5. Now close the Scrapbook by clicking the Close button.

Tip

If you plan to use several images from the Scrapbook, minimize it to the Windows 95 taskbar by clicking the Minimize button. When you need another image, click the Scrapbook button to restore the Scrapbook to the screen.

As you noticed, the initial Clipart tab in Scrapbook has very few images available. For almost all Scrapbook applications, you'll want to locate an image on the Corel WordPerfect Suite 8 CD.

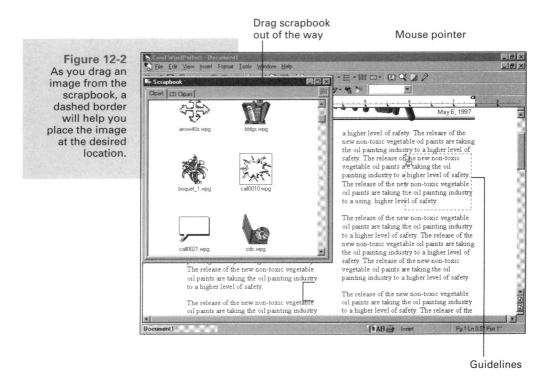

Figure 12-2 As you drag an image from the scrapbook, a dashed border will help you place the image at the desired location.

Scrapbook has a nasty habit of remaining on top of all other applications as you open them. This means that if you open another application while Scrapbook is still active, the newly started program will appear behind the Scrapbook applet. Since you can't move the Scrapbook to a subordinate position, you'll need to minimize it to the taskbar, then restore it when you need to work with it again.

Hands On: Adding a Scrapbook Image from the CD

To locate and add an image from the Corel WordPerfect Suite 8 CD, use these steps:

1. Start the Scrapbook applet, then click the CD Clipart tab. The CD Clipart folder display will open as shown in Figure 12-3.

CHAPTER 12 • ADDING GRAPHICS TO A NEWSLETTER   351

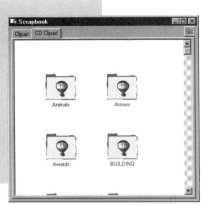

Figure 12-3
The CD Clipart collection organizes images into 38 Scrapbooks. Scroll though the collection to also view the Clipart images included in the default Compact Scrapbook.

Note

The first time you use the CD Clipart tab, Scrapbook may not be able to locate the CD. You'll be prompted to provide the location of the CD. Once you enter the location the first time, you will not be required to provide it again. Of course, if you click the CD Clipart tab without the Corel WordPerfect Suite 8 CD in the drive, you will again be prompted since WordPerfect doesn't know whether the CD is missing, or whether you want to access the Clipart from an alternate location.

2. Double-click the LEISURE folder to display two subfolders, then double-click the Hobbies folder to preview the clipart images contained in the folder. You may find it easier to preview the images if you maximize Scrapbook to a full screen display. Figure 12-4 displays a maximized Scrapbook.

3. Copy or drag the image symb058.wpg (4 paint tubes) to your document. Don't worry too much about placement yet. In the next few hands-on activities you'll learn how to position your images, and how to edit them.

Adding an Image from a File

In addition to using the Scrapbook to locate and insert Corel images, you can use WordPerfect's Graphics from File feature. This is especially useful if you want to use an image from another program.

Returns to previous folder

Figure 12-4 Maximizing the Scrapbook allows you to view more images.

Almost all image types will automatically be converted for use within WordPerfect. When you add a graphic to a WordPerfect document, a copy of the file is actually created in .WPG format. If your file cannot be converted for some reason, open the graphic in the program that was originally used to create it, then save it to a format that is recognized by WordPerfect. If there still isn't a format you can use, open the file in its native program, then select the entire graphic. Use the copy command to store the copied graphic in the Clipboard, then paste the image in WordPerfect. In combination with Presentations, WordPerfect 8 can automatically convert these graphic types:

Extension	Type
.BMP	Microsoft Windows (3.x) and OS/2 Presentation Manager bitmap
.CAL	CALs bitmap
.CDR	CorelDraw file
.CDT	CorelDraw template
.CGM	Computer Graphics metafile
.CH3	Harvard Graphics (chart)
.DRW	Micrografx Designer

Chapter 12 • Adding Graphics to a Newsletter

.DXF	AutoCAD format
.EMF	Enhanced Windows metafile
.EPS	Encapsulated PostScript
.GIF	Graphics Interchange Format
.HPG	Hewlett-Packard Graphics Language Plotter file
.IMG	GEM Paint bitmap
.JPG	Joint Photographic Experts Group
.MAC	MacPaint bitmap
.PAT	CorelDraw
.PCD	Kodak Photo CD bitmap
.PCT	Macintosh PICT format
.PCX	PC Paintbrush format
.PIC	Lotus 1-2-3 PIC format
.PNG	Portable Network Graphics
.PP4	Picture Publisher 4 bitmap
.PPT	PowerPoint
.PRS	Harvard Graphics for Windows, version 1, 2, or 3
.SY3	Harvard Graphics 3.0 for DOS (symbol file)
.TGA	TrueVision TARGA
.TIF	Tagged Image File Format
.TP3	Harvard Graphics 3.0 for DOS (template)
.WMF	Windows metafile format
.WPG	WordPerfect Graphics format
.WVL	Wavelet bitmap

The .WPG files tend to be smaller and more efficient than other graphics formats. Unfortunately, not all drawing or graphic programs export correctly to .WPG files. You may find when opening a .WPG file from another program that not all of the image elements were correctly converted. If this is the case, open the file again in its original program and try saving it to another format which is also recognized by WordPerfect.

Note

WordPerfect will automatically convert many of these image types to a .WPG graphics file when inserting them in a document. If, however, the graphic you want to insert is not accepted by WordPerfect, try importing the graphic in Presentations. Often Presentations will convert the graphic. Then choose File, Save (in Presentations) to save the image. It will automatically be saved to a .WPG format.

Hands On: Adding a Drop Cap and a Graphic Image from a File

A number of interesting textures and backgrounds can be found in the photo collection on the Corel WordPerfect Suite 8 CD. Use these steps to create an interesting drop cap at the beginning of the article and then add a texture behind the drop cap:

1. If the paint newsletter.wpd file is not already open, open it. Place the insertion point at the beginning of the first line in the article.

2. Choose Format, Paragraph, Drop Cap, or press Ctrl+Shift+C. The first character will immediately turn into a three-line, descending drop cap and the Drop Cap property bar will appear. Figure 12-5 displays a four-line drop cap—one line up and three lines down.

3. Click the Drop Cap Style button, displaying the style palette. Then select the one-up, two-down drop cap style (last tile in the top row) or a drop cap style you like. The drop cap will update to reflect your choice.

   The borders and fills for drop caps are the same ones you used for columns, paragraphs, and pages. Nice, but with only a few choices. The photo collection contains several files that can be used as a background for the drop cap, enhancing its appearance.

4. Choose Insert, Graphics, From File. The Insert Image file management dialog box will open at the location for your Corel Clipart. Using the Look In drop-down list, locate your CD-ROM drive.

5. Double-click the Photos folder, then double-click the Colors folder to open the list of photo files.

6. Click the Preview button in the toolbar to initialize the file viewer. The viewer pane will open on the right side of the file management dialog box.

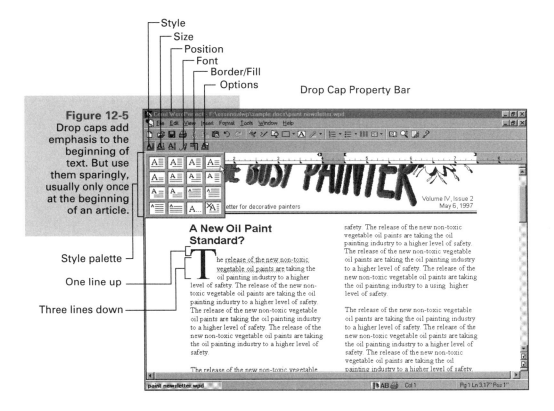

Figure 12-5
Drop caps add emphasis to the beginning of text. But use them sparingly, usually only once at the beginning of an article.

7. As you click a filename, a preview of the photo will appear in the viewer pane.

In all of the Corel photo file lists, two versions of each photo are available. One file is a bitmap, with the extension .bmp; the other is a JPEG file, with the extension .jpg. JPEGs are slower to view and considerably larger than bitmap files (which are low-resolution images). But the quality of a JPEG file is much better. Therefore, click a .bmp file to see the image in the viewer, then double-click the .jpg file as the choice to be added to your document.

8. Since quality of the image isn't critical for this sample newsletter, double-click file 754025.bmp (an oil slick texture) to add it to the newsletter. After a brief pause while WordPerfect converts the file to a .WPG image, the photo will appear in the newsletter.

The next hands-on activity will assist you in sizing the photo file and placing it behind the drop cap.

Adding images to the newsletter greatly increases its file size. If you know that the same CD will be available in the same location each time you print or open the newsletter, click the Image on Disk check box. This links the newsletter to the CD file for the image.

Manipulating the Images

When added to your document, graphics are sized by WordPerfect so that they retain their proportions. You can manipulate the images in any number of ways from within WordPerfect, stretching and contorting them to fit your needs. You can place images in front of text, or behind the text, contour text to follow the outline of the image, or prevent text from wrapping around an image.

While three images have been added to the newsletter, nothing has been sized or placed. Figure 12-6 shows before and after images of the newsletter. Your newsletter possibly resembles the *before* image in Figure 12-6. After placing and sizing the images and setting options for text wrapping, the newsletter will more closely resemble the *after* side of Figure 12-6.

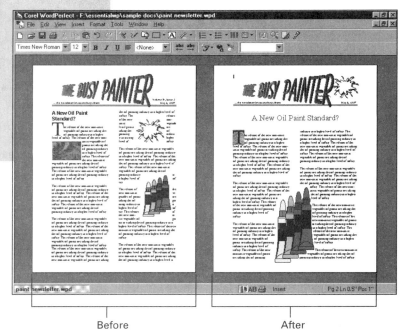

Figure 12-6 Before sizing and placing the images, the newsletter is a jumble of text and graphics. After careful placement, the newsletter is more appealing.

Before   After

CHAPTER 12 • ADDING GRAPHICS TO A NEWSLETTER **357**

WordPerfect enables you to place graphics exactly where you want them to be by dragging them to the desired location, or by explicitly setting the location through menu choices. Typically you'll use a combination of both. It's often easiest to first drag the graphic to the location you want it to appear, then, using QuickMenus, lock the location so that the graphic stays in the correct location.

Sizing Graphics and Placing Them Effectively

Before you can manipulate a graphic in any way, you must first select the graphic. To do so, click the graphic image once. A set of eight graphic *handles* (small black squares) will appear around the perimeter of the graphic, as shown in Figure 12-7.

When selecting a graphic, be careful to only click the graphic image once. Double-clicking will launch the OLE server associated with the graphic, usually Presentations. If you accidentally launch the OLE server, click in the document outside of the graphic image to return to your document, then try again.

If you have difficulty single-clicking to select, try pointing to an unselected box, then right-click. Handles surround the box and the graphic QuickMenu will simultaneously appear. On the QuickMenu, choose Select Bo_x_. The QuickMenu will close and the box will remain selected.

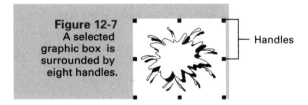

Figure 12-7
A selected graphic box is surrounded by eight handles.

Handles

The handles indicate the size of the current graphic *box* or *frame*. The box is used to control the size and appearance of the graphic within WordPerfect. WordPerfect enables you to change the border and fill of the graphic box. Images or other elements such as text, TextArt, lines or shapes, appear inside the box. To change the appearance of the graphic image, you must launch the program which was used to create the box, usually by double-clicking the image. The OLE server for the graphic type will then launch.

When you select a graphic, a new property bar appears. See Table 12-1 to identify each button.

Table 12-1 The Graphics Property Bar

Button	Purpose
Graphics ▾	Opens a drop-down menu of Graphics editing choices. Use this menu to change the stack order of graphic images, or to flip the graphic image from left to right or top to bottom. You can also group or separate graphic images using this menu. The remaining choices are also available on the graphics QuickMenu.
	Selects the Previous graphic box
	Selects the Next graphic box
	Opens the Border Style palette from where you can select a Border style. Selecting More from the palette opens the Box Border/Fill dialog box.
	Opens a palette of fill styles and patterns. This is an alternate route to the Box Border/Fill dialog box.
	Creates a caption by inserting a box counter in the caption location and opens the Text Editing property bar
	Flips the image from left to right
	Flips the image from top to bottom
	Opens the Image Tool palette from where you can edit the attributes for the image within a graphic box
	Changes the order of objects by moving the selected box forward one in the stack
	Changes the order of objects by moving the selected box backward one in the stack
	Opens a palette to text wrap options
	Creates a hyperlink

Moving and Positioning a Graphic Box

You can move a selected graphic by pointing to the center of the graphic (the mouse changes to a four-headed arrow), then dragging the graphic to the new location. As you drag the graphic, the mouse pointer changes to the drag and drop pointer. When you release the mouse button, text and other images shift to allow room for the new graphic. Changing the wrap settings for the affected graphics will prevent them from moving. Figure 12-8 displays an image being moved using the mouse.

CHAPTER 12 • ADDING GRAPHICS TO A NEWSLETTER

Figure 12-8
A guideline illustrating the perimeter of the graphic box is visible when dragging a graphic to a new location.

Copy a graphic by pressing Ctrl while dragging. When you release the mouse button, a copy of the graphic will appear in the new position, leaving the original graphic intact.

A graphic image is automatically attached to a location on a page when it is inserted in a WordPerfect document. This means that as you add or delete text, the graphic may move to a different page. You can force a graphic image to stay on the page on which it was placed, or you can attach a box to a paragraph so that it moves with the paragraph as the document is edited. You can further designate a graphic as a character so that it moves with a line of text similar to any other typed character.

To position a graphic or attach a graphic to a set location, use these steps:

1. Select the graphic by clicking the image.
2. Right-click to display the QuickMenu or open the Graphics drop-down menu on the toolbar. Now select Position. The Box Position dialog box will open as displayed in Figure 12-9.
3. Using the Attach Box To drop-down control, select the attachment type to which you want the box to be assigned. As you make your choices, the Box Position dialog box updates. Table 12-2 lists the options and actions available for each attachment type.

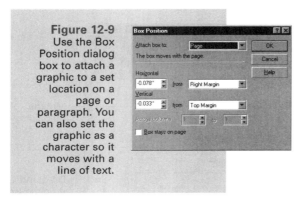

Figure 12-9 Use the Box Position dialog box to attach a graphic to a set location on a page or paragraph. You can also set the graphic as a character so it moves with a line of text.

Hands On: Positioning the Graphic Elements on the Newsletter

The graphic images copied from the scrapbook and the \Photo folder earlier inserted from file need to be appropriately placed on the newsletter. Refer to Figure 12-6 (the before and after figure) periodically for approximate locations. Use these steps to experiment with various methods of positioning graphics:

1. Open the newsletter file, then select the paint splash scrapbook image.

2. Drag the image to the right side of the TextArt masthead. Depending on the current settings for the TextArt box, the paint splash may be forced to appear below the masthead. Don't worry for now. You'll learn more about wrap options later in this section.

3. With the image still selected, right-click to display the QuickMenu, then choose Position. The Box Position dialog box will open.

4. Verify that the box is attached to the Page, then fine-tune the position by setting the Horizontal distance to 0" from the Right Margin. You can use the spin controls on the measurement control, although it's usually easiest to type the distance. An approximate Vertical measurement is sufficient.

5. Click Box Stays on Page to ensure that the box will not move from the first page of the newsletter. Then click OK to return to the document window. The graphic box may shift slightly, snapping to the right margin.

6. Now select the paint tubes graphic image, then again open the Box Position dialog box. This image should also be attached to the Page.

7. Select Centered in Columns from the Horizontal drop-down list, then be sure that the Horizontal distance is set to 0".

Table 12-2 Options for Graphic Attachment Types

Attach to/Option	Causes this effect
Page	
Hori**z**ontal	Allows you set the graphic a specific distance, left to right from the Left Edge of Page, Left or Right Margins, or centered between the margins or in relationship to defined columns.
Vertical	Sets an exact location for the graphic box from either the top or bottom margin, the top edge of the paper, or equidistant between the top and bottom margins.
Box Stays on Page	Check this option to be sure that the box does not move from page to page as text is edited around the box. When not checked, the box can move to the same location on another page as the surrounding text is edited.
Paragraph	As you drag a box assigned to a paragraph to a new position, a thumbtack and dotted guideline will appear indicating the place where the box is attached. Then as you drag to other paragraphs, the thumbtack will jump from the beginning of one paragraph to the next paragraph maintaining a paragraph attachment.
Hori**z**ontal	Horizontal positioning sets the box location from left to right within the paragraph.
Vertical	Vertical positioning indicates how far from the top of a paragraph the box should appear.
Character	The Character positioning options also include a preview window which illustrates the position you have selected.
Top	Top positioning sets the top of the graphic box at the same height as a capital letter in the text.
Centered	The middle of the graphic box rests on the baseline of the text line; half of the box is above the baseline and half is below the baseline.
Bottom	Bottom placement puts the bottom of the graphic box on the text baseline.
Content Base**l**ine	Sets the bottom of the image within the box on the text baseline.
C**u**stom	Use Custom to set an exact vertical position on a line, in percentages. A .4 setting positions 40% of the box above the baseline while .8 positions 80% of the box above the baseline.

8. Align the graphic with the Bottom Margin in the <u>V</u>ertical F<u>r</u>om drop-down list control. Then verify that the distance is 0".
9. Set columns 1 to 2 in the Acros<u>s</u> Columns controls, then check the <u>B</u>ox Stays on Page check box.

PART IV • CREATE A NEWSLETTER

10. Click OK to return to the document window. The graphic box will appear between the columns, centered at the bottom margin on the page.

It's helpful to change the zoom to Full Page view periodically while positioning graphics. This allows you to get a better sense of how the graphic affects the complete page.

11. Finally, position the oil slick image that will be used as a background for the drop cap. Attach the box as a Character, then assign a custom vertical alignment position of about **.3**.

All graphic boxes are now placed in their approximate permanent positions. The next section will assist you in finalizing the box positions by determining how text or other boxes interact.

Wrapping Text Around or Through a Graphic Box

Wrap settings determine how text and other graphic boxes treat the selected image. You can choose to wrap text around all or any of the box edges, in front of, behind, or contoured around the image within the box. Use a rigid, square wrap type to allow the maximum white space around the graphic box. Use contour to form a tighter relationship between the box and text. Figure 12-10 displays these text wrap choices.

Wrap settings can be accessed through either the Wrap button on the property bar, or by selecting W*r*ap from the graphic QuickMenu. See Figure 12-11.

Hands On: Setting Text Wrap Options for the Newsletter Graphic Boxes

Use these steps to align the text and graphic boxes in the *The Busy Painter* newsletter:

1. The paint splash image and the masthead both share the same approximate space at the top of the newsletter. Wrap options must be set for both boxes so that they can exist in the same location. First, click the TextArt box to select it.

2. Click the Wrap button on the property bar, or right-click, then choose W*r*ap from the QuickMenu.

Chapter 12 • Adding Graphics to a Newsletter

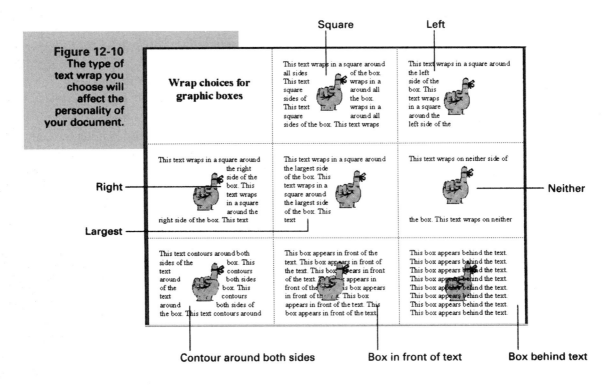

Figure 12-10 The type of text wrap you choose will affect the personality of your document.

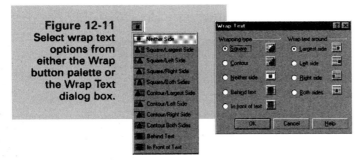

Figure 12-11 Select wrap text options from either the Wrap button palette or the Wrap Text dialog box.

Tip — If you cannot select a graphics box, point to the image and right-click to display the QuickMenu. Then choose Select Box. If more than one box appears in the same approximate location, you may need to choose Select Other from the QuickMenu, then choose the box you want to select from the resulting list of graphic boxes.

3. Select Behind Text to force the TextArt image to allow other text or images to wrap over the top of the image.

PART IV • CREATE A NEWSLETTER

4. Now select the paint splash and set the wrap option to In Front of Text. You may need to reposition the paint splash image after changing its wrap options.

5. Next, select the oil slick photo. Set the wrap options to Behind Text. The text of the first paragraph will adjust, appearing over the top of the color image. In the next section you will learn how to size the image.

6. Finally, select the paint tubes image. Set wrap options to Contour on Both Sides. The text will readjust slightly, wrapping words around the perimeter of the image rather than the perimeter of the box.

Sizing a Graphic Box

A selected graphic can be sized or moved using the mouse. To size a graphic, place the mouse pointer over one of the handles, drag the handle until the image is the desired size, then release the mouse button. The mouse pointer will change to a double-headed arrow when placed over a handle. Dragging a corner handle allows the graphic to remain proportionate; the height and width of the graphic maintain the same relation to each other. Dragging a middle handle stretches the graphic box and the image within the box. Note that you can drag boxes smaller as well as larger. Figure 12-12 illustrates the effect of using the corner handles and side handles to size a box.

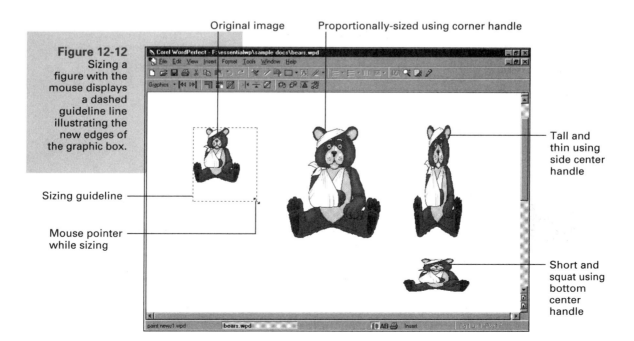

Figure 12-12 Sizing a figure with the mouse displays a dashed guideline line illustrating the new edges of the graphic box.

You can also size a graphic by selecting Size from either the Graphics drop-down button or the QuickMenu which appears when you right-click an image. Either choice opens the Box Size dialog box displayed in Figure 12-13. Size a graphic by typing the exact Width and Height measures you want to use in the Set text boxes. Selecting Full stretches the image to the margins; Full Width stretches the image to the current left and right margins; Full Height stretches the image to the top and bottom page margins. Maintaining proportions sizes the box proportionately to the size set in either Width or Height. Setting an exact width and proportionate height for a box results in a box that is the width you indicated with the height automatically maintaining the correct relationship to the width. Click OK when your measurements are complete.

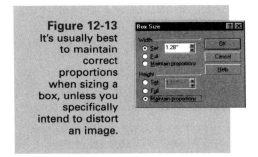

Figure 12-13
It's usually best to maintain correct proportions when sizing a box, unless you specifically intend to distort an image.

Hands On: Sizing Images on the Newsletter

Use these steps to size the three graphics in the newsletter:

1. Start by sizing the paint tubes image. First, select the paint tubes box.
2. So that you can more easily view the result of your sizing efforts, click the Zoom button on the property bar, then select Full Page. The document window will update displaying the complete first page of the newsletter.
3. Position the mouse pointer over one of the top corner handles and drag the image until it is about one-third of the page height. Then release the mouse. The text will rewrap, contouring around the image.
4. Now, using the top center handle, stretch the paint tubes until they appear slightly elongated. When complete, you'll probably need to reposition the image so that it returns to the center of the columns. You can use the Position dialog box from the QuickMenu, or just drag the image to the correct location.

> If you accidentally move an image when you meant to size it, don't worry. You can easily reposition the image at any time by dragging it back to its original location, or by using the Position control from either the Gr<u>a</u>phics menu or the QuickMenu.

5. Next, return to a 100% view (or larger!) using the Zoom button so that you can easily see the drop cap and the background image. Now scroll through the page as necessary until you can see both the drop cap and the oil slick photo.

> Before changing Zoom settings, click in the area you want to see enlarged. When the document window updates, the insertion point location will be at the bottom of the window.

6. An image whose wrap is set to Behind Text cannot be selected by clicking on the image. Point to the background image, right-click, then choose Select <u>B</u>ox from the resulting QuickMenu. Handles will appear around the box.

7. Using the right side center box handle, squeeze the image until it appears only slightly larger than the drop cap. You may want to also shorten the image using the top center handle so that it does not overwhelm the letter in height.

> Placing and sizing an image precisely behind text sometimes requires a bit of patience and trial-and-error. As you size an image that is set as a Character type, occasionally the image wants to jump around in a somewhat unstable manner. It then becomes rather difficult to place using the mouse to drag it around. There are two things you may need to do to place the box at its correct location. First, you may need to open the Box Position dialog box and again place the image exactly where it should be. Then open Reveal Codes and locate the `[Box]` code. Cut the code, then paste it where it should go (in this case, immediately after the `[Dropcap Definition]` code).

8. If needed, add more or less space to the bottom of the image, by changing the percentage of vertical positioning you assigned to the image when attaching it to the text as a character graphic. To do so, right-click the image, then choose <u>P</u>osition. Try incrementing the C<u>u</u>stom setting, clicking OK between each increment until the box appears at just the correct position.

CHAPTER 12 • ADDING GRAPHICS TO A NEWSLETTER **367**

9. When you are satisfied with the position of the background image, click outside the image to deselect it. The drop cap character will appear on top of the image. In the next section you will learn how to manipulate the image so that it appears lighter, improving the visibility of the drop cap letter.

Your newsletter will now appear similar to Figure 12-14.

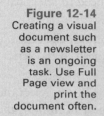

Figure 12-14
Creating a visual document such as a newsletter is an ongoing task. Use Full Page view and print the document often.

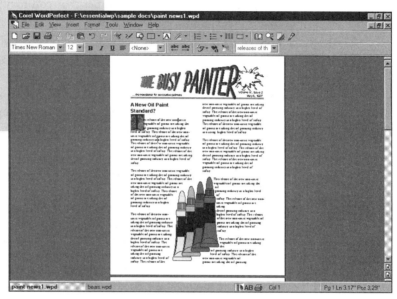

Changing the Stack Order of Images

Although you can probably see both images in the masthead of your newsletter, the TextArt image and the paint splash actually sit one behind another. This is called the stack order of the boxes. Other objects can also be stacked. For example, if your document contains an OLE object such as a spreadsheet and then you added a graphic image which is to print in the corner of the spreadsheet, two objects actually exist in the same location on the page. When you print your document, it's entirely possible that the graphic image won't appear on the printed copy. It really *is* there, but it appears behind the spreadsheet. By changing the stack order the graphic image can be moved to the top of the stack, thus allowing it to print on top of the spreadsheet.

When stacking objects, you can send an object all the way to the back or front of the stack, or move them one position forward or backward at a time. If you have several images in the same area, you might need to experiment a little to determine where in the stack each image must reside in order for them to print correctly.

> **Hands On: Placing the Images in the Correct Order**

The paint splash clipart added to the masthead must appear over the top of the TextArt image used to create the masthead. If it is not, it will not appear when the newsletter is printed—it will be hidden behind the masthead. Use these steps to stack the images correctly:

1. Select the paint splash image. Remember that you may need to select it using the QuickMenu.
2. Since only two images must actually be manipulated, you can click the Forward One button on the property bar to move the splash to the very top of the stack.
3. Try printing your newsletter. Does the paint splash print? If not, select the image again. To be sure that no other text or objects appear in front of the image, click the Graphics drop-down menu on the property bar and choose To Front.

Tip

Once you've stacked your objects, select all of the objects by [Shift]+clicking each object. Then open the Graphics drop-down menu on the property bar and select Group. (If Group is disabled, you don't really have more than one image selected. Click somewhere outside the images and try again; this is usually best accomplished by selecting the smallest image first.) This will prevent the objects from accidental individual modification. If you later need to modify an individual object in a Group, select the image group, then choose Separate from the Graphics drop-down menu.

Changing Graphic Attributes

Similar to font attributes, graphic attributes control the appearance of a graphic box and its contents. Attributes include such settings such as the brightness or contrast of an image, whether the image is transparent, black and white, or color. You can flip, rotate, or size the image within the box. Each application you create using graphics will require a different attribute setting, although almost all boxes and images are correctly configured without any intervention on your part.

Several tools can be used to change the appearance of your graphics. For example, the Border and Fill buttons on the graphics property bar allow you to manipulate the box without modifying the image within the box. In fact, the image within the box and the box itself are two different elements, although tied closely together. The Box Fill has nothing to do with the fill of the image within the box. Figure 12-15 illustrates this point.

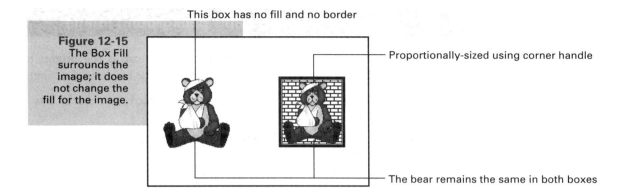

Figure 12-15 The Box Fill surrounds the image; it does not change the fill for the image.

To add a fill and border to a box, use these steps:

1. Select the image to which you want to add a fill and border.
2. Click either the Box Border or Box Fill button on the property bar.
3. From the resulting palettes, make the appropriate selections. Clicking More on the palette opens the Box Border/Fill dialog box from where you can customize the appearance of both the border and the fill.
4. Click Apply to view the results of your choices without closing the dialog box. Click OK to close the dialog box and return to the document window.

Most attributes for the *image* are accessed through the Image Tools tool palette. To open the palette, right click on a selected graphic then choose Image Tools from the QuickMenu. The Image Tools palette will open (you'll see this palette displayed in the next Hands On activity).

As you modify images using the Image Tools, you are not changing the original image—you only change the way the image looks within the graphic box.

Changing the Brightness or Contrast of an Image

An image is added to a WordPerfect document in the same colors and hues in which it was originally created. For almost all applications, the color brightness, or intensity, is acceptable. For some uses, such as using an image as a background for text, you'll need to fade the colors slightly, projecting them with more light on the image. Removing light from the image makes it darker, as if in a shadow.

Contrast controls modify the relationship between the colors in the image. The more contrast between colors, the darker the image will appear. Less contrast will fade the image toward white.

PART IV • CREATE A NEWSLETTER

Hands On: Fading the Drop Cap's Background Image

In the newsletter, the oil slick appearing behind the drop cap is too bright; it obscures the readability of the text. Here's how to change the brightness setting:

1. In the newsletter, select the oil slick box. You might need to select the box using the QuickMenu.
2. Right click to the graphic QuickMenu, then choose I<u>m</u>age Tools. The Image Tools palette will open.
3. Click the <u>B</u>rightness button to open the Brightness palette, shown in Figure 12-16.

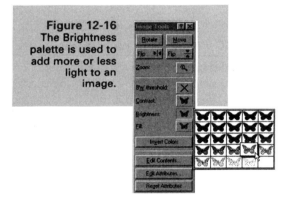

Figure 12-16 The Brightness palette is used to add more or less light to an image.

4. Click a tile from the palette which has enough light added to it to cause the image to fade slightly (Figure 12-16 suggests a possible tile choice). As soon as you make your selection, the image assumes your setting. You may need to experiment with different brightness tile choices until the image displays the effect you want.
5. Now click the <u>C</u>ontrast button to open the contrast palette. It appears similar to the Brightness palette. Experiment with various contrast tiles, lightening and darkening the contrast until you find a setting you like.
6. The Image Tools palette remains open until you click the Close button on the Image Tools title bar or until you deselect the graphic box by clicking in a new location in the document window. If you are satisfied with your settings, click the Close button to return to the document window.

CHAPTER 12 • ADDING GRAPHICS TO A NEWSLETTER 371

You can alternately set the brightness and contrast controls using typed value settings. To do so, from the Image Tools palette click the E_dit Attributes button to open the Image Settings dialog box. Click _C_olor Attributes to access the color attribute controls. In the _B_rightness control, type a value between -1 (black) and 1 (white), or click the Brightness button to open the brightness palette. Similarly in the Contrast control, type a value between -1 (no contrast) and 1 (highest contrast), or click the contrast button to open the contrast palette. As you make choices using the Image Settings dialog box, the preview window illustrates their effect.

The appearance of a printed document is often slightly different than it appears on screen. Print your document periodically so that you can see the full effect of your modifications.

So that you have an image to experiment with while learning about a few of the remaining image tools, open a new, blank document window. Then, using the Scrapbook, locate and copy a Clipart image to the new document. The image used in the hands-on activities and in the figures is `sling2.wpg`, found in the CD Clipart collection in the `Home, Misc` folder. Be sure to save this new document, perhaps naming it **bear** so that you can start over at any time, testing the editing tools as they are presented in the activities.

Using Image Tools, you can also rotate (freehand a full 360 degrees or in 90-degree increments) or flip an image (reverse the image top-to-bottom or left-to-right). You'll want to experiment with both of these controls to determine exactly which one provides the effect you're after when editing a graphic image.

You should also play a bit with the _M_ove and _Z_oom controls on the Image Tools palette. Moving or zooming an image within the box allows you to emphasize a particular portion of a complete image. After clicking the _M_ove button, use the mouse to drag the image through the box until it appears in the desired location. The _Z_oom control shrinks or enlarges the image within the box. It's useful for isolating a particular area of an image. Referring to Figure 12-15, for example, you could zoom the bear's nose to completely fill the box.

Rotating and Flipping an Image

Rotating an image changes its axis *within* the graphic box. It does not rotate the box. Therefore, an image that is tall and narrow will be cut off when rotated 90 degrees since the graphic box size maintains the same axis and dimensions.

Flipping an image reverses its appearance either left-to-right or top-to-bottom.

Hands On: Rotating an Image in a Graphic Box

To rotate the bear within the box, use these steps:

1. Select the graphic box, right-click the QuickMenu and select Image Tools.
2. Click the Rotate button to add rotation handles to the image. You might find it helpful to drag the Image Tools palette away from the image giving yourself adequate room to work.
3. Position the mouse pointer over one of the rotation handles (it changes to a double-headed arrow) then drag the image either clockwise or counter-clockwise. As you drag the image, a guideline appears showing you the position the image will take when you release the mouse. See Figure 12-17.

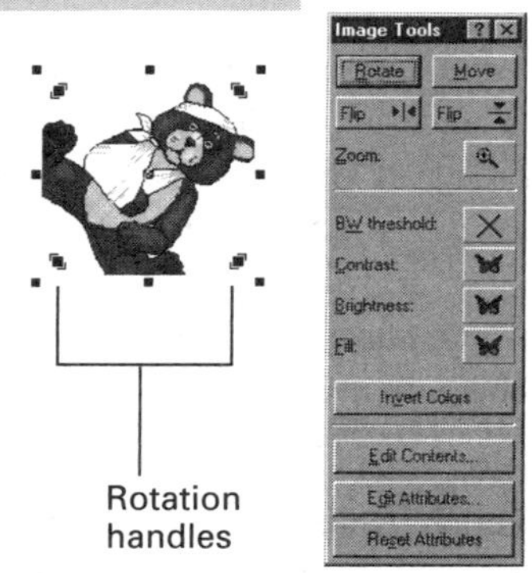

Figure 12-17 Rotating an image sometimes results in edges of the image being cut off by the edges of the box.

Rotation handles

To reset an image back to its original appearance, open the Image Tools palette, then click Edit Attributes. The Image Settings dialog box will open. Now click the Reset All button. Click OK, then close the Image Tools palette to return to your document window.

4. When the image is correctly rotated, release the mouse button.
5. To flip, or *mirror*, the image, click one of the Flip buttons on the Image Tools palette. The image will flip, mirroring its appearance either top to bottom or left to right.
6. Close the Image Tools palette by clicking the Close button on the Image Tools title bar.

Moving and Zooming an Image

Moving or zooming an image within the box allows you to emphasize a particular portion of a complete image. Using the mouse, you can drag the image through the box until it appears in the desired location. Zoom shrinks or enlarges the image within the box. It's useful for isolating just an area of an image.

Hands On: Moving and Zooming an Image

To isolate the face of the bear in the sample image, use these steps:

1. Select the image, right click to display the QuickMenu, then open the Image Tools palette.
2. Click the Zoom button. A three-tile palette will open; Figure 12-18 identifies the purpose for each of the tiles.

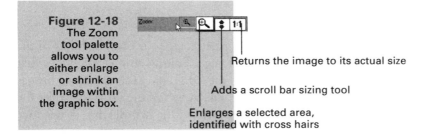

Figure 12-18 The Zoom tool palette allows you to either enlarge or shrink an image within the graphic box.

Returns the image to its actual size
Adds a scroll bar sizing tool
Enlarges a selected area, identified with cross hairs

3. Click the magnifying tool tile, then point to the image. The mouse pointer will resemble a magnifying glass with a set of cross hairs.
4. Position the pointer so that the cross hairs describe the top and left edges of the area to be enlarged.
5. Now press and drag the mouse diagonally across the area — to the bottom right corner of the bear's face. A guideline box will appear to assist you in properly describing the area.
6. Release the pointer. The described area will appear within the box and the box will resize its height, maintaining the proportions of the enlarged area.
7. Now move the image slightly within the box so that it's centered better. Click the Move button, then point back to the image. The mouse pointer appears as a four-headed arrow, as shown in Figure 12-19.

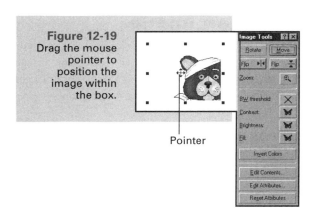

Figure 12-19
Drag the mouse pointer to position the image within the box.

Pointer

8. Press and drag the pointer through the box. As you do so, the image will appear within the dimensions of the box. When you can see the area of the image you want in the box, release the mouse.

Editing an Image

REFER TO CHAPTER 10 FOR MORE INFORMATION ABOUT OLE.

Each of the tools used in the Image Tools palette apply or edit attributes to the image, but they don't actually change the image. Editing an image requires that you open its OLE server. Presentations 8 is the OLE server for all Clipart images supplied with WordPerfect 8. PhotoHouse will launch as the OLE server for the photos. Because the OLE server will appear within the WordPerfect 8 window, before editing you'll want to zoom the WordPerfect document window to the largest size possible while being able to view the complete image on the window.

Editing an image requires that you know a few graphic principles. WordPerfect supports both *vector* and *bitmap* images. A vector image is made from lines and shapes which are mathematically computed for speed and clarity. A vector image is usually very clean and crisp. A bitmap image, most often created from a scanned image, is comprised of thousands of dots, called *pixels*. Bitmap images tend to look ragged with rough, jagged edges. When editing, you can change the color of the pixels, altering the shape of the image.

When you edit a WordPerfect graphic, you are usually working with vector images. The graphic image may be made up of several layers of shapes which are carefully stacked to provide the final image. Some shapes are complex, using many corners called *points*, which act as pivot or turning positions for a line. You can edit the points, adding or deleting points as needed, then dragging the points resulting in a change of shape. For example, in a simple square shape, four points are obvious—the four corners. If you drag any one of the corners, the shape can no longer be described as a square. See Figure 12-20 for an illustration of this.

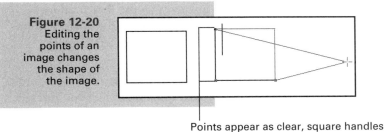

Figure 12-20 Editing the points of an image changes the shape of the image.

Points appear as clear, square handles

Similar to working with a WordPerfect graphic box, you'll use a pointer tool to select all or part of the image you are editing. But some images are made of many layers of shapes which are grouped together to form the complete image. Some images contain many different groups of shapes within an even larger group. Before you can edit the image, therefore, you must separate the shapes so that you can isolate the shape you want to change.

Learning to edit, or create, computer drawings is beyond the scope of this book. I'm a very poor artist at best, but by using some of the tools provided with Presentations, I can make simple changes to the clipart images. The sections which follow provide two examples of the types of editing I find to be most commonly needed; simple modifications to images which someone else has already drawn!

A Simple Fill Example

Adding or changing the colors, or *fills,* of an image can change the complete personality of the graphic. As you've learned, within WordPerfect the only graphic fills you can modify are those attached to the graphic box. You can't edit the fill of the image. However, by launching Presentations, you *can* edit the image, changing its fill, line styles, and so on.

Hands On: Adding a Gradient Fill to the Paint Splash

In the *Busy Painter* newsletter, a paint splash was added to the masthead. But the paint splash uses a solid white fill. Not too exciting in a masthead. Use these steps to add a gradient fill to the paint splash:

1. Open the `paint newsletter.wpd` file you created earlier. Using the Zoom button on the toolbar, change the zoom to at least 200%. Now using the scroll bars, position the paint splash approximately in the center of the document window.

2. Double-click the paint splash graphic box to open the Presentations drawing window. A slanted border will appear around the image and the menus, title bar, toolbar and property bars will update reflecting the Presentations editing choices.

3. Click the image within the box to select the image. A set of image handles will appear within the selected graphic box. Remember that you can see both the WordPerfect selected graphic box and the selected image *within* the box. Making changes to the image does not change the box. Figure 12-21 identifies the handles for both the box and the image along with the buttons to be used in this Hands On activity. Remember that you can rest the mouse pointer on any button to view a QuickTip identifying the button name and purpose.

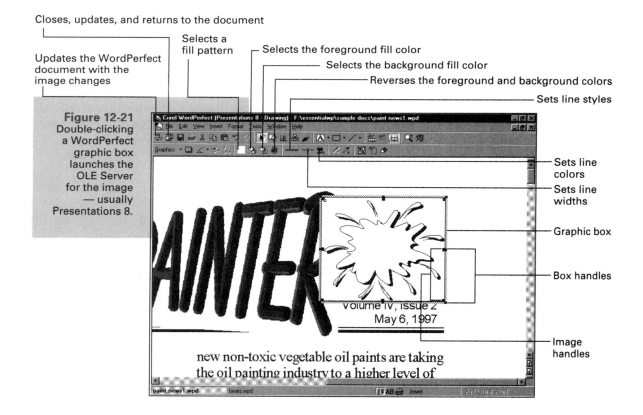

Figure 12-21 Double-clicking a WordPerfect graphic box launches the OLE Server for the image — usually Presentations 8.

CHAPTER 12 • ADDING GRAPHICS TO A NEWSLETTER 377

Similar to WordPerfect, Presentations displays context sensitive toolbars and buttons. Because the current fill color for the paint splash is white, you can't start by selecting a fill pattern. All tiles on the fill palette appear to be solid white—the current foreground and background fill colors. You need to select a temporary fill color so that you can see the fill patterns on the fill style palette.

4. Click the Foreground Fill Color button, then select any bright fill color (such as bright blue or red—anything except white). The color you select will be used by the Fill Style Palette button to display fill patterns.

5. Now click the Fill Style button to open the fill style palette and select one of the gradient fills, such as the centered, rectangular gradient. Alternatively, you can click the More button on the palette to open the Object Properties dialog box, then click the Gradient button to display a larger selection of predefined gradient styles.

6. Next, select both a foreground and a background fill color for your gradient, using the appropriate toolbar buttons.

7. Experiment with several gradient patterns and fill combinations until you are satisfied with your image. To update the WordPerfect document and return to the document editing window, click the OLE close button.

8. Now return the document Zoom size to Full Page so that you can view the effect of your changes. (You need to use View, Zoom rather than the Zoom button while the box is selected.) If you like the changes, deselect the box by clicking somewhere else in the document. Or zoom back to a large size and edit the image again.

A Simple Editing Example

Changing the shape of a clipart image involves editing the image points. Once again, because you are editing an actual image, you must first launch the OLE server associated with the image.

Hands On: Editing the Paint Tubes Image

To remove the tall, pointy caps from the top of each of the paint tubes so that they look a little more like oil paint tubes, use these steps:

1. Zoom to 200%, scroll to the paint tubes image, then double-click the figure to launch Presentations.

PART IV • CREATE A NEWSLETTER

2. Select the image within the box; then, if necessary, drag the image within the box until you can see the top of each tube. This does not actually move the image within the box—it merely acts as a method of scrolling to other areas of the image.

3. Right-click to display the QuickMenu, then choose Separate Objects so that you can edit each item within the group.

You can alternately choose Edit Group which allows you to edit each object within the group without separating the objects. An additional set of handles and grouping box will appear.

4. Click the yellow paint tube (the first tube on the left), right-click to display the QuickMenu, and again choose Separate Objects.

5. Right-click again, then choose Edit Points. The points used to describe the image will be displayed.

6. To allow more precise editing, click the Zoom button, select Zoom to Area, then zoom around the top of the paint tube cap. Your editing window should look similar to Figure 12-22, which also displays the guideline identifying the area to be deleted, described in the next step.

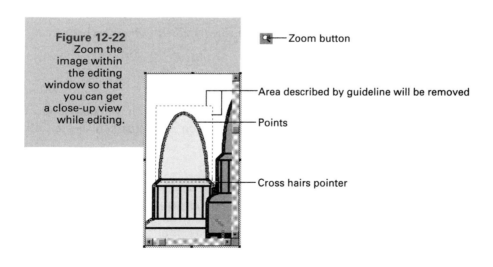

Figure 12-22
Zoom the image within the editing window so that you can get a close-up view while editing.

CHAPTER 12 • ADDING GRAPHICS TO A NEWSLETTER

7. Although you can individually click and delete each point, it's easiest to select a group of points and then delete them as a unit. To do so, drag the mouse pointer over the cap enclosing all points for the cap within the guidelines (refer to Figure 12-22). When you release the mouse, the points will be selected.

Tip

If you make a mistake and accidentally drag a point rather than selecting it, release the mouse button then press Ctrl+Z to undo your accidental change.

8. Press Del to remove the points, resulting in a squared-off paint cap! Don't like it? Press Ctrl+Z to undo your change, then edit the points and try again.
9. Now, scroll to each tube, and then, repeating steps 4-8, remove the rounded tips from each paint cap.
10. When satisfied with your changes, close the Presentations window by clicking the Close OLE button. The edited paint tubes will appear in the document.
11. Finally, use the Image Tools, Move and Zoom buttons to position the paint tubes neatly within the graphic box. When complete, your newsletter should resemble Figure 12-23.

Figure 12-23
Almost done, but the headline looks a little lost.

Moving the Headline Provides the Final Touch

It's a pretty common practice to span a headline over the columns which contain the text for the article. When learning about columns, however, the headline was included within the column; it wrapped and looked okay until the drop cap and background were added. Before calling the newsletter complete, reposition the headline removing it from the first column and centering it across both columns.

You could certainly include the headline in a text box graphic box, but it's really not necessary in this instance. Text boxes will be discussed in the next example.

Hands On: Placing the Headline Over Both Columns

Use these steps to remove the headline text from the first column and center it over both columns:

1. Position the insertion point at the beginning of the headline. Now open Reveal Codes so that you can view the exact formatting instructions while you cut and paste the headline to its new position.

2. Press ← to position the insertion point *before* any font codes surrounding the text.

You can cut, copy, and paste codes just as though they were text. If graphic box codes of any type follow the font face code or font size code, select and cut the box code. Then, using the cursor arrows, place the insertion point just prior to or just after the [Dropcap Definition] code and paste the box to this new location. You may need to edit the oil slick position to correct its location.

3. Select and cut the complete headline, including any of the font codes which surround it. Delete any extra [HRt] codes which may follow the column definition code.

4. Press ↑ once to place the insertion point on a blank line, then press Enter four times to open a few lines of blank space.

5. Press ↑ twice to move to the second blank line, then paste the headline. It now appears prior to the column definition.

6. Press Home, Home to move to the absolute beginning of the line, prior to the font codes, then press Shift+F7 to center the line.

7. Now, if desired, change the font face or font size for the headline. Figure 12-24 shows the completed newsletter, using Times Roman, bold, 30 pt for the headline text.

Don't use center justification here unless you first select the line! Doing so will force the entire newsletter to use center justification.

Figure 12-24
The completed newsletter shows off your graphic talents!

Adding a Screen Shot to Documentation

As you learn WordPerfect 8, you may find that documenting new computer procedures is one of your duties. As you type instructions for other users, it's often helpful to include pictures of the actual screens users will work with, including lines or arrows (called *callouts*) pointing to important areas. You can use a number of methods to capture screens, including Windows 95's Alt + Print Screen capability. What makes WordPerfect powerful, however, is its ability to edit the screens, zooming to only important areas of the screen, then adding borders, fills, callouts, and captions.

This section will introduce you to WordPerfect 8's drawing layer. You'll learn how to draw shapes, add lines with pointing arrows on the ends, add text boxes for callout text, and how to create captions for your figures.

Alt+Print Screen is an effective method of grabbing just the active dialog box or active window. If you need complete screens, such as the background window behind a dialog box, or images of the cursor or mouse pointer, you'll need to purchase a snap shot program specifically designed for that task. You can then edit the resulting graphic files in WordPerfect or Presentations.

Hands On: Capturing a Screen, Then Pasting It to a Document

Use these steps to capture a WordPerfect screen and then add it to a document:

1. In a new document window, type:

    You can copy, move, print, and delete files and folders using a file management dialog box such as Open File, displayed in the next figure:

2. Now, click the File Open button on the toolbar to open the Open File dialog box. Press Alt+Print Screen to take a snapshot of the dialog box. It doesn't appear that anything has happened, but Windows 95 has copied a picture of the active dialog box to the Clipboard.

3. Click the Close button to close the dialog box, then press Ctrl+V to paste the screen image from the Clipboard to your document. After a brief pause the figure will appear in your document. Don't be deceived! That's a picture of the dialog box, not the real one! You may need to adjust your zoom size so that you can view the complete figure.

4. Select the figure, then using the QuickMenu, attach the graphic to the paragraph and align it with the right margin. Size the box proportionally with the width set to 4.5". Then save your document using the filename `documentation.wpd`. Your document should look similar to Figure 12-25.

Adding a Callout to the Figure

WordPerfect 8 has a complete set of drawing tools similar to those you find in most drawing programs. You can use these tools to draw simple and complex lines, closed shapes such as polygons, circles and ellipses, and arrows. The shapes can be edited in the same manner you edit any other graphic. You can add borders and fills, colors and shadows. You can drag the shapes to new positions, use the figure handles to size the shape, and so on. Choose Insert, Shape to open the menu of drawing tools shown in Figure 12-26.

CHAPTER 12 • ADDING GRAPHICS TO A NEWSLETTER   383

Figure 12-25
At a 75% Zoom display, the documentation page should resemble this figure. Your screen image may look different, however.

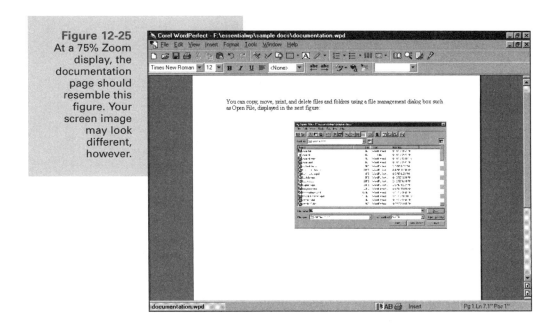

Figure 12-26
The drawing tools menu lists the shapes you can add to a WordPerfect document.

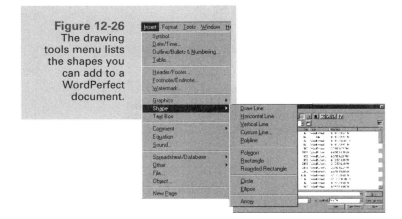

As you can see by viewing the menu, several basic shapes can be drawn. Figure 12-27 illustrates and identifies the shapes for you.

If you need to create more complicated shapes than WordPerfect allows, choose Insert, Graphics, Draw Picture to launch Presentations 8.

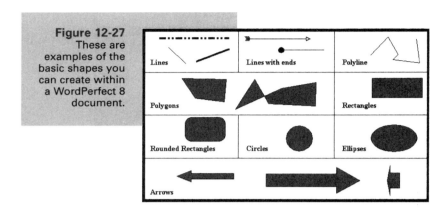

Figure 12-27 These are examples of the basic shapes you can create within a WordPerfect 8 document.

Drawing Lines

Inserting or drawing lines in a WordPerfect document is very simple. But the steps involved vary slightly depending on the line type you are creating. All lines are drawn using the Insert, Shape menu. When you select one of the line types, the Drawing Line Shape property bar appears, offering several buttons for your use in editing a line. Figure 12-28 identifies these buttons for you.

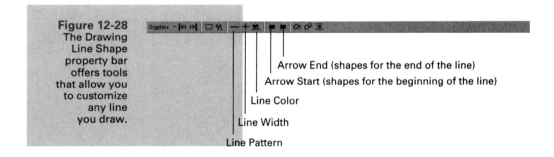

Figure 12-28 The Drawing Line Shape property bar offers tools that allow you to customize any line you draw.

Here's a list of the steps for creating the various line types:

- Horizontal and vertical lines extend automatically from margin to margin at the insertion point. These lines are useful when creating a rule to separate different topics in a column, for example. To insert either a horizontal or vertical line, choose Insert, Shape, then choose either Horizontal Line or Vertical Line. A line will appear in the document.

Tip

If QuickFormat is enabled, type a series of either ------- (hyphens) or ========== (equal signs) to insert a single or double horizontal line at the insertion point.

Tip

When creating a header or footer, a line button is visible on the property bar, which, when clicked, also creates a horizontal line at the insertion point.

- To draw a line, choose Insert, Shape, Draw Line. The mouse pointer changes to a cross hair. Point with the mouse at the position you want the line to begin, then drag the pointer across the window until the line reaches the length you need. Then release the mouse. You can constrain the line in 45-degree increments by pressing [Shift] as you drag the mouse pointer.
- When Custom Lines is chosen from the Shape menu, the Create Graphics Line dialog box opens from which you can define all of the line attributes you want to use such as the line style, width and color. Custom lines also require you to type the length you want the line to assume and to refine the placement for the line at the insertion point. For example, when creating a horizontal line, you can place the line at the baseline of the current font face, or you can set an exact location measured from the top edge of the paper.
- Polylines are lines with angles. They break at corners and then continue in a new direction until you are done. To create a polyline, first choose Polyline from the Shapes menu, then drag the mouse pointer creating the first line segment. Release the mouse button to break the segment, then drag in a new direction. Continue dragging and releasing until all line segments have been created, then double-click to finish the polyline.

To edit any of the line lengths, right-click to display the QuickMenu, then choose Edit Points. Drag a point on the line to change its length.

Hands On: Adding a Callout to the Screen Capture

To add a callout identifying the Details button on the captured Open File dialog box, use these steps:

PART IV • CREATE A NEWSLETTER

1. With the documentation document open, increase the zoom view to a size large enough to allow you to easily see the toolbar buttons.
2. Choose Insert, Shape, Draw Line. The mouse pointer changes to a cross hair.
3. Point to the Details button on the screen capture image of the Open File dialog box.
4. Press and drag the mouse pointer past the left edge of the box. Release the mouse when the line is the correct length. The line will remain selected with its box handles around the perimeter of the graphic box. Your screen image may look similar to Figure 12-29.

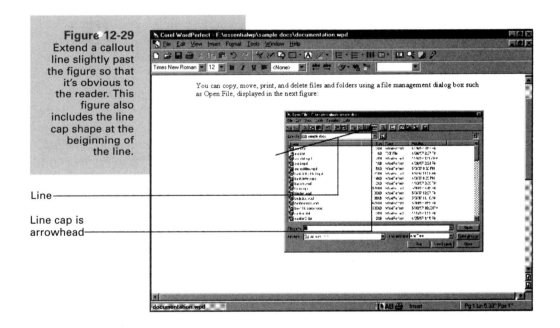

Figure 12-29 Extend a callout line slightly past the figure so that it's obvious to the reader. This figure also includes the line cap shape at the beiginning of the line.

Line

Line cap is arrowhead

5. There are a number of different standards for callouts, but I like to include an arrow pointing to the selected item so that the reader knows just what I'm talking about. To add an arrow to the beginning of the line, click the Arrow Start button. Its palette will open as shown in Figure 12-30.
6. Click the tile for the arrowhead you like. It will appear at the beginning of your line.
7. If necessary, drag a corner handle to resize or pivot the line.

Figure 12-30
The Arrow Start and Arrow End buttons each display this palette of line end choices.

8. To group the line and the figure so that they remain together (and so accidental edits don't move the callout away from its intended button), leave the line selected, then Shift+click while pointing to the screen capture figure. The group of handles will appear around the perimeter described by both figures together.

9. Click the Graphics drop-down menu on the toolbar, then choose Group. The menu will close. Click elsewhere in the document to deselect the figure group.

Creating a Text Box to Describe the Callout

Text boxes are special graphic boxes in which you can type text. They're especially useful when creating visual documents such as newsletters or flyers since you can freely place text by dragging the text box around rather than attempting to position text using formatting commands. I've used them frequently when creating business card layouts, advertising flyers, and even lengthy brochures. They also provide a method of including a table that spans several columns in a newsletter. You can include almost every text formatting command in a text box, setting tabs, font faces and attributes, and so on.

To create a text box, choose Insert, Text Box. A graphic box will appear in your document with the insertion point blinking inside, ready for you to type the content of your text. The text box is usually about the length of half a text line and sized appropriately for one line of text. As text lines wrap within the box, the box expands vertically to accommodate the text. You must size the box yourself, however, by dragging a handle if you want the box to be wider or more narrow.

Tip

For text boxes that will contain lengthy or complicated text, it's easiest to create the text in a document window, then cut and paste it into a text box. In this method you can easily retain formatting without being bound by the constraints of the text box size.

Hands On: Adding a Description to the Callout

Use these steps to describe the detail button for your screen shot callout:

1. Click in the document window, but be sure that the screen shot figure is not selected.
2. Choose Insert, Text Box. A text box will open in the document. Don't worry about its placement yet.
3. In the text box, first select an appropriate font face and size for the callout, something like Arial 10pt will work nicely. As you change the point size for your font, the text box will adjust vertically reflecting your change.
4. Now type: **The Detail button shows you the details for each file on the list**. As you type this lengthy text, the text box expands vertically adjusting for multiple lines.
5. Click outside the text box so that you can now manipulate the text box as a figure box, moving it to the correct position in the document. The border around the box is removed and the box is deselected.
6. Click the box, then position the mouse pointer over the box until it appears as a four-headed arrow. Drag the text box to the left side of the screen shot figure, then release the mouse. The text box will now overlap the screen shot, as displayed in Figure 12-31.

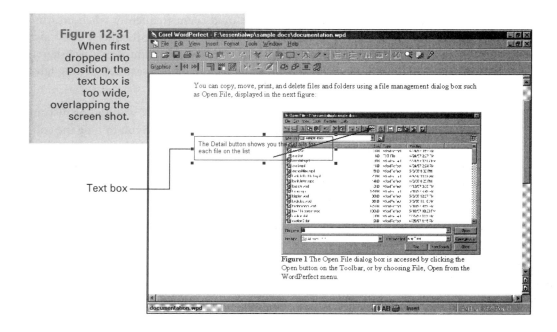

Figure 12-31 When first dropped into position, the text box is too wide, overlapping the screen shot.

CHAPTER 12 • ADDING GRAPHICS TO A NEWSLETTER **389**

7. Using the side and bottom center handles, size the box until the descriptive text is three or four lines in height and the box fits nicely against the left margin without overlapping the screen shot.

8. Using the Border button on the graphics property bar, remove the border for the text box.

9. Now group the text box with the screen shot and the callout line. (You'll need to select both figures first.)

Drawing Shapes

As you saw in Figure 12-27, many different types of shapes can be created using the drawing tools. Shapes differ from lines in that they are closed—the lines meet at all corners so that the center of a shape can contain a fill. When first created, all closed shapes contain a fill. You can change the fill, change the colors for the fill, and also add shadows to a closed shape. When creating a closed shape, the property bar updates with buttons used to edit the attributes for a shape.

All closed shapes are started from the Insert, Shapes menu. While similar, the various shapes require slightly different steps when creating. Here are the shapes and the steps used to create them:

- *Polygons* are flat shapes surrounded by three or more straight lines. To create a polygon, first choose Polygon from the Shapes menu. The mouse pointer changes to a cross hair. Press and drag the pointer to describe the first line, then release the mouse button to form the first corner. Now press and drag to form a three-sided polygon. Release the mouse pointer again when the second line is complete, then drag and release the mouse pointer for each segment of the polygon until the shape is complete. Double-click to finish the polygon.

- *Rectangles* are also polygons, but are limited to four sides. After selecting Rectangle from the Shape menu, the mouse pointer changes to a cross hair. Press and drag the mouse pointer over the area that describes the rectangle, then release the mouse button. Create a square by pressing (Shift) while dragging the mouse pointer.

- *Rounded rectangles* create rectangles with rounded corners. They are created in exactly the same manner as a rectangle.

- *Circles* and *Ellipses* are similarly created in the same fashion. After selecting the desired shape from the Shape menu, press and drag the mouse pointer, creating the shape.

- *Arrows* are special shapes. You create an arrow by first selecting it from the Shapes menu. Then press and drag the mouse to create the arrow. As you drag to the left, the arrowhead points to the right. Drag to the right and the arrowhead points to the left. As you drag up or down you define the height of the arrow shape.

Hands On: Adding a Shape to the Callout

Use these steps to add an ellipse as a border around the callout text:

1. Choose Insert, Shape, Ellipse. The mouse pointer appears as a cross hair.
2. Position the pointer to the upper left corner of the callout text, then press and drag the mouse pointer over the callout text. Don't worry if you can't cover the text exactly. You can adjust the dimensions of the ellipse after it has been created. When the ellipse is approximately the correct shape, release the pointer. The filled ellipse shape now covers the callout text.
3. Remove the fill from the ellipse by clicking the Fill Style button on the property bar. Click the first tile in the palette, marked with an x (see Figure 12-32). The fill will be removed.

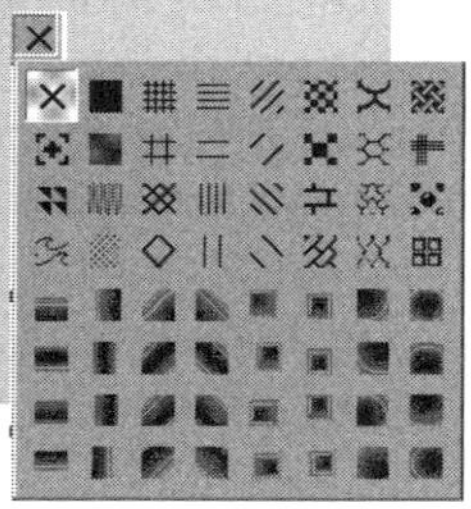

Figure 12-32 Select the solid, black shape to create a solid fill; click X to make the shape transparent.

4. Using the box handles, adjust the ellipse shape and position until the callout text is centered within the ellipse.
5. You may want to separate the remaining images and reposition the callout line so that it meets the edge of the ellipse. Figure 12-33 displays the ellipse with the text and callout line in place.
6. Finally, add the ellipse to your object grouping. The group should now include all of the elements—the screen figure, the callout line, the callout text, and the ellipse surrounding the callout text. This grouping makes up the complete object.

CHAPTER 12 • ADDING GRAPHICS TO A NEWSLETTER **391**

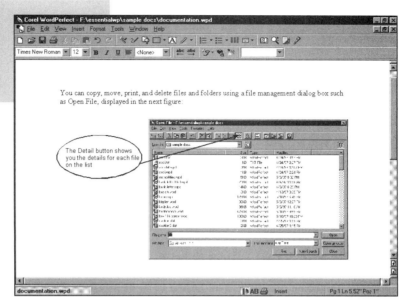

Figure 12-33
Adding a shape such as an ellipse draws attention to the callout text.

Adding a Caption to the Screen Shot Figure

> FOR ADDITIONAL INFORMATION ABOUT CREATING LISTS, REFER TO CHAPTER 10.

Readers benefit from figure captions which describe the figure or provide other pertinent information about the image being presented. Including a caption also adds a figure number of some type to the box. This figure number can be automatically included when generating lists.

In WordPerfect, captions can appear on any of the four sides of a graphic box, either inside or outside of the box boundary. If a border is included with the graphic box, adding a caption inside the box boundary adds the caption inside the border. You can also rotate a caption at any of the four sides.

Hands On: Adding a Caption to the Screen Shot Figure

With all objects grouped, the caption will still be placed on one of the four sides of the graphic box. Use these steps to add a caption to the bottom of the box:

1. Select the object, right-click to display the QuickMenu, then choose Caption. The Box Caption dialog box will open (see Figure 12-34).

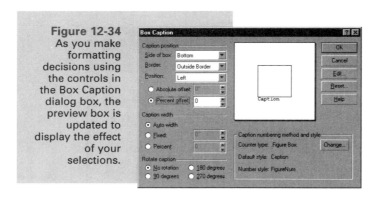

Figure 12-34 As you make formatting decisions using the controls in the Box Caption dialog box, the preview box is updated to display the effect of your selections.

The caption for a grouped object can only be created through the Box Caption dialog box. A simple caption for a single graphic box can be created by clicking the Caption button on the graphics property bar. However, you can only create the caption text with the Caption button. You'll still need to use the Box Caption dialog box to format the caption's location and position.

2. Click the Edit button to add the figure number to the bottom of the screen capture figure. The insertion point appears after the figure number so that you can type the text for the caption.

3. Press the space bar, then type this text: **The Open File dialog box is accessed by clicking the Open button on the Toolbar, or by choosing File, Open from the WordPerfect menu.**

4. Click outside the caption to deselect it, adding it to the figure. The completed screen shot appears in Figure 12-35.

Including a Graphic on Every Page Using a Watermark

To WordPerfect, a watermark is a special code, similar to a header or footer, which appears on every page of a document once it has been created. It prints behind the text or contents of a document, often containing a graphic such as a logo. Although you can include text in a watermark, be careful with its placement so that it doesn't interfere with the text of the document itself.

Chapter 12 • Adding Graphics to a Newsletter

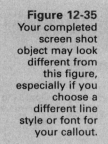

Figure 12-35
Your completed screen shot object may look different from this figure, especially if you choose a different line style or font for your callout.

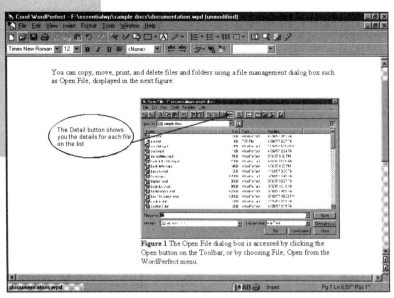

Two watermarks can be active at the same time in a document, designated as Watermark A and Watermark B. Both watermarks can appear on every page, or can be defined so that one watermark appears on odd numbered pages while the other watermark appears on even numbered pages.

Adding a watermark that contains a clipart image to a document is simple. Use these general steps:

1. Click the insertion point on the page where you want the watermark to begin.
2. Choose Insert, Watermark. The Watermark dialog box will open, allowing you to Create, Edit, or Discontinue either Watermark A or Watermark B.
3. Click either Watermark A or Watermark B, then click Create. The window will update, displaying a blank page in Full Page Zoom view. The Watermark buttons appear on the property bar. Figure 12-36 identifies these buttons for you.
4. Click the Image button to open the Insert Image dialog box.
5. Locate and select a graphic file, then click Insert to add the file to the watermark page. The image appears in the watermark page, lightly shaded and formatted at full size so that it fills the page.

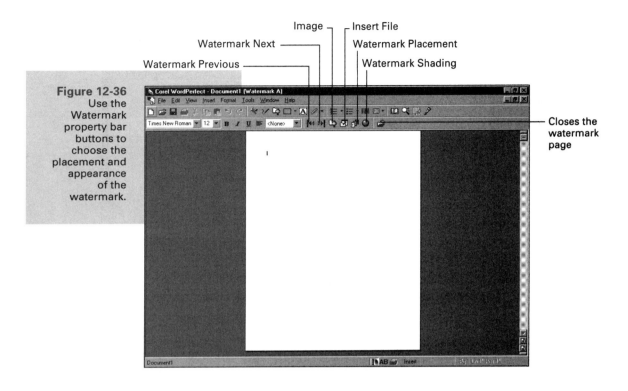

Figure 12-36 Use the Watermark property bar buttons to choose the placement and appearance of the watermark.

> You can't add an image from the Scrapbook while creating a watermark. If you want to use a Scrapbook image, it's easiest to add the image to the document, then cut and paste it into the watermark page. You may need to adjust the image shading so that the image does not overwhelm the text, making it impossible to read.

6. If desired, size and place the image, or make any other editing changes as you would normally to a graphic image. Click outside the image to deselect it. The Watermark property bar buttons reappear.

7. To increase or decrease the image brightness, click the **Watermark Shading** button. Both text and image shading are set to 25% of normal. To make the image brighter, increase the percentage. Click OK to return to the watermark page.

8. When you are satisfied with the watermark, click the Close button to return to your document. The watermark image will now appear behind each remaining page of text of the document.

PART V
Tell Me More

13 USING WORDPERFECT TO CONNECT TO THE WORLD.... **397**

14 EQUATIONS—A SPECIAL TYPE OF GRAPHIC........... **435**

15 AUTOMATING DAILY WORK WITH SIMPLE MACROS **449**

16 UNDERSTANDING TEMPLATES AND PROJECTS.......... **481**

13
Using WordPerfect to Connect to the World

IN THIS CHAPTER

- Creating Web Pages with WordPerfect
- Linking Web Pages Using Hyperlinks
- Publishing Your Web Pages

Unless you have been hiding in a cave for the last few years, you have heard about the World Wide Web: a globe-girding complex of computers and communication links that you can access with a special tool called a *browser*. The *World Wide Web* (*WWW* or just *Web* for short) is arranged into *sites*, with each site containing information provided by the site's owner. Most sites are nothing more than individual pages of information (much like the pages in a WordPerfect document) linked together with special connections called *hyperlinks*. In fact, although the Corel WordPerfect Suite provides many tools specifically for maintaining Web sites, you can build a credible Web site for yourself using only WordPerfect 8.

In this chapter, you'll learn how to create Web pages using the tools provided by WordPerfect, and how to link those pages to form a complete Web site.

Creating a Web Document

You can create Web pages either by converting existing WordPerfect documents into Web format (known as HTML) or by creating the Web pages from a WordPerfect template. The built-in WordPerfect Web templates provide customized menus and toolbars to make working with Web pages easier.

HTML stands for *HyperText Markup Language*, a simple programming language used to describe Web page text, graphics, and formatting. Actually writing HTML code can be very complicated, but WordPerfect writes all the code for you.

HTML does have some formatting limits, so not everything you can see in a WordPerfect document can be translated into a Web page.

To surf the World Wide Web, you need a *browser*. The two most popular browsers available are Netscape Navigator and Microsoft's Internet Explorer. A browser should be provided to you by your Internet Service Provider (ISP). Here's where you can download the latest version of each of these browsers:

http://www.microsoft.com/ie/download/
http://www.netscape.com/cgi-bin/123.cgi

CHAPTER 13 • USING WORDPERFECT TO CONNECT TO THE WORLD 399

Publishing a WordPerfect Document to HTML

If you have lots of WordPerfect documents that you want to publish on your Web site, you can convert them to Web format. After the conversion, you need to reopen the document in WordPerfect and edit it (as discussed later in this chapter) to adjust any formatting that HTML cannot handle properly.

To save an existing WordPerfect document in Web page format, follow these steps:

1. Choose File, Open.
2. Select the file to convert from the Open File dialog box. WordPerfect displays the document. For example, Figure 13-1 shows the selection of a heavily formatted page that uses graphics, multiple fonts, bullets, and a table with a background color.

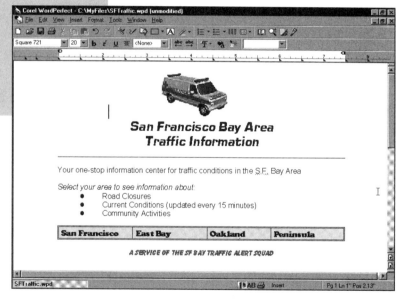

Figure 13-1
The first step in converting a document to Web format is to open the document in WordPerfect.

3. Choose File, Internet Publisher to open the Internet Publisher dialog box (see Figure 13-2).
4. Select Format as Web Document. The resulting document gives you some idea how the page will look in a Web browser, but the view is not entirely accurate. For example, the document shown in Figure 13-3 still shows the blue background on the table—but the browser version of this document

does not include the background. And remember, if people viewing your Web page don't have the fonts you used, the page won't look the same on their computers.

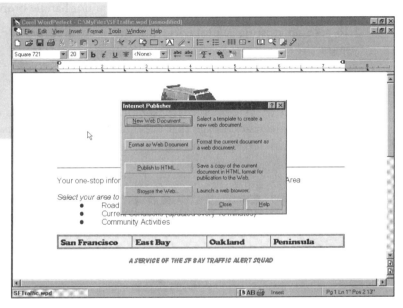

Figure 13-2
The Internet Publisher dialog box enables you to work with your WordPerfect document in Web format.

If you save a file after choosing to format it as a Web document, you will wipe out your original WordPerfect file and replace it with this "converted" file because the filename is the same as your original document. To avoid this problem, save the file with a different name.

5. Choose File, Internet Publisher, and click Publish to HTML. WordPerfect displays the Publish to HTML dialog box. The suggested file name is the same as the original document with an HTM extension.
6. Click OK and WordPerfect makes the conversion.
7. To see the converted document, choose File, Open and choose the newly created document. Choose OK when the Convert File Format dialog box opens to convert the file from HTML. WordPerfect displays the page as it will look in a Web browser (see Figure 13-4).

CHAPTER 13 • USING WORDPERFECT TO CONNECT TO THE WORLD **401**

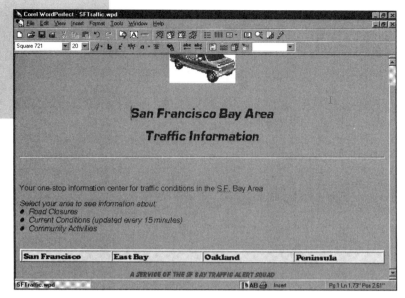

Figure 13-3
This is approximately how the heavily formatted document will look in a Web browser.

Note

It is possible to skip step 4 and convert the original document without first previewing the document in Web format. However, for some reason, much more formatting is lost when you do this. For example, the bullets and table borders are lost, along with some (but not all) of the special font information.

Note

As you can see from Figure 13-4, much of the formatting from our WordPerfect document was lost when we converted to Web format. Centering, tabs, line spacing, and the table background color all disappeared. It is possible to put back most of the special formatting using the tools available for Web pages. However, you should try to build heavily formatted pages destined for the Web directly in Web format, as we will discuss in the next section.

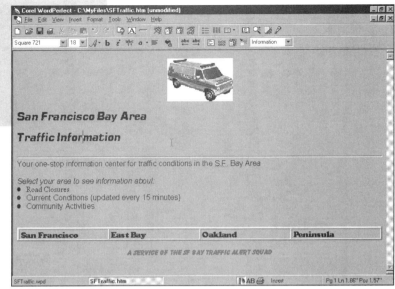

Figure 13-4
The WordPerfect document in Web (HTML) format has lost some of the formatting from the original document.

Creating a New Document Using a Web Template

WordPerfect enables you to create Web-format pages directly using special Web-format templates. As you saw earlier, this is the preferred method of creating Web pages when you need to use any special formatting. When you create a Web page using the Web templates, your formatting options are largely limited to selections that work well in HTML. In addition, you get a pretty good idea of what your Web page will look like in a browser as you work.

Hands On: Creating a New Web Page

To create a new Web page, follow these steps:

1. Choose File, Internet Publisher to open the Internet Publisher dialog box.
2. Select New Web Document. WordPerfect opens the Select New Web Document dialog box. Select the template you want to use from the Select Template list.
3. Choose Select. WordPerfect presents the selected template, ready for you to add your changes.

CHAPTER 13 • USING WORDPERFECT TO CONNECT TO THE WORLD 403

Working with Text Elements

Of course, a blank Web page isn't very interesting, so you can use WordPerfect's tools to add content. Typing text into a Web page is done just as it is in a regular WordPerfect document. However, specifying the attributes of the text works a little differently. While you *can* choose a font and size from the toolbar, your selections might not be preserved in the HTML document. Instead, it's best to use the Web-specific formats provided by the template. You'll see how to do this when you add a text heading and some explanatory text to the page.

Hands On: Adding Text to the Web Page

To add text to the Web page, follow these steps:

1. Press [Enter] three times to move the cursor down the page so that you have room at the top for adding a graphic later.
2. Type **San Francisco Bay Area**, press [Enter], and then type **Traffic Information**.
3. Select the lines you've just typed; click the Font/Size button on the toolbar to drop down a list of Web styles (see Figure 13-5). Select Heading 1.

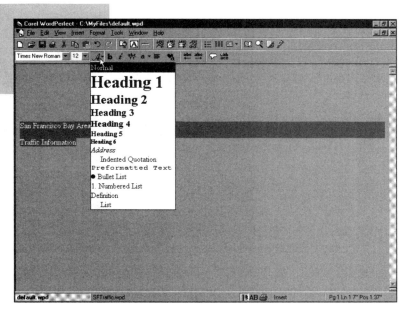

Figure 13-5
Use the Font/Size button to select Web font styles.

Part V • Tell Me More

4. Reselect your text (if necessary) and choose Format, Justification, Center (or click the Justification button on the toolbar and select Center).
5. Move to the next line and select Heading 4 from the Font/Size icon.
6. Type **Your one-stop information center for traffic conditions in the S.F. Bay Area**.

Note

Notice that you can apply formatting to text either before or after typing the text—just as in a regular WordPerfect document.

7. Press Enter, select left alignment, and type **Select your area to see information about:**.
8. Select this line, select Heading 5 from the Font/Size icon, and click the Italic button to italicize the text. Figure 13-6 shows what your Web page looks like so far.

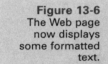

Figure 13-6 The Web page now displays some formatted text.

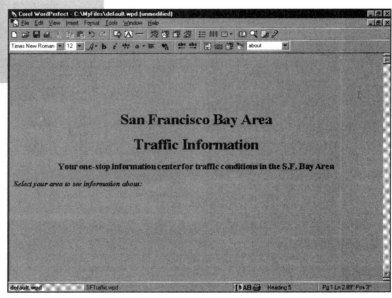

CHAPTER 13 • USING WORDPERFECT TO CONNECT TO THE WORLD **405**

9. Choose File, Save to save the Web page. Name the page **Default**. If you have a browser installed and want to see exactly what the page will look like when someone accesses it on the Web, click the View in Web Browser button on the toolbar; close your browser when you're finished.

Each Web site has a *home page*—the main page for the site. By naming your home page `Default`, you ensure that a visitor's browser will automatically access that page when the visitor specifies the address of your Web site without indicating a particular filename.

Adding Bulleted Items

As with any other document, bullets can highlight important lists of information in a Web page.

Hands On: Adding Bulleted Items to a Web Page

To add a bulleted list to your Web page, follow these steps:

1. Position the cursor one line below the line that reads `Select your area to see information about:`. If you are continuing from the last Hands On, you can just press (Enter).
2. From the Font/Size button, select `Bullet List`. WordPerfect places a bullet on the page, ready for you to type the first item in the list.
3. Type **Road Closures** and press (Enter) to move to the next line. Notice that another bullet automatically appears.
4. Type the other two items in the list: **Current Conditions** and **Community Activities**. Press (Enter) after each entry to move to the next line.
5. Press (←Backspace) or select Normal from the Font/Size button to get rid of the extra bullet on the last line.
6. To make the bulleted items larger, select the entire bulleted list, click the Font Attributes button on the toolbar, and select `Large` from the list. Figure 13-7 shows how the Web page looks now.

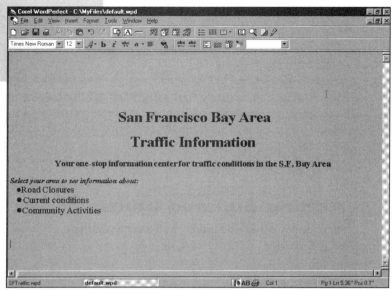

Figure 13-7 The Web page now has a list with bullets to attract the eye.

Including Columns

One major limitation of HTML is that it doesn't support fancy text formatting. However, you can use WordPerfect's column feature to create multiple columns of text in a Web page. By combining multiple columns with other WordPerfect capabilities, you can create side-by-side bulleted or numbered lists.

Hands On: Including Columns in a Web Page

To add columns to a Web page:

1. Type the text you want to appear in columns. For this example, include two columns of descriptive text about the San Francisco Bay area. You can copy this text from Figure 13-9 or just add your own text.

2. Select the text. You can click the Columns button on the toolbar and drag to select the number of columns you want. Alternatively, choose Format, Columns, Format to open the Web Columns dialog box (see Figure 13-8).

3. Set the number of columns by typing **2** in the Columns box. Optionally, you can set the total width of the columns on the page in either pixels or as a percentage of the page width. Finally, you can set the Spacing Between Columns. Figure 13-9 shows how the Web page looks now.

Chapter 13 • Using WordPerfect to Connect to the World

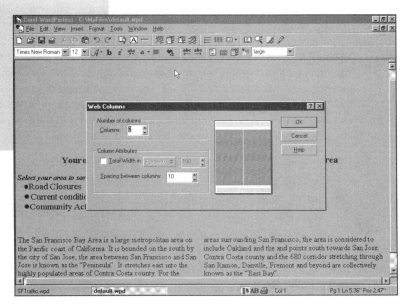

Figure 13-8
The Web Columns dialog box enables you to choose the number of columns you want and set other column attributes.

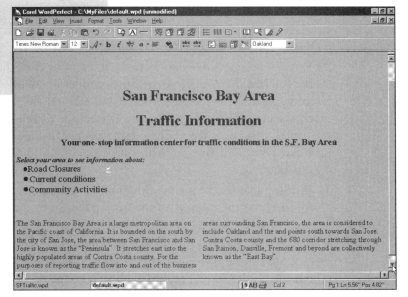

Figure 13-9
WordPerfect's Columns feature helps you lay out text the way you want.

Using Tables for an Organized Display

You can use tables to exercise considerable layout control over the information displayed in a Web page. You can specify the number of rows and columns, as well as background colors and border properties. You can align text within a cell, and set the width of each cell independently.

You can place text in virtually any configuration you want on a Web page by making use of a table with invisible borders. You then can type the text into various cells of the table. All the viewer sees is the information presented in the layout you want.

All the table controls that work under HTML are available from the HTML Table Properties dialog box (reached by choosing T<u>a</u>ble, F<u>o</u>rmat).

Hands On: Adding a Table to a Web Page

To add a table to the example Web page, follow these steps:

1. Place the cursor where you want to insert the table. In this case, place the cursor on the line just after the bulleted list.
2. You can create a table two ways. First, you can click the Table button on the toolbar, then drag to define the number of columns and rows you want. This technique gives you a table with the default properties for colors and borders. The second way to create a table is to choose <u>I</u>nsert, <u>T</u>able. This opens the HTML Table Format dialog box (see Figure 13-10) where you can define the table properties. You use the second method in this example.
3. Set the Table size by setting the number of columns using the <u>C</u>olumns spinner, and the number of rows using the <u>R</u>ows spinner. For the example, set both to **2**.
4. You can set the table appearance by using the spinners for Table <u>B</u>orders, Cell S<u>p</u>acing, and Inside Cell <u>M</u>argins. Table Borders sets the width of the outside border for the table. Cell Spacing sets the border around each cell internally in the table. Inside Cell Margins sets the amount of space between the border of the cell and the text in the cell. For this example, leave these all set to **1**.

CHAPTER 13 • USING WORDPERFECT TO CONNECT TO THE WORLD 409

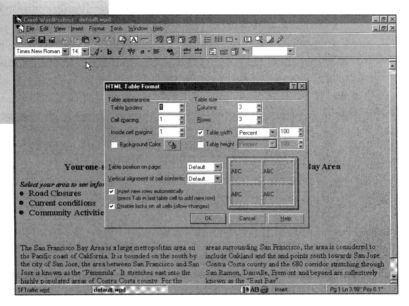

Figure 13-10
The HTML Table Format dialog box enables you to set all the table properties that HTML supports.

5. Set the background color for the table by selecting the Background Color radio button, then clicking the Fill Color button to display a palette of fill colors. Select light blue.

6. If you want, you can set Table Position on Page by selecting `Default`, `Left`, or `Right` from the drop-down list. You can also set Vertical Alignment of Cell Contents to `Default`, `Top`, `Center`, or `Bottom`. For this example, leave both of these set to `Default`.

7. You can set the width and height of the table by choosing Table Width or Table Height. These quantities can be set as either a percentage of the width or height of the page, or directly in pixels. For this example, leave these set to `Default`.

Note

If you decide to set the table height or width, it is usually best to set them as a percentage. The problem with setting the table width in pixels is that you don't know what resolution the person viewing your page will be using. Thus, if you set the table width to 700 pixels and the person is using 640x480 (standard VGA), the Web page will be too wide for them to view on-screen.

PART V • TELL ME MORE

8. When you are done setting the table properties, choose OK to place the table into the Web page.

9. To complete the table, type the following into the four cells (see Figure 13-11) : **San Francisco**, **Peninsula**, **Oakland**, and **East Bay**.

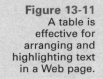

Figure 13-11
A table is effective for arranging and highlighting text in a Web page.

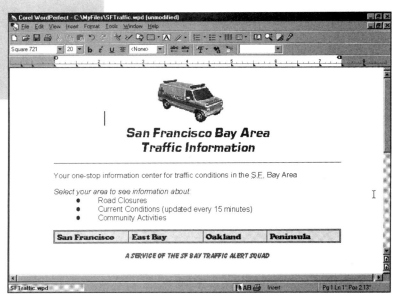

As you can see, the table you've built doesn't look quite right. For one thing, the text is not centered in the cells. Also, the cells are too big for their text. Another problem appears when you view the page in a Web browser (click the View in Web Browser button on the toolbar)—that nice blue background you chose doesn't show up!

We need to make some adjustments to our table! We can make these changes by choosing Table, Format to reopen the HTML Table Properties dialog box. Notice that some additional tabs are now displayed (see Figure 13-12).

In addition to the table properties discussed earlier, you now can adjust the following items:

- Individual row properties, such as Row Height (by percentage or pixels), Row Background Color, and Horizontal or Vertical alignment of the text in the row.

- Individual column properties, such as Column Width (by percentage or

Chapter 13 • Using WordPerfect to Connect to the World 411

pixels), Column Background Color, and Horizontal or Vertical alignment of the text in the column.

- Individual cell properties, such as Horizontal or Vertical alignment of text, and Cell Background Color. You also can specify if you want to Ignore the Cell When Calculating a formula, Use Header Text Format (a heavier text format), and have No Text Wrap in Cell.

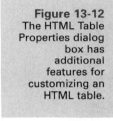
Figure 13-12 The HTML Table Properties dialog box has additional features for customizing an HTML table.

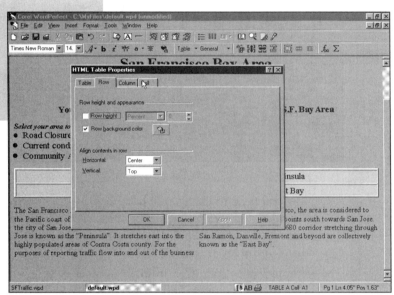

Hands On: Adjusting the Table Dimensions

To adjust the table you created in the previous exercise, follow these steps:

1. Click the upper-left cell of the table and drag to highlight all four cells.
2. Choose Table, Format from the toolbar to open the HTML Table Properties dialog box.
3. Click to select the Cell tab.
4. Change the Horizontal option to Center.
5. Select the Cell Background Color check box. Click the Fill button and choose a light blue from the pop-up color palette.
6. Choose OK to examine the changes you've made (see Figure 13-13). The blue background now shows up in the Web browser as well.

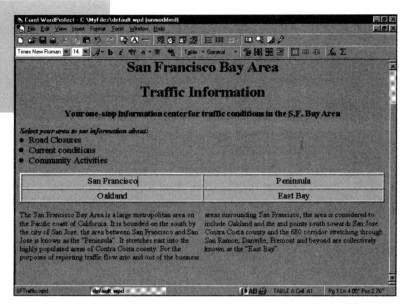

Figure 13-13
After the latest changes, the cell background color works, and the text is centered.

7. Now you need to change the table again—this time to use the first row as a "header" (an area for a label) and the second row to hold the various localities. The first step is to add more cells to the second row. Place the cursor in the lower-left cell (Oakland).

8. Choose Table, Split, Cell from the toolbar to bring up the Split Cell dialog box. Choose Columns and set the quantity to **2** (you could split the cell into multiple rows here, as well, but don't for this example). Choose OK.

9. To split the East Bay cell (lower-right cell), use a different technique. Click QuickSplit Column on the toolbar. Move the cursor to a point about two-thirds of the way across the bottom row of the table, and click. WordPerfect splits the middle cell on the bottom row in two, resulting in four cells in the bottom row.

10. Type the four localities into the cells in the bottom row of the table in the following order: **Oakland**, **San Francisco**, **Peninsula**, and **East Bay**. Delete San Francisco and Peninsula from the top row of the table.

11. Next, you'll combine the two cells in the top row into a single cell. Select the two cells by clicking and dragging across the cells to highlight them.

12. Choose Table, Join, Cell from the toolbar. The two cells are combined into a single cell.

CHAPTER 13 • USING WORDPERFECT TO CONNECT TO THE WORLD **413**

13. In the top row of the table, type **Traffic Localities**. Highlight the contents of this cell and click Bold on the toolbar. Figure 13-14 shows the current Web page.

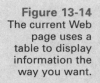

Figure 13-14
The current Web page uses a table to display information the way you want.

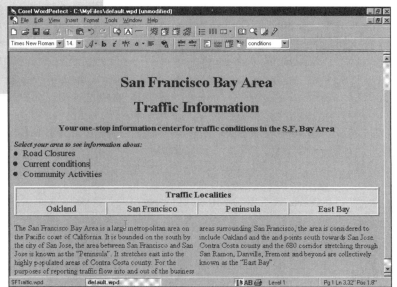

Adding Images

Text communicates information well, but a Web page without any graphics does not look very interesting. A few colorful graphics can really dress up a Web page and catch the viewer's eye. Try to limit your graphics usage, because graphics files can be quite large—which increases the amount of time it takes for a page to load into the browser.

Graphics serve several purposes. In addition to "dressing up" the page, they can be used as buttons to activate links to other Web pages. You can even add special animated graphics to a page. You can place these special files (called "animated GIFs") on a Web page just like any other graphic, but when loaded into a browser, the animation plays automatically, adding interest to the page. There are tools for creating your own animations and packaging them into an animated GIF file, including CorelMove, a tool that comes with Corel's Web.Graphics Suite.

Web browsers only understand two image formats: JPG and GIF. However, you can add graphics to a WordPerfect Web page in other formats. When you publish the page as a Web document in HTML, WordPerfect automatically converts the graphic into one of the supported formats (you have your choice of which one you want to use).

Note

Most ISPs host Web sites for individuals and businesses. Essentially, your Web site is just a folder of Web-format files on the ISP's computer, which has a connection to the Internet. When you contract with an ISP to provide you with space on their computer, most provide a utility to upload your files. To make it easier to keep things organized, you should keep all your Web files in a single folder (or subfolders of a single folder) on your computer, and then use the provided utility to simply upload the entire folder to the ISP.

WordPerfect enables you to place graphics on your Web page from many sources:

> CHAPTER 12 OFFERS INFORMATION ON CLIPART AND THE GRAPHICS EDITOR.

- Clipart collection.
- Graphics File. WordPerfect supports quite a few graphics formats, and you can select a graphics file in any of these formats.
- TextArt. The TextArt application (only available if you installed it when you ran Setup) enables you to create art from text—combining fonts, fills, outlines, and 3D effects into an eye-catching text message.
- Draw Picture. WordPerfect comes with a simple graphics editor that you can use to create your own diagrams right in the Web page.
- Chart. You can easily insert a chart created in either a WordPerfect datasheet or a spreadsheet such as Quattro Pro.

> SEE CHAPTER 9 FOR DETAILS ON INSERTING CHARTS.

Hands On: Adding Graphics to a Web Page

To insert some graphics in the example Web page, follow these steps:

1. Position the text cursor at the very top of the document, where you want to insert the graphic.
2. You want the graphic to appear centered on the page, so click the Justification button on the toolbar and select Center.
3. Choose Insert, Graphics, From File to select a graphic file. Follow along and select one of the Clipart graphics unless you have another graphic you want to use. WordPerfect opens the Insert Image dialog box.

CHAPTER 13 • USING WORDPERFECT TO CONNECT TO THE WORLD   415

You can import clipart that came with WordPerfect by choosing Insert, Graphics, Clipart. WordPerfect opens the scrapbook to display previews of the clipart. Simply drag the graphic you want into the WordPerfect document.

4. Navigate to the folder containing the file you want to use and select the file. Choose Insert.

5. Remove any extra lines at the top of the document and examine the current look of the Web page (see Figure 13-15).

Figure 13-15
You've inserted a graphic on the page. Doesn't it look better now?

6. Click the graphic to select it, right-click, and choose HTML Properties. WordPerfect opens the HTML Properties dialog box (see Figure 13-16).

7. In the Alternate Text field, type **Golden Gate Bridge**. This text will display instead of the graphic if the viewer has graphics turned off in the browser. This text also will display until the graphic downloads, so the viewer has an immediate idea what the graphic is going to display.

PART V • TELL ME MORE

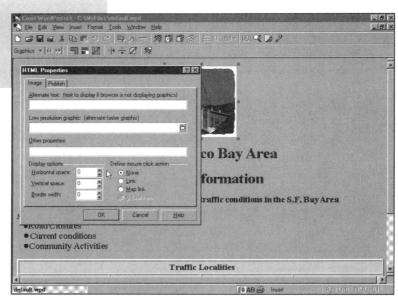

Figure 13-16
This dialog box enables you to set properties for the graphic.

8. You can increase the space around the graphic by adding values to the spinners beside <u>H</u>orizontal Space, <u>V</u>ertical Space, and <u>B</u>order Width.

Note

The Publish tab of the HTML Properties dialog box makes several more options available. The most interesting is the Interlaced option, available when you choose to save or convert a graphics file in GIF format. *Interlaced* is a special variation of the GIF format that downloads a low-detail version of the entire graphic, and then, as additional data is downloaded, the graphic becomes more and more detailed, until it is complete. Using interlaced format is considered a courtesy to viewers, as they can get an idea of the complete graphic before it fully downloads.

Next, you'll add a graphic "button" to the bottom of the page using WordPerfect's TextArt feature so that you can attach a link to another Web page later.

CHAPTER 13 • USING WORDPERFECT TO CONNECT TO THE WORLD **417**

Hands On: Adding a TextArt Button

To add a TextArt button to the Web page, follow these steps:

1. Position the text cursor at the very bottom of the document, below the columns you inserted earlier.
2. Choose Format, Justification, Center to center the text cursor at the bottom of the page.
3. Choose Insert, Graphic, TextArt. WordPerfect opens the TextArt application at the bottom of the screen (see Figure 13-17).

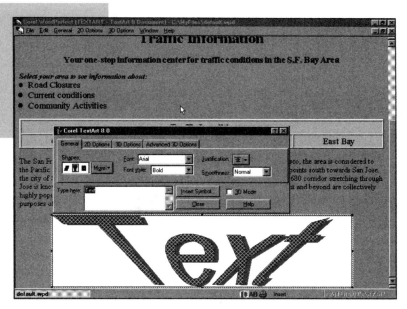

Figure 13-17 The TextArt application enables you to create fancy text effects and add them to a Web page as graphics.

4. Use the tools in TextArt to create a graphic that says **Feedback**. You'll use this graphic later as a button to jump to a page where the viewer can provide their opinion of your Web site (that is, if you want to know!).
5. Click the Close button in TextArt. WordPerfect places the graphic at the bottom of the Web page (see Figure 13-18).

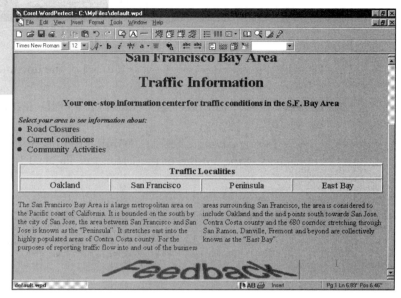

Figure 13-18 This graphic created in TextArt will later be used as a button.

Inserting Lines

You can insert horizontal lines into a Web page to break up blocks of text.

Hands On: Inserting Lines in the Web Page

To insert a line in your Web page, follow these steps:

1. Position the text cursor at the end of the line Traffic Information.
2. Choose <u>I</u>nsert, <u>H</u>orizontal Line. WordPerfect inserts a line below Traffic Information that stretches across the screen.

Changing the Text or Background Colors

Graphics add interest to a Web page, but all that plain black text presents a problem—how do you highlight important items on your Web page? And, while you're at it, try to do something about that boring gray background!

Chapter 13 • Using WordPerfect to Connect to the World

Hands On: Changing the Text and Background Colors

First, change the text color. You can change the color of just some selected text, or of all the text on the page. To change the color of just selected text, use the following steps:

1. Click and drag to select the `Traffic Information` line.
2. Choose the Font Color button on the toolbar. From the pop-up color palette, select dark blue. WordPerfect changes the color of the text to dark blue.
3. Optionally, you can change the color of all the text on the page. To do so, choose Format, Text/Background Colors. WordPerfect opens the HTML Document Properties dialog box (see Figure 13-19).

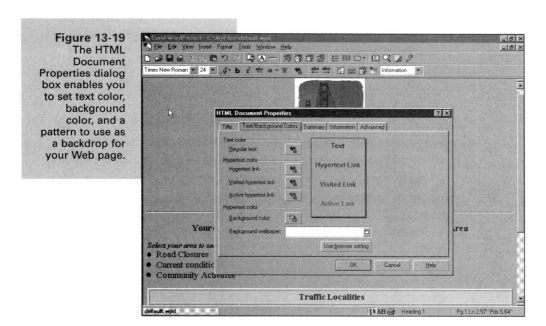

Figure 13-19 The HTML Document Properties dialog box enables you to set text color, background color, and a pattern to use as a backdrop for your Web page.

4. To change the color of all the regular text on the page, choose the Regular Text fill button, and select the color you want from the pop-up color palette. However, any text you changed previously using the technique presented in step 2 will remain its chosen color.

Note

The Hypertext Link colors refer to a special kind of text that enables you to jump between Web pages. This is discussed in the next section.

5. To rid yourself of that gray background color, click the Background Color fill button, and select a color from the pop-up palette.
6. You can use almost any graphic file as a background for the Web page. First, click the small folder button beside the Background Wallpaper text field. WordPerfect opens the Background Wallpaper dialog box. A good source of background textures is the `Corel/Suite8/Graphics/Texture` folder (assuming you used the default installation path).
7. Select the `Paper` folder and double-click to list the files inside. Select `Gray Fibers.bmp` and click Select. WordPerfect returns to the HTML Document Properties dialog box and shows you a preview of the pattern you've selected.
8. Choose OK to return to the Web page and see how your new background looks

Note

Although WordPerfect provides many backgrounds to choose from, most are not appropriate for a Web page. The main problem is that many are too dark (obscuring the text) or too busy, making it difficult to read the Web page. Choose your backgrounds with care!

Working with Hyperlinks

While a single, well-designed Web page is pretty nice, the real power of a Web site is the ability to link multiple pages together into a coherent whole, so the viewer can navigate around the site as he or she chooses. What makes it possible to navigate through the pages on a Web site are invisible links that connect the pages together. These links are called *hyperlinks*. The links can take many forms:

- *Hypertext* is specially-marked text (usually blue in color) that links to another Web page. Clicking the text navigates to the destination Web page.

Chapter 13 • Using WordPerfect to Connect to the World

- A *graphic* can link to another Web page. In fact, the buttons that you often find on Web pages are nothing more than ordinary graphics that have a hyperlink attached.
- An *image map* is a special version of a graphic. Within an image map there can be many different links. Where you navigate to depends on exactly where in the graphic you click. For example, you could use a map of the San Francisco Bay Area as a graphic, and define the graphic as an image map, so that viewers would be able to click the city of Oakland to go straight to the Oakland Web page, and so on. Unfortunately, WordPerfect does not have the ability to build pages with image maps in them. You can, however, build image maps in other tools, including Corel Presentations, and include those pages along with the pages you build in WordPerfect.

Note

As the designer of the Web site, it's up to you to define the hyperlinks and ensure that the pages they link to actually exist. If a hyperlink points to a nonexistent page, the viewer's browser displays an error message—which makes the Web site designer (you!) look pretty clueless.

First of all, you'll need some additional pages or you won't have anything to link to. Build two additional pages—one for East Bay (see Figure 13-20) and one for San Francisco (see Figure 13-21). If you want, you can build pages for the other two localities as well.

Hands On: Adding Web Pages for Linking

To create the additional pages, follow these steps:

1. Create a blank web page by choosing File, Internet Publisher and then clicking the New Web Document button. Select a template and choose Select.
2. Place the elements on the page, as shown in Figure 13-20 (for the first page) or Figure 13-21 (for the second page). It really doesn't matter what you put on the page, except that there should be a text line on each page that reads `Back to Main`.
3. Save the file as `EastBay.wpd` (first page) or `SanFrancisco.wpd` (second page).

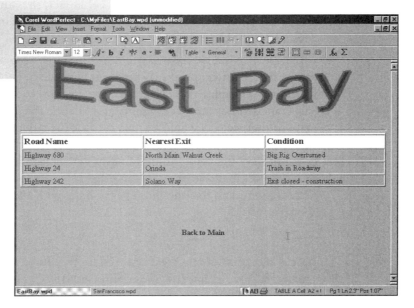

Figure 13-20 This is the Web page for the East Bay.

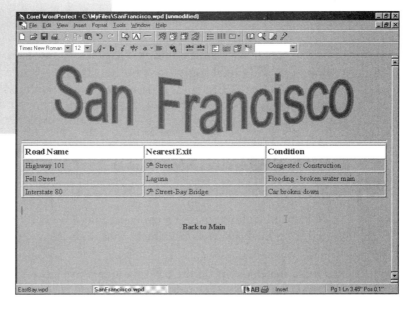

Figure 13-21 This is the Web page for San Francisco. The text `Back to Main` near the bottom of the page will come in handy later.

CHAPTER 13 • USING WORDPERFECT TO CONNECT TO THE WORLD **423**

Adding Text Hyperlinks

First, you're going to build text hyperlinks from the default page to each of the locality pages (East Bay and San Francisco).

Hands On: Creating a Text Hyperlink

To create a text hyperlink, follow these steps:

1. Click and drag to select the text that will become the starting point (source) for the link. For this example, select `San Francisco` in the table near the bottom of the default (traffic information) Web page.
2. Choose Tools, Hyperlink or select the Hyperlink button on the toolbar. WordPerfect displays the Hyperlink Properties dialog box (see Figure 13-22).

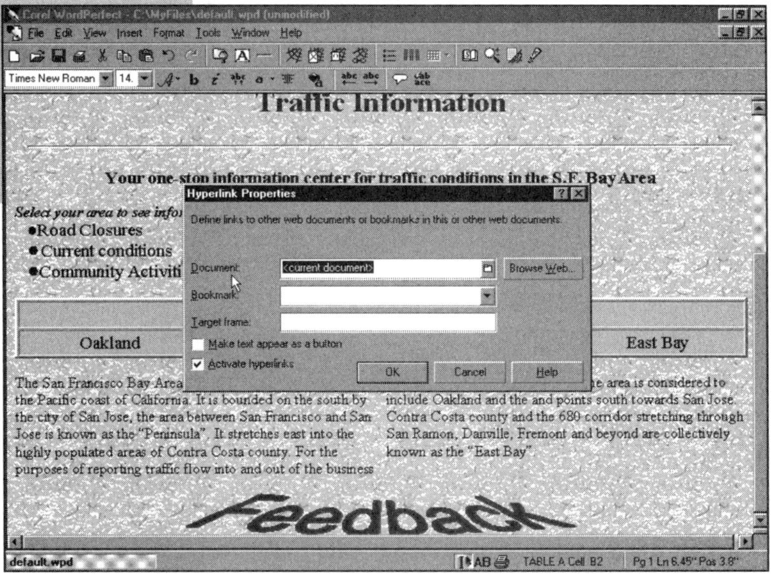

Figure 13-22
Use the Hyperlink Properties dialog box to specify the destination for a hyperlink.

3. Click the browse button (marked with a small folder) beside the Document text field. WordPerfect opens the Select File dialog box.
4. Select the file that will be the target of your hyperlink—that is, the file that will appear when a visitor clicks the hyperlink. For this example, select `SanFrancisco.wpd`. WordPerfect returns to the Hyperlink Properties dialog box, displaying the name of the selected file in the Document field.

PART V • TELL ME MORE

Note: Notice that you can select a destination anywhere on the World Wide Web by clicking the Browse <u>W</u>eb button. However, you must have your Web connection active in order for this to work.

5. Choose OK. WordPerfect returns to the document. Notice that the hypertext now looks different. Unless you've changed the default hypertext properties, the text is blue and underlined (see Figure 13-23).

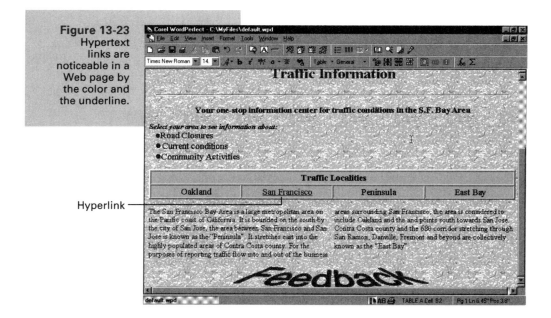

Figure 13-23 Hypertext links are noticeable in a Web page by the color and the underline.

Hyperlink

6. Repeat steps 1 through 5 above to link `East Bay` to the `EastBay.wpd` page.
7. Save the page (choose <u>F</u>ile, <u>S</u>ave). You can now click the hypertext you've just built to jump to either locality page.

Editing a Text Hyperlink

You can change the properties of a text hyperlink (or any hyperlink) by returning to the Hyperlink Properties dialog box and changing information, such as the target of the hyperlink (you'll explore some of the other options in a moment). However, getting to the dialog box can be problematic, because WordPerfect's default behavior is to open the linked document when you click a hyperlink.

There are two ways to edit a hyperlink. First, you can right-click the hyperlink and choose Edit Hyperlink from the pop-up menu. Second, you can temporarily deactivate the hyperlink by deselecting the Activate Hyperlinks check box in the Hyperlink Properties dialog box. If you deactivate the hyperlink, you can then edit the hyperlink by clicking to select it and then choosing Tools, Hyperlink.

Adding Button Hyperlinks

You can also place hyperlinks in Web pages by turning text into "buttons." Once you've built text button hyperlinks, they work just like the hypertext links discussed previously.

Hands On: Adding a Text Button Hyperlink

To build a text button hyperlink, follow these steps:

1. Open the `SanFrancisco.wpd` Web page.
2. Highlight the words `Back to Main` near the bottom of the page.
3. Choose Tools, Hyperlink to open the Hyperlink Properties dialog box.
4. Click the browse button (marked with a small folder) beside the Document text field. Select `Default.wpd` as the target of the hyperlink.
5. Select the Make Text Appear as a Button check box; click OK.
6. WordPerfect creates the hyperlink and formats the `Back to Main` text as a button (see Figure 13-24).
7. Make the same changes to the East Bay page.

Note

The "button" you just created is actually a WordPerfect *text box*. You can edit the properties of the text box by right-clicking it to access the QuickMenu. As discussed in Chapter 12, you can change the text content, position, size, HTML, and border/fill properties. However, none of the border/fill options—except for changing the Available Border Styles and Line Style, both in the Box Border/Fill dialog box—translate properly into a Web page.

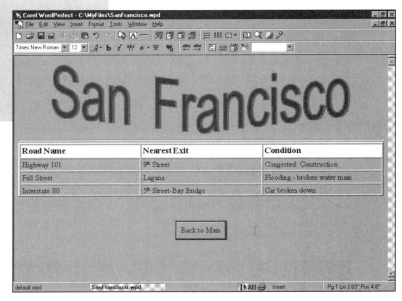

Figure 13-24 You can easily convert hypertext to a button for a more professional appearance.

Adding Graphic Hyperlinks

Another way to insert a hyperlink into a Web page is to attach the link to a graphic. This is my favorite way to implement hyperlinks, because small, carefully chosen graphics really inform viewers exactly what they're choosing.

Hands On: Attaching a Graphic to a Hyperlink

To attach a graphic to a hyperlink, follow these steps:

1. Create a simple Web page named `Feedback`. To do so, choose File, Internet Publisher and choose New Web Document. Select a template, then add the heading **Feedback** to the page. Save the page.
2. Switch to the `Default` page and click the `Feedback` graphic at the bottom of the page.
3. Choose Tools, Hyperlink to open the Hyperlink Properties dialog box.
4. Select the browse button (marked with a small folder) beside the Document text field to open the Select File dialog box. Select `Feedback.wpd` as the target of the hyperlink and click Select.
5. You now can click the `Feedback` graphic to jump to the `Feedback` page.

Using Bookmarks

One of the things you may have noticed is that, up until now, your hyperlinks always jump to another page, and the new page appears flush with the top of the document window. You can combine "bookmarks" with hyperlinks, however, to jump to any location on another page—or even to jump to another location on the same page.

Bookmarks can be very handy. For example, you can use bookmarks and hyperlinks to navigate through a long document. Here's how you might set this up:

1. First, create a long document—perhaps by converting a WordPerfect document into a Web page.
2. At the top of the document, insert a table of contents that includes each of the major headings in the document.
3. Go through the document and place a bookmark at each major heading.
4. Finally, turn each table-of-contents entry into a hyperlink that links to the appropriate heading bookmark.

Hands On: Adding Bookmarks to Hyperlinks

You're going to modify two existing hyperlinks by adding bookmarks to make them more useful. One problem with the local traffic conditions pages (San Francisco and East Bay) is that when a viewer clicks the `Back to Main` hyperlink, they're taken to the top of the `Default` page. It would be better if the links returned to the Traffic Localities table, so that viewers could pick another locality to check without scrolling down the `Default` page. To fix this situation, follow these steps:

1. On the `Default` Web page, place the text cursor at the end of the table heading that reads `Traffic Localities`.
2. Choose Tools, Bookmark to open the Bookmark dialog box (see Figure 13-25).
3. Click Create to open the Create Bookmark dialog box (see Figure 13-26). The default name for the bookmark is the first few words following the bookmark on the page. You can, of course, change the name if you like, but for this example, use the default name.
4. Choose OK to close the Create Bookmark dialog box and create the bookmark.

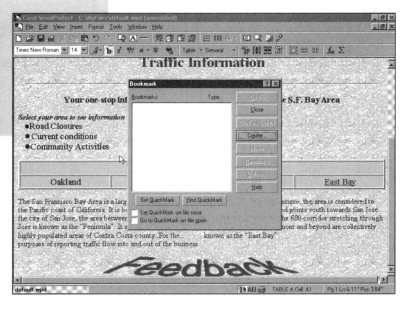

Figure 13-25
The Bookmark dialog box enables you to create bookmarks that mark a particular point in a Web page.

Figure 13-26
Create the bookmark name in the Create Bookmark dialog box.

Note

You can't see bookmarks on a Web page, so they can be pretty hard to find. To locate a bookmark, choose Tools, Bookmark to display a list of existing bookmarks, then select the bookmark you want from the list, and choose Go To. Alternatively, choose View, Reveal Codes. The Reveal Codes window displays a special marker for each bookmark.

5. Open the SanFrancisco.wpd document.
6. Right-click the Back to Main button and choose Edit Hyperlink from the QuickMenu. WordPerfect opens the Hyperlink Properties dialog box.

7. Move to the Bookmark text field and either type the name of the bookmark you want (**Traffic Localities**) or select it from the drop-down list.
8. Click OK. Now, when you move the mouse pointer over the `Back to Main` button, a QuickTip shows that the destination of the hyperlink is the `Traffic Localities` bookmark on the `Default` Web page.
9. Repeat the steps above to add the bookmark to the hyperlink on the `EastBay.wpd` page.

Adding Other Objects to Your Web Page

WordPerfect enables you to add many kinds of objects to a document—embedded spreadsheets, many formats of graphics, animations, and the output of virtually any OLE-enabled application. However, a Web browser has no way to show most of these types of objects, so if your ultimate goal is to publish your pages on the WWW, it doesn't make sense to add these types of objects to a Web page.

There are exceptions to these guidelines, however. Both of the most popular browsers support helper programs (plug-ins in Netscape Navigator and ActiveX components in Microsoft Internet Explorer) that enable them to view more graphic formats, view animations, and do various other things. If you know that your viewers have access to the appropriate plug-ins, then you can add these types of objects to your Web page. One way you can be certain that your viewers have the appropriate plug-ins is if your Web pages are posted on an internal company Web (called an *intranet*) and the plug-ins are installed along with the browsers on the corporate machines.

You can, however, add two types of objects that virtually any standard browser can handle: sound clips and Java applets.

Java applets are beyond the scope of this book, but once you've mastered the basics of putting together a Web site, you might want to pick up one of the many Java books on the market, and learn how to use applets to add functionality to your site.

You can add a sound clip to a Web page in order to provide voice explanations for instructions on that page. For this chapter's example, however, you'll do something more fun: add a sound effect to the page.

PART V • TELL ME MORE

Hands On: Adding a Sound Clip to a Web Page

To add a sound clip to a Web page, follow these steps:

1. Open the Web page to which you want to attach a sound clip. Use the `EastBay` page, just because it's less crowded than the `Default` page.
2. Position the cursor where you want the sound clip inserted. As you'll see in a moment, WordPerfect inserts a small icon where the sound clip is attached. For this example, position the cursor just below the `Back to Main` button.
3. Choose Insert, Sound. WordPerfect opens the Sound Clips dialog box (see Figure 13-27).

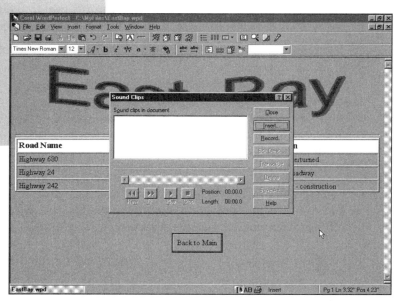

Figure 13-27
The Sound Clips dialog box enables you to insert sounds into a document, as well as listen to sounds and even record your own sounds.

4. If your computer has a properly-equipped sound card, you can click Record and use your microphone or other sound hookup to record a new sound on the spot. For this example, however, you're going to insert a sound that is already stored in a file. Click Insert. WordPerfect opens the Insert Sound Clip into Document dialog box.
5. Type **Traffic Sounds** as the Name for the sound clip.
6. Click the browse button (marked with a small folder) beside the File text box. WordPerfect opens the Select Sound File dialog box.

CHAPTER 13 • USING WORDPERFECT TO CONNECT TO THE WORLD **431**

7. Select the sound file you want to include. In this case, `Carhorn.wav` from the `Corel/Suite8/Sounds` folder. Click Select to return to the Insert Sound Clip into Document dialog box.

Note

There are two additional buttons in the Insert Sound Clip into Document dialog box, Link to File on Disk and Store in Document. For the purposes of publishing a Web page, it doesn't matter which one you choose; the process of publishing the page in Web format places a copy of the sound file in the same folder as the page file regardless of which option you choose.

8. Choose OK. WordPerfect places a small sound icon on the page. To hear the sound, simply click the icon.

Tip

To edit the sound, right-click the sound icon and choose Edit from the QuickMenu.

Publishing Pages to Your Web Site

In the final analysis, your goal is to create a set of files (preferably in a single folder) that you can move to an ISP's computer to create or modify your Web site. For an interactive Web site with hyperlinks (such as the one you've built in this chapter), this means that you need to publish the Web site using HTML.

Note

For a Web site based on a Corel Presentations slide show, however, you could publish the slide show to a Web site using Corel Barista.

Right now, you have a set of WPD files (WordPerfect document files). Unfortunately, WordPerfect does not make it easy to convert these files to a set of working HTML Web pages. Any way you proceed, there are several manual steps you need to perform.

The first difficulty is how to get all your Web files into a single folder. There are two ways to approach this:

- Convert each page to HTML, directing the HTM file into the folder you have designated for your Web pages, and directing the converted graphics and sound files into that folder as well. Unfortunately, graphics that do *not* need to be converted (GIF and JPG files) are not automatically added to the Web folder—so you have to copy those files manually.
- Create the folder for your Web pages and copy all the WPD files and their supporting files (sound, GIF, JPG, and other graphics files, as well as any Java classes or other supporting files you need) into the new folder. Then convert each WPD file to an HTML file. After you have finished the conversion, remove the WPD files from the Web folder (you don't want to upload them to your ISP).

The next issue you have to deal with is redirecting your hyperlinks. If you've been following all the "Hands On" exercises, you've been building hyperlinks—but they're directed at other WordPerfect documents. For example, the Feedback graphic on the Default page is hyperlinked to the file Feedback.wpd. You need to open each .htm file and edit all hyperlinks to point to the .htm version of the target files.

A good way to avoid having to convert files and redirect the hyperlinks is to *only* work with HTML files. That is, immediately upon creating your new, blank WordPerfect Web page (which is a WPD file), use Internet Publisher to Publish to HTML. Then, work *only* with the HTML version of the file. After building all your pages this way, the last step is to designate your hyperlink targets as the appropriate HTML Web pages. For example, you would have created Default.wpd and Feedback.wpd, converted them (as blank pages) to Default.htm and Feedback.htm. You then would have completed building each page in HTML format, and added the hyperlink from the Feedback graphic on the Default.htm page to the Feedback.htm page. This technique, however, limits you to the formatting options that work with HTML, so it's only appropriate when the *only* use of the files you're creating is to establish a Web site.

Hands On: Converting Web Pages to HTML Format

It's time to translate the Web site to HTML format. Follow these steps:

CHAPTER 13 • USING WORDPERFECT TO CONNECT TO THE WORLD **433**

1. Create a new folder named **MyWebSite** to hold the files that comprise your Web site. Copy any GIF or JPG files that you've used in constructing your Web site into the new folder. You've only used the GIF for the Golden Gate bridge, so copy that GIF into the new folder.
2. Open the Default.wpd file.
3. Choose File, Internet Publisher and select Publish to HTML. WordPerfect opens the Publish to HTML dialog box. In the Publish To field, type the destination (MyWebSite) where you want the HTML file saved. In the Save New Images and Sound Clips In field, type where you want images and sound clips saved. These two folders should be the same (see Figure 13-28).

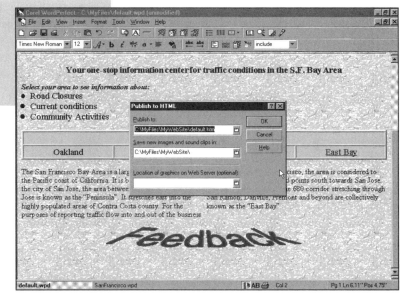

Figure 13-28
Use the Publish to HTML dialog box to designate where the files for your Web site should be saved.

4. Repeat steps 2 and 3 for the other WordPerfect files that comprise your Web site. When you're done, you should have a complete set of HTML files and supporting files in your Web folder.
5. Choose File, Open and select Default.htm.
6. Right-click the San Francisco hyperlink and choose Edit Hyperlink from the QuickMenu. WordPerfect opens the Hyperlink Properties dialog box.

7. Modify the Document field to point to the SanFrancisco.htm file (use the browse button to locate the file if necessary).
8. After you have located the new hyperlink target document, click OK.
9. Repeat steps 6 through 8 to redirect the East Bay and Feedback hyperlinks.
10. Repeat steps 5 through 8 for the East Bay page and San Francisco page (each has only a Back to Main hyperlink, which must point to Default.htm).

You're done converting the Web pages to HTML format; your first complete Web site is ready to face the world!

14
Equations—A Special Type of Graphic

IN THIS CHAPTER

- **Starting the Equation Editor**
- **Understanding the Equation Editor Tools**
- **Mechanics of Building and Editing Equations**
- **Adding Equations to a Document**

For many of us, the last time we had to deal with complex equations was in a math class in high school or college. Nevertheless, the world is full of equations, and sooner or later you'll probably have to include an equation in a WordPerfect document. Equations you're likely to run into include:

PART V • TELL ME MORE

- Financial equations, including loan payments, present or future value of investments, and many others
- Complex equations that are often found in calculations used in electronics and computer design
- "Physical law" equations, such as acceleration, kinetic energy, momentum, gravity, and quantum/speed of light equations

Even if you don't understand what many of these equations do, you might end up having to create a document (perhaps for someone else) containing equations.

Fortunately, WordPerfect includes a powerful Equation Editor. With the Equation Editor, you can build complex equations that include multiple-sized characters, special symbols, and multiple text styles. And, since these equations are a special form of graphic, you can even apply graphic properties to the result to make the equation stand out exactly as you want it to.

You can embed an equation directly in a WordPerfect document just like any other graphic element (see Figure 14-1).

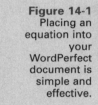

Figure 14-1
Placing an equation into your WordPerfect document is simple and effective.

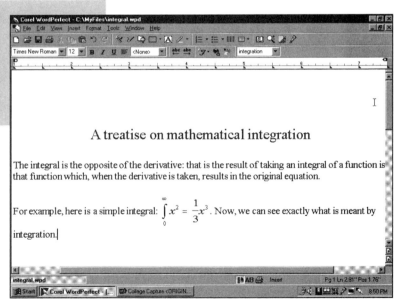

CHAPTER 14 • EQUATIONS—A SPECIAL TYPE OF GRAPHIC **437**

Starting the Equation Editor

The first step is to open or create the WordPerfect document into which you want to insert the equation. When you're ready to insert an equation into your document, position the cursor where you want to insert the equation and choose Insert, Equation. WordPerfect opens the Equation Editor window (see Figure 14-2).

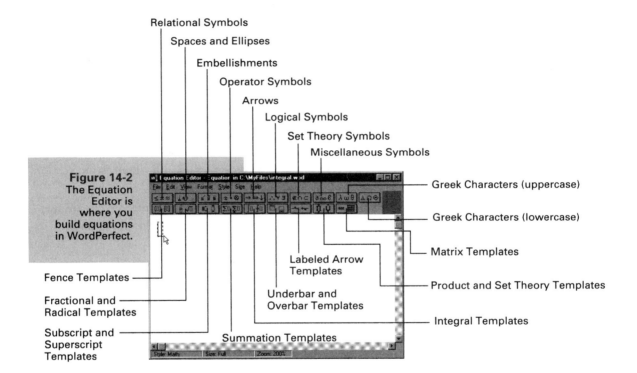

Figure 14-2
The Equation Editor is where you build equations in WordPerfect.

Understanding the Equation Editor Toolbar

The Equation Editor toolbar can be pretty overwhelming. There are a large number of buttons (refer to Figure 14-2), each with its own purpose. Clicking a button causes a drop-down list of symbols to appear. Here's an explanation of what each button provides:

- The Relational Symbols button provides a variety of symbols that are useful in comparing portions of equations. These include equal, not equal, approximately equal, precedes, follows, proportional, equivalence, and subgroup.

- The Spaces and Ellipses button provides various sizes of spaces and various configurations of ellipses (the three-dot symbols).
- The Embellishments button provides a set of symbols that can be used to modify how a particular character is displayed. Most of the embellishments represent symbols that appear above a character, such as prime, double-prime, hat, tilde, overbar, backprime, and arrows. Other embellishments include strikethrough and slash symbols.
- The Operator Symbols button provides symbols for addition, subtraction, multiplication, division, bullets, and angles.
- The Arrow Symbols button provides (surprise!) a variety of arrow symbols, including single and double arrows, bent arrows, and vertical arrows.
- The Logical Symbols button provides a variety of symbols you can use in constructing logic equations. These include Therefore, Since, Exists, Such That, Logical And, and Logical Or.
- The Set Theory Symbols button provides symbols for use in equations for constructing sets. These symbols include Element Of, Intersection, Union, Subset, Superset, and Empty Set.
- The Miscellaneous Symbols button provides several buttons that are very useful, but difficult to classify. Examples include partial differential, gradient, infinity, degree, summation, and product.
- The Greek Characters (lowercase) button provides a set of lowercase Greek characters.
- The Greek Characters (uppercase) button provides a set of uppercase Greek characters.
- The Fence Templates button provides symbols such as parentheses, brackets, braces, vertical bars, and double bars.
- The Fraction and Radicals Templates button provides symbols for fractions (like $1/3$) and radicals (square root, cube root, and so on).
- The Subscript and Superscript Templates button provides various combinations of small subscript and superscript symbols.
- The Summation Templates button provides the summary symbol with various types of limit templates.
- The Integral Templates button provides single, double, and triple integrals, with various flavors of limits on the integration. It also provides contour integrals.
- The Underbar and Overbar Templates button provides overbars and underbars.

CHAPTER 14 • EQUATIONS—A SPECIAL TYPE OF GRAPHIC **439**

- The Labeled Arrow Templates button provides left- and right-facing arrows with slots for adding text to the arrows.
- The Product and Set Theory Templates button provides product, union, and intersection, with many different types of limits.
- The Matrix Templates button provides a set of empty matrix templates so that you can add your own values to a grid.

Understanding Style and Size in the Equation Editor

As you'll see shortly, the Equation Editor is capable of creating complex and impressive equations. You have quite a bit of control over exactly how the Equation Editor renders the equations. You can use the Style menu and Size menu to make adjustments to the appearance of the equations.

Changing the Style of an Equation

The Equation Editor's Style menu supports six styles: Math, Text, Function, Variable, Greek, and Matrix-Vector. You may pick one of the items in the menu to specify the text style.

The appearance of each of the six styles is under your control. To view the settings or change them, choose Style, Define. WordPerfect opens the Styles dialog box (see Figure 14-3). From this dialog box, you can change the font and specify whether to use the bold and italic effects when that style is chosen.

To type a brief English phrase into the Equation Editor, use the Text style. Text style is the only style for which the space bar works.

If you want to just pick a font without going through styles, you can choose Style, Other and then select a font and effects from the dialog box that appears.

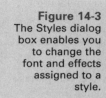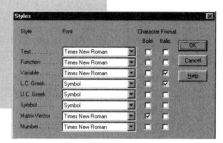

Figure 14-3
The Styles dialog box enables you to change the font and effects assigned to a style.

If you decide to redefine the font for a style, be very careful. Many fonts don't have the special symbols that you may need to render the equations properly. For example, if you define a regular font for the Greek style, it won't look right.

Changing the Size of an Equation

The Equation Editor's Size menu also has a set of predefined sizes for the equations: Full, Subscript, Sub-Subscript, Symbol, and Sub-Symbol. You may choose from one of the items in the menu to specify the size of the text in the equation.

Each of these sizes is under your control. To view the settings or change them, choose Size, Define. WordPerfect opens the Sizes dialog box (see Figure 14-4). From this dialog box, you can change point size (there are 72 points in an inch). As you click each size, the sample in the window changes to show you which part of an equation you'll be changing.

If you want to pick a size without going through the Sizes dialog box, choose Size, Other and then select a size from the dialog box that appears.

CHAPTER 14 • EQUATIONS—A SPECIAL TYPE OF GRAPHIC **441**

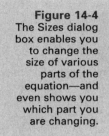

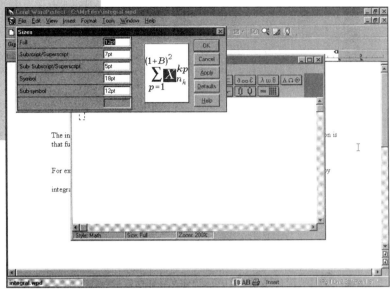

Figure 14-4
The Sizes dialog box enables you to change the size of various parts of the equation—and even shows you which part you are changing.

Creating a Simple Equation

The best way to learn how to use the Equation Editor is to go ahead and try it. Follow the instructions in this section carefully, because editing in the Equation Editor isn't quite like editing in a regular WordPerfect document. After you build the equation, you'll use it in a later exercise to learn how to edit an equation.

Hands On: Creating a New Equation

To create a new equation, follow these steps:

1. Position the cursor where you want the equation to appear.
2. Choose Insert, Equation. WordPerfect opens the Equation Editor window. A blinking cursor and dashed box indicate where the first character in the equation will go.

Note

If you decide that you don't want to create an equation, you can exit the Equation Editor. However, a small graphic box is left behind in the document. To get rid of this box, select it and press Del.

3. Click the Integral Templates button. The Equation Editor presents a list of integration symbols. Choose Definite Integral with Overscript and Underscript Limits (the middle symbol in the top row of the drop-down list). The integral symbol appears in the Equation Editor (see Figure 14-5). The blinking cursor appears in the dashed square in front of the integral.

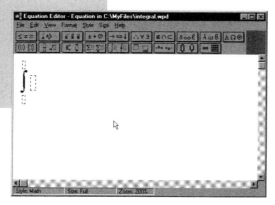

Figure 14-5
An integral symbol with upper and lower limits is the starting point for the equation.

4. Press ↑. The cursor moves to the upper limit box. Click the Miscellaneous Symbols button. Select the infinity symbol (which looks like an "8" lying on its side). WordPerfect places the infinity symbol into the upper limit box.
5. Press ↓ twice to move the cursor to the lower limit box. Type **0**.
6. Press ↑ once to move the cursor back to the box in front of the integral. Type **x**.
7. Click the Subscript and Superscript Templates button. Select the Superscript symbol (upper-left corner of the drop-down list). Notice that a new dashed square appears as a superscript of x.
8. Type **2** in the superscript. Figure 14-6 shows the equation as it looks now.
9. Press → to move the cursor away from the superscript. Type an equal sign (=).
10. Click the Fraction and Radical Template button. Select the full-size vertical fraction symbol (upper-left corner of the drop-down list). As you would expect, this symbol provides two places to type a number—above and below the fraction line.

CHAPTER 14 • EQUATIONS—A SPECIAL TYPE OF GRAPHIC **443**

Figure 14-6
The equation is beginning to take shape!

11. Type **1** above the fraction line. Press ↓ to move the cursor to the bottom fraction. Type **3**.

12. Press → and type another **x**.

13. Click the Subscript and Superscript Templates button again, and select the Superscript symbol. Type **3**. This finishes the sample equation. Figure 14-7 shows how it looks.

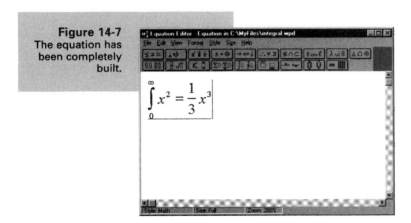

Figure 14-7
The equation has been completely built.

14. To place the equation in the document, choose File, Exit. The Equation Editor closes and updates the document with the equation (see Figure 14-8).

PART V • TELL ME MORE

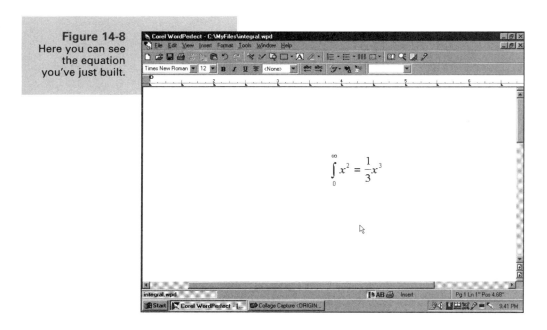

Figure 14-8
Here you can see the equation you've just built.

Understanding How to Edit in the Equation Editor

As you were building the equation in the Equation Editor, you may have noticed some unusual cursor behavior as you navigated through the equation. As you use the arrows to move through an equation, the blinking cursor changes size, and the blinking underline changes to indicate which portion of the equation you are currently working with. To take a good look at this, you'll edit the equation you just built.

Hands On: Editing an Equation

To edit the equation, use the following steps:

1. Click the equation to select it. Sizing handles appear around the equation when it is selected.
2. Right-click the selected equation and choose Open Equation Object from the QuickMenu. WordPerfect reopens the Equation Editor with the equation highlighted.

CHAPTER 14 • EQUATIONS—A SPECIAL TYPE OF GRAPHIC **445**

3. Press → once to remove the highlighting. Notice that now the blinking underline spans the entire equation. Press ←Backspace. The superscript 3 is highlighted. If you were to press ←Backspace again, the 3 would be deleted (so don't do that). Press → to remove the highlighting.

4. Press ← until the blinking cursor is just to the left of the superscript 3, then press it again so that the cursor is just to the right of the x. If you were to press ←Backspace now, the x would be removed.

Note

If you press ←Backspace or Del when the blinking cursor doesn't refer uniquely to a single character, the Equation Editor highlights the character(s) that will be affected, to give you a chance to confirm your action. For example, if the cursor is just to the right of the $^1/_3$, two characters will be affected if you press ←Backspace (the superscript 1 and the subscript 3), so the Equation Editor highlights the entire $^1/_3$. However, if you move the cursor just to the right of the $^1/_3$, and then press ↑ so that the cursor is alongside only the superscript 1, pressing ←Backspace will erase the 1 without a confirmation highlight from the Equation Editor.

5. Press ← until the cursor won't go any further left. Press Del. Once again, the entire equation is highlighted, and if you pressed any other key, the equation would be replaced by that character.

Setting the Graphic Properties of an Equation

As mentioned earlier, each equation that the Equation Editor places in your document is a graphic. As such, you can edit the graphic to dress it up. Of course, if you reopen the equation in the Equation Editor, you see only the text, but the graphic enhancements reappear when you return to the document.

Hands On: Formatting the Equation

To add graphic formatting to your equation, follow these steps:

1. Click the graphic to select it.
2. Position the mouse pointer over the lower-right sizing handle. The mouse pointer becomes a two-headed diagonal arrow.

PART V • TELL ME MORE

3. Click and drag down and to the right. When you release the mouse button, WordPerfect resizes the equation to its new, larger size (see Figure 14-9).

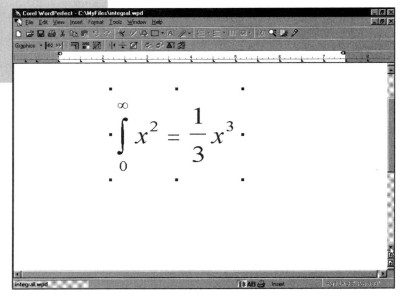

Figure 14-9
Need a bigger equation? Just drag it to the size you want!

4. Click the Border Style button from the property bar and pick the lower-left option as the border for your equation.
5. Right-click the equation and choose Border/Fill from the QuickMenu. Click to select the Fill tab. Select a fill style (for this exercise, the fifth from the left on the bottom row) and a Foreground fill color (try a nice bright yellow). If you want, you also can select a Background fill color.
6. Click OK to return to the main document.
7. Click the Caption button in the property bar. WordPerfect enables you to type a caption (see Figure 14-10). Type **This is one big integral!** and then click outside the graphic.

CHAPTER 14 • EQUATIONS—A SPECIAL TYPE OF GRAPHIC **447**

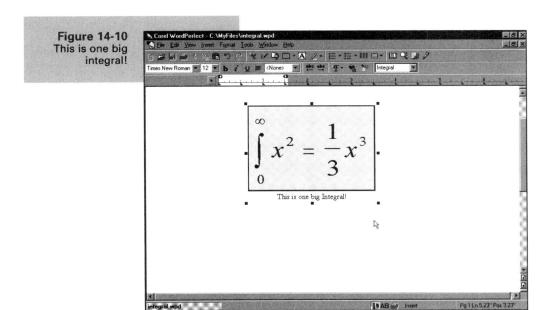

Figure 14-10
This is one big integral!

15
Automating Daily Work with Simple Macros

IN THIS CHAPTER

- **Record Simple Macros**
- **Understand Macro Syntax**
- **Debug a Macro When It Fails to Compile**
- **Edit a Macro**
- **Use the PerfectScript Command Inserter and Macro Help Files**

The amount of repetitive work performed on computers is staggering, especially in a word processing program. The same basic shell is used for most of the letters written. Memos and fax cover pages use the same layout almost every time. The same names, signature blocks, and phrases are typed over and over again. Perhaps you have a set of forms that you use repeatedly, filling in unique data for each use. Or maybe it's necessary to complete several forms using the same information. These few examples illustrate just a fraction of the tedious repetition that takes place daily, perhaps in your office?

This chapter will guide you in developing some simple macros while learning techniques that you can apply to your routine word processing tasks. You will learn to record a macro while creating a basic fax cover sheet, then use the fax cover sheet while learning a little about editing a macro and the macro command language.

Macros are just one of the automation tools in WordPerfect; merges, styles, templates, and projects are also important automation tools. These five tools together should be considered when you're looking at methods of automating, simplifying, and maintaining some sort of quality control measures for your work. Each of these tools has specific strengths; consider these strengths as you design your automation plan.

- Macros are ideally suited for those occasions where decision-making is important. Assume, for example, that each principal in your firm has his or her own custom letterhead and his or her own preferred method of closing a letter (such as "Very truly yours" or "Sincerely yours"). A macro can ask you for the name or initials of the principal for whom you are creating the letter, then automatically go get all of the various pieces required for that individual's letterhead paper.

- Macros can perform error checking. What if the user types the state abbreviation in uppercase and lowercase? A macro can check the case of an entry, then correct it to all uppercase.

- A macro is not necessarily the best tool to use for typing lengthy text in a document. You can include as much text as you need in a macro file, but a macro file can be tricky to edit. Neither is a macro the best choice when you want to edit the pattern text frequently. You *can* program the macro to insert other documents or files that do contain text, however!

- Styles are used to apply formatting commands to text. But *you* must determine which style to apply at what time. And they're not ideally suited to actually typing the text. A macro can test for the type of response you've provided, apply the style, either prompt you for the text or supply it, and then properly turn off the style.

REFER TO CHAPTER 5 TO LEARN ABOUT STYLES.

CHAPTER 15 • AUTOMATING DAILY WORK WITH SIMPLE MACROS **451**

> **CHAPTER 16 FOCUSES ON PROJECTS AND TEMPLATES.**

> **SEE CHAPTER 7 FOR MORE INFORMATION ABOUT MERGING.**

- Templates and projects each create a new document in a new document window. They can prompt for information, and provide options for formatting. But they're not suited for making changes to a current document, and they lack decision-making abilities. You can instruct a macro to use a template or project. And a template or project can contain macros which are unique to the template.

- Merges are ideally suited where you want to reuse a form with different information each time or send the same document to many different people. They can prompt for information, and they can even play macros. So why not use a merge for everything? Merges require a little more work to get started. You must name the form document and a data document, if there is one. But you can ask a macro to start a merge!

The tools can be used together to provide sophisticated solutions for your automation requirements.

Macro Basics

The Corel WordPerfect Suite 8 CD contains a number of predefined macros for your use. Several of them are automatically installed when you choose a Typical installation, while the others can be marked to copy to your system when you choose a Custom install. You can locate a list and description of the macros in the WordPerfect Help index by searching for `macro`, then clicking `macros included with Corel WordPerfect`.

Creating your own macros involves these steps:

1. Plan the macro.
2. Create the macro.
3. Compile the macro.
4. Play the macro.
5. Edit the macro, if necessary, and compile it again.

Planning the Macro

Planning is the most important step in successful macro creation. While macros can be edited easily, you'll find that far less time will need to be spent fixing problems if you start by thinking through what the macro should accomplish.

You should also give some thought to how you plan to use the macro. If you begin recording a macro while the select feature is active, it may fail if you play the macro while select is inactive! You can include commands in the macro to test for various environment settings when the macro begins. Basic environment testing, including testing for the location of the insertion point, is usually part of a well-designed macro. As you plan your macro's purpose, therefore, also think about unexpected circumstances that might be encountered when the macro is used.

Many different techniques are used by professionals before they begin writing programs. However, merely writing down in a logical order what you want the macro to do is effective. This chapter will present a fax cover sheet as an example for recording and editing a macro. This solution is not complete (the address book won't be linked to the macro), but it's a good start to understanding how to record and edit a macro. Here's a simple plan for the fax cover sheet:

1. The sender's name, organization, address, and return telephone number must be included.
2. The macro must pause so that the user can complete three fields: the name of the person to whom the fax is directed, their fax number, and the number of pages being sent.

As part of planning the macro, you should create a practice document. This "dry run" helps you determine just how to actually perform all of the functions necessary to make the macro work properly. You need to try out the keystrokes to be sure you know exactly what it is you want to do and how to do it. While recording, you can use the mouse only to make menu or dialog box choices. You cannot use it in the document window to select text, for example. It's best, therefore, to practice the steps required to create a document using only the keyboard in the typing area.

APPENDIX A CONTAINS A LIST OF KEYBOARD SHORTCUTS.

Figure 15-1 displays the fax cover sheet which will be created in the hands-on activities in this chapter.

Refine your planning stage by including these formatting steps:

1. The personal information on the cover sheet is formatted flush right. The name is italicized; the firm name is in boldface.
2. The title for the document uses a large, display font face, such as Futura, bold, 40 points.
3. Format the recipient information so that multiple names can be included in the Fax To and Fax Number fields. Using a table allows for multiple-line entry without disrupting the remaining form.

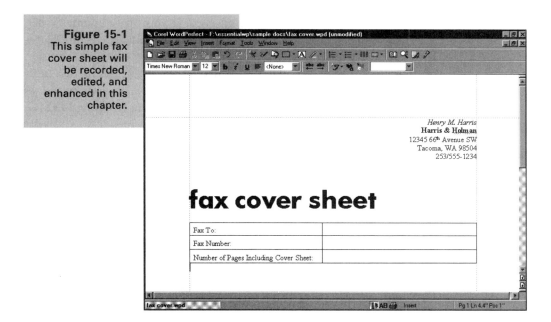

Figure 15-1 This simple fax cover sheet will be recorded, edited, and enhanced in this chapter.

Understanding Macro Types

Macros can be created and edited using two different methods, or using a combination of the two. Commands and text can be recorded using WordPerfect's macro record function; or all macro commands can be typed from scratch in a WordPerfect document window.

Three types of macros exist. The types are identified by the macro type assigned when you record or create and save your macro.

Macros on Disk

Macros on disk are available to any document. They are recorded by choosing Tools, Macro, Record. Unless specifically directed otherwise, macros on disk are created and stored in the current default macro folder named in Tools, Settings, Files, Merge/Macro.

When you create a macro on disk, either by recording keystrokes or by typing programming commands, you are creating a file. You can, therefore, use any Windows 95 allowable characters (up to a maximum of 255 characters including the path) as the filename for your macro. You should avoid using any of the reserved characters in a filename, such as /, \, *, ?, :, ;, +, =, and |.

WordPerfect automatically adds the extension .wcm to your macro name. When you are ready to use your macro, you do not need to type the extension; WordPerfect automatically searches for a macro filename ending with the extension .wcm. For example, suppose you've created a macro to type the closing of a business letter. You've named the macro MYSIG, which is stored on your system as MYSIG.WCM. When you play the macro, you can do so by simply typing **MYSIG**; WordPerfect knows to look for MYSIG.WCM.

Older versions of WordPerfect allowed you to name a macro using (Alt) plus a single character. In Windows 95 programs, however, the (Alt)+ key combination is usually used to open a menu ((Alt)+(F) opens the File menu, for example). This key combination is, therefore, unavailable when you name a macro file.

There are two methods of assigning shortcut keys to macros. You can rename the actual macro file to a (Ctrl)+ or (Ctrl)+(Shift)+ key combination. To do so, choose Tools, Macro, Play. The Macro Play dialog box opens, from which you can perform any typical file management task. Select the macro you want to rename, then right-click to display the QuickMenu. Select Rename, then type `Ctrlx` or `Ctrlsftx` where *x* is a single character. Press (Enter) and the new name is assigned to the file.

You need to be cautious when assigning (Ctrl)+ and (Ctrl)+(Shift)+ key combinations. Your new file will only work if no other WordPerfect function uses the key combination. For example, assume that you rename a macro file as `Ctrls`. When you attempt to play the macro by pressing (Ctrl)+(S), the WordPerfect Save File function appears. You can avoid some of this duplication by using the customize keyboard feature to assign macros to key combinations.

To play a shortcut key macro, just press the key combination at the location you want the macro to start.

Using the customize keyboard feature, you can assign named macros to almost any shortcut key combination you can think of, even overriding a default feature or function already using that key combination. While using the customize keyboard feature, you'll be able to view the feature assigned to each key; you can then decide whether you want to reassign the key combination to your macro.

When adding macros to a custom keyboard definition, a toolbar, or a menu, you have the option of Saving the Macro With Full Path. Doing so stores the location of the macro with the keyboard, toolbar, or menu you are editing. This means that you can freely edit the macro and the changes will appear in the keyboard, toolbar, or menu.

Chapter 15 • Automating Daily Work with Simple Macros

> **Appendix A lists the WPWin 8 keyboard shortcut keys used by WordPerfect.**

However, if you choose not to save the macro with its path, WordPerfect will look for the macro in its macro folder search string. Refer to the sidebar below titled "Where are Macro Files Created?"

> **See Chapter 2 for help in assigning macros to a keyboard.**

Where are Macro Files Created?

During installation, the predefined macros were copied to a folder on your hard drive, usually `\Corel\Suite8\Macros\WPWin`. You can verify the default location by choosing Tools, Settings, Files and then clicking the Merge/Macro tab. The Default Macro Folder contains the predefined macros, unless you've copied the macros to an alternate location. As you create new macros, they are also stored in the default macro folder.

WordPerfect can actually play macros from one of several locations without needing to know the exact path to the macro. When you ask to play a macro, WordPerfect first looks in the default macro folder, then looks to the supplemental macro folder. If the macro is not found in either of these two locations, WordPerfect then looks in the folder that contains the `WPWIN8.EXE` file, and finally in the default document folder. This means that you can store macros in a number of locations and play them by typing the filename (without the path) in the Play Macro dialog box, then pressing Enter or clicking the Play button.

When you create a new macro, the macro is automatically created in the default macro folder named in Files Settings. If your predefined macros also reside in the same directory, your personal macros will commingle with the macros provided by WordPerfect. That's not necessarily bad, but think how difficult it might be to isolate *your* macros from those that were installed with WordPerfect 8.

If you work on a stand-alone version of WordPerfect 8 and don't share your macro files with other users, at the very least you should create your own folder for macros you create. Then change the folders named in the Files Settings dialog box. Name the current default location as the supplemental macro location, and name your personal

> macro directory as the default macro directory. Doing this will force your new macros to be automatically stored in a separate location from the predefined macros.
>
> If you work on a network sharing files and macros with other users, then consider moving the predefined macros to the same directory/folder as the `WPWIN8.EXE` file. (The predefined macros can reside in a read-only folder.) Then, store your network-wide custom macros in the supplemental macro folder which resides on a network drive. Finally, create a personal macro folder (usually on your own hard drive) as your default macro folder. Using this structure makes it easy to remove the predefined macros when software is updated.

> **SEE CHAPTERS 3 AND 16 FOR MORE INFORMATION ON USING PROJECTS AND TEMPLATES.**

Template Macros

Template macros are stored with either the current template or the default template. A template macro is accessible only in the template in which it was created or copied (associated). Template macros are an especially useful method of assembling macros that all have something in common. You might want to include a set of macros specific to a particular form, for example. You can create the form as a template, then associate, record, or copy all pertinent macros to that template.

A template macro is recorded by choosing Tools, Template Macro, Record. When editing an existing macro or creating a macro file from scratch, you can store the macro as a template macro using the Options button on the Macro toolbar.

The QuickMacro

The QuickMacro is temporary—only one QuickMacro exists at a time. Each time you create a new QuickMacro, you replace the previous QuickMacro. The QuickMacro resides only in memory; it's not saved to a file and cannot be edited. The QuickMacro is deleted when you exit WordPerfect. The QuickMacro is especially useful for tasks that you need to use repeatedly, but only once, such as a series of identical edits to various locations in the current document.

Unless you add the QuickMacro Record and Play buttons to a toolbar, they're not necessarily *quick*. Recording and playing the QuickMacro each require several steps. To record a QuickMacro, choose Tools, Template Macro, Record, then click Record again without typing a name for the macro. To stop recording, choose <u>T</u>ools, Templ<u>a</u>te Macro, <u>R</u>ecord. If you plan to use the QuickMacro feature, be sure to add the QuickMacro Play and QuickMacro Record buttons to your normal toolbar or menu.

Recording and Playing Macros

A recorded macro writes into the macro file all the text and commands you enter from the keyboard or select with a mouse. Rather than actually recording keystrokes, however, a macro writes programming commands that document the features you used when creating the macro. This prevents the macro from needing to interpret the various ways that a feature can be implemented: typed from the keyboard using shortcut keys and menus, selected using a mouse, or some combination of both.

Macro Recording Basics

There's nothing tricky about recording a macro. You start the macro recorder, then type the text or choose the features you want the macro to remember, then stop recording. As you record these steps, you are actually typing or editing on a document window. When the macro is complete, you can discard the "blackboard" document or the changes you made to the existing document. Remember that a macro is a new file of recorded steps; it is not dependent on the appearance of the blackboard for its success.

> **Because you are actually modifying a document while recording a macro, be sure to save any open documents before starting to record. This will allow you to recover your document should you accidentally discard or unacceptably change an open document in some fashion while recording the macro.**

Every recorded macro uses the same basic steps:

1. Choose <u>T</u>ools, <u>M</u>acro, <u>R</u>ecord, or press `Ctrl`+`F10`. The Record Macro dialog box opens so that you can name your macro (see Figure 15-2).
2. Type the name you want to use for the macro, then press `Enter` or click Record. The mouse pointer becomes unavailable within the editing window and the Macro Toolbar appears at the top of the current document editing window. Some of the buttons on the Macro toolbar can be used when recording a macro, but most are used when editing a macro or creating a macro from scratch. Table 15-1, which follows this procedure, identifies the toolbar buttons and the mouse pointer during macro recording.

Figure 15-2 Your macro will be created in the folder name listed in the title bar.

Type macro name here.

3. Perform the keystrokes necessary to complete the steps for the macro. If you make a minor mistake, don't worry too much about it. You can always edit the macro file later, correcting any mistakes. Depending on how major your mistake is, however, you may find it better to just quit recording and start over.

4. Choose <u>T</u>ools, <u>M</u>acro, <u>R</u>ecord or press Ctrl+F10 (or click the Stop Recording button on the macro property bar). The record feature stops.

Table 15-1 Buttons on the Macro Toolbar

Button	Used for
⊘	The mouse pointer is unavailable in the document window while recording a macro
■	Stops playback or recording of the current macro
●	Starts recording to the current macro
▶	Plays the macro currently on-screen
▮▮	Pauses the current macro
Dialog Editor...	Opens the Dialog Editor dialog box, from which you can create or edit your own dialog boxes for use by your macros
Commands...	Click the Co<u>m</u>mands button to open a dialog box list of the Corel PerfectScript commands; you can also open the Corel PerfectScript commands dialog box by pressing Ctrl+M
Save & Compile	Saves and compiles the macro currently on the editing window
Codes...	Allows you to include macro functions normally associated with WordPerfect codes only, such as date codes or search strings
Options ▼	From the Op<u>t</u>ions button you can save your macro file, save it as a template macro, close the macro file, or remove the Macro toolbar

CHAPTER 15 • AUTOMATING DAILY WORK WITH SIMPLE MACROS 459

Hands On: Recording the Fax Cover Sheet Macro

Follow these steps to record the basic fax cover sheet macro you saw in Figure 15-1:

1. On a new document window, choose <u>T</u>ools, <u>M</u>acro, <u>R</u>ecord or press Ctrl+F10. The Record Macro dialog box opens.
2. Type **faxform** as the name for your fax macro. Then press Enter or click Record. If you type a name that is already used by a macro file, WordPerfect displays a prompt box asking you whether you want to replace the existing macro file. Be careful not to accidentally replace macros you still use!
3. After a brief pause, the Macro toolbar appears and the mouse pointer is indicated to be unavailable in the document editing window.
4. Begin by choosing Fo<u>r</u>mat, <u>J</u>ustification, <u>R</u>ight. Then type the name and address for the firm, using the text that follows this paragraph. Use the keyboard shortcuts for italic (Ctrl+I) and bold (Ctrl+B), starting and stopping each attribute before typing each line of text, and then turning it off at the end of each line. Press Enter to complete each line, including the last line.

   Henry M. Harris
   Harris & Holman
   12345 66th Avenue SW
   Tacoma, WA 98504
   253/555-1234

5. Return to left justification by choosing Fo<u>r</u>mat, <u>J</u>ustification, <u>L</u>eft. Press Enter three times to open some space between the return address and the fax cover sheet title.
6. Type **fax cover sheet** as the title line text.
7. With the insertion point appearing at the end of the title text, press Shift+Home to select the title text while moving the insertion point to the beginning of the title line.
8. Now select a font face similar to Futura Md BT, set the font size to 40 points, and add the bold attribute.
9. Turn off the select feature by pressing F8, then press End to move to the end of the title line. Press Enter twice to complete the line.
10. Using the table button, create a table two columns wide and three rows high. The table appears in the document and the insertion point is placed in the first table cell.

> REVIEW CHAPTER 4 FOR ASSISTANCE IN SELECTING FONTS.

> **SEE CHAPTER 9 FOR MORE INFORMATION ABOUT CREATING TABLES.**

11. Type the heading for the first row, **Fax To:**, then press Tab to move to cell B1.
12. Pausing a macro during playback allows you to type the necessary information. When you press Enter the macro continues to play. To record the pause into the macro, click the Pause button on the Macro toolbar, or choose <u>T</u>ools, <u>M</u>acro, Pa<u>u</u>se. Now click the Pause button again, or choose <u>T</u>ools, <u>M</u>acro, Pa<u>u</u>se again.
13. Press Tab to move to cell A2, then type **Fax Number:**. Press Tab to move to cell B2, then repeat step 12 to add another pause to the macro. Remember that it takes two pause steps (<u>T</u>ools, <u>M</u>acro, Pa<u>u</u>se; <u>T</u>ools, <u>M</u>acro, Pa<u>u</u>se) to actually add the pause to the macro.
14. Press Tab to move to cell A3, type the prompt text **Number of Pages Including Cover Sheet:**, press Tab to move to the next cell, and then add the last pause.
15. From cell B3 (the last cell in the table), press ↓ once to move the insertion point after the table. Press Enter to add a blank line.
16. To stop recording, click the Stop Recording button, or choose <u>T</u>ools, <u>M</u>acro, <u>R</u>ecord (or press Ctrl+F10). After a brief pause, the Macro toolbar closes and the mouse pointer returns.
17. Close the document window you used as a blackboard while recording your macro. Choose <u>N</u>o when prompted to save changes.

Playing a Macro

The last step in creating a new macro is to play it, ensuring that your steps were accurate. Usually the macro performs correctly, but occasionally you find that you need to edit the macro. Or, if the macro does not meet your needs at all, you may decide to re-record it.

The first step to playing a macro is the same for all three macro types. You must position the insertion point at the location you want the macro to start. The position varies depending on the actions of the macro. For example, if your macro assigns new fonts to selected text, you need to select the text, then play the macro. If your macro creates a letterhead, you probably want to open a new document window before playing the macro.

The remaining steps to play a macro depend on the macro type you've created:

- To play a macro on disk, use one of these two methods:

  If the macro you want to play was one of the last nine macros played, choose <u>M</u>acro. The macro submenu appears, with the last nine macros

Chapter 15 • Automating Daily Work with Simple Macros

listed at the bottom of the menu. Press the number assigned to the macro on the list, or double-click the macro name. See Figure 15-3.

Or

Choose <u>T</u>ools, <u>M</u>acro, <u>P</u>lay. The Play Macro dialog box opens. If you know the name of the macro you want to play, simply type the macro name and press [Enter]. Alternately, you can select a macro from the file list, then press [Enter] or click <u>P</u>lay.

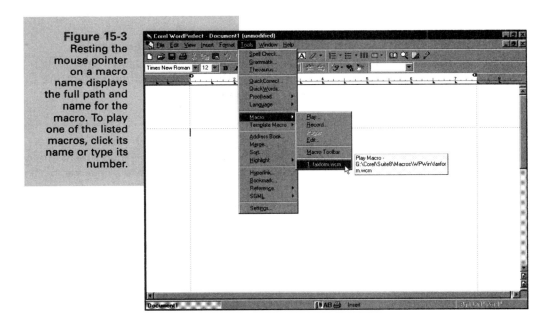

Figure 15-3
Resting the mouse pointer on a macro name displays the full path and name for the macro. To play one of the listed macros, click its name or type its number.

- To play a template macro, choose <u>T</u>ools, Tem<u>p</u>late Macro, <u>P</u>lay. Type or select the macro name, then press [Enter]. Similarly, if the template macro you want to play was one of the last nine template macros used, you can select it from the Template Macro submenu.

- To play the QuickMacro, choose <u>T</u>ools, Tem<u>p</u>late Macro, <u>P</u>lay, <u>P</u>lay or click the QuickMacro Play button if you've added it to your toolbar.

Hands On: Playing the `faxform` Macro

To test the fax form macro, use these steps:

1. Open a new document window, then choose <u>T</u>ools, <u>M</u>acro, <u>P</u>lay or press [Alt]+[F10]. The Play Macro dialog box opens.

2. Type **faxform** and press Enter; or, select the faxform macro filename from the file list, then press Enter or click Play. The first time the macro plays, a very brief pause occurs while the macro compiles. Compiling a macro checks the macro syntax (the proper form of all commands), and writes a header to the resulting compiled macro file. Then the macro begins.

You can view the status of a macro by looking at the General Status button in the application bar.

3. The macro pauses at the first location where you recorded a pause instruction. Type some sample data in the *Fax To* pause, then press Enter. The macro immediately continues, pausing at each location in sequence until all commands in the macro file are finished.

At any time during macro play, press Esc to interrupt the macro. Be aware, however, that two macro commands exist that can be used when programming a macro to disable the action of the cancel key, thus preventing your ability to stop a macro. CANCEL(Off!) turns off the action of the cancel key during macro execution and prevents the user from interrupting a macro. ONCANCEL causes a macro to jump to another macro action if the user presses Esc during playback. Usually pressing Ctrl+Break will interrupt macros that contain either of these two programming commands.

Editing a Macro

A macro file can be opened in a document window just like any other WordPerfect file. Editing a macro allows you to add or change the macro commands contained within the file.

The steps used to open the macro file vary depending on whether you want to edit a macro on disk or a template macro:

- To open a macro on disk for editing, choose Tools, Macro, Edit, then locate the file and click Edit. You can also click the File Open button or choose File, Open. Then locate the folder which contains the macro and click Open.

CHAPTER 15 • AUTOMATING DAILY WORK WITH SIMPLE MACROS **463**

By default, when you select a file from a different folder, that folder will open automatically the next time you choose File, Open. You can turn off the change default folder option by choosing File, Open to open the Open File dialog box. If the menu's not already displayed, toggle it on by clicking the Toggle Menu On/Off button, then choose Edit and click the Change Default Folder menu choice, removing its checkmark.

FOR ADDITIONAL INFORMATION ABOUT TEMPLATES, SEE CHAPTER 16.

- To edit a template macro, you must first open the template to which the macro is attached. Then choose Tools, Template Macro, Edit. Select the macro file name from the file list displayed and click Edit.

Hands On: Opening the `faxform` Macro File for Editing

To open the `faxform` macro for editing, use these steps:

1. Choose Tools, Macro, Edit. The Edit Macro file management dialog box opens.
2. Select the `faxform` file in the file list area, then click the Edit button. The `faxform` macro file opens (see Figure 15-4).

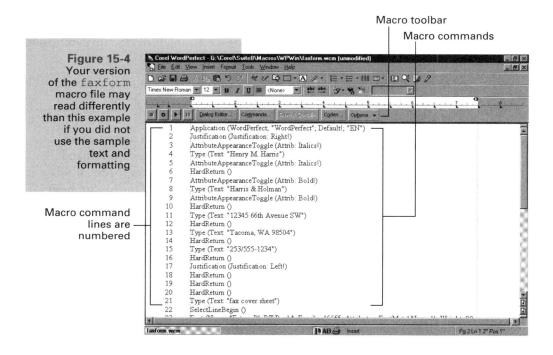

Figure 15-4 Your version of the `faxform` macro file may read differently than this example if you did not use the sample text and formatting

Macro command lines are numbered

Macro toolbar
Macro commands

Understanding Macro Commands

The WordPerfect 8 macro language, PerfectScript, is a *command-based* language rather than a *keystroke-based* language. This means that whether you choose to record a macro or type a macro, you are working with commands from WordPerfect's programming language (*PerfectScript*) rather than the procedures used to access a command.

Using commands eliminates possible errors or confusion in the macro stemming from the various methods WordPerfect 8 provides to accomplish its functions. For example, if you want to change tab settings, you can do so in any of the following ways: by choosing Format, Line, Tab Set; by dragging a tab marker on the ruler bar; or by double-clicking an existing [TabSet] code in the Reveal Codes pane. Imagine the confusion that would result if WordPerfect stored each key press or mouse click! Rather, WordPerfect simply records the command TabSet and all of its associated parameters and members.

Learning Syntax Rules While Reviewing the faxform Macro

Each macro command must follow very precise syntax rules. You'll especially need to know these rules when you begin typing macros from scratch. For now, however, briefly skim these rules so that you'll be more comfortable with the commands recorded in the faxform macro.

In general, the syntax rules you must follow when typing PerfectScript commands are:

- Any command that has the possibility of parameters must include the parentheses, even if they are empty. For example, look at the HardReturn() command on Line 6 of the macro.
- Text that will be typed in a document, that will appear anywhere on-screen (such as a prompt), or that is needed to complete a command, must be surrounded by double quotes (not smart quotes!). Text of this sort is referred to as a *string*. For example, in Line 4 of the macro, notice the command Type(Text: "Henry M. Harris").
- Parameters that indicate enumerated types must end with an exclamation point. An *enumeration* is a parameter value provided by PerfectScript. You can view the enumerations for a command in the WordPerfect Macro Help, or in the Command Inserter (both discussed in the next section). Review Line 2 of the faxform macro. The Justification command uses a required enumerated parameter which specifies the type of justification set by the command.

- Required parameters must be typed in the exact order required by the command. For example, in Lines 23 through 25, the Font command requires parameters which fully identify the font face.
- It is not necessary to include the parameter name when typing a macro command. For example, Line 8 is correct if typed **Type (Text: "Harris & Holman")** or **Type ("Harris & Holman")**.
- Be very careful where you place each colon (:), semicolon (;), or quotation mark (") in your command. These must follow exact command syntax, or the command will not compile properly. View Lines 23 and 24, part of the Font command, for an illustration of a command with several parameters separated by semicolons. Notice that the parameter name ends with a colon.

While command syntax is very precise, you can be reasonably *imprecise* with the actual appearance of the commands. This allows you to format your macro in a manner that makes it easy for you to read and edit. Here are a few typing tips that may be helpful as you begin to create your own macros:

- Macro commands may be typed in any combination of uppercase and lowercase. For example, the following three forms of the `MacroStatusPrompt` command are all acceptable:

    ```
    MacroStatusPrompt(On!; "this is the prompt")
    MACROSTATUSPROMPT(On!; "this is the prompt")
    macrostatusprompt(On!; "this is the prompt")
    ```

- You can use any font or attribute within your command. An attribute used in the macro will not affect the macro command. It can sometimes be helpful, for example, to place all text which will appear anywhere in the macro or document in bold or italic. For example, the command ***Type("Harris & Holman")*** will type the words `Harris & Holman` into the document in normal typeface, not in bold or italic.
- Macro commands can wrap from line to line. If you use a hard return in the macro command, WordPerfect will assume that the command is complete and begin compiling the next line as a separate command. It can be helpful to use a hanging indent sequence (F7, Shift+Tab) to start a command which will wrap so that you can easily find the beginning of each command line.
- It can also be helpful to include a space after a semicolon (;) to assist in word-wrapping a long command.

Understanding the Syntax in the `faxform` Macro

Macro commands are quite logical and easy to read. As you review the `faxform` macro, you can see that every command is a straightforward presentation of the feature or function you are using in the macro.

In a recorded macro, each macro command begins on a new line. Some parameters (specific settings for each command) will wrap to subsequent lines. A semicolon separates each parameter. When you type macro commands, the commands can appear sequentially as long as they are separated by spaces, tabs, indents, or hard returns. These *white space* codes also make your macro easier to read!

The `faxform` macro contains about a page of PerfectScript commands. It can be confusing to assimilate the complete macro in one reading. It's easiest to try to isolate each command until you understand exactly what is happening at that stage in the macro. Learning to write your own macros isn't difficult, but it helps to examine the predefined macros and every other macro example you can find. You'll rapidly see that imitation is definitely the best way of learning to write macros.

> **Find it Online**
>
> Outstanding examples of macros can be found at several Internet sites, such as the Corel FTP publications site (**ftp://ftp.corel.com/pub**) and the WordPerfect Magazine site (**http://www.wpmag.com**). You also should look in the library section of the CompuServe WordPerfect Users forum (**GO WPUSERS**). The message section of the WPUSERS forum is an excellent place to ask macro questions of other WordPerfect users and macro experts.

Now that you've been introduced to macro syntax, look at a few of the `faxform` macro commands:

Line 1. The first line of the macro reads `Application(WordPerfect; "WordPerfect"; Default!; "EN")`. Every macro you record in WordPerfect will begin with this line. It identifies for the PerfectScript compiler the name of the application to use in the macro. It must precede any of the commands specific to WordPerfect, such as justification commands.

Line 2. The line `Justification(Justification: Right!)` illustrates a simple, one parameter command. The command name is `Justification`. The enumerated parameter is typed within parentheses.

Line 3. The `AttributeAppearanceToggle(Attrib: Italics!)` line is another example of a WordPerfect command with a required enumerated parameter. The name of the parameter is `Attrib` which is properly followed by a colon. The enumerated value is `Italics!`. Other examples of attribute enumerations are `Bold!`, `Underline!`, and `Redline!`.

Lines 23-25. The `Font` command is extensive, including several required parameters, some with enumerated values, and some using values you supply. Notice that the complete command actually requires three lines.

Line 36. The `PauseKey(Key: Enter!)` line instructs the macro to pause playback and then start again when the user presses Enter.

Recording a Change to the `faxform` Macro

By far the simplest method to make changes or additions to a macro is to record new commands directly into the existing macro file. Recording commands requires these steps:

1. Open the macro file you want to modify.
2. Position the insertion point in the macro where you want the new commands to be inserted.
3. Click the Record button on the Macro toolbar. A temporary document window opens for you to use while recording your commands.
4. Perform all the commands, or type any text you want to add to your macro.
5. When you have completed all commands and text, click the Record button again to stop recording. The temporary document window closes, and the commands and text you've recorded are added to the existing macro at the insertion point.

After playing the `faxform` macro, you might realize that you need to include a footer that contains text that tells the recipient what they should do if they get the fax in error. You could easily type new commands and text into the macro, but it's much easier and more accurate to record macro commands wherever possible, thus ensuring their correctness.

PART V • TELL ME MORE

Note

Because a new, empty document window is opened when you record from a macro window, sometimes it's almost impossible to record the correct keystrokes at the correct time. For example, suppose you want to add an additional table row to the `faxform` macro. If you record from the macro, a new document window opens—without the table. You must re-create the table, add the new row, then stop recording. All of the table creation steps are also recorded to the original macro, even though they already exist in the macro. You then need to locate and delete all of the extraneous rows in the original macro when you stop recording.

It might be more expedient, therefore, to manually create a new, temporary document, set up the table, then record a macro from the point in the temporary document where the macro steps should be recorded. Then cut and paste the commands from the newly created macro back to the macro to which you want the changes made.

Hands On: Adding a Footer to the `faxform` Macro

Use these steps to add a footer to the `faxform` macro:

1. Open the `faxform` macro file if it is not already open.
2. A footer is usually created at the beginning of a document; therefore, position the insertion point at the beginning of Line 2, the first line after the identifying product command.

Tip

If you can't see the line numbers in your macro file, make sure that they haven't just scrolled off the left edge of the window. You might also try changing the zoom percentage you're currently using so that you're displaying the full width of the page. To do so, click the Zoom button on the toolbar, then select Page Width.

3. Click the Record button on the Macro toolbar. A new document window opens.

Chapter 15 • Automating Daily Work with Simple Macros

4. Choose Insert, Header/Footer, then click Footer A on the Headers/Footers dialog box. Click Create.

5. Type this text for the footer:

   If the reader of this message is not the intended recipient, or an employee responsible for delivering the facsimile, please notify me immediately by telephone. Thank you.

6. Click the footer Close button (it appears at the end of the header/footer property bar) to complete the footer.

7. The changes to the macro are now complete, so click the Stop Recording button on the Macro toolbar. You are returned to the macro document and the footer commands you've used are added to the macro (see Figure 15-5).

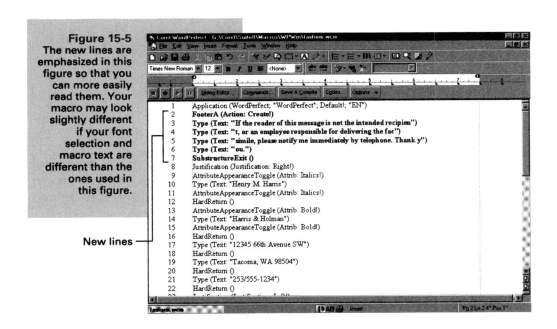

Figure 15-5
The new lines are emphasized in this figure so that you can more easily read them. Your macro may look slightly different if your font selection and macro text are different than the ones used in this figure.

New lines

Notice that the Type command lines wrap the text from line to line without regard to full words. Macro lines can be a maximum of 255 characters, but, when recording, they are typically shortened to about 80 characters. You can carefully edit these lines so that the text is more logically formatted, as shown in Figure 15-6. (Notice the use of the hanging indent in the new lines to help you visually identify the long command line.)

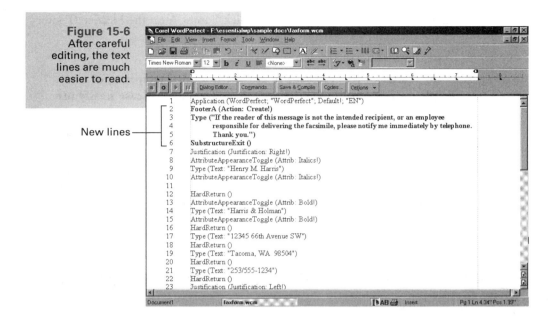

Figure 15-6
After careful editing, the text lines are much easier to read.

New lines

Compiling the `faxform` Macro

WordPerfect automatically compiles a macro at the time it is saved, at the time recording is finished, or when it is played for the first time. A macro must be compiled before it is played. Each time a macro is edited, it must be recompiled. When a macro is compiled, WordPerfect checks the macro language for any possible errors and adds a section to the macro file that only a computer can read. This machine language causes the macro to quickly execute when it is played.

A brief message appears on the General Status button in the application bar that says `Compiling Macro` when you stop recording a macro or when you play a macro that has not been previously compiled.

Occasionally an error is found during the compiling process. When this happens, a dialog box appears that states the type and location of the error. You have the option to edit the macro or to continue compiling the remainder of the macro. Correct any errors that were found, then recompile the macro by clicking the Save and Compile button on the Macro toolbar.

One of the most common errors points to a missing parenthesis or quotation mark. Carefully check the syntax of the line referenced by the error. If the missing punctuation is not apparent, also check the preceding line.

Chapter 15 • Automating Daily Work with Simple Macros

As you review the macro looking for the error, make sure that all quotation marks, commas, and ending parentheses are in place. If the identified line looks correct, look one or two lines prior to the numbered line to find the error. Probably the most common macro errors are due to typing errors causing a syntax problem. For example, if you omit an ending parenthesis, PerfectScript assumes that the current command still continues to the next line and attempts to compile the macro until an ending parenthesis *is* found. Of course, the parenthesis found belongs to the wrong command, which then confuses things further.

Figure 15-7 illustrates just such an example. The PerfectScript compiler has found a syntax error, but it's pointing to the wrong line. The error actually occurs at the end of Line 5, where an ending parenthesis is missing.

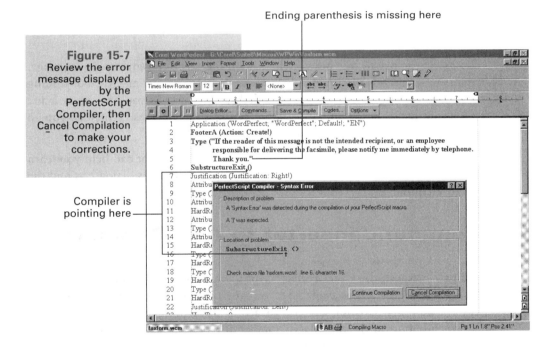

Figure 15-7 Review the error message displayed by the PerfectScript Compiler, then Cancel Compilation to make your corrections.

Tip

Look up the topic **macro errors** in the Macro Help text for more information about common macro compiling errors. Refer to the next section, "Getting Macro Help," to learn more about installing the macro help file if you haven't already done so.

> **Hands On: Saving and Compiling the Macro Changes**

With the changes complete to the `faxform` macro, you should save and compile the macro so that you can test your modifications. Use these steps:

1. Click the Save & Compile button on the Macro toolbar.
2. After a brief pause, the Save & Compile button is disabled and the Macro Play button on the toolbar is enabled.

If your macro does not compile successfully, an error prompt box appears which identifies the location and suspected error encountered. You must review the macro syntax, correct the mistake, then Save & Compile the macro again.

Getting Macro Help

The `faxform` macro touches very lightly on the macro programming language. There are thousands of commands you can include in your macros, but finding them and learning to use them takes a dedicated effort. As you have seen, many of the commands have required parameters and enumerations. Where do you go to find out about these commands?

There are two sources within Corel WordPerfect Suite 8 that can help you learn to write effective macros, the Corel PerfectScript Commands dialog box and the Macro Help file.

Using the Command Inserter to Add Commands to a Macro

The first method, the Corel PerfectScript Commands dialog box (referred to as the *Command Inserter*), is available to you any time you edit an existing macro or create a new macro from scratch. To access the Command Inserter, click the Commands button on the Macro toolbar (or press Ctrl+M). The Corel PerfectScript Commands dialog box opens.

In the Command Inserter, macro commands are separated into two categories, selected from the Command Type drop-down list:

> *PerfectScript* commands are common to all programs in Corel WordPerfect Suite 8. Sometimes referred to as *programming commands*, these commands include functions that control how a particular application interacts with the user, such as building a menu, or commands that evaluate a condition.

Chapter 15 • Automating Daily Work with Simple Macros

Product commands for Presentations, Quattro Pro, and WordPerfect include commands that are specific to the selected program. For example, a `FlushRight` command is specific to WordPerfect, while a command to advance a single slide in a slideshow is specific to Presentations.

As you select various commands from the Command Inserter, the dialog box is updated, listing any Parameters and Enumerations specific to the selected command.

To use the Command Inserter:

1. Click the Commands button on the Macro toolbar or press Ctrl+M to open the Command Inserter.
2. From the Command Type drop-down list, select the group of commands you want to use.
3. Locate and select the command you want to use from the Commands list.
4. Click Edit to add the command to the Command Edit text box.
5. Double-click each parameter in turn, choosing any associated enumerations. Or, where appropriate, type the string or value necessary to complete the command.
6. When the command is complete, click Insert to add the command to your macro. Then, when you are finished inserting commands, click Close to close the Command Inserter.

The `faxform` macro is missing several steps that typically occur in a well-planned application. One of these missing steps is that the macro doesn't test to determine whether the current document is blank before creating the fax form. Using the Command Inserter, this important test can be added to the macro. Of course, you can alternately type the complete syntax into the macro without using the Command Inserter.

Steps involving PerfectScript product commands, such as the `Error` command, cannot be recorded; they must be either typed manually or inserted using the Command Inserter.

To complete the steps in the hands-on activity which follows, you first need a quick introduction to system variables and a simple `IF` test.

In brief, *variables* are pieces of information (values) that are stored in memory. Each variable is referenced by a name which is then used to access or manipulate the variable value. Two types of variables are available—user variables and system variables.

PART V • TELL ME MORE

A *user variable* is created by you. You control the name and value of the variable. For example, a macro can be programmed to ask a question, such as "Do you want to continue?" The response, yes or no, is stored in a variable—perhaps named answer—that you named in the command. You can then query the answer variable, checking for its value.

A *system variable* is named by PerfectScript and, when included in a macro, can return the status of some aspect of WordPerfect or your system. This is useful, for example, when a successful macro depends on Insert being disabled, or the insertion point not residing in a header page.

In the faxform macro, you'll use the system variable ?DocBlank to check the status of the current document window. This system variable will be combined with a simple IF test command syntax.

Hands On: Adding an IF Test to the faxform Macro

Use these steps to add a test to the faxform macro which tests for a blank document, then opens a new document window if the current document is not blank:

1. Position the insertion point at the beginning of Line 2 of the faxform macro file.
2. Press Enter to open a blank line for the new command, then press ↑ to return to the blank line.
3. Click Co*m*mands (or press Ctrl+M) to open the Corel PerfectScript Commands dialog box.
4. Verify that the Command *T*ype drop-down list displays PerfectScript-EN, then locate the IF command in the *C*ommands list. You can either scroll through the list or type **IF** to quickly locate the command.
5. Select the IF command, then press Enter or click the *E*dit button (or just double-click the command). The IF command sequence is added to the Command Edit text box.

Note

Because the IF command is a simple one, the only required parameter is the actual test. Unfortunately, the Command Inserter cannot build command strings based on more than one command.

CHAPTER 15 • AUTOMATING DAILY WORK WITH SIMPLE MACROS **475**

6. Click **I**nsert to add the `IF()` command to the macro. Now click between the open and close parentheses so that the next command is inserted in the correct position.

You can move freely between the Command Inserter dialog box and the text of your macro. The Corel PerfectScript Commands dialog box remains open until you specifically close it.

7. In the Command Inserter, select `WordPerfect-EN` as the Command **T**ype. The **C**ommands list updates, displaying the first of over 2,000 commands which relate specifically to WordPerfect.

8. Locate and **E**dit the system variable command `?DocBlank`. It is added to the C**o**mmand Edit text box.

All system variables start with a question mark (?).

9. Click in the C**o**mmand Edit text box, then position the insertion point after the ending parenthesis.

   The `?DocBlank` command returns a text string value of either `True` or `False`, depending on the condition found. If the current document *is* blank, `?DocBlank` returns the value `True`; if the document *is not* blank, the returned value is `False`. Both `True` and `False` are text strings and, following syntax rules, must be included in quotes. Because the macro is testing for the value of the system variable, the test needs to be added to the command.

10. Type **="False"**. The complete command now reads `?DocBlank ()="False"`.

11. Click **I**nsert to add the command to the macro. The complete command line now reads `If(?DocBlank ()="False")`. The ending parenthesis typically wraps to the next line in the macro. It's okay to leave it there, but it's really much neater to include it at the end of the full command line. Go ahead and adjust your text so that the complete command appears on a single line.

    The command as it is now entered can be read as *If the current document is not blank*. No action has been specified, but the test line itself is complete. The next few lines must tell the macro what to do if the current document is not blank.

12. After the ending parenthesis for the `IF` command, press Enter to move to a new blank line.
13. Locate and Insert the macro command `FileNew()` in the Commands list for `WordPerfect-EN`. (`FileNew()` opens a new, blank document window.)
14. Press Enter after the command line in the macro to complete the command.
15. All `IF` tests must have an ending command which tells PerfectScript that the test is complete. Locate the `ENDIF` command in the `PerfectScript-EN` Command Type list, then choose Insert.
16. Click the Close button to close the Command Inserter. Figure 15-8 shows the added commands.
17. Finally, Save & Compile your macro, then test it to be sure it properly opens a new document when played within an existing document.

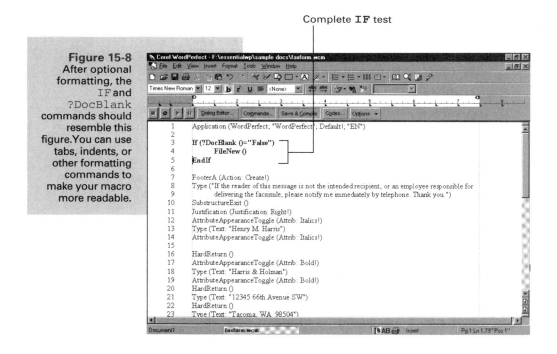

Figure 15-8
After optional formatting, the `IF` and `?DocBlank` commands should resemble this figure. You can use tabs, indents, or other formatting commands to make your macro more readable.

Using Macro Help

The Macro Help file is a full reference manual, complete with examples, listing each of the PerfectScript commands. It's by far my favorite method of researching the commands needed to perform a specific task in a macro. Unfortunately, the Macro Help file is not automatically copied to your system when you choose a Typical installation. To add the Macro Help file to your system, you need to return to the Corel WordPerfect Suite 8 Setup utility, choose Custom Install, and select Macro Help from the WordPerfect 8 component list.

Once installed, open the Macro Help file by choosing Help, Help Topics; then double-click the Macros book on the Contents tab. Then select About Macros or Macro Programming. About Macros provides general macro information, such as listing the changes in commands between versions. Macro Programming provides lists and help text for all of the PerfectScript and product commands.

After you select Macro Programming, a new help file opens for Corel WordPerfect 8 Macros Help. From this help window, you can locate specific help for every possible macro command by double-clicking the Lists of Commands book from the Contents tab. Then select System Variables, Product Commands, or Corel PerfectScript Programming Commands. If you've used other WordPerfect versions, you can view a list of commands that were added to WordPerfect 8 in the New Corel WordPerfect Commands item. Finally, you can print complete paper manuals that list and describe each system variable, product command, or programming command (the PerfectScript commands). This takes a lot of paper and time, though, so be prepared!

Looking for a command using the Lists of Commands requires you to know the name of the command you need. Especially when you are learning to write macros, you'll probably find that you have no idea what command you are looking for.

It's far easier, therefore, to use either the Index or Find tab, type a general word or a keyword that represents a concept, and then skim through the responses until you find the command that meets your requirements. The Index is especially useful for locating macro command information without knowing exactly what command you want to use.

Hands On: Using Macro Help to Find a Particular Command

Use these steps to locate a command in Macro Help when you're not quite sure what command you need:

1. Choose Help, Help Topics; then double-click Macros on the Contents tab, and select Macro Programming to open Help Topics: Corel WordPerfect 8 Macros Help.

2. Click the Index tab, then type **print** in the Type the First Few Letters of the Word You're Looking For text box. As you begin to type, the list of index entries updates, locating the first entry that matches your search word.

3. Scroll through the list until you reach the subentry for page. Then click Display. The help text for Print: Page opens (see Figure 15-9).

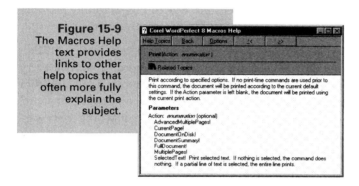

Figure 15-9
The Macros Help text provides links to other help topics that often more fully explain the subject.

4. After reading the help text, click the Related Topics icon to open a list of other, related help text items.

Tip — Some help text items also provide examples. You may want to print the examples so that you can study them.

Converting Macros from Previous Versions

Macros written in WordPerfect 5.1 for DOS require conversion before they will run in WordPerfect 8. A helpful utility for converting 5.1 macros, `mc5x6x.exe`, is available at the Corel FTP site:

`FTP://ftp.corel.com/pub/wordperfect/wpwin/70/%21index.htm`

Download this utility to your system, then run it to convert your WordPerfect 5.1 DOS-based macros to the PerfectScript command language used by WordPerfect 6, 6.1, 7, and 8.

CHAPTER 15 • AUTOMATING DAILY WORK WITH SIMPLE MACROS **479**

You may find, however, that your macros do not convert acceptably even after running the conversion utility. WordPerfect 8 is a far more powerful program than was WordPerfect 5.1. Because WordPerfect 8 also uses the Windows 95 or Windows NT operating system, many—if not all—of the system commands used by the WordPerfect 5.1 macro language have changed. If your previous macros were very basic, perhaps only typing text, they probably will convert correctly. However, if your previous macros displayed menus or checked for environment status, they probably will require some editing.

Macros created with WordPerfect 6.1 or 7 do not require conversion before they'll play in WordPerfect 8; however, some commands used in previous versions are now obsolete. You can find a list of obsolete, added, or changed commands by choosing Help, Help Topics, then double-clicking Macros on the Contents tab, and selecting Macro Programming. Then click Upgrade Help, What's New in Corel WordPerfect 8 Macros. Also look at the About Converting Macros item in the same Help book.

16

Understanding Templates and Projects

IN THIS CHAPTER

- **Create a Custom Template**
- **Include Prompts to Ask for Fill-in-the-Blank Information**
- **Associate Macros and Triggers with a Template**
- **Add and Remove Projects**

The selection of predefined WordPerfect projects is reasonably comprehensive, but it would be foolish to assume that every form or task you use appears in the selection. There are, no doubt, forms and tasks in your office that are unique to the work you do. This chapter will walk you through the techniques you need to know to design and create a custom template, or to edit one of the predefined templates. You'll learn how to add a new project to an existing category.

What are Projects and Templates?

Think of *templates* as skeleton documents for documents you use repeatedly. You can create templates for standard business documents, school reports, announcements, and so on.

Templates can:

- Include text and graphics
- Prompt you for "fill-in-the-blank" information
- Refer to Address Book entries
- Automatically complete portions of the template based on personal information (such as your name and address) from an Address Book entry
- Play macros based on events which occur while you use the template

All documents in WordPerfect 8 are based on a template. Templates define a new document's default formatting, including margins, tab settings, and so on. In addition, templates define which toolbars, menus, styles, or macros are used or displayed when a new document is based on a template. When you create a new document, the properties for the template remain with that document, even after the document is saved and subsequently reopened. A template, therefore, forms the complete basis for the document.

A *project* is any document, spreadsheet, template, macro, or application that appears when you choose File, New. The predefined projects are compiled files which can contain templates, executable files, and, optionally, the PerfectExpert. These projects are created by Corel or third-party developers. You can add new compiled projects to the project list, obtaining them from the Corel Web site for WordPerfect 8 or from other developers. These existing projects can be copied, moved, or removed from the project list. Additionally, you can add a document, spreadsheet, template, macro, or application to the list as a new project. But you cannot create your own compiled projects which include the PerfectExpert in the Standard version of Corel WordPerfect Suite 8.

You see a list of both projects and templates when you choose File, New. Most of these projects use a template by the same filename. For example, the Business Letter project file, named `BusLet.ast`, refers to the template `BusLet.wpt`. (Template files all use the extension `.wpt`; projects use the extension `.ast` or `.asx`.) You can edit the templates, making whatever changes you require, but you cannot edit a compiled project file.

You cannot tell by looking at the project and template list which items on the list are compiled project files and which are template files. It can be frustrating, therefore, if you want to make a small change to an existing project. By displaying the properties for a project, however, you can determine the type of file that comprises the project and then determine whether the file is editable. Here's how:

1. Choose File, New. The New dialog box opens.
2. As necessary, select the category which contains the project you want to review. Then select the project from the project list.
3. Click the Options button, then select Project Properties. The Modify a Project dialog box opens, displaying the name of the project, its description, and the name of the file which controls the project. (You can edit the project Display Name and Description.)
4. When finished, click OK to return to the project list.

There's a trick here, however. Almost all of the projects which are included with Corel WordPerfect Suite 8 also reference a template file. Template files *can* be edited, which gives you an avenue to making minor changes to these predefined projects. Review the list of files in the default template folder (usually Corel\Suite8\Template—choose Tools, Settings, Files and select the Template tab), evaluating the file extensions to determine whether the project also uses an editable template. For example, when reviewing the file list, you see two files for the business letter project: BusLet.ast and BusLet.wpt. You can edit the template file, BusLet.wpt, but not the project file, BusLet.ast.

Note

Not all predefined projects and templates are copied to your system during a Typical or Custom installation. If you select a project from the list, you may see a prompt box advising you to insert the Corel WordPerfect Suite 8 CD in your CD-ROM drive. You can avoid this prompt by copying all projects from the CD (in the \Corel\Suite8\Template folder) to your default template folder.

When you create a new, blank document in WordPerfect 8, the document is based on the settings in the default WordPerfect 8 template, named wp8us.wpt, usually stored in the folder \Corel\Suite8\Template\Custom WP Templates. If you use a version other than the U.S. language version, your default (standard) template is named using the two-letter abbreviation for the language, such as wp8ce.wpt for the Canadian English version. If you are working on a network installation of WordPerfect 8, your default template is located in the Windows template folder.

> An additional template can be assigned as a second default template. You can share customized toolbars or menus stored in your own default template by naming your default template (and its location) as the Additional Objects template on other systems. Assign the template as the Additional Objects template by choosing Tools, Settings, Files, Template tab, Additional Objects Template. You can find more information about the Additional Objects template in WordPerfect Help.

You can create, edit, delete, and rename templates. You can also create categories to logically organize templates.

Creating the Personal Letterhead Template

The real power of templates occurs when you create templates that do *exactly* what *you* want them to do. You can base a custom template on an existing document, or on an existing template. Creating a template generally requires the following steps:

1. Design the form, including all text, graphics, formatting, and so on. For example, if your form will be based on a set of margins and styles, it's easiest to create the form in a standard document window and then use it as a source for your new template.
2. Create the template, insert the document, then add any necessary custom prompts.
3. Copy any objects you want included into the template. Objects can be macros, styles, QuickWords, toolbars, menus, or keyboards.
4. Associate any features you want associated with those copied toolbars, menus, or keyboards which will be active in the template. For example, assume that you have created a custom toolbar containing buttons you use when typing a business letter. You can copy the custom toolbar to your new template, then associate it so that it's the default toolbar when creating a letter.
5. Associate any macros with events that will occur while you use the template. If you've created a macro that prompts you to save your document, for example, you can associate that macro so that it plays before you print a document.
6. Save and exit the template, assigning a description, template name, and template category.

The two letter projects included with WordPerfect 8 are extensive. They allow you to customize your letter, including closing signatures, and text formatting styles such as modified or full block. They even include boilerplate text to help you write your letter. But they don't allow a method of including your own custom letterhead. You may have already designed a computer version of your letterhead, complete with a scan of your logo. It's easy to take that letterhead and turn it into a template, adding links to the Address Book to personalize the letterhead for each user, and use entries for the addressee.

It is generally easiest to base a template on an existing file. To create the custom letterhead template, you can either create the letterhead as a standard WordPerfect document, or copy an existing letter and delete the text of the letter. Either method provides you with a raw file that can be used as the basis for the template.

> **CHAPTER 4 COVERS THE BASICS OF FONT FACES AND FONT SIZES.**

The hands-on examples in this chapter will guide you through creating a custom template based on the Midvalley Children's Clinic letterhead example displayed in Figure 16-1. As you refer to this letterhead, notice the areas that will be completed each time the letterhead is used; the text is between two braces ({ }) and is included only to illustrate the areas where prompts or ties to the Address Book will be added. You do not need to type these placeholders.

You can create the Midvalley letterhead and follow along step by step, or use a letterhead you have already created for your company.

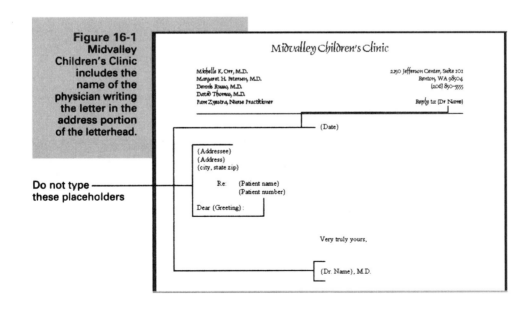

Figure 16-1 Midvalley Children's Clinic includes the name of the physician writing the letter in the address portion of the letterhead.

Do not type these placeholders

Create the Midvalley letterhead using these settings:

- The complete letterhead uses the font face Dauphin, one of the fonts available on the Corel WordPerfect Suite 8 CD.
- The name of the clinic, `Midvalley Children's Clinic`, is centered and sized to 20 points.
- The list of doctors and the address are created within a one-row, two-column table. Right-align the text in the second column. Size all text to 11 points.
- All lines in the table are hidden, except the bottom line. The bottom line uses the Thick line style.

> REFER TO CHAPTER 9 FOR ADDITIONAL INFORMATION ABOUT TABLES.

When your letterhead is complete, save and close the letterhead, naming the file **letterhead.wpd**.

Creating a Category for Your Templates

Templates are organized in categories or *groups* of templates. Templates you create are automatically stored in the `Corel\Suite8\Template\Custom WP Templates` folder. Creating a category creates a folder within the `Corel\Suite8\Template\Custom WP Templates` folder, further organizing your templates into logical groups. You might want to create one category for your business letterheads, another for advertising pieces, another for client forms, and so on.

Categories can be manually created by creating a new folder in the `Corel\Suite8\Template\Custom WP Templates` folder, or by choosing File, New, Options, Create Category.

Hands On: Creating a Category for Your Custom Letterhead

To create a category to organize any templates you create for Midvalley, use these steps:

1. Choose File, New. The New dialog box opens, similar to Figure 16-2.
2. Click the Options button, the click Create Category. The Add a Project dialog box opens.
3. Type **Midvalley Templates** as the name for your category (see Figure 16-3).
4. Click OK to return to the New dialog box.

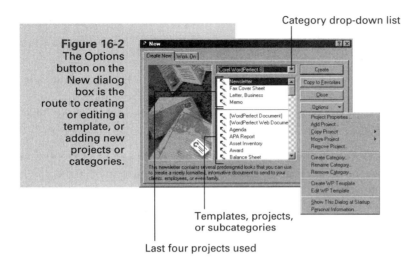

Figure 16-2
The Options button on the New dialog box is the route to creating or editing a template, or adding new projects or categories.

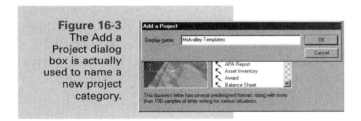

Figure 16-3
The Add a Project dialog box is actually used to name a new project category.

5. Verify your category by clicking the category drop-down list button. You should see your new category in the list. Clicking your new category opens its list of templates, which is empty at the moment.

Creating the Template

With the category defined, you can now create the template. You can create a template from scratch in the Template editing window, insert an existing document into a template, or a combination of both.

Hands On: Creating the Letterhead Template

Creating a template from an existing file is easy and quick. Use these steps:

1. From the File, New dialog box, click the Option button. Now choose Create WP Template. After a brief pause, the Template property bar opens

PART V • TELL ME MORE

in a blank document window. Table 16-1, which follows this procedure, identifies the buttons on this bar.

2. Click the Insert File button, then locate the `letterhead.wpd` file.

3. Click <u>I</u>nsert to add the file to your template. A prompt box appears which asks `Overwrite current styles?`—respond <u>Y</u>es to be sure that your template contains the styles used in the original letterhead document. The letterhead document appears in the template.

> While editing or creating a template, include a QuickMark at the location in the template where you want the insertion point to be whenever you create a new document based on that template. To do so, position the insertion point in the template, then choose <u>T</u>ools, <u>B</u>ookmark, Set <u>Q</u>uickMark.

4. Click the Close button to name and save your template. When prompted `Save Changes to Template1?`, respond <u>Y</u>es. The Save Template dialog box opens.

5. Type a description and a name for the template. The <u>D</u>escription will be displayed in the project list box on the New dialog box. The name you list in the Template <u>N</u>ame text box will be used as the filename for the template.

Table 16-1 Template Property Bar Buttons

Button	Purpose
(Insert File)	Opens the Insert File dialog box, from which you can select a file to be added to the template
Build Prompts...	Opens the Prompt Builder dialog box, enabling you to create prompts for your template
Copy/Remove Object...	Opens the Copy/Remove Template Objects dialog box, from which you can copy objects from the default template to your new template
Associate...	Allows you to associate toolbars, menus, or keyboards with specific WordPerfect features; or to associate macros with WordPerfect events such as printing or file open
Description...	Allows you to change or add a description for the template, to be displayed in the New dialog box
(Close)	Closes the current template, prompting you to save and name a new or modified template

6. Scroll through the Template Group list until you see the Midvalley Templates category. Figure 16-4 shows the completed Save Template dialog box.
7. Click the category, then click OK. The template closes and you are returned to the document window.

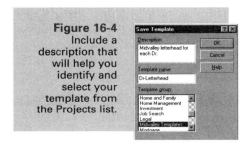

Figure 16-4 Include a description that will help you identify and select your template from the Projects list.

Using Your Custom Template

Selecting and using a template you create is identical to selecting a predefined WordPerfect project.

Hands On: Using the Letterhead Template

To use the Midvalley letterhead template, complete these steps:

1. Choose File, New. The New dialog box opens, displaying the predefined templates and projects.
2. Click the category drop-down list, then select Midvalley Templates.
3. Select the Midvalley letterhead template from the project list, then click Create. A new document window opens and the letterhead is ready to use!

Enhancing the Letterhead Template with Prompts

A common practice in many businesses is to create a skeleton document, then open it to serve as a new document, eventually saving the new document with a new name. This works reasonably well and is easy to set up. Unfortunately, you run the risk of accidentally saving your new file over the top of the old skeleton document.

The Midvalley letter created in the previous hands-on activity is usable, but not much better than just copying an existing document. The greatest advantage to using the template is that it *does* create a new document, thus preventing you from accidentally saving your new file over an old one.

Adding prompts to the letterhead, asking you for the name of the addressee and so on, adds very basic programming to the template. The prompts can be linked to the Address Book, enabling you to complete information such as the address directly from entries in the Address Book. You can also personalize the template by linking personal information, such as your name and phone number, to other template prompt areas. All prompts you create will appear in a dialog box at the time you use the template.

As you create the prompts, you paste each of them on the template at the location where that data needs to appear when the template is used.

The Midvalley letterhead must ask for this information:

- The name of the doctor writing the letter—this information will appear both as the signature in the letter and in the letterhead Reply To field
- The name, address, city, state, and ZIP code for the person to whom the letter is being sent
- The name to be used as the Greeting on the letter
- The name of the patient about which the letter is being written
- The patient's identification number

The name, address, and greeting for the person to whom the letter is written should be linked to the Address Book. This allows you to select an Address Book entry, quickly completing all related linked fields. The name of the physician and the Reply To name can also be linked to the Address Book as *personal information*. Personal information is linked to an entry in the Address Book which is selected or completed the first time you use a template that requires personal information. It remains selected until you choose an alternate entry from the Address Book. This allows you to use the same template for many different people without customizing the template for each person.

Hands On: Adding Prompts to the Letterhead Template

Adding prompts to a template follows a simple, logical sequence. Use these steps:

1. Open the Midvalley letterhead for editing by choosing File, New. Locate the Midvalley letterhead template in the project list (you may need to open the Midvalley Templates category first), then click the Options button.

Chapter 16 • Understanding Templates and Projects

Now choose Ed*i*t WP Template. The template opens with the Template property bar in place.

2. Start by adding the date code to the template at the location where you want the current date to appear each time you use the template. To do so, position the insertion point at the correct location, then choose Insert, Date/Time. The Date/Time dialog box opens. Click the check box for Automatic Update, then click Insert. Alternately, press Ctrl+Shift+D to add the automatic date code to the document. Today's date appears in the template now, but because you've selected an automatic date, the current date will appear each time the template is used.

3. Delete any *placeholder* text you included in your document, such as the placeholder text shown in Figure 16-1.

4. Click the Build Prompts button on the Template property bar. The Prompt Builder dialog box opens (see Figure 16-5).

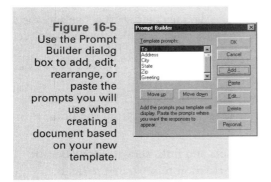

Figure 16-5
Use the Prompt Builder dialog box to add, edit, rearrange, or paste the prompts you will use when creating a document based on your new template.

Note

The macro `prompts.wcm` **must exist in one of the four possible macros folders. (See Chapter 15 for help with macro folders.) If it cannot be found, WordPerfect displays an error box and abandons the Build Prompts instruction. If necessary, use the Windows 95 Find Files and Folders utility to locate the** `prompts.wcm` **file, then copy it to your macros folder. Then start the Build Prompts function again.**

5. Click Add to open the Add Template Prompt dialog box shown in Figure 16-6.

6. Type **To** as the text for the Prompt.

Part V • Tell Me More

Figure 16-6
Make your prompts descriptive, but keep their length to about 35 characters or less so that the complete prompt is visible when the template is used.

7. Click the drop-down list for Link to Address Book Field, then select Name. Click OK to add the prompt text to the Prompt Builder Template Prompts list.

> *Tip:* The Link to Address Book Field drop-down list displays the default list of fields for the Address Book. Clicking the Show All Available Fields check box adds the complete list of available Address Book fields to the Link to Address Book Field drop-down list.

8. Click Add again, then type **Address** as the prompt text. This field also links to an entry in the Address Book. Select Address from the Link to Address Book Field drop-down list.

9. Continue adding the remaining prompts and links shown below. Be sure to include any necessary spaces or punctuation to separate the fields.

Prompt	**Link to**
City	City
State	State
Zip	ZIP Code
Greeting	Greeting
Patient Name	None
Patient Number	None

> *Tip:* The Template Prompts list displays the prompts in the order they will appear when the template is used. If you create a prompt out of order, select it in the Template Prompts list, then click the Move Up or Move Down button until the prompt appears in the correct location in the list.

CHAPTER 16 • UNDERSTANDING TEMPLATES AND PROJECTS **493**

One additional field must be added to the letterhead—the name of the doctor who will sign the letter and whose name will be included in the Reply To field. This name, while also supplied from the Address Book, is considered personal information. Personal information remains the same for this and all other templates until it is changed.

10. Click <u>P</u>ersonal to open the list of Personal Fields shown in Figure 16-7. Select Name, then click in the letterhead area, after the text `Reply To:`. Then click <u>P</u>aste in the Personal Fields dialog box. The personal field `<Name>` is inserted in the document. Now also insert the personal field `Name` in the signature block area.

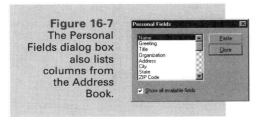

Figure 16-7
The Personal Fields dialog box also lists columns from the Address Book.

11. Click <u>C</u>lose to return to the Prompt Builder dialog box.

    The Prompt list is complete. Now you need to paste the field associated with each prompt into the document text at the location where you want the data to appear.

12. Click in the document at the location where the name of the person to whom you are writing should be inserted.

13. Select the prompt `To` in the <u>T</u>emplate Prompts list, then click <u>P</u>aste to add the prompt to the letterhead. The prompt appears in the letterhead as `[To]` (see Figure 16-8).

14. Continue clicking in the document at the correct location for each field, selecting the appropriate field from the <u>T</u>emplate Prompts list, and pasting the field into the document until all prompts have been correctly located. You need to add returns or punctuation where appropriate, such as pressing (Enter) after each line of the address, and adding a comma and space between the City and State fields.

15. When all prompts have been placed, click OK. WordPerfect displays a Please Wait dialog box while it prepares the template, adding numbered bookmarks at each prompt location. After a brief pause, the insertion point is returned to the template and the Prompt Builder closes.

PART V • TELL ME MORE

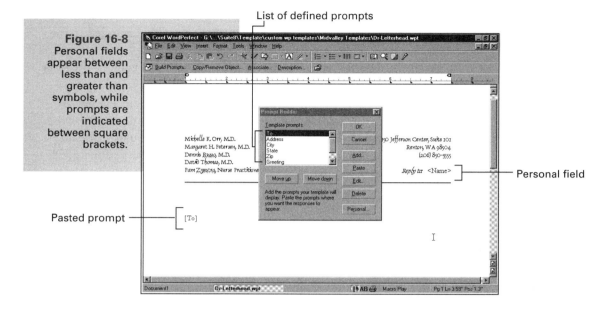

Figure 16-8
Personal fields appear between less than and greater than symbols, while prompts are indicated between square brackets.

The `prompts.wcm` macro builds bookmarks for each prompt, sequentially numbering them. You can view the bookmarks by opening Reveal Codes. Figure 16-9 shows the template with all of the prompt fields and personal fields in place.

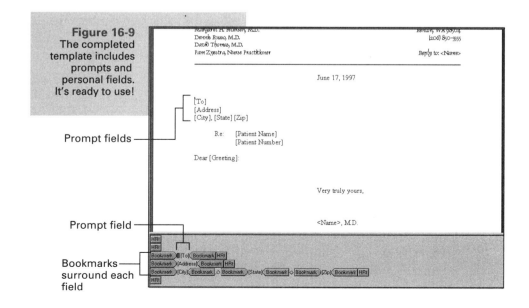

Figure 16-9
The completed template includes prompts and personal fields. It's ready to use!

16. Click the Close button, saving your changes to the template. The template design window closes, returning you to a document window.

The final step in designing any template is to test it to be sure everything works as you intended.

Hands On: Using the Letterhead Template

To test the template, use these steps:

1. Choose File, New, select the Midvalley letterhead from the projects list, then click Create. The letterhead opens and immediately displays the Template Information dialog box, shown in Figure 16-10.

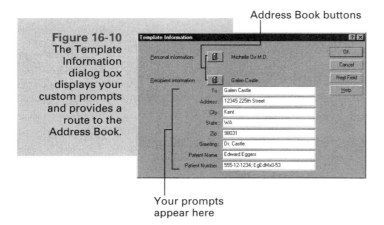

Figure 16-10 The Template Information dialog box displays your custom prompts and provides a route to the Address Book.

2. Verify the Personal Information for the template. If it is incorrect, click the Address Book button, then select your name (or the name of the person from whom the letter is being sent). If you do not have an entry for yourself in the Address Book, click the Add button, select Person as the entry type, and complete the New Personal Properties dialog box. When your entry is complete, click OK to return to the Address Book. Then select your name and click Select. Your name appears in the Personal Information field.

3. Now complete the entries for the Recipient, using the Address Book as required for the recipient information.

4. The Patient Name and Patient Number fields are not linked to the Address Book, so you need to provide the appropriate information. In the Patient Name field, type **Edward Eggers**. In the Patient Number field, type **555-12-1234; EgEdMxO-53**.

5. Click OK to transfer the information from the Template Information dialog box to the letterhead. The dialog box closes and your letter is ready for the text!

Associating a Macro with the Template

Although the vast majority of the templates you create will be complete with the inclusion of prompts, you may want to consider adding macros to templates to further enhance their usability. You can group any type of macros you want with a template. In a letterhead template such as the Midvalley Children's Clinic letterhead, you might want to add several macros for custom signature blocks, macros with often-used text phrases, and so on. These macros can be played by choosing Tools, Template Macro, Play, or can be added to a toolbar or menu. If you choose to add a macro to a toolbar or menu, you also must copy the toolbar or menu to the template.

In addition, you might consider associating a macro with a template *trigger*. A trigger is a WordPerfect event such as opening or closing a document, creating a table, or printing. A common macro based on a trigger is one that saves a document when a print request is issued, before the document is printed.

Adding Objects to the Template

Macros, styles, QuickWords, toolbars, menu bars, and keyboards can be copied from one template to another. Macros on disk can also be added to a template. Objects must be added to the template if you need them to be available when the template is used.

All objects available in the default template are automatically available to all new templates. This means that all of the predefined toolbars, menus, and so on can be selected, used, and edited even when a custom template is selected. You might, therefore, want to *remove* certain objects from a custom template to prevent a user from accessing features you don't want them to use.

Copying any object type to a template requires these basic steps:

Chapter 16 • Understanding Templates and Projects

1. Open the template for editing.
2. Click the <u>C</u>opy/Remove Object button on the Template property bar. The Copy/Remove Template Objects dialog box opens, as shown in Figure 16-11.

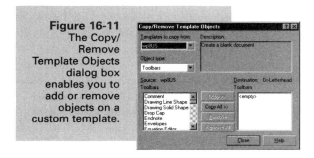

Figure 16-11
The Copy/Remove Template Objects dialog box enables you to add or remove objects on a custom template.

3. Select the template from which you want to copy the object (you can only copy from the default or additional objects template) from the <u>T</u>emplates to Copy From drop-down list.
4. Select the object type you want to copy from the O<u>b</u>ject Type drop-down list.
5. Select the specific object or objects you want to copy from the <u>S</u>ource list.
6. <u>C</u>opy the object or objects to the <u>D</u>estination template (the current template being edited).

Similarly, removing an object requires that you open the template for editing, then click the <u>C</u>opy/Remove Object button. Select the object type to be removed, then locate and select the object in the <u>D</u>estination list. Finally, click the <u>R</u>emove button; the object is removed from the current template.

Hands On: Creating a File Save Macro

To complete the next "Hands On" activity, "Hands On: Adding a Macro to a Template," a File Save macro must be created and saved. You may need to refer to Chapter 15 for additional information regarding macros. Use these steps to create the File Save macro:

1. On a blank document window, choose <u>T</u>ools, <u>M</u>acro, <u>M</u>acro Toolbar. The Macro toolbar appears at the top of the document edit area and the first line of the macro file is numbered.
2. Type this macro command: **FileSave()**

PART V • TELL ME MORE

Although you normally would type an `Application` command as the first command in a macro (thus identifying to the compiler the application to be used), for a simple macro such as the one being presented here, you can get away without it.

The `FileSave()` macro command forces a Save As dialog box to appear if the document has not previously been saved and named. If the document has been named, the `FileSave()` command updates the file.

3. Now click the Save & Compile button on the Macro toolbar. The Macro Save As dialog box opens.
4. Name the macro `filesave` and click the Save button. You are returned to the macro document.
5. Close the macro document to return to a blank document window.

With the macro created, you can now add the macro to the Midvalley letterhead as a template macro.

Hands On: Adding a Macro to a Template

To add the `filesave` macro to the Midvalley letterhead template, use these steps:

1. Open the template for editing by choosing File, New. Select the Midvalley letterhead template, then click the Options button and select Edit WP Template. The template opens with the Template property bar at the top of the document editing window.
2. Click the Copy/Remove Object button on the Template property bar. The Copy/Remove Template Objects dialog box opens.
3. From the Object Type drop-down list, select `Macros on Disk`. The dialog box updates, displaying the Macros on Disk control in the Source group.

All objects other than Macros on Disk are copied from the default template to the template currently being edited.

CHAPTER 16 • UNDERSTANDING TEMPLATES AND PROJECTS **499**

4. Click the Folder button on the Macros on Disk control, then locate and select the `filesave.wcm` macro file you created earlier. Click the Select button. The macro filename (including the full path) appears in the Macros on Disk control.
5. You must next copy the macro to the template. With the macro filename appearing in the Macros on Disk control, click the C_opy button. The macro name appears in the _Destination list (see Figure 16-12).
6. Click _Close to close the Copy/Remove Template Objects dialog box.

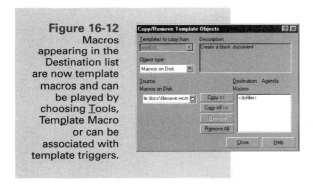

Figure 16-12
Macros appearing in the Destination list are now template macros and can be played by choosing _Tools, Temp_late Macro or can be associated with template triggers.

Understanding Associations

Two types of associations can be made in a template. You can associate toolbar, menu, or keyboard objects with WordPerfect features; or you can associate macro objects with a WordPerfect event.

Associating an object with a feature means that it will automatically appear when that feature is used. For example, assume that you have created a custom toolbar. You've associated that toolbar with the Headers feature. Now, when you create or edit a header, that custom toolbar will appear. You can associate objects with these features:

Comments

Endnotes

Equation Editor

Footers

Footnotes

Graphics

Headers

The main document editing window

Outlines

Tables

Watermarks

Remember that you can use and see toolbars, menus, or keyboards from the default template when you use another template. You cannot, however, associate their appearance with a WordPerfect feature in another template, unless they were also copied as objects to that template. Therefore, before you can associate the object, you must use the Copy/Remove Object button to copy the object to the template. Review the previous section for the necessary steps.

Associating an object with a feature uses these steps:

1. Edit the template, then click the Associate button. The Associate dialog box opens (see Figure 16-13).

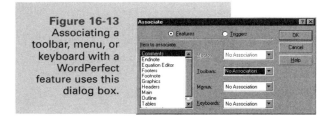

Figure 16-13 Associating a toolbar, menu, or keyboard with a WordPerfect feature uses this dialog box.

2. Select the object you want to associate from the Toolbars, Menus, or Keyboards drop-down list.
3. Select the WordPerfect feature with which you want to associate the object from the Item to Associate list.
4. Click OK to return to the template editing window.

Macro objects can be associated with a template only when certain functions take place. These functions are referred to as *events* or *triggers*. For example, a macro can automatically play in a template-based document immediately after you create a table, before you close the document, or before you print the document. These functions are examples of *triggers*.

You can associate a macro with a trigger, provided the macro has been copied to the template. The previous "Hands On" activity copied the `filesave` macro object to the Midvalley letterhead. The `filesave` macro can, therefore, now be associated with a trigger. Table 16-2 lists the triggers with which a macro can be associated. Remember that triggers occur in documents based on the template that contain the trigger association.

Table 16-2 Template Triggers

Trigger	Does this
Post Close	The Post Close trigger plays a macro after you close the document. A document is closed by choosing File, Close, or by clicking the Close button on the document window.
Post New	Post New plays a macro immediately after a new document is created based on the template. The text and graphics in the template document are displayed before the macro plays.
Post Open	When a template has a macro that is associated with the Post Open trigger, the macro plays only after the template document is first created, saved, and closed… and then opened. The trigger executes immediately after you open the saved template document.
Post Print	Post Print plays a macro immediately after the template document is submitted to print. If the macro writes to the template document, the changes occur after the document has spooled to the printer.
Post Startup	Post Startup plays a macro immediately after starting WordPerfect 8. This trigger must reside in the default template.
Post Switch Doc	The Post Switch Doc trigger plays the macro when you switch from the template document to another document window. The macro plays *each* time you switch!
Post Tables	Post Tables plays a macro immediately after a table is created. The macro plays in the first cell of the table.
Pre Close	The Pre Close trigger plays a macro immediately before closing the template document. If the template document contains changes since its last save, the macro executes prior to the `Save changes` prompt.
Pre New	This trigger only works in the default template. The macro plays immediately after you choose File, New.
Pre Open	The template on which this trigger is based must be open in the current document window. The macro then plays immediately after you choose File, Open to open another file.
Pre Print	The Pre Print trigger plays a macro just prior to submitting a document to the print spooler. If the macro writes to the document, the changes appear in the current print, although it appears that printing has already begun before the text is added to the document.
Pre Switch Doc	Pre Switch Doc plays a macro immediately when you choose to switch to another document window, open another document, or create a new document. This trigger also plays a macro when the template document is minimized while another document is maximized.
Pre Tables	Pre Tables plays a macro before a new table is written to the template document.

Hands On: Associating a Macro with the Pre Print Trigger

Associating the `filesave` macro with the Pre Print trigger forces the macro to play before a letter based on the Midvalley letterhead template prints. Use these steps to add the association:

1. Open the Midvalley letterhead template for editing, then click the Associate button on the Template property bar.
2. Click Triggers, then select Pre Print in the Item to Associate list.
3. Select the `filesave` macro from the Macros drop-down list. Figure 16-14 displays the Associate dialog box with these selections.

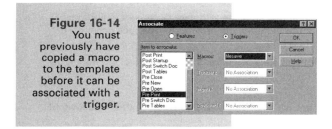

Figure 16-14 You must previously have copied a macro to the template before it can be associated with a trigger.

4. Click OK to return to the template editing window.
5. Close the template, saving your changes. Now, create a new document based on your custom template, and send it to print. The `filesave` macro plays, opening a File Save As dialog box because the document has not previously been named and saved.
6. Name and save your document, naming it **trigger**. The `trigger` document then prints. Close the `trigger` document and then reopen it. Make a simple change to the document, such as typing your name at the end, then again send the document to print. The `filesave` macro plays again, this time updating the saved file, and the revised document prints.

Managing Projects

As you've learned, a full list of projects appears when you choose File, New. While many of these projects are helpful tools to your daily work, you'll very likely find that you only work with a few of them. Perhaps you would like to remove some of these unused projects, making it easier to locate those projects you *do* regularly use.

You've also learned that you can create a template and include it as a project on the list as it is created. But you can also include other types of files in the list of projects. A project can consist of a document, template, macro, or application.

Of course, there are other management tasks you can perform to keep your projects logically organized and appropriate to the tasks at hand. You can copy or move projects between categories, and even rename or remove categories.

This section will guide you through the basic steps required to remove a project and then add it back to the project list.

Removing a Project

Removing a project deletes it from the category list, but doesn't actually delete the project file from the disk. Only one project can be removed at a time, but you might want to make the investment of time and clean out all those projects that you never use.

Hands On: Removing a Project from the Corel WordPerfect 8 Category

Use these steps to remove a project:

1. From the WordPerfect document window, choose File, New. The New dialog box opens. Verify that the Create New tab is on top.
2. Select `Corel WordPerfect 8` from the category drop-down list if it is not already selected.
3. Select `Agenda` from the list of projects.
4. Click Options, then click Remove Project. The Remove This Project from the Current Category? dialog box opens, as shown in Figure 16-15.

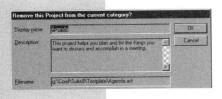

Figure 16-15 Verify that you've selected the correct project before removing it from the category.

PART V • TELL ME MORE

5. Click OK. The project disappears from the list of projects for the displayed category.

6. As desired, repeat steps 2 through 5 for each project you want to remove.

Adding a Project

As you know, projects can consist of compiled project files (which end in an `.ast` or `.asx` extension), other applications, macros, documents, spreadsheets, or templates. You may have templates which were created in WordPerfect 7 that you want to add to the project list (probably in their own category), or you may want to add a full application.

 Look in the Freebies section at the Corel Web Site to locate additional projects:

http://www.corel.com/products/wordperfect

Hands On: Adding a Project

In the previous "Hands On" activity, you removed the Agenda project from the `Corel WordPerfect 8` category. Use these steps to add it back to the category project list:

1. From the WordPerfect document window, choose File, New to open the New dialog box.
2. Select `Corel WordPerfect 8` from the drop-down category list if it is not already selected.
3. Click Options, then click Add Project. The Add New Project dialog box opens, as shown in Figure 16-16.

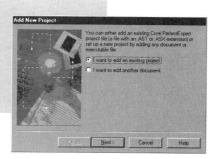

Figure 16-16
The Add New Project dialog box is used to add all project types to the project list.

> Only two choices are possible in the Add New Project dialog box. You can add an existing project (a compiled project file that uses the .ast or .asx extension), or you can add another document. This is a bit misleading. The choice I Want to Add Another Document is used to add *all* other project types—applications, documents, templates, macros, or spreadsheets.

4. Choose I Want to Add an Existing Project, then click Next.
5. Click the Browse button to access the Open File file management dialog box. Locate the folder which contains your WordPerfect 8 templates (usually \Corel\Suite8\Template), then select Agenda.ast and click Open. The full path and filename for the project are added to the Add an Existing Project dialog box (see Figure 16-17).

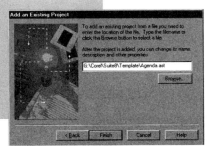

Figure 16-17 The Add an Existing Project dialog box is used to add compiled project files to the project list.

6. Click Finish. A Corel PerfectExpert dialog box appears, verifying that the project was added to the Corel WordPerfect 8 category.
7. Click OK. The New dialog box reappears with Agenda added to the project list.

Part VI
Appendixes

A KEYBOARD SHORTCUT KEYS 509

B PREDEFINED TOOLBARS AND PROPERTY BARS 517

C GLOSSARY 533

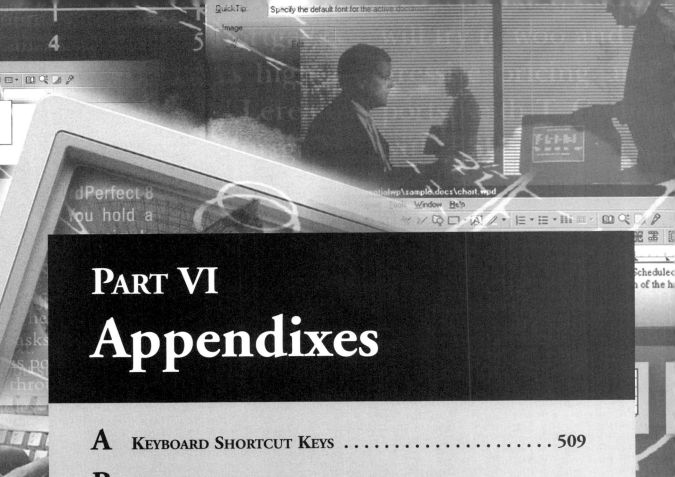

A

Keyboard Shortcut Keys

WordPerfect 8, like its predecessors, allows you to use the keyboard to perform all of the most commonly used (and some of the less frequently used) features. Table A-1 lists the shortcut keys you can use with the WPWIN 8 default keyboard to perform these features.

PART VI • APPENDIXES

For a printable Function Key template, refer to the Corel FTP site:

ftp://ftp.corel.com/pub/

You'll then need to access the area for the Corel suites or for WordPerfect.

This table lists the shortcut keys logically by feature. This should allow you to quickly locate the keystroke you need by looking through the first column to find the feature and task you want to do. An ellipsis (…) sometimes guides you to the next logical thought in the process. For example, notice that there are several variations listed for the Go To feature. You should logically think, "I want to Go To *where*?" This will help you determine the correct keyboard shortcut for the particular task at hand.

Any commas in the feature/task column are to facilitate logical sorting of the list. This enables you to skim through the list looking for the primary feature that interests you, then quickly locate the specific task to be performed for that feature. For example, the entry "Table, Create" directs your attention to the general feature (working with tables) and then to the particular task (creating a table).

> CHAPTER 2 PROVIDES INFORMATION ABOUT SELECTING KEYBOARDS.

Some features and tasks can be accomplished in a number of ways. In that case, you'll see multiple shortcut keys presented; for example, seeing "Ctrl+C or Ctrl+Insert" in the second column means that you can either press Ctrl+C or press Ctrl+Insert to perform the task.

Table A-1 List of Shortcut Keys, Sorted By Feature/Task

Feature/Task	Shortcut Key(s) Using the WPWIN 8 (Default) Keyboard
Bars, Hide	Alt+Shift+F5
Bars, Show (after hiding)	Esc
Bold Toggle	Ctrl+B
Case Toggle	Ctrl+K
Center Line	Shift+F7
Close	Ctrl+F4
Copy	Ctrl+C or Ctrl+Insert
Cut	Ctrl+X or Shift+Del
Date, Automatic	Ctrl+Shift+D

Appendix A • Keyboard Shortcut Keys

Feature/Task	Shortcut Key(s) Using the WPWIN 8 (Default) Keyboard
Date Text	Ctrl+D
Delete	Del
Delete ... Next Character	Del
Delete ... Table, Row	Alt+Del
Delete ... to End of Line	Ctrl+Del
Delete ... to End of Page	Ctrl+Shift+Del
Display Popup Menu (Dialog Box)	Shift+F10
Double Indent Paragraph	Ctrl+Shift+F7
Drop Cap	Ctrl+Shift+C
Edit Graphic Box	Shift+F11
Exit WordPerfect	Alt+F4
Feature Bar	Alt+Shift+F10
Find and Replace	Ctrl+F or F2 or Ctrl+F2
Find Next	Shift+F2 or Ctrl+Shift+F
Find Previous	Alt+F2 or Alt+Ctrl+F
Flush Right Line	Alt+F7
Font	F9
Generate	Ctrl+F9
Go to ...	Ctrl+G
Go to ... Character, Next	→
Go to ... Character, Previous	←
Go to ... Column, Bottom	Alt+End
Go to ... Column, Next	Alt+→
Go to ... Column, Previous	Alt+←
Go to ... Column, Top	Alt+Home
Go to ... Document, Bottom	Ctrl+End
Go to ... Document, Next Open	Ctrl+F6
Go to ... Document, Previous Open	Ctrl+Shift+F6
Go to ... Document, Top	Ctrl+Home
Go to ... Document, Top (before formatting)	Ctrl+Home, Ctrl+Home
Go to ... Line, Beginning	Home
Go to ... Line, Beginning (before formatting)	Home, Home
Go to ... Line, End	End
Go to ... Line, Next	↓
Go to ... Line, Previous	↑
Go to ... Page, Next	Alt+Pg Dn
Go to ... Page, Previous	Alt+Pg Up
Go to ... Pane, Next	F6

Table A-1 Continued

Feature/Task	Shortcut Key(s) Using the WPWIN 8 (Default) Keyboard
Go to ... Pane, Previous	Shift+F6
Go to ... Paragraph, Next	Ctrl+↓
Go to ... Paragraph, Previous	Ctrl+↑
Go to ... Screen Down	Pg Dn
Go to ... Screen Up	Pg Up
Go to ... Scroll Left	Ctrl+Pg Up
Go to ... Scroll Right	Ctrl+Pg Dn
Go to ... Table, Cell Down	Alt+↓
Go to ... Table, Cell Next	Alt+→ or Tab
Go to ... Table, Cell Previous	Alt+← or Shift+Tab
Go to ... Table, Cell Up	Alt+↑
Go to ... Table, Column, Next	Alt+→ or Tab
Go to ... Table, Column, Previous	Alt+← or Shift+Tab
Go to ... Up	↑
Go to ... Word, Next	Ctrl+→
Go to ... Word, Previous	Ctrl+←
Grammatik	Alt+Shift+F1
Graphics ... Insert Line, Horizontal	Ctrl+F11
Graphics ... Insert Line, Vertical	Ctrl+Shift+F11
Graphics, Create Text Box	Alt+F11
Hanging Indent Paragraph	Ctrl+F7
Help Topics	F1
Help, What Is?	Shift+F1
Hyphen Character	Ctrl+-
Hyphen Soft	Ctrl+Shift+-
Hyphenation Cancel	Ctrl+/
Indent Paragraph	F7
Insert Bullet	Ctrl+Shift+B
Insert Image From File	F11
Insert Paragraph Number	Ctrl+Shift+F5
Italic Toggle	Ctrl+I
Justify ... Center	Ctrl+E
Justify ... Full	Ctrl+J
Justify ... Left	Ctrl+L
Justify ... Right	Ctrl+R
Line Break	Ctrl+Shift+L

Feature/Task	Shortcut Key(s) Using the WPWIN 8 (Default) Keyboard
Macro Play	Alt+F10
Macro Record	Ctrl+F10
Margins	Ctrl+F8
Merge	Shift+F9
New, Blank Document	Ctrl+N or Shift+F4
New Document	Ctrl+Shift+N or Ctrl+T
Open	F4 or Ctrl+O
Outline Body Text	Ctrl+H
Paste	Ctrl+V or Shift+Insert
Paste Simple (without attributes)	Ctrl+Shift+V
Print	Ctrl+P or F5
Print Document (directly to printer)	Ctrl+Shift+P
Print History Dialog Box	Ctrl+Shift+H
QuickCorrect	Ctrl+Shift+F1
QuickFind Next Current	Alt+Ctrl+N
QuickFind Previous Current	Alt+Ctrl+P
QuickMark Find	Ctrl+Q
QuickMark Set	Ctrl+Shift+Q
QuickWords Insert	Ctrl+Shift+A
Redisplay	Ctrl+F3
Redo	Ctrl+Shift+R
Reveal Codes Open/Close	Alt+F3
Ruler Toggle	Alt+Shift+F3
Save	Ctrl+S or Shift+F3
Save All	Ctrl+Shift+S
Save As	F3
Select On/Off	F8
Select ... All	Ctrl+A
Select ... Character, Next	Shift+→
Select ... Character, Previous	Shift+←
Select ... Column, Next	Alt+Shift+→
Select ... Column, Previous	Alt+Shift+←
Select ... Beginning of Line	Shift+Home
Select ... Beginning of Line (before formatting)	Shift+Home, Shift+Home
Select ... End of Line	Shift+End
Select ... Line, Next	Shift+↓
Select ... Line, Previous	Shift+↑
Select ... Page, Next	Alt+Shift+Pg Dn

Table A-1 Continued

Feature/Task	Shortcut Key(s) Using the WPWIN 8 (Default) Keyboard
Select … Page, Previous	Alt+Shift+Pg Up
Select … Paragraph, Next	Ctrl+Shift+↓
Select … Paragraph, Previous	Ctrl+Shift+↑
Select … Screen Down	Shift+Pg Dn
Select … Screen Up	Shift+Pg Up
Select … Table, Cell	Shift+F8
Select … Table, Cell, Down	Alt+Shift+↓
Select … Table, Cell, Up	Alt+Shift+↑
Select … Table, Cell, Next	Alt+Shift+→
Select … Table, Cell, Previous	Alt+Shift+←
Select … Word, Next	Ctrl+Shift+→
Select … Word, Previous	Ctrl+Shift+←
Select to … Column, Bottom	Alt+Shift+End
Select to … Document, Bottom	Ctrl+Shift+End
Select to … Document, Top	Ctrl+Shift+Home
Show ¶	Ctrl+Shift+F3
Sort	Alt+F9
Spell Check	Ctrl+F1
Styles	Alt+F8
Symbol, Insert WP Character	Ctrl+W
Tab Hard Decimal	Alt+Shift+F7
Table, Create	F12
Table, Decrease Column	Ctrl+, or Ctrl+Shift+,
Table, Increase Column	Ctrl+. or Ctrl+Shift+.
Table, QuickSum	Ctrl+=
Table, Borders/Fill	Shift+F12
Table, Calculate Document	Alt+Shift+F12
Table, Format	Ctrl+F12
Table, Numeric Format	Alt+F12
Table, QuickFill	Ctrl+Shift+F12
Table, Row Append	Alt+Shift+Insert
Table, Row Delete	Alt+Del
Table, Row Insert	Alt+Insert
Thesaurus	Alt+F1
Typeover Toggle	Insert
Undelete	Ctrl+Shift+Z

Feature/Task	Shortcut Key(s) Using the WPWIN 8 (Default) Keyboard
Underline Toggle	Ctrl+U
Undo	Ctrl+Z
View, Draft	Ctrl+F5
View, Page	Alt+F5
WP Character	Ctrl+W
Zoom Full Page	Shift+F5

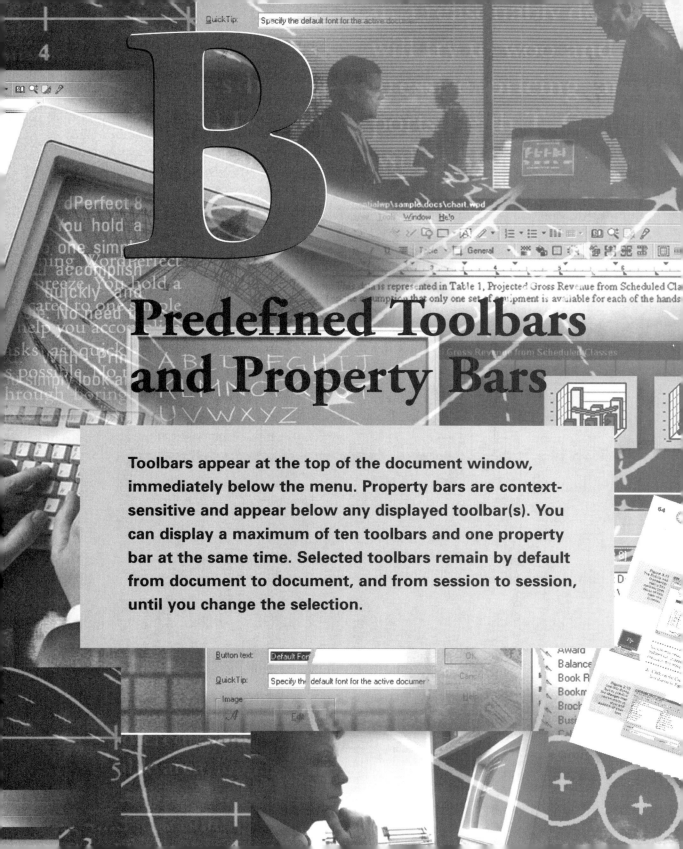

Predefined Toolbars and Property Bars

Toolbars appear at the top of the document window, immediately below the menu. Property bars are context-sensitive and appear below any displayed toolbar(s). You can display a maximum of ten toolbars and one property bar at the same time. Selected toolbars remain by default from document to document, and from session to session, until you change the selection.

Predefined Toolbars

CHAPTER 2 EXPLAINS HOW TO CUSTOMIZE A TOOLBAR BY ADDING OR DELETING BUTTONS.

To display a specific toolbar, right-click the current toolbar and select the toolbar you want to display from the QuickMenu list; or choose View, Toolbars to display the Toolbars dialog box, then check those toolbars you want to display, and click OK.

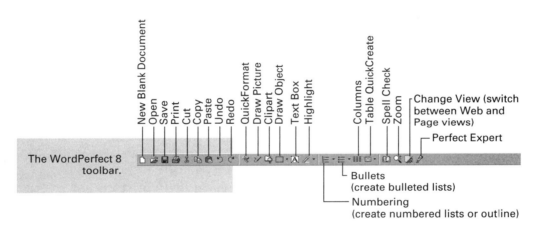

The WordPerfect 8 toolbar.

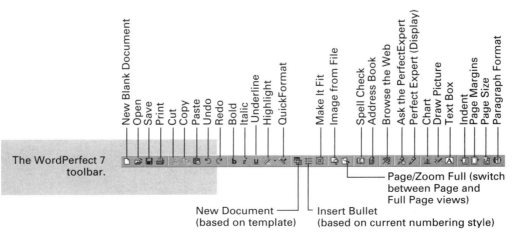

The WordPerfect 7 toolbar.

APPENDIX B • PREDEFINED TOOLBARS AND PROPERTY BARS

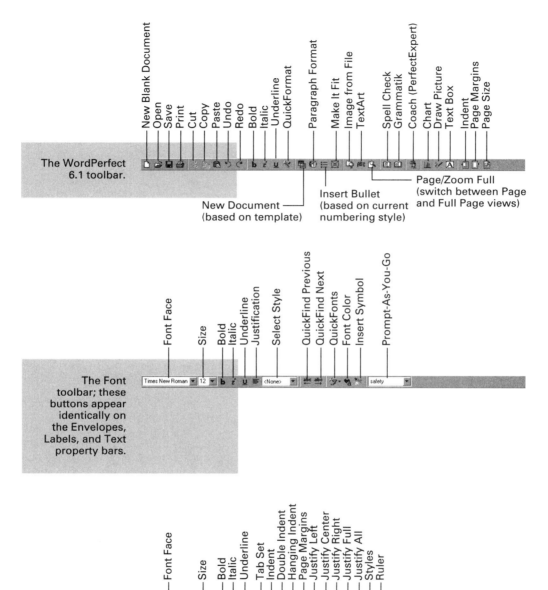

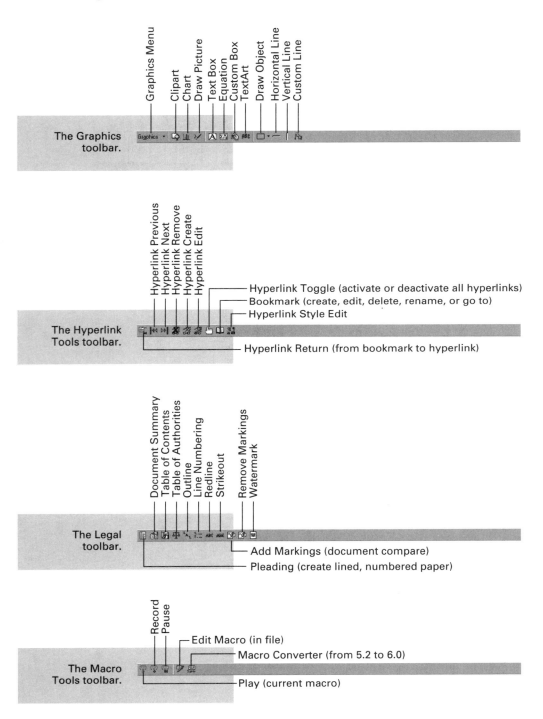

Appendix B • Predefined Toolbars and Property Bars

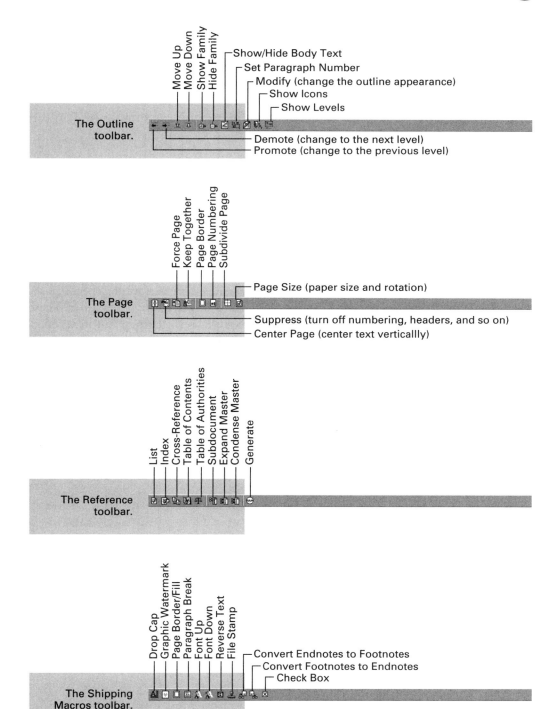

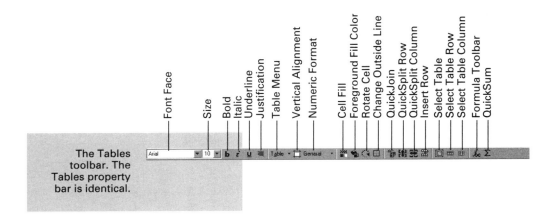

The Tables toolbar. The Tables property bar is identical.

Property Bars

Property bars usually appear one at a time when you are performing specific tasks in WordPerfect that might require the buttons displayed on a given bar. These bars are context-sensitive, appearing automatically as the current feature or operation requires. Similarly, buttons on the bars vary automatically depending on the current settings of the feature you're working with.

Note

Previous versions of WordPerfect referred to these bars as *feature bars* or *power bars*. Some portions of the WordPerfect help text still mention these previous names rather than *property bars*.

The bars in this section are roughly grouped by feature. If property bars are not automatically visible, choose View, Toolbars and then check Property Bar in the Available Toolbars list.

A complete suite of property bars, not pictured in this appendix, is available when creating or editing SGML documents.

APPENDIX B • PREDEFINED TOOLBARS AND PROPERTY BARS **523**

Bars for Working with Graphic Features

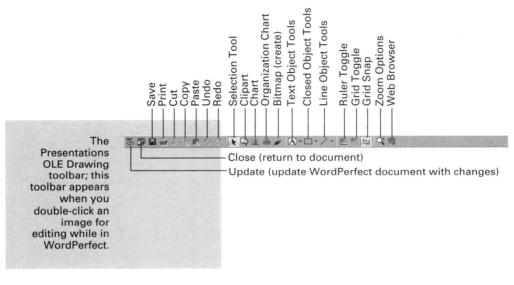

The Presentations OLE Drawing toolbar; this toolbar appears when you double-click an image for editing while in WordPerfect.

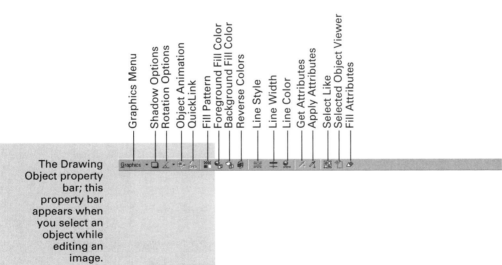

The Drawing Object property bar; this property bar appears when you select an object while editing an image.

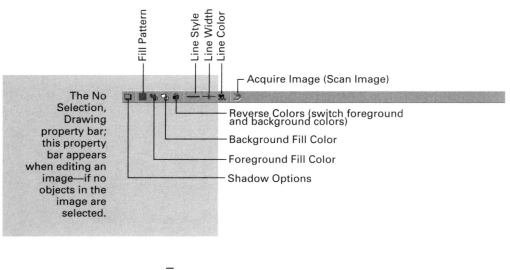

The No Selection, Drawing property bar; this property bar appears when editing an image—if no objects in the image are selected.

The Drop Cap property bar.

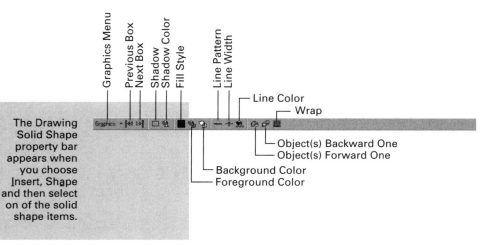

The Drawing Solid Shape property bar appears when you choose Insert, Shape and then select on of the solid shape items.

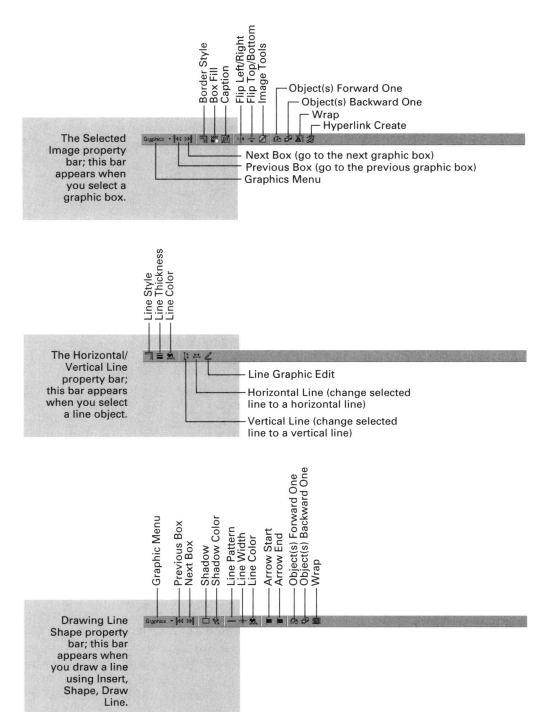

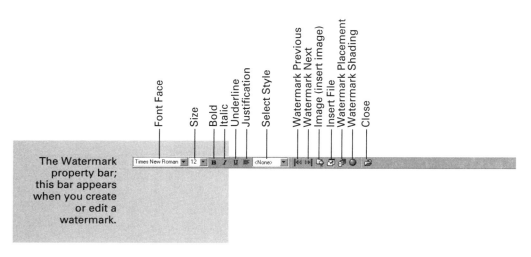

The Watermark property bar; this bar appears when you create or edit a watermark.

Formatting Property Bars

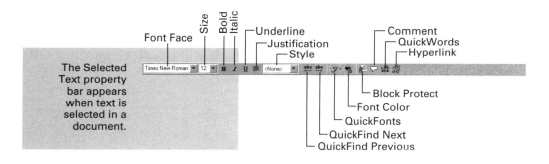

The Selected Text property bar appears when text is selected in a document.

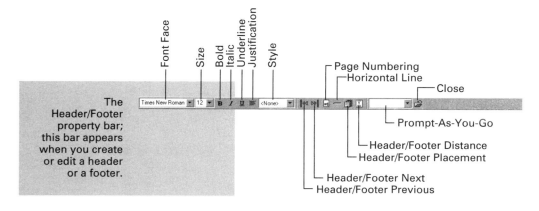

The Header/Footer property bar; this bar appears when you create or edit a header or a footer.

Appendix B • Predefined Toolbars and Property Bars

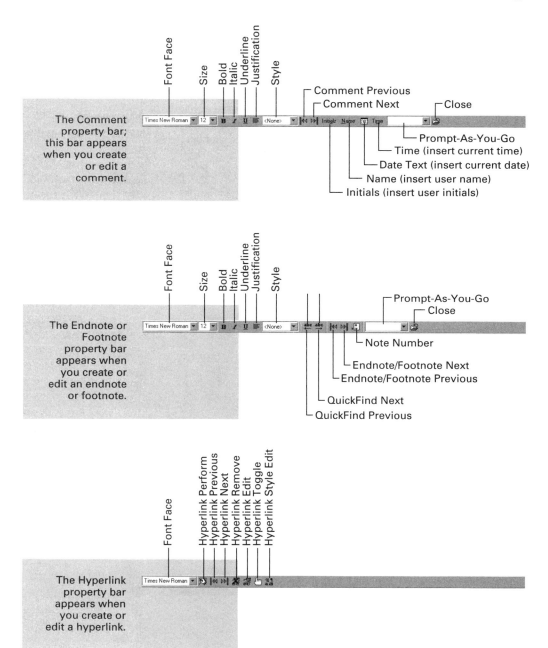

The Comment property bar; this bar appears when you create or edit a comment.

The Endnote or Footnote property bar appears when you create or edit an endnote or footnote.

The Hyperlink property bar appears when you create or edit a hyperlink.

Internet Publisher Property Bars

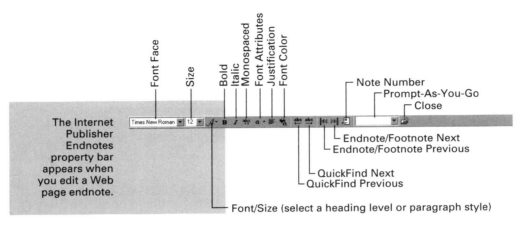

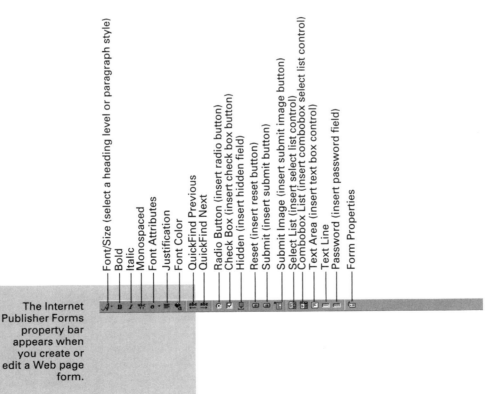

Appendix B • Predefined Toolbars and Property Bars

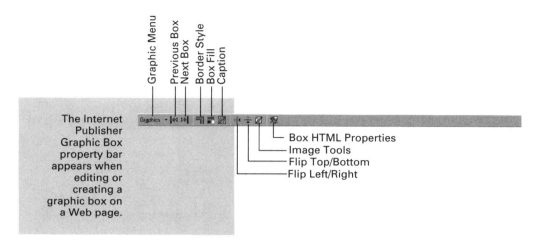

The Internet Publisher Graphic Box property bar appears when editing or creating a graphic box on a Web page.

Labels: Graphic Menu, Previous Box, Next Box, Border Style, Box Fill, Caption, Box HTML Properties, Image Tools, Flip Top/Bottom, Flip Left/Right

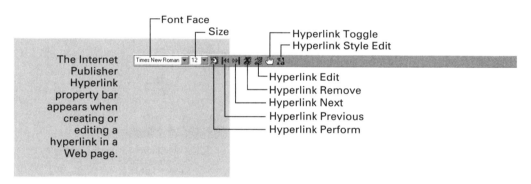

The Internet Publisher Hyperlink property bar appears when creating or editing a hyperlink in a Web page.

Labels: Font Face, Size, Hyperlink Toggle, Hyperlink Style Edit, Hyperlink Edit, Hyperlink Remove, Hyperlink Next, Hyperlink Previous, Hyperlink Perform

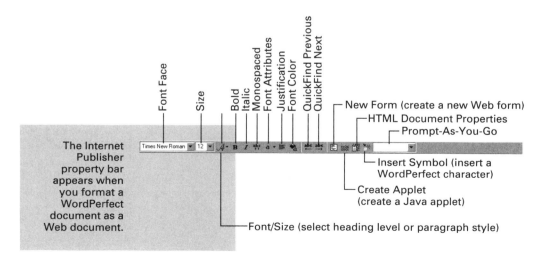

The Internet Publisher property bar appears when you format a WordPerfect document as a Web document.

Labels: Font Face, Size, Bold, Italic, Monospaced, Font Attributes, Justification, Font Color, QuickFind Previous, QuickFind Next, New Form (create a new Web form), HTML Document Properties, Prompt-As-You-Go, Insert Symbol (insert a WordPerfect character), Create Applet (create a Java applet), Font/Size (select heading level or paragraph style)

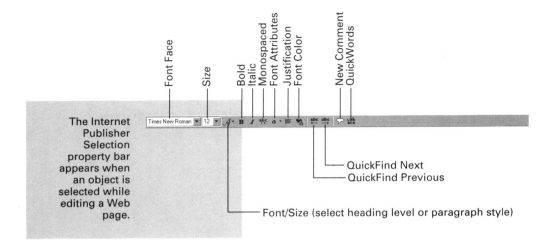

The Internet Publisher Selection property bar appears when an object is selected while editing a Web page.

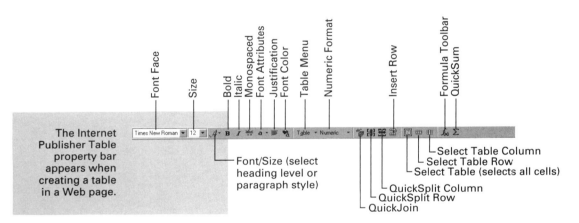

The Internet Publisher Table property bar appears when creating a table in a Web page.

APPENDIX B • PREDEFINED TOOLBARS AND PROPERTY BARS

Tables Property Bars

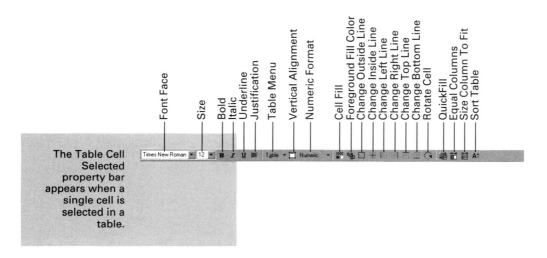

The Table Cell Selected property bar appears when a single cell is selected in a table.

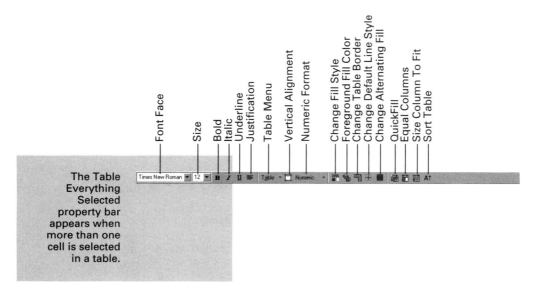

The Table Everything Selected property bar appears when more than one cell is selected in a table.

Specialty Property Bars

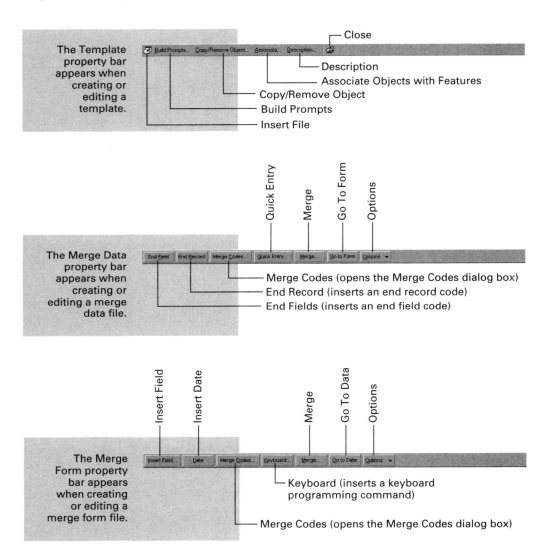

Glossary

2D. Two-dimensional. A flat-looking image, especially expressed with graphics or Text Art, displaying only height and width.

3D. Three-dimensional. An effect used with an image to add the appearance of having depth as well as height and width.

Alignment. The arrangement of text or an object in relation to a document's margins, columns, or the edges of text in a table cell.

Applet. A small program that is available only within its host program. Java applets are an example of small programs that can be added to a WordPerfect Web file.

Application Bar. The bar that appears at the bottom of the document window holding buttons for each open document, the position of the insertion point, and the general status of WordPerfect at any given time.

Auto-Play. A program that starts when a CD-ROM disk is placed in a CD-ROM drive.

Axis. (pl. **axes**) In a graph or chart, one of two value sets, usually measured as an x-axis or a y-axis. (See also *Y-axis* and *X-axis*.)

Barista. A Corel Internet publishing program that allows you to use Java to publish WordPerfect documents for the Internet or an intranet, complete with all formatting and graphics.

Bold. A font attribute that applies a thicker, heavier effect to text. Adding the bold attribute to text creates a pair of codes, [Bold‡] and [flBold], which work together to define the area to which bold is applied.

Border. A visible frame surrounding text or objects. A border can be lines, shadows, or graphic images.

Bullet. A symbol that precedes an item in a list. Bullets can be any of over 1,500 symbols available in WordPerfect. Most commonly, bullets are small, black filled circles.

CapsFix. A feature in WordPerfect that corrects accidental usage of Caps Lock.

Case. The capitalization status of text, including uppercase, lowercase, and mixed case.

Cell. The intersection of a row and column in a table.

Chart. Sometimes called a *graph*, a chart usually provides a visual representation of numerical data. However, charts are not necessarily a graphical representation. They can also be numeric or text representations.

Clipart. An image that can be inserted in a WordPerfect document.

Clipboard. A temporary storage area in memory where text and/or graphics can be placed while you copy or cut them.

Code. A button inserted in Reveal Codes that indicates the position where a feature or function occurs.

Column. A set of cells running vertically down a table, or a vertical section of text running down a page.

Contrast. The amount of black and white in an image that can be adjusted to modify the relationships between the colors in the image.

Control. An element appearing in a dialog box.

DAD bar. Short for *Desktop Application Director*, the DAD bar displays icons used to launch programs from the Windows taskbar status area.

Data. Information, either numerical or factual.

Data Source. One of many types of data files; in a merge function, the data source is the file used to store and reference data records.

Desktop. The *screen* area of Windows 95 typically used to open and manage files or programs.

Dialog box. A window that appears containing various controls, from which a user can select options or perform commands or tasks.

Drag and drop. A method of moving text or objects by pressing and holding a mouse button, moving the mouse, and releasing the mouse button when the object is in the desired location.

Drop Cap. A special format emphasizing the first letter(s) in a paragraph.

E-mail. Short for *electronic mail.* Messages distributed and received over a computer network or system of networks, such as the Internet.

Em dash. A long dash (—) based on the width of an uppercase M, used to set off portions of a sentence.

En dash. A short dash (–) based on the width of an uppercase N, used to separate words.

Field. A placeholder for corresponding data that will be automatically inserted, usually in a merge operation.

Fill. A color, shade, or pattern which can be placed in the interior of objects.

Flush right. Aligns the right edge of text with the right margin on a page, in a column, or in a cell.

Font. A design set of letters, symbols, and numbers.

Footer. Text, graphics, or other objects placed at the bottom of the page, immediately above the bottom margin, that repeats on consecutive pages until discontinued.

Form document. The programming side of a merge document, the form document contains all text, formatting, and merge programming that will appear when a merge is executed.

Format. The overall layout of a document or object, including margin settings, font settings, and so on.

Full Page View. Accessed through Zoom, this view displays the current page of a document in a size that enables you to see the complete page while editing.

Generate. The process in WordPerfect of collecting all entries and creating a table of contents, index, list, or table of authorities, or updating all cross-references.

Go To. A feature in WordPerfect that allows you to place the insertion point at a desired location in a document.

Gradient. A shading effect that moves from lighter to darker.

Grammatik. A program within WordPerfect that proofreads documents, or parts of documents, looking for grammatical errors and offering suggestions for possible correction.

Graph. See *Chart*.

Graphic. A file that contains visual data, such as a line drawing or photograph, rather than text. An *image*.

Graphics box. A WordPerfect element that holds an image or text and can be freely placed in a document.

Guideline. A WordPerfect feature, appearing as dashed lines, that displays and allows you to edit the location of margins, columns, tables, headers, and footers. Guidelines also appear when you drag tab, margin, or paragraph symbols on the ruler bar.

Handles. Small squares that appear when you select an object, allowing the object to be edited, moved, or resized.

Hard page break. A code in WordPerfect, appearing as [HPg] in Reveal Codes, which is created by pressing Ctrl+Enter. A hard page break forces text to split, moving remaining text to the top of the next page.

Hard return. Created by pressing Enter, a hard return forces a new line to begin. The hard return code appears as [HRt] in Reveal Codes. See Soft return.

Header. Text, graphics, or other objects placed at the top of the page, immediately below the top margin, that repeats on consecutive pages until discontinued.

Highlight. A feature that marks text for emphasis, similar to marking written text with a highlighting pen.

HTML. Short for *HyperText Markup Language*, a common programming language used to create Web pages. Comprehensive HTML support is available in Corel WordPerfect Suite 8, allowing easy creation of HTML documents and forms (and editing of HTML documents) from WordPerfect.

Hyperlink. Text, graphic, or other object on which the user can click to quickly move to a specific linked location; this location may be in the current document, in another local file, or on a file server halfway across the world. See *Jump*.

Hypertext system. A system of integrated documents designed to be navigated through the use of *hyperlinks*.

Icon. A graphic used to represent a particular function. Icons allow visual identification of an application, as a picture on a button in a toolbar, and so on.

Image. A graphic; an individual piece of clipart.

Indent. To align the first and subsequent lines of paragraph text away from the left margin.

Insertion point. The location in a document where text or editing will occur, typically represented by a blinking vertical bar.

Internet. A globally connected system of computer networks allowing online access to various types of documents and e-mail.

Internet Publisher. A feature in WordPerfect allowing you to create and edit Internet Web pages through HTML, Java, or Barista.

Intranet. A company-wide version of the Internet, an intranet may include all the same kinds of services: hypertext and other types of documents, e-mail capabilities, FTP, and so on.

Italic. A font attribute that applies a *slanted* effect to text.

Java. An object-oriented programming language commonly used to create animated effects on the Internet.

Jump. Within a hypertext system, to move from one hypertext area to another using hyperlinks.

Justify. To line up text in relation to the left and right margins. Left, Right, Center, Full, and All Justification are supported by WordPerfect. See Chapter 4 for examples of each type.

Key. A rule in sorting situations that determines how data should be analyzed for sorting. A maximum of nine keys can be defined in WordPerfect.

Label. A descriptive text element often added to a chart to help the reader understand a visual element. Also refers to headings in a row or column, or sections in a macro file.

Label (mailing). A defined WordPerfect page that contains formatting for mailing labels. A number of predefined mailing labels are included with WordPerfect, but you can also define your own.

Landscape. Orientation of a document so that, when printed, text runs from left to right along the longest edge of the paper.

Legend. In a chart, a feature that defines for the reader the relationship of the graphic symbols to the data elements.

Line style. Effects using width, patterns, and arrows that can be applied to a line.

Link. The connection between two objects, such as a WordPerfect document and a Presentations graphic.

Logical page. An area inside a *physical page* (a piece of paper) that acts as though it were a full piece of paper. In a sheet of labels, for example, each individual label is a logical page, while the entire sheet comprises the physical page.

Macro. A recorded or programmed file that stores a series of commands using WordPerfect's PerfectScript macro programming language.

Make It Fit. A feature in WordPerfect that shrinks or expands a document to fit a designated number of pages.

Margin. An edge of a page, cell, column, or graphic which is blank.

Master document. A feature in WordPerfect that allows you to assemble and generate subdocuments.

Merge. A procedure whereby a form document and a data source file combine, producing an output file.

Object. Any graphic, file, drawing, chart, or other file placed in a WordPerfect document.

OLE. Short for *Object Linking and Embedding*, a technology that allows you to embed or link an object to a WordPerfect document.

Order. The hierarchy of how images are placed on a page relative to one another. Order can make one object seem to be placed in front of or behind another object.

Orientation. A setting that designates whether a document will print with text running along the long or short side of a piece of paper. See also *Landscape* and *Portrait*.

Outline. A hierarchy of lines of text that suggests major and minor ideas. WordPerfect enables you to create outlines based on its predefined outline styles, or on custom styles you create.

Paint. The act of dragging a mouse pointer across a section of a document is often referred to as *painting*. In WordPerfect, you can paint the format of a heading or paragraph over other areas of the document using the QuickFormat paintbrush pointer.

Page setup. A collection of settings that relate to how the pages of your document are set up, including margins, orientation, paper size, and so on.

Password. A word selected by a WordPerfect user to protect a document. After a document is protected, the correct password must be entered before you're allowed to modify the document.

Paste. To copy the contents of the Windows Clipboard into a document.

Paste Link. To place a copy of a file in a WordPerfect document while establishing a link to the original file.

Pattern. An arrangement of dots or lines that can be used to fill an object.

PerfectExpert. A Corel WordPerfect Suite 8 feature that provides shortcuts to certain features while using a *project*; also a search tool used in WordPerfect Help, enabling you to ask questions in sentence form.

PerfectScript. WordPerfect's programming language.

Physical page. A full piece of paper. (Compare with *Logical page*.)

Pie chart. A round chart type in which each pie wedge represents a value.

Portrait. An orientation that places text from left to right along the short side of a piece of paper.

Program. A software package often referred to as an *application.*

Project. Collection of files that can include documents, templates, macros, programs, and the PerfectExpert; can be accessed when you choose File, New.

Properties. Information about an object.

Property Bar. A context-sensitive collection of buttons that usually appears below the toolbar, most commonly used with a mouse to access frequently used features.

QuickBullets. A feature in WordPerfect that creates lists and outlines as you type.

QuickCorrect. A feature in WordPerfect that provides a shortcut method of automatically correcting typographical errors as you type.

QuickFormat. A feature in WordPerfect that picks up formatting from one paragraph or heading and allows you to *paint* that set of formatting over other parts of the document.

QuickLinks. A feature in WordPerfect that creates hyperlinks to the Internet while you type.

QuickMacro. A macro that is available only during the current session of WordPerfect. Only one QuickMacro exists; it has no name and cannot be edited.

QuickMenu. A context-sensitive list of menu choices that appears when you right-click an object.

QuickOrdinals. A feature in WordPerfect that changes ordinals (for example, the st in 1st) to superscript.

QuickSymbols. A feature in WordPerfect that changes -- or ---, respectively, to an en dash or em dash.

QuickTip. An identifying box that provides a help tip when you rest the mouse pointer on a button, menu item, or other area in WordPerfect that has a related QuickTip.

QuickWords. A feature in WordPerfect, similar to an abbreviation, that replaces characters with formatted text as you type the characters.

Redo. To proceed with an action that you have undone using the Undo command.

Reveal Codes. A pane of the document editing window used to view formatting or feature codes.

Revisions. Highlighting effects applied to indicate any changes between document versions.

Rotate. To move an object along a 360-degree path.

Row. A set of cells running from left to right across a table.

Ruler. An on-screen feature that allows you to view and change tabs, margins, tables, and column settings by clicking and dragging.

Save As. To save a previously saved document with a new name or properties.

Scan. To electronically record a hard copy image as a graphic file; this file then can be opened and manipulated in WordPerfect.

Scrapbook. A condensed collection of images from which individual images can be copied to a WordPerfect document.

Scroll bar. A mechanism used with a mouse for navigating a document horizontally or vertically.

Shadow. A drawing effect that appears to place a shadow alongside an object.

Shadow cursor. A lightly-shaded cursor that travels in relation to the mouse pointer, indicating where the insertion point will go if you click.

SmartQuotes. Curly quotes, as opposed to the straight quote style used for foot or inch marks.

Soft page break. A code in WordPerfect that is automatically created at the location where text is split between two pages; appears as [SPg] in Reveal Codes.

Soft return. Created automatically by WordPerfect, a soft return code, [SRt], appears at the location where text wraps to the next line.

Sort. To arrange data alphanumerically or numerically, in either ascending or descending order.

APPENDIX C • GLOSSARY **543**

Spell-As-You-Go. A feature of WordPerfect that checks spelling as you type, flagging unknown words with dashed lines. Right-click a flagged word to see a possible list of replacement spellings.

Spell Checker. A feature of WordPerfect that checks the spelling of words in your document against a dictionary (and any word lists you provide), flagging possible errors and offering suggestions for correction.

Stack. A series of graphic images that rest one on top of another. You can change the order of the graphics, thus changing the stack order.

Style. A group of formatting instructions that can be applied to text through various WordPerfect features.

Subdivided page. A physical page divided into logical pages.

Subdocument. One of a series of documents that can be combined using a master document.

Symbol. One of a possible 1,500 special WordPerfect characters, accessed by pressing Ctrl+W.

Tab. A setting that can be placed along the width of a line that allows you to easily align text at a specific location.

Table. A collection of columns and rows, forming cells at all points of intersection; usually used to organize sets of data, or to format text.

Taskbar. In Windows 95, the bar that runs across the bottom of the desktop, which dynamically creates buttons for all open programs.

Template. A predefined collection of formatting, style settings, macros, toolbars, and keyboards. Each WordPerfect document is based on a template.

Text box. A floating text object that can be manipulated like any other graphic box.

Text wrap. This feature forces remaining text in a paragraph to wrap (move) to the next line when the text reaches the right margin as you type or edit. See *Soft return*.

TextArt. A WordPerfect applet used to add special effects to text.

Toolbar. A collection of buttons used with the mouse, providing easy methods of accessing WordPerfect features and functions. Several predefined toolbars are installed with WordPerfect 8.

Undo. To reverse the last action performed.

Views. In software, various displays of documents or information that allow you to see different perspectives of the same material.

Watermark. A special page in WordPerfect, often containing graphics, that provides a background image for a document page. Once defined, watermarks continue to run for each page until discontinued.

Web. See *World Wide Web*.

Word count. A tally of the number of words in a document.

World Wide Web. A hypertext system of documents transmitted and accessed over the Internet.

Wrap. See *Text wrap*.

X-axis. In a chart, the horizontal axis.

Y-axis. In a chart, the vertical axis.

Zoom. To modify view settings so that what you see on-screen is a percentage (larger or smaller) of a document page's actual size.

Index

A

absolute cell references, formulas, 250
actions, undoing last, 63, 211, 261, 379
Add an Existing Project dialog box, 505
Add New Project dialog box, 504
Add Template Prompt dialog box, 491-492
Address Book, 87-91
    accessing, 87
    address layout format selections, 90-91
    address types, 88
    custom field addition, 184
    first time access, 88
    first time project/template use personal information, 50
    label print merge, 162-163
    merge entry selections, 180-182
    My Address Book, 88
    My Addresses Address Book, 177
    name searches, 90
    Organization address type, 88
    Person address type, 88
    records, 173
    Sales Letter merge data source, 176-177
    template links, 492
Address Book and New Entry dialog box, 50
Address Book button, 87
Address Book Cardfile, 5
After the Fact typos, correcting, 62
alignment, text, 108-110
Alt key
    macro non-support, 454
    menu item selections, 22
alternative words, Thesaurus, 129-132
antonyms, Thesaurus alternatives, 129-132
applets, 6, 305, 429
application bar, 28
    CAPS button, 28

    document status information, 28
    editing, 33-35
    Insert/Typeover mode selection, 28
    QuickTips, 28
Application Bar Settings dialog box, 40-41
applied styles, 141
Arabic numerals, page numbers, 110
archived documents, retrieving/storing, 57-58
archives, described 54-55
arithmetic operators, formulas, 250
arrows, described, 389-390
As You Type typos, correcting, 62
ASCII Delimited file format, 40, 187-190
Associate dialog box, 500
Associate Form and Data dialog box, 176-177
associations, template, 496-502
ast/asx (projects) filename extension, 482
asymmetric columns, 338-340
attachments, e-mail, 166-168
authorities, described, 286
automatic
    character styles, described, 140
    date codes, templates, 491
    file backup settings, 52
    typing tools, 134-139
Avery label definitions, 159-160

B

background
    colors, changing in Web pages, 418-420
    fills, table cells, 239-241
Backspace key
    correcting typing mistakes, 62
    deleting outline levels, 206
backup folder, automatic file backup settings, 52
balanced newspaper columns, described, 327
bar codes, POSTNET, 157-158

Barista, 5, 7
    publish Corel Presentations slide show, 431
bars
    adding/removing commands, 33-34
    button arrangements, 34
    described, 22
    keystroke additions, 35
    macro additions, 36
    program additions, 35-36
    property, 522-532
    Separators, 34
bitmap images, described, 374
Bitstream Font Navigator 2.0, 5, 101
Blank Document window, document creation, 47
block protection, newspaper columns, 328
body text, outlines, 211-212
boldface text, 103-104
booklets, printing, 155-156
Bookmark dialog box, 428
bookmarks, 310-312, 427-429
borders, columns, 335-337
Box Caption dialog box, 391-392
Box Position dialog box, 359-360
Box Size dialog box, 365
briefs, described, 286
browser, 397-398
bugs, leaving PerfectExpert panel open when attempting to use a project, 118
bulleted lists, 97-99
    adding to Web page, 405-406
Bullets and Numbering dialog box, 204
Bullets or Numbering button, 97
Bullets palette, 97
bullets, list styles, 97-99
Business Letter project, 50, 114-118
business letters, 80-118
    address additions, 86-92
    body text formatting, 92-96
    bulleted/numbered list insertion, 97-99
    Business Letter project creation, 114-118
    creating from scratch, 80-114
    date addition, 85-86
    e-mail address/hypertext link conversion, 85
    full block with full justification style, 81
    inserting Windows Messaging/Exchange address, 91-92
    letterhead addition, 84-85
    margin settings, 83-84
    modified block style, 81
    page numbers, 110-114
    paper size selections, 81-83
    selected text font size/type editing, 102-103
    symbol insertion, 107-108
    text justification, 108-110
buttons
    adding/removing from bars, 34
    appearance modifications, 34-35
    hypertext links, 309-310
    keystroke additions, 35

C

Calendaring & Scheduling, 5
callouts
    captions, 391-392
    described, 381
    drawing shapes, 389-391
    line styles, 384-387
    text box addition, 387-389
CAPS button, application bar, 28
caption files, data entries, 191-196
CD Clipart, adding to newsletter, 350-351
CD-ROM, installation process, 8-10
cells
    background fills, 239-241
    floating, 251-253
    formula entry, 249
    joining/splitting, 237-238
Center Page(s) dialog box, 162
character styles, described, 140
characters
    colon (:), 465
    deleting in Equation Editor, 445
    double quotes ("), 464
    ellipsis (...), 22
    exclamation point (!) enumeration, 464
    parentheses (and), 464
    reserved, 52
    semicolon (;), 465
    symbols, 106-108

COMMANDS **547**

Chart toolbar, 255
charts
    labels, 258
    perspective views, 259
    previewing changes, 256
    subtitles, 258
    table data creation, 253-260
    titles, 258
checking styles, Grammatik, 133
circles, described, 389
clipart, 5
    CD Clipart newsletter addition, 350-351
    importing to Web pages, 415
    paint splash image, 349
    Scrapbook, 348-351
    wpg filename extension, 347
Clipboard
    copying table data to a chart, 255
    cutting/copying/pasting text, 71
Close button, WordPerfect 8 window, 17
codes
    paragraph formatting, 95-96
    reading Reveal Codes contents, 31-32
colon (:) character, macro commands, 465
colors
    background, changing, 418-420
    changing text, 418-420
    Reveal Codes window, 30
Column border/Fill dialog box, 335
Columns dialog box, 333-334
columns
    adding to Web page, 406-407
    appearance enhancements, 331-332
    asymmetric, 338-340
    borders, 335-337
    fills, 335-337
    gutter space, 328-329
    justification, 330
    lines as separators, 337
    naming conventions, 226
    navigating, 331
    newsletters, 327-335
    sizing, 234-237, 332-333
    summing, 246-247
    table addition, 233-234
    tables, 226
Command Inserter, 472-476
commands
    adding/removing from bars, 33-34
    Chart, Subtitle, 258
    Edit, Copy, 71
    Edit, CustomFields, New, 184
    Edit, Cut, 71
    Edit, Find and Replace, 64
    Edit, Paste, 71
    Edit, QuickMenu, 33
    Edit, Undo/Redo History, 63
    ellipsis (...) characters, 22
    File, Document, Condense Master, 303
    File, Document, Expand Master, 302-304
    File, Document, Subdocument, 299
    File, Internet Publisher, 399
    File, Move to Folder, 58
    File, New, 48, 115, 482
    File, New, Options, Create Category, 486
    File, Open, 60, 399
    File, Page Setup, 81
    File, Print, 152
    File, Save, 52
    File, Save As, 52
    File, Send To, 167
    File, Version Control, Retrieve Current, 57
    File, Version Control, Save Current, 66
    Format, Envelope, 156
    Format, Font, 104
    Format, Labels, 160
    Format, Line Flush Right, 109
    Format, Line, Center, 109
    Format, Line, Tab Set, 464
    Format, Page, Center, 162
    Format, Page, Delay Codes, 114
    Format, Page, Numbering, 111, 295
    Format, Page, Page Setup, 81
    Format, Page, Suppress, 114
    Format, Paragraph, Drop Cap, 354
    Format, Paragraph, Format, 96
    Format, Styles, 145
    GoTo, 331

Help, Ask the PerfectExpert, 73
Help, Help Topics, 477
Help, PerfectExpert, 74
Insert, Date/Time, 86
Insert, Equation, 437
Insert, Graphics, Chart, 254
Insert, Graphics, Clipart, 348
Insert, Graphics, Draw Picture, 383
Insert, Graphics, From File, 354
Insert, Graphics, TextArt, 321
Insert, Header/Footer, 112
Insert, Object, 305
Insert, Outline/Bullets & Numbering, 204
Insert, Shape, Draw Line, 385
Insert, Shape, Ellipse, 390
Insert, Text Box, 387
Insert, Watermark, 339, 393
Insert, Watermark, Discontinue, 340
Inset, Shape, 382
macro, 464-467
mnemonic selection letters, 22
PerfectScript product, 472-473
QuickTips, 22-23
Settings, Printers, 164
Settings, Save as Application Default, 153
Size, Define, 440
size, Other, 440
Start, Documents, 11
Style, Define, 439
Style, Other, 439
Tools, Address Book, 87, 162
Tools, Bookmark, 311, 428
Tools, Bookmark, Set QuickMark, 488
Tools, Grammatik, 133
Tools, Hyperlink, 309, 423
Tools, Macro, Edit, 462
Tools, Macro, Macro Toolbar, 497
Tools, Macro, Play, 454, 461
Tools, Macro, Record, 453, 457
Tools, Merge, 176
Tools, Proofread, 122
Tools, Proofread, Grammar-As-You-Go, 132
Tools, QuickCorrect, 125, 137
Tools, QuickLinks, 312
Tools, QuickWords, 135
Tools, Reference, Generate, 295, 301
Tools, Reference, Index, 282
Tools, Reference, Lists, 278
Tools, Reference, Table of Authorities, 288
Tools, Reference, Table of Contents, 270
Tools, Settings, 37, 52, 164
Tools, Settings, Files, 455
Tools, Settings, Files, Merge/Macro, 453
Tools, Sort, 262
Tools, Spell Check, 127
Tools, Template Macro, Play, 461
Tools, Template Macro, Record, 456
Tools, Template, Macro, Edit, 463
Tools, Thesaurus, 130
Undo, 211
View, Guidelines, 20
View, Hide Bars, 15
View, Page, 112
View, Reveal Codes, 30
View, Ruler, 20
compact.scb file, 349
complex equations, 436
components
    CorelCENTRAL, 4
    installation types, 9-10
    Professional Suite version, 5
    Standard Suite, 4-5
compressed documents, retrieval times, 55
CompuServe
    Corel technical support, 75
    WordPerfect Users forum macros, 466
    WPUSERS technical support, 75
computations, table math, 245-251
computers, won't restart after installation, 10
concordance file, 281-284
Condense/Save Subdocuments dialog box, 303
Control Panel, Corel Versions access, Windows 95, 55
controls, TextArt, 324-325
conventions
    document naming, 51-52
    file name excluded characters, 52
conversions
    e-mail address/hypertext link, 85
    files, 6, 40

previous WordPerfect version macros, 478-479
supported image types, 345-354
Convert Settings dialog box, 40
Copy/Remove Template Objects dialog box, 497
Corel, Web site URLs, 75
Corel Barista. *See* **Barista**
Corel Magazine, Web site URL, 75
Corel Versions
accessing, 55
file archiving, 54-58
Help system, 58
retrieving archived documents, 57-58
storing another version of documents, 56-57
Corel WordPerfect Suite 8
components, 4-5
installation, 7-10
Professional Suite components, 5
Standard Suite components, 4
starting, 10-11
system requirements, 7-8
uses, 5-7
versions, 4
CorelCENTRAL
Professional Suite enhancements, 4
Standard Suite components, 4
Create Bookmark dialog box, 311-312, 428
Create Data File dialog box, 191
Create Format dialog box, 215
Create Merge File dialog box, 176
cross-references
described, 266
location pointers, 292-294
Ctrl key, macro assignments, 454
Ctrl+Shift keys, macro assignments, 454
current printer, setting as default printer, 152-154
cursors, shadow, 18-19
Custom installation, 9-10, 50
Customize Button dialog box, 34
Customize Settings dialog box, 41-43

D

DAD (Desktop Application Director) bar, 11
data extraction sort, 263-264
data file, 172
data series, QuickFill table entries, 228-229
data sources, 172
ASCII delimited file, 187-190
creating from scratch, 190-197
merges, 184-198
Paradox database, 185-198
databases
merges, 185-187
Paradox as data source, 185-187
supported types, 185
Date/Time dialog box, 86
dates
adding to templates, 491
business letters addition, 85-86
formats, 85
default printer, disabling document reformat, 164
Define Index dialog box, 285
Define List dialog box, 279
Define Table of Authorities dialog box, 288-289
Define Table of Contents dialog box, 274-275
definitions
Avery label, 159-160
custom outline creation, 213-214
legal brief, 214-222
outline, 202-212
saving, 220-222
styles, 141-142
switching between, 213
Thesaurus words, 129-132
Del key, correcting typing mistakes, 62
Delay Codes, suppressing codes, 114
delimiters, file conversions, 40
desktop, WordPerfect 8 start up, 10
dialog boxes, field QuickTips, 37
discontinue code, subdocument header/footer entry, 296
Display Settings dialog box, 30, 37-38

document icons, described, 16
document styles, described, 140
Document Summary Settings dialog box, 40
document transfers, FTP site URL, 75
Document Word List, Spell Checker, 124
documents
- address additions, 86-92
- application bar status information, 28
- archiving, 54-58
- automatic file backup, 52
- automatic typing tools, 134-139
- Blank Document window creation, 47
- body text formatting, 92-96
- booklet printing, 155-156
- bookmarks, 310-312
- business letters, 80-118
- closing, 51-54
- compressed, 55
- compressing current version when archiving, 55
- conventions used in book, 46
- converting without previewing in Web format, 401
- creating, 46-51
- cross-reference location pointers, 292-294
- date addition, 85-86
- default formatting, 47
- described, 46
- disabling reformat when printing, 164
- dragging text between, 70-71
- editing, 59-60
- electronic, 6
- e-mail attachments, 166-168
- excluded filename extensions, 52
- exiting, 17
- fax printing, 168-169
- finding/replacing text, 63-66
- first time save, 52-54
- grammar checking, 132-134
- graphics design guidelines, 348-349
- grouping copies when printing, 153
- hypertext links, 308-310
- indexes, 280-286
- inserting Windows Messaging/Exchange address, 91-92
- item lists, 276-280
- links, 6
- list insertion, 97-99
- mailing address, 156
- margin settings, 83-84
- master, 296-304
- multiple version tracking, 54-58
- naming conventions, 51-52
- navigating, 60-61
- OLE links, 304-307
- opening, 59-60
- page numbers, 110-114
- paper size selections, 81-83
- permanent archive, 55
- practice macros, 454
- predefined styles, 142-144
- printing, 152-156
- printing troubleshooting, 163-166
- proofreading tools, 120-134
- publish to HTML, 399-402
- reference types, 266-295
- renaming when saving, 53
- repositioning insertion point after scrolling, 27
- retrieving archived, 57-58
- save in Web page format, 399-402
- saving, 51-54
- saving when exiting program, 17
- screen shot additions, 381-392
- scrolling, 27
- selected text font size/type editing, 102-103
- spell checking, 126-129
- subdocuments, 296
- summaries, 40
- symbol insertion, 107-108
- table of authorities, 286-292
- templates, 482-506
- temporary archive, 55
- text justification, 108-110
- text selection, 62-63
- title bar status display, 16
- two-sided printing, 155
- typing tools, 134-139
- updating links, 309
- versus files, 46

Web, 398-434
white space, 347
wpd (WordPerfect) filename extension, 52
Documents list, opening WordPerfect 8 from, 11
Documents menu, recently edited file list, Windows 95 taskbar, 60
double quotes (") characters, macro commands, 464
double-head pointer, dragging/sizing windows, 16
double-indent, described, 99
drag and drop
    graphics copy, 361
    mouse techniques, 69-71
Drawing Line Shape property bar, 384
drop caps
    background fading, 370
    newsletters, 354-356

E

Edit Page Size dialog box, 82
electronic documents, viewing with Envoy 7, 6
electronic help, Web site URLs, 75
elements, WordPerfect 8 window, 14-28
ellipsis (...) characters
    command dialog box, 22
    described, 389
e-mail
    described, 167
    document attachments, 166-168
e-mail address
    hypertext link conversion, 85
    technical support, 75
embedded objects, versus links, 304-305
Enter key
    hard break, 206
    paragraph formatting, 92-93
Envelope dialog box, 156-157, 183
Envelope Options dialog box, 157-158
envelopes, 156-159
    creating, 156-158
    mailing address, 156
    merge addition, 182-184
    POSTNET bar codes, 157-158
    printing, 158-159

    troubleshooting print problems, 159
    ZIP code printing, 157-158
Environment Settings dialog box, 39
Envoy 7 Viewer, 4, 6
Envoy printer driver, 5
Equation Editor
    deleting characters, 445
    editing in, 444-447
    exiting if you change your mind, 441
    keyboard, 41
    starting, 437
    style and size, 439-441
    window, 437
Equation Editor toolbar, understanding, 437-439
equations, 435-447
    adding captions, 446-447
    building, 437
    changing style, 439-440
    deleting graphic box, 441
    dragging to desired size, 446
    drawbacks to changing fonts, 440
    formatting, 555-557
    placing in documents, 436
    setting graphic properties, 445-447
    simple, 441-444
    Size menu, 439
    Style menu, 439
    Text style, to use English phrase, 439
Esc key, interrupting macro playback, 462
events, template triggers, 500-502
Exchange/Windows Messaging Address Book, 87, 91-92
exclamation point (!) enumeration character, macro commands, 464
Expand Master Document dialog box, 302
Explorer
    opening files, 60
    WordPerfect 8 start up, 11
EXPNDALL.WCM macro file, 137

F

families, outline, 207-209
Favorites List, file/folder addition, 59
Fax Cover Sheet project, 50
fax, printing, 168-169

faxform macro, 459-472
feature bars, 522-532
　See also property bars
field names, merge, 173
fields
　　Address Book addition, 184
　　dialog box QuickTips, 37
　　form letters, 178-180
　　legal caption data file merge, 191-193
　　margins, 84
　　merge, 173
　　Quick Data Entry, 192
　　required, 50
file formats
　　ASCII Delimited, 40
　　image types, 351-356
　　merge, 172
　　wpg (WordPerfect clipart), 347
File menu
　　functions, 22
　　recently edited file list, 60
File Settings dialog box, default extension, 52
filename extensions
　　ast/asx (projects), 482
　　excluded, 52
　　wcm (macro), 454
　　wpd (WordPerfect), 52
　　wpg (WordPerfect clipart), 347
　　wpt (template), 482
Files Settings dialog box, 40
files
　　ASCII delimited, 187-190
　　automatic file backup settings, 52
　　compact.scb, 349
　　concordance, 281-284
　　conventions used in book, 46
　　conversions, 6, 40
　　document summaries, 40
　　excluded filename extensions, 52
　　EXPNDALL.WCM, 137
　　Favorites list addition, 59
　　folder creation, 59
　　image formats, 351-356
　　legal caption data, 191-193

　　Macro Help, 476-478
　　management, 58-59
　　MISSPELL.WPD, 122-124
　　moving between folders, 58-59
　　naming conventions, 52
　　opening as a copy, 60
　　opening upon start up, 11
　　prompts.wcm, 491
　　recently edited list, 60
　　renaming when saving, 53
　　saving after conversion to web document, 400
　　selecting, 58
　　selecting alternative types when saving, 54
　　sorting, 59
　　title bar display, 16
　　versus documents, 46
　　WP8US.WPT, 135
　　wpd (WordPerfect) filename extension, 52
fills
　　Alternating Fill, 242
　　columns, 335-337
　　described, 239
　　images, 375-377
　　table cell backgrounds, 239-241
financial equations, 436
Find and Replace Text dialog box, 64
floating cells, tables, 251-253
folders
　　backup, 52
　　creating, 54, 59
　　default document, 40
　　Favorites List addition, 59
　　management, 58-59
　　moving files between, 58-59
　　tree display, 59
　　Web pages, 432
Font (F9) key, 104
Font dialog box, 103-106
Font Face button, 100, 102
font faces (typefaces)
　　described, 100
　　displaying installed, 102
　　editing existing, 102-103
　　versus fonts, 100-101

fonts, 4
    attribute settings, 102
    described, 100
    drawbacks to changing in equations, 440
    editing size/type, 102-103
    finding/replacing, 65-66
    installation, 101
    monospace, 94
    newsletter titles, 329
    point size measurement, 102
    proportional, 94
    resident, 163
    Reveal Codes window, 30
    selecting, 403
    size type listings, 102
    sizing, 102
    TrueType, 163
    versus typefaces, 100-101
footers
    described, 110
    page numbers, 112-114
    subdocuments, 296
form document, 172
form file, 172
form letters
    Address Book as data source, 176-177
    alternate data source selection, 177
    creating, 174-180
    field additions, 178-180
    merge form creation, 175-176
Format Address dialog box, 91
Format-As-You-Go, 137-138
formats, table, 238-239
Formatting property bars, 526-527
forms
    merge, 172
    pleading, 196-198
Formula toolbar, 248
formulas
    arithmetic, 250
    absolute cell references, 250
    gross revenue table, 249-251
    relative cell references, 250
    tables, 245-251
forums, WordPerfect, 75

fractions, decimal conversions, 84
FTP sites
    Corel macros, 466, 478
    document transfers/program patches, 75
    Windows 95 Exchange program update, 87
full block with full justification, business letter style, 82
functions, Properties for Table Format dialog box, 232-233

G

glossary, 533-544
gradient fills, images, 375-377
grammar checking, 132-134
Grammar-As-You-Go, 132-133
Grammatik, 133-134
Graphic features property bars, 523-526
graphic hyperlinks, Web pages, 426
graphic properties, setting in Equation Editor, 445-447
graphics, 421
    attachment options, 361
    attributes, 368-374
    box sizing, 364-367
    copying while dragging, 359
    design guidelines, 346-347
    handles, 357
    interlaced, 416
    newsletters, 345-394
    setting properties, 416
    single versus double clicking, 357
    sizing/placing, 357-368
    text wrapping, 362-364
    watermarks, 392-394
    Web pages, 413-418
    white space, 347
Graphics property bar, 358
guidelines, 19-20
    default document format settings, 47
    displaying/hiding, 20
Guidelines dialog box, 20
gutter space
    newsletter columns, 328-329
    width settings, 333-334

H

handles
    graphics, 357
    graphics box sizing, 364-367

hands on
    adding a bookmark-based hypertext link to a document, 311-312
    adding a callout to the screen capture, 385-387
    adding a caption to the screen shot figure, 391-392
    adding a clipart image to a newsletter, 348-350
    adding a description to the callout, 388-389
    adding a drop cap and a graphic image from a file, 354-356
    adding a footer to the faxform macro, 468-470
    adding a gradient fill to the paint splash, 375-377
    adding a hypertext link to the business plan, 308-310
    adding a letterhead, 84-85
    adding a macro to a template, 498-499
    adding a QuickCorrect entry, 125-126
    adding a QuickLink to your document, 313
    adding a Scrapbook image from the CD, 350-351
    adding a shape to the callout, 390-391
    adding a sound clip to Web pages, 430-431
    adding a text button hyperlink, 425-426
    adding a TextArt button, 417-419
    adding an IF test to the faxform macro, 474-476
    adding an object to the business plan, 305-307
    adding body text to the business plan, 211
    adding bookmarks to hyperlinks, 427-429
    adding bulleted items to Web page, 405
    adding columns to a table, 233-234
    adding envelopes to the Sales Letter merge, 182-183
    adding field locations to a form letter, 178-180
    adding fills to the title and header rows, 239-240
    adding graphics to Web pages, 414-416
    adding lines between the columns, 337
    adding names to your Address Book, 88-90
    adding new outline items to the business plan, 210-211
    adding prompts to the Letterhead template, 490-495
    adding tables to a Web page, 408-411
    adding text to Web page, 403-405
    adding today's date to your letter, 85-86
    adding Web pages for linking, 421-422
    adjusting table dimensions, 411-413
    archiving a document, 55-56
    associating a macro with the Pre Print trigger, 502
    associating the Address Book with the form letter, 176-177
    attaching a graphic to a hyperlink, 426
    capturing a screen, then pasting it to a document, 382
    changing font faces and font sizes for existing text, 102-103
    changing page margins, 83-84
    changing text and background colors, 419-420
    choosing an outline definition for a business plan, 204-205
    converting Web pages to HTML format, 432-434
    creating a category for your custom letterhead, 486-487
    creating a concordance file, 284
    creating a file save macro, 497-498
    creating a floating cell that calculates payments, 252-253
    creating a legal caption data file and adding the data, 193-196
    creating a legal caption data file/defining field names, 191-193
    creating a legal pleading form, 196-198
    creating a master document, 299-300
    creating a master document and subdocuments, 297-299

creating a masthead using a table for layout, 320
creating a masthead with TextArt, 321-324
creating a memo using the Memo project, 48-51
creating a merge data file from an ASCII delimited file, 188-190
creating a merge form from the letter, 175-176
creating a new Web page, 402
creating a QuickFormat style, 147-148
creating a QuickStyle, 148-150
creating a QuickWords entry, 135-137
creating a sample business plan, 267-268
creating a sample document for style practice, 143-144
creating a script using parallel columns, 341-343
creating a simple equations, 441-443
creating a table, 225
creating a text hyperlink, 423-424
creating a title row, 237-238
creating an article for your newsletter in columnar format, 329-330
creating an effective chart using table data, 254-257
creating an envelope, 156-158
creating and naming a custom definition, 215-216
creating asymmetric columns, 339-340
creating headers or footers, 112-114
creating simple bulleted or numbered lists, 97-98
creating the gross revenue formula, 249-251
creating the Letterhead template, 487-489
creating the sample document, 120-121
defining (or modifying) level styles for a level brief, 217-220
defining a table of authorities page, 287-290
defining an index, 285-286
defining the list, 279-280
defining the table of contents location, 274-276
editing an equation, 444-447
editing the paint tubes image, 377-379

editing the predefined styles, 144-146
enhancing the chart, 258-260
expanding/contracting the master document, 302-304
fading the drop cap's background image, 370
find and replace to change a font face throughout a document, 65-66
formatting the equation, 445-447
generating references from a condensed master document, 301
generating the references, 295
hiding and displaying outline levels, 208-209
hiding and redisplaying body text, 211-212
hiding the guidelines, 20
including a cross-reference in a report, 292-294
including columns in Web page, 406-407
including table of content marks in a style, 272-273
including WordPerfect characters, 107-108
inserting an Address Book entry in a document, 90-91
inserting lines in the Web page, 418
locking in column settings, 333-336
marking items for a table of authorities, 290-292
marking text for a list, 278
marking words and phrases for an index, 282-283
modifying table lines, 241-243
naming and saving the memo, 52-54
opening the faxform macro file for editing, 463
placing the headline over both columns, 380-381
placing the images in the correct order, 368
playing the faxform macro, 461-462
positioning the graphic elements on the newsletter, 360-362
preparing a document for a list of tables, 276-278
printing the current document to the default printer, 152
rearranging the business plan outline, 207-208

recording the fax cover sheet macro, 459-460
removing a project from the Corel WordPerfect 8 category, 503-504
renumbering the document page, 295
retrieving an archived document, 57-58
rotating an image in a graphic box, 372
rotating text, 230
saving and compiling the macro changes, 472
saving the legal brief definition, 221
selecting a different outline definition, 213
selecting a label definition, 160
selecting a paper size, 81-83
selecting Address Book entries and performing the merge, 180-182
sending an e-mail message, 167-168
sending the current document as a fax, 169
setting number types and aligning text, 244-245
setting text wrap options for the newsletter graphic boxes, 362-364
simple alphabetic or numeric sort, 261
sizing and placing the masthead, 326-327
sizing images on the newsletter, 365-367
sizing the columns and gutter widths, 333
sizing the row heading column, 236-237
sorting by the second word in a column, 262-263
spell checking a document, 126-129
Spell-As-You-Go and Prompt-As-You-Go misspelling correction, 122-124
storing another version, 56-57
summing rows, 246-247
suppressing the header from page 1 of the letter, 114
typing and printing address labels, 162-163
typing the business plan outline, 206-207
typing the letter, 175
using a Paradox database as data source, 186-187
using a saved style file in another document, 221-222
using center, flush right, and justification, 109-110
using find and replace to change text, 65
using Grammar-As-You-Go, 132-133
using keyboard Quick Keys to add common attributes, 104
using macro help to find a particular command, 477-478
using QuickFill to complete a series of months, 229
using sort to extract data, 263-264
using tabs to align text, 94-95
using the Business Letter project, 114-118
using the Font dialog box, 106
using the letterhead template, 489
using the letterhead template, 495-496
using the predefined heading styles, 144
using the Windows Messaging/Exchange Address Book, 91-92

hanging indent
described, 99
tab settings, 100

hard disks
image storage requirements, 347
storage space requirements, 7-8

hard page breaks, 95
header rows, excluding from table sort, 260
header styles, 142-143
headers
default margin settings, 47
described, 110
guidelines, 19
page numbers, 112-114
subdocuments, 296
suppressing from page 1 of the letter, 114

Headers/Footers dialog box, 112
headlines, newsletter placement, 380-381
Help (F1) key, 71
Help system, 71-75
accessing, 71-72
Command Inserter, 472-478
Corel Versions, 58
macro descriptions, 451
macros, 472-478
online help, 74-75
PerfectExpert, 72-75
QuickTips, 22-23, 28
Sample Formulas, 248
topic searches, 72

INSERT SYMBOL BUTTON

Help Topics dialog box, 71-72
Hide Bars Information dialog box, 15
home pages, Web page, 405
horizontal lines, call outs, 384
HTML (Hypertext Markup Language), 398
    documents converted to, 399-402
    formatting limits, 398
    to avoid converting files, 432
HTML Document Properties dialog box, 419
HTML Table Properties dialog box, 408, 411, 416
Hyperlink Properties dialog box, 309
hyperlinks, 400, 420-429
    See also links
    adding bookmarks, 427-429
    creating text, 423-424
    editing text, 424-425
hypertext, 420
Hypertext codes, viewing in Reveal Codes window, 85
hypertext links, 307-312
    See also links
    bookmarks, 310-312
    button format, 309-310
    colors, 420
    convert to text button, 426
    described, 85
    e-mail address conversion, 85

I

icons, outline levels, 208
Image Editor dialog box, 34-35
image map, 421
Image Tools palette, 369-374
images
    attachment options, 361
    bitmap, 374
    brightness settings, 369-371
    contrast settings, 369-371
    editing, 374-379
    fills, 375-377
    flipping, 371-372
    forcing TextArt images over a table, 327
    handles, 357
    inserting from files, 351-356
    installation, 347
    JPEG versus bitmap, 355
    manipulating, 356-381
    moving, 373-374
    newsletter addition, 347-356
    paint splash, 349
    pixels, 374
    points, 374-375
    previewing, 348
    resetting, 372
    rotating, 371-372
    sizing, 365-367
    sizing/placing, 357-368
    stack order, 367-368
    supported types, 351-356
    toolbar buttons, 34-35
    vector, 374
    Web pages, 413-418
    zooming, 373-374
Import Data dialog box, 188-189
Indent (F7) key, 99
indents, 99
indexes
    concordance file, 281-284
    creating, 280-286
    definition additions, 285-286
    described, 266
    document reference, 266
    entry marking, 282-283
indicators, table column/row, 226
Inert button, application bar, 28
information, personal, 50
ink-jet printers, no-print zone, 163
in-place editing, described, 305
Insert Columns/Rows dialog box, 234
Insert Field Name or Number dialog box, 179, 183
Insert mode, 28
Insert Object dialog box, 305-306
Insert Paragraph Number dialog box, 211
Insert Sound Clip into document dialog box, 431
Insert Symbol button, 106

insertion point
  repositioning after scrolling document, 27
  Reveal Codes, 30-31
  shadow cursor, 18-19
  installation, 7-10
  images, 347
  Netscape Navigator, 167
  projects, 483
  templates, 483
interlaced, 416
Internet Publisher dialog box, 400
Internet Publisher property bars, 528-530
intranets, online reference libraries, 5-6
ISP (Internet service Provider), 398, 414
italic text, 103-104
item lists, 276-280
items, outline additions, 209-212

J

Java applets, 6, 429
jumps, hypertext links, 307-312
justification
  newsletter columns, 330
  text, 108-110

K

keyboard shortcut keys, 509-515
Keyboard Shortcuts dialog box, 42
keyboards
  customizing, 41-43
  Equation Editor, 41
  moving/copying text, 71
  predefined types, 41
  shortcut key assignments, 42-43, 509-515
  toolbar non-support, 24
  Windows key, 17
  WPDOS 6.1, 41
  WPWIN 7, 41
  WPWIN 8, 41
keys
  Alt, 22, 454
  Backspace, 62, 206
  Ctrl, 454
  Ctrl+Shift, 454
  Enter, 92-93, 206
  Esc, 462
  F1 (Help), 71
  F7 (Indent), 99
  F8 (Select), 104
  F9 (Font), 104
  F9 (Underline Tabs), 196
  Select (F8), 62
  Shift+Tab, 98, 206
  shortcut, 509-515
  shortcut assignments, 42-43, 509-515
  sort, 262
  space bar, 94
  Tab, 92-93, 98, 206
  table navigation, 228
  Windows, 17
keystrokes, bar additions, 35

L

labels, 159-163
  Address Book merge, 162-163
  Avery definitions, 159-160
  charts, 258
  physical page versus logical page, 161
  text entry, 161-163
Labels dialog box, 160
landscape orientation, 82
Laser Printed labels, 160
laser printers, no-print zone, 163
layouts
  business plan outline, 206
  keyboards, 41-43
  predefined table formats, 238-239
left margin guideline, 19
left margin symbol, rulers, 21
legal brief definitions, outline, 214-222
legal caption data files
  data entries, 193-196
  merges, 191-193
Letter PerfectExpert, Business Letter project, 115-118
letterheads, business letters, 84-85
letters
  address additions, 86-92
  body text formatting, 92-96
  business, 80-118

    date addition, 85-86
    inserting Windows Messaging/Exchange address, 91-92
    list insertion, 97-99
    margin settings, 83-84
    page numbers, 110-114
    paper size selections, 81-83
    selected text font size/type editing, 102-103
    symbol insertion, 107-108
    text justification, 108-110

levels
    hiding/displaying, 208-209
    outline, 202-204, 209-212
    style definitions, 216-220
    subordinate, 207
    table of contents, 269

libraries, online reference, 5-6

lines
    adding/hiding in tables, 241-243
    call out, 384-387
    inserting in Web pages, 418
    length editing, 385
    newsletter column separators, 337

linked objects, versus embedded objects, 304-305

links
    See also hyperlinks and hypertext links
    documents, 6
    hypertext, 307-312
    OLE objects, 304-307
    updating, 309
    versus embedded objects, 304-305
    Web pages, 6

lists, 276-280
    bulleted, 97-99
    document insertion, 97-99
    document references, 266, 276-280
    numbered, 97-99
    reference item definitions, 276-280
    versus outlines, 204

logical page, labels, 161

logos, creating, 6-7

M

macro commands, 464-467
    colon (:) character, 465
    double quotes (") character, 464
    exclamation point (!) enumeration character, 464
    line wrapping, 465
    parameter order, 464-465
    parentheses (and) characters, 464
    semicolon (;) character, 465
    strings, 464
    syntax rules, 464-467
    system variables, 474
    user variables, 474
    variables, 473-474

Macro toolbar, 458

macros, 449-480
    adding to bars, 36
    advantages, 450-451
    Alt+ key combination non-support, 454
    Command Inserter, 472-476
    command syntax rules, 464-465
    commands, 464-467
    compiling, 470-472
    CompuServe WordPerfect Users forum library, 466
    converting from previous WordPerfect versions, 478-479
    Corel FTP site address, 466
    Ctrl/Ctrl+Shift key assignments, 454
    default folder storage, 455-456
    described, 36
    disk storage, 453-455
    editing, 462-472
    events/triggers, 500-502
    EXPNDALL.WCM file, 137
    faxform, 459-472
    file save, 497-498
    help, 472-478
    Help system descriptions, 451
    interrupting playback, 462
    keystroke planning, 451-453

MACROS

keystroke-based language, 464
Macro Help file, 476-478
naming conventions, 453-455
PerfectScript language, 464
playing, 460-462
practice document creation, 452
predefined, 451
QuickMacro, 456-457
recording, 457-460
renaming, 454
shortcut key assignments, 454
status viewing, 462
template, 456
template associations, 496-502
types, 453-457
uses, 449-450
variables, 473-474
versus other automation tools, 450-451
wcm filename extension, 454
WordPerfect Magazine Web site address, 466

mailing address, documents, 156

margins
default settings, 47
element settings, 47
mouse editing techniques, 67-68
repositioning guidelines, 19
setting, 83-84

master document
creating, 297-300
described, 296
expanding/contracting, 302-304
reference generation, 301
subdocuments, 296, 299-300

mastheads, 318-327
content, 318-319
development, 318-327
placing, 326-327
sizing, 326-327
table creation, 319-320
TextArt creation, 320-327

Maximize button, WordPerfect 8 window, 17

measurements
margin fields, 84
points, 102

Memo PerfectExpert prompt box, 50-51

Memo project, memo creation, 48-51
memory, requirements, 7
memos, creating, 48-51
menu bar, 22-23
display appearance, 33
editing, 33-35
function groupings, 22
switching between, 23

menus
ellipsis (...) characters with command items, 22
item selection techniques, 22
QuickTips, 22-23
right-click access, 23
submenus, 22
switching between, 23

Merge dialog box, 176

merges
Address Book as data source, 176-177
Address Book entry selections, 180-182
Address Book records, 173
ASCII delimited files, 187-190
blank line prevention, 182
data file scratch creation, 190-197
data file sources, 172
database, 185-187
database supported types, 185
envelope addition, 182-184
external data sources, 184-198
fields, 173
form letter creation, 174-180
legal caption data file, 191-193
Paradox database as data source, 185-187
records, 173
Sales Letter, 174-184
saving entries to named groups, 181
spreadsheet supported types, 185
storing merge layouts, 184
supported file formats, 172
terminology, 172-174
versus macros, 451

Microsoft Internet Explorer, 398
Minimize button, WordPerfect 8 window, 17
MISSPELL.WPD file, 122-124
misspelled words, wavy red lines, 121

mistakes
- After the Fact corrections, 62
- As You Type corrections, 62
- correcting, 62-66
- undoing last action, 63, 211, 261, 379

mnemonic letters, command selections, 22
modified block style, business letter style, 82
monospace fonts, 94
Monthly Calendar project, 50
mouse
- double-headed pointer, 16
- drag and drop graphics copy, 359
- drag and drop techniques, 69-71
- dragging text between documents, 70-71
- file selections, 58
- graphics box sizing, 364-367
- margin/tab settings, 67-69
- moving/copying text, 70
- Reveal Codes access, 30
- right-click menu access, 23
- right-click QuickMenus, 28-29
- shadow cursor, 18-19
- toolbar button access, 24

My Address Book, 88
My Addresses Address Book, 177
My Computer
- opening files, 60
- WordPerfect 8 start up, 11

N

Netscape
- Collabra, 5
- Communicator 4, 5
- Composer, 5
- Conference, 5
- Messenger, 5
- Navigator, 167, 398

New dialog box, 48-49, 115, 486-487
New Entry dialog box, 89
New Message dialog box, 167-168
New Organization Properties dialog box, 89
New Person Properties dialog box, 89
New Sort dialog box, 262, 264
New Version dialog box, 55-56
newsgroups, Corel WordPerfect, 75

Newsletter project, 50
newsletters, 317-394
- asymmetric columns, 338-340
- CD Clipart addition, 350-351
- column appearance enhancements, 331-332
- column creation, 329-330
- column styles, 327-335
- drop caps, 354-356
- file image insertion, 354-356
- graphic attribute modifications, 368-374
- graphics, 345-394
- graphics attachment options, 361
- graphics box sizing, 364-367
- graphics design guidelines, 346-347
- gutter space, 328-329
- headline placement, 380-381
- image addition, 347-356
- image manipulation, 356-381
- image stack order, 367-368
- justification, 330
- line separators, 337
- masthead, 318-327
- navigation, 331
- parallel column scripts, 338-341
- Scrapbook clipart, 348-351
- screen shot addition, 381-392
- sizing/placing graphics, 357-368
- title font faces, 329
- watermarks, 339-340, 392-394
- wrapping text around/through graphics, 362-364

newspaper columns, described, 327
no-print zone, printers, 163
numbered lists, 97-99
numbers
- list styles, 97-99
- table alignment, 243-245

O

object groups, editing, 378
objects
- add to Web pages, 429-431
- described, 304
- linking versus embedding, 304-305
- OLE, 304-307

OBJECTS

selecting, 368
stacking, 367-368
template, 496-499
ODBC (Open Database Connectivity), 172
OLE (Object Linking and Embedding), 304-307
document links, 304-307
object stacking, 367-368
servers, 305
online help, Web site URLs, 74-75
online reference libraries, 5-6
Open File button, 60
Open File dialog box, 60
open styles, 141
operators, data extraction sort, 264
Organization address type, Address Book, 88
Outline property bar, 205
outlines, 202-222
appearance enhancements, 212-222
body text, 211-212
custom definitions, 213-214
definitions, 202-212
families, 207-209
hiding/displaying levels, 208-209
item additions, 209-212
level icons, 208
level styles, 204
levels, 202-204
saving custom definitions, 220-222
style level definitions, 216-220
subordinate levels, 207
switching definitions, 213
text entry, 205-207
versus lists, 204

P

page breaks, 95
page numbers, 110-114
counter types, 110
footers, 112-114
headers, 112-114
Page Setup dialog box, 81-82
Page View, enabling, 112
pages
numbering, 110-114

printing non-adjacent, 155
publishing to Web site, 431-434
paint splash image, described, 349
paired codes, described, 141
paired styles, 141
paper size, selecting, 81-83
paper source, selecting, 82
paper
custom definitions, 83
orientation, 82
Paradox 8, 5, 185-187
Paragraph Format dialog box, 96
paragraph format symbol, rulers, 21
paragraph formatting
codes, 95-96
disadvantages, 95
Enter key, 92-93
hard page breaks, 95
monospace fonts, 94
proportional fonts, 94
space bar paragraph alignment, 94
Tab key, 92-93
text alignment, 108-110
text wrapping, 98
paragraph styles, described, 140
parallel columns, described, 328
scripts, 338-341
parallel with block protect columns, described, 328
parentheses (and) characters, macro commands, 464
PerfectExpert, 72-75
bugs, 118
described, 48, 73
PerfectExpert dialog box, required fields, 50
PerfectScript Commands dialog box, 472-476
PerfectScript language
compiling macros, 470-472
macro command syntax rules, 464-467
macros, 464
variables, 474
PerfectScript product commands, 472-473
Perform Merge dialog box, 180-181
permanent archive, described, 55

Person address type, Address Book, 88
personal information, first time project/template use, 50
Personal Letter project, 50
Personal Letterhead template, 484-502
Personalize Your Templates dialog box, 50
Perspective dialog box, 259
perspective views, charts, 259
Photo House 1.1, 4
phrases, adding to QuickCorrect, 125-126
physical law equations, 436
physical page, labels, 161
pixels, described, 276
Play Macro dialog box, 461
pleading forms, creating, 196-198
pointers, double-headed, 16
points
    described, 374-376
    font size measurement, 102
polygons, described, 389
polylines, call outs, 385
portrait orientation, 82
POSTNET bar codes, printing, 157-158
power bars, 522-532
predefined styles, document inclusion, 142-144
predefined toolbars, 518-522
Presentations 8, 4
    accessing, 383
    logo creation, 6-7
Print dialog box, 152-154
Print Status and History dialog box, 165
printers
    custom paper definitions, 83
    default, 152-154
    ink-jet, 163
    laser, 163
    no-print zone, 163
    paper source selections, 82
    resident fonts, 163
    selecting, 152-153
    setting as default, 164
printing, 151-170
    booklets, 155-156
    checking status/history of print jobs, 165-166
    default settings, 153-154
    envelopes, 158-159
    fax services, 168-169
    landscape orientation, 82
    non-adjacent pages, 155
    portrait orientation, 82
    POSTNET bar codes, 157-158
    report references, 294-295
    troubleshooting, 163-166
    two-sided, 155
    ZIP codes, 157-158
Professional Suite version, components, 5
program icons, described, 15
program patches, FTP site URL, 75
programs
    adding to bars, 35-36
    exiting, 17
    saving documents when exiting, 17
    title bar display, 16
projected gross revenue table, 224-238
projects, 502-505
    adding, 504-505
    ast/asx filename extensions, 482
    Business Letter, 50, 114-118
    category listing, 48-49
    Corel Web site additions, 504
    Custom installation, 50
    described, 48, 482
    document creation, 48-51
    Fax Cover Sheet, 50
    first time use personal information, 50
    installation, 483
    Memo, 48-51
    Monthly Calendar, 50
    Newsletter, 50
    Personal letter, 50
    removing, 503-504
    template file references, 482-483
    templates, 48-51
    Typical installation, 50
    versus macros, 451
    versus templates, 482
Prompt Builder dialog box, 491
Prompt-As-You-Go, error-checking, 121-124

prompts
- Address Book/templates links, 492
- automatic date codes, 491
- personal fields, 493-494
- prompts.wcm file, 491
- template, 489-496

prompts.wcm file, 491

proofreading tools, 120-134
- Document Word List, 124-125
- grammar checking, 132-134
- Grammatik, 133-134
- misspelled word-checking methods, 121
- Prompt-As-You-Go, 121-124
- QuickCorrect, 124-126
- Spell Checker, 126-129
- Spell-As-You-Go, 121-124
- Thesaurus, 129-132
- User Word List, 124-125

Properties for Table Format dialog box, 230-231

property bars, 27, 522-532
- button keyboard access, 27
- editing, 33-35

proportional fonts, 94

Publish to HTML dialog box, 433

Q

Quattro Pro 8, 4

Quick Data Entry dialog box, 192

Quick View Plus, 5

QuickCorrect dialog box, 125-126, 135-136, 312-313

QuickCorrect, typographical error correction, 124-126

QuickFill, table data series entries, 228-229

QuickFonts button, 104

QuickFormat, style creation, 147-148

QuickJoin, joining/splitting table cells, 237-238

QuickLinks
- described, 304
- World Wide Web, 312-313

QuickMacro, 456-457

QuickMark, template insertion point, 488

QuickMenus, described, 28-29
- display appearance, 33
- right-click access, 28-29
- Spell-As-You-Go, 123-124
- switching between, 23

QuickStyle, style creation, 148-150

QuickSum, row/column sums, 246-247

QuickTips
- application bar, 28
- commands, 22-23
- dialog box fields, 37

QuickWords, 135-137

R

recently edited file list, 60

Record Macro dialog box, 457-458

records, Address Book merge, 173

rectangles, described, 389

Reference Center, 5

reference lists, 276-280

reference marks, document text, 267

relative cell references, formulas, 250

Remove This Project from the Current Category? dialog box, 503

reports, 201-222
- cross-references, 292-294
- document references, 266-295
- indexes, 280-286
- item lists, 276-280
- master documents, 296-301
- outlines, 202-222
- reference generation, 294-295
- section management, 296-304
- table of authorities, 286-292

required fields, PerfectExpert dialog box, 50

reserved characters, file naming conventions, 52

resident fonts, described, 163

Restore button, WordPerfect 8 window, 17

Retrieve Version dialog box, 57

Reveal Codes window, 28-32
- accessing, 30
- color settings, 30
- customizing, 30
- described, 28-29
- double-indent code, 99
- hanging indent code, 99
- hard page break (HPg), 95
- Hypertext codes, 85

indent code, 99
insertion point, 30-31
paragraph formatting codes, 95-96
reading code contents, 31-32
style editing, 144-146
Tab codes, 99
right margin guideline, 19
right margin symbol, rulers, 21
right-click menus, accessing, 23
right-click QuickMenus, 28-29
Roman numerals, page numbers, 110
rounded rectangles, described, 389
rows
naming conventions, 226
summing, 246-247
table addition, 226, 233-234
title, 237-238
rulers, 20-22
default document format settings, 47
displaying/hiding, 20
margin symbols, 21
tab symbols, 21
viewing current tab settings, 69

S

Sales Letter merge, 174-184
Save File dialog box, 52-53
Save Template dialog box, 489
Scrapbook
clipart, 348-351
compact.scb file, 349
locating/adding CD images, 350-351
minimizing, 349-350
paint splash image, 349
screen shots, 381-392
callouts, 381-391
captions, 391-392
scripts, parallel columns, 338-341
scroll bars, 27
searches
Address Book names, 90
finding/replacing text, 63-66
font find/replace, 65-66
Help system topics, 72
Spell Checker wild card, 128-129
word form find/replace, 64
second default template, 484
Select (F8) key, 62, 104
Select Destination Folder for Move dialog box, 58
Select Page Numbering Format dialog box, 111
selection letters, command, 22
semicolon (;) character, macro commands, 465
Separators, bars, 34
Series Properties dialog box, 256-257
servers, OLE, 305
Settings dialog box, 37-43
Application Bar Settings, 40-41
Convert Settings, 40
Customize Settings, 41-43
Display Settings, 37-38
Environment Settings, 39
Files Settings, 40
Summary Settings, 40
shadow cursor
date positioning, 86
insertion point location, 18-19
shape palette, TextArt, 322
shapes, drawing, 389-391
Shift+Tab key
moving back one level, 98
outline levels, 206
shortcut keys, 509-515
Bold (Ctrl+B), 103
Bullet (Ctrl+Shift+B), 98
center (Shift+F7), 108
Close (Ctrl+F4), 113
Column Break (Ctrl+Enter), 331
Command Inserter (Ctrl+M), 472
Copy (Ctrl+C), 71
Ctrl+Shift+D (automatic date code), 491
Cut (Ctrl+X), 71
date code (Ctrl+Shift+D), 86
date text (Ctrl+D), 86
Delete (Ctrl+Del), 62
Delete Entire Word (Ctrl+Backspace), 62
double-indent (Ctrl+Shift+F7), 99
Drop Cap (Ctrl+Shift+C), 354
Find and Replace (Ctrl+F), 64
flush right (Alt+F7), 108

Format menu (Alt+R), 15, 22
GoTo (Ctrl+G), 331
Grammatik (Alt+Shift+F1), 133
hanging indent (Ctrl+F7) or (F7, Shift+Tab), 99-100
hard page breaks (Ctrl+Enter), 95
Hide Bars (Alt+Shift+F5), 15
Insert Paragraph Number (Ctrl+Shift+F5), 211
Insert Row (Alt+Insert), 237
Italic (Ctrl+I), 103
Line break (Shift+Ctrl+L), 206
macros, 456
Move Left (Alt+left arrow), 331
Move Right (Alt+right arrow), 331
Name Search (Ctrl+F), 90
New (Ctrl+Shift+N), 115
Open (Ctrl+O), 60
Paste (Ctrl+V), 71
Print (Ctrl+P), 152
Print (Ctrl+Shift+P), 152
Print Screen (Alt+Print Screen), 381-382
Record Macro (Ctrl+F10), 457
Reveal Codes (Alt+F3), 30, 144
Save (Ctrl+S), 52
single-level hanging indent (Ctrl+F7), 99
Sort (Alt+F9), 262
Spell Check (Ctrl+F1), 127
Start menu (Ctrl+-), 17
Style List (Alt+F8), 145
Symbols (Ctrl+W), 106
Thesaurus (Alt+F1), 130
Underline (Ctrl+U), 103, 195
Undo (Ctrl+Z), 63, 211, 261, 379
shortcuts, key assignments, 42-43, 509-515
signature lines, creating, 195
Size buttons, 102
Size menu, Equation Editor, 440
Sizes dialog box, 440-441
SmartQuotes, 138-139
soft page breaks, 95
Software Development Kit, 5
Sort dialog box, 262
sorts
    concordance file, 284
    data extraction, 263-264
    files, 59
    keys, 262
    table data, 260-264
    undoing, 261
Sound Clip dialog box, 430-431
sound clips, 430-431
source applications, linked objects, 305
space bar key
    Equation Editor, 439
    font alignment, 94
special characters, 106-108
Specialty property bars, 532
Specific Codes dialog box, 66
Spell Checker, 126-129
    Document Word List, 124
    manual text editing, 129
    replacement suggestions, 127-129
    starting, 127
    User Word List, 124
    wild card word search, 128-129
Spell-As-You-Go, error-checking, 121-124
Standard Suite version, components, 4-5
status area, DAD bar icons, 10-11
strings, macro commands, 464
styles, 140-150
    applied, 141
    bullets/numbering, 97-99
    business letter layout, 80-81
    custom creation, 146-150
    editing, 144-146
    header, 142-143
    master document, 296
    open, 141
    outline level definitions, 204, 216-220
    paired, 141
    QuickFormat, 147-148
    QuickStyle, 148-150
    SpeedFormat, 238-239
    system, 142
    table alignment, 244-245

table of contents, 272-273
types, 140
versus macros, 450
Styles dialog box, 440
Styles Editor dialog box, 145-146
subdocuments, 296, 299-300
submenus, 22
subordinate levels, outlines, 207
subtitles, charts, 258
Summary Settings dialog box, 40
Suppress dialog box, 114
Symbols dialog box, 106
symbols, special characters, 106-108
synonyms, Thesaurus alternatives, 129-132
system requirements, 7-8
system styles, 142
system variables, macro commands, 474

T

Tab key
    moving back one level, 98
    outline levels, 206
    paragraph formatting, 92-93
Tab QuickMenu, 69
tab symbols, ruler, 21
table formatting, 238-245
    adding/hiding section lines, 241-243
    Alternating Fill, 242
    background fills, 239-241
    number alignments, 243-245
Table Functions dialog box, 249
table of authorities, 286-292
    definitions, 287-290
    described, 266
    document reference, 266
    entry marking, 290-292
    full form entry, 290
    short form entry, 290
table of contents
    creating, 268-276
    described, 266
    document reference, 266, 268-276
    level limitations, 269
    level markings, 274

    location definition, 274-276
    marking entries, 269-273
    styles, 272-273
Table property bars, 531
Table SpeedFormat dialog box, 238-239
tables, 224-264
    adding to Web page, 408-411
    adjusting dimensions, 411-413
    appearance enhancements, 238-245
    chart creation, 253-260
    column sizing, 234-237
    column/row additions, 233-234
    column/row naming conventions, 226
    creating, 224-238
    data extraction sort, 263-264
    excluding header rows from sort, 260
    floating cells, 251-253
    for organized display, 407-413
    forcing TextArt images, 327
    formulas, 245-251
    introductory text, 224
    invisible borders, 410
    item lists, 276-280
    joining/splitting cells, 237-238
    masthead creation, 319-320
    math computations, 245-251
    navigation keys, 228
    predefined formats, 238-239
    projected gross revenue, 224-238
    Property bar buttons, 227
    QuickFill data series entries, 228-229
    QuickSum row/column sums, 246-247
    revenue projection, 224-251
    row/column indicators, 226
    row/column sums, 246-247
    sort keys, 262
    sorting entries, 260-264
    summing, 246-247
    text rotation, 229-233
    title row creation, 237-238
tabs
    described, 99
    hanging indent settings, 100
    mouse editing techniques, 68-69
    types, 69

targets, cross-reference, 292-294
taskbar
    DAD bar status area icons, 10-11
    Documents list, 60
    WordPerfect 8 window, 17
technical support
    e-mail address, 75
    online help Web site URLs, 75
Template Information dialog box, 495
template macros, 456
Template Property bar, 488
templates, 48-51, 482-506
    Address Book links, 492
    category creation, 486-487
    category listing, 48-49
    creation, 484-489
    date/time addition, 491
    described, 48, 482
    events, 500-502
    first time use personal information, 50
    installation, 483
    macro associations, 496-502
    objects, 496-499
    personal field prompts, 493-494
    Personal Letterhead, 484-502
    prompts, 489-496
    prompts.wcm file, 491
    QuickMark insertion, 488
    second default, 484
    triggers, 500-502
    versus macros, 451
    versus projects, 482
    viewing information, 495-496
    Web pages, 402-429
    WP8US.WPT file, 135
    wpt filename extension, 482
temporary archive, described, 55
terms, 533-544
    alignment, 108-110
    applying formatting, 404
    automatic wrapping, 98
    boldfacing, 103-104
    cross-reference item marking, 292-294
    dragging between documents, 70-71
    finding/replacing, 63-66
    hypertext links, 309-310
    index entry marking, 282-283
    italicizing, 103-104
    justification, 108-110
    list reference marking, 278
    moving/copying, 70-71
    newsletter column entry, 331
    outline entry, 205-207
    replacing all instances, 65
    selecting, 62-63
    special characters, 106-108
    table of authority entry marking, 290-292
    table of contents reference marking, 267-273
    TextArt masthead effects, 320-327
    underlining, 103-104
    wrapping, 205
    wrapping around images, 362-364
text button hyperlinks, Web pages, 425-426
text colors, changing in Web pages, 418-420
text elements, Web pages, 403-405
text hyperlinks
    add to Web pages, 423-424
    editing, 424-425
text rotation, tables, 229-233
TextArt, 305, 417-418
    2D controls, 324
    3D controls, 325
    forcing images over a table, 327
    masthead creation, 320-327
    shape palette, 322
    wrapping text around/through graphics, 362-364
Thesaurus, 129-132
Time Line, 5
times, adding to templates, 491
title bar, described, 16
titles
    charts, 258
    newsletter font face guidelines, 329
    newsletter masthead, 318-327
    table rows, 237-238
Toolbar Editor dialog box, 33-35
Toolbar Options dialog box, 25-26

toolbars, 23-26
    Address Book button addition, 87
    display options, 24-26
    editing, 33-35
    Equation Editor, 437-439
    keyboard non-support, 24
    maximum row display, 25-26
    mouse-only editing aid, 24
    moving, 24-25
    predefined, 518-522
    selecting, 24
top margin guideline, 19
Tractor-Fed labels, 160
triggers, templates, 500-502
troubleshooting
    computer won't restart after installation, 10
    envelope printing, 158-159
    print job sent to printer did not print, 165-166
    Print Text Only option selection, 154
    printed document looks different than it did on screen, 163
    printing problems, 163-166
TrueType fonts, 163
two-sided printing, 155
typefaces (font faces), described, 100, 102
Typeover mode, 28
Typical installation, 9-10, 50
typing tools, 134-139
    Format-As-You-Go, 137-138
    QuickWords, 135-137
    SmartQuotes, 138-139
typos, correcting, 62

U

Underline Tabs (F9) key, 196
underlined letters, command selection, 22
underlined text, 103-104
undo items, storage settings, 63
undoing last action, 63, 211, 261, 379
user variables, macro commands, 474
User Word List, Spell Checker, 124

V

variables, macro commands, 473-474
vector images, described, 374
Version Properties dialog box, 57
Versions, 5
vertical lines, call outs, 384

W

Watermark dialog box, 339
Watermark property bar, 394
watermarks, 339-340, 392-394
wavy red lines, misspelled words, 121
wcm (macro) filename extension, 454
Web Columns dialog box, 407
Web pages
    adding links, 421-422
    adding objects, 429-431
    applying text formatting, 404
    background colors, changing, 418-420
    backgrounds, 420
    bookmarks, 427-429
    bulleted items, 405-406
    columns, 406-407
    converting without previewing in Web format, 401
    create with Web template, 402-429
    creating, 398-434
    editing text hyperlink, 424-425
    graphic hyperlinks, 426
    graphics, 413-418
    home page, 405
    hyperlinks, 420-429
    images, 413-418
    import clipart, 415
    inserting lines, 418
    Java applets, 429
    links, 6
    losing formatting during conversion, 401
    putting in single folder, 432
    sound clips, 430-431
    tables, using, 407-413
    text button hyperlinks, 425

text colors, changing, 418-420
text elements, 403-405
text hyperlinks, adding, 423-424
TextArt button, adding, 417-418

Web sites
Corel, 74-75, 313, 504
electronic help, 75
Microsoft Internet Explorer, 398
Netscape Navigator, 398
publishing pages to, 431-434
WordPerfect Magazine, 466

Web templates, to create a new document, 402-429

WEB.SiteBuilder, 5-6

white space, graphics guidelines, 347

wild cards, Spell Checker search, 128-129

Windows 95
Control Panel, 55
WordPerfect 8 window universal elements, 15-17

Windows key, Start menu access, 17

Windows Messaging/Exchange Address Book, 87, 91-92

windows
Blank Document, 47
described, 16
full/partial-screen display, 17
maximizing/minimizing, 17
Reveal codes, 28-32
sizing, 16
WordPerfect 8, 14-28

word forms, finding/replacing, 64

word meanings, Thesaurus, 129-132

WordPerfect 8 window
application bar, 28
bars, 22-28
Close button, 17
customizing display appearance, 32-43
display settings, 37-38
document icon, 16
document-editing elements, 18-21
elements, 14-28
exiting, 17
guidelines, 19-20

Maximize button, 17
menu bar, 22-23
Minimize button, 17
program icon, 16
property bars, 27
QuickMenus, 28-29
Restore button, 17
Reveal Codes, 28-32
ruler, 20-22
scroll bars, 27
shadow cursor, 18-19
title bar, 16
toolbars, 23-26
Windows 95 taskbar, 17
Windows 95 universal elements, 15-17

WordPerfect Draw, 305

WordPerfect Magazine, Web site URL, 75

WordPerfect SGML Layout Designer, 5

WordPerfect symbols, 106-108

words
adding to QuickCorrect, 125-126
adding to Spell Checker, 124
replacing all instances, 65
Thesaurus alternatives, 129-132

World Wide Web, 397
QuickLinks, 312-313
selecting destination, 424

WP8US.WPT file, 135

wpd (WordPerfect) filename extension, 52

WPDOS 6.1 keyboard, 41

wpg (WordPerfect clipart) filename extension, 347

WPWIN 7 keyboard, 41

WPWIN 8 keyboard, 41

Wrap Text dialog box, 363

wrapped text, 98, 205

wrapping, text around graphics, 362-364

Z

ZIP codes, printing, 157-158

zones, no-print, 163

Zoom tool palette, 373

zooms, image percentages, 373-374

NOTES

NOTES

NOTES

NOTES

NOTES

NOTES

NOTES

NOTES

The Essential WordPerfect 8 Book

YOUR COMMENTS
Send Us

Dear Reader:

Thank you for buying this book. In order to offer you more quality books on the topics *you* would like to see, we need your input. At Prima Publishing, we pride ourselves on timely responsiveness to our readers' needs. If you'll complete and return this brief questionnaire, *we will listen!*

Name: (first) _____ (M.I.) _____ (last) _____

Company: _____ Type of business: _____

Address: _____ City: _____ State: _____ Zip: _____

Phone: _____ Fax: _____ E-mail address: _____

May we contact you for research purposes? ❏ Yes ❏ No
(If you participate in a research project, we will supply you with your choice of a book from Prima CPD)

---

❶ How would you rate this book, overall?

❏ Excellent ❏ Fair
❏ Very Good ❏ Below Average
❏ Good ❏ Poor

❷ Why did you buy this book?

❏ Price of book ❏ Content
❏ Author's reputation ❏ Prima's reputation
❏ CD-ROM/disk included with book
❏ Information highlighted on cover
❏ Other (Please specify): _____

❸ How did you discover this book?

❏ Found it on bookstore shelf
❏ Saw it in Prima Publishing catalog
❏ Recommended by store personnel
❏ Recommended by friend or colleague
❏ Saw an advertisement in: _____
❏ Read book review in: _____
❏ Saw it on Web site: _____
❏ Other (Please specify): _____

❹ Where did you buy this book?

❏ Bookstore (name) _____
❏ Computer Store (name) _____
❏ Electronics Store (name) _____
❏ Wholesale Club (name) _____
❏ Mail Order (name) _____
❏ Direct from Prima Publishing
❏ Other (please specify): _____

❺ Which computer periodicals do you read regularly? _____

❻ Would you like to see your name in print?

May we use your name and quote you in future Prima Publishing books or promotional materials?

❏ Yes ❏ No

---

❼ Comments & Suggestions: _____

PRIMA PUBLISHING
Computer Products Division
3875 Atherton Rd.
Rocklin, CA 95765

PLEASE PLACE STAMP HERE

⑧ Where do you use your computer?

Work	❏ 100%	❏ 75%	❏ 50%	❏ 25%
Home	❏ 100%	❏ 75%	❏ 50%	❏ 25%
School	❏ 100%	❏ 75%	❏ 50%	❏ 25%

Other _____

⑨ How do you rate your level of computer skills?

❏ Beginner
❏ Advanced
❏ Intermediate

⑩ What is your age?

❏ Under 18
❏ 18-24   ❏ 40-49
❏ 25-29   ❏ 50-59
❏ 30-39   ❏ 60-over

⑪ I would be interested in computer books on these topics

❏ Word Processing   ❏ Database
❏ Networking   ❏ Spreadsheets
❏ Desktop Publishing ❏ Web site design

Other _____

SAVE A STAMP

Visit our Web Site at: **http://www.primapublishing.com**
and simply fill in one of our online Response Forms

Other Books from Prima Publishing, Computer Products Division

ISBN	Title	Price
0-7615-0801-5	ActiveX	$40.00
0-7615-0680-2	America Online Complete Handbook and Membership Kit	$24.99
0-7615-0915-1	Building Intranets with Internet Information Server and FrontPage	$45.00
0-7615-0417-6	CompuServe Complete Handbook and Membership Kit	$24.95
0-7615-0849-X	Corporate Intranet Development	$45.00
0-7615-0743-4	Create FrontPage Web Pages in a Weekend	$29.99
0-7615-0692-6	Create Your First Web Page in a Weekend	$29.99
0-7615-0428-1	The Essential Excel 97 Book	$24.99
0-7615-0969-0	The Essential Office 97 Book	$27.99
0-7615-0695-0	The Essential Photoshop Book	$35.00
0-7615-0752-3	The Essential Windows NT Book	$27.99
0-7615-0427-3	The Essential Word 97 Book	$24.99
0-7615-1008-7	Excel 97 Visual Learning Guide	$16.99
0-7615-0955-0	Hands-On Visual Basic 5 for Web Development	$40.00
0-7615-1005-2	Internet Information Server 3 Administrator' Guide	$40.00
0-7615-0815-5	Introduction to ABAP/4 Programming for SAP	$45.00
0-7615-0901-1	Leveraging Visual Basic with ActiveX Controls	$45.00
0-7615-0690-X	Netscape Enterprise Server	$40.00
0-7615-0691-8	Netscape FastTrack Server	$40.00
0-7615-0852-X	Netscape Navigator 3 Complete Handbook	$24.99
0-7615-1162-8	Office 97 Visual Learning Guide	$16.99
0-7615-0759-0	Professional Web Design	$40.00
0-7615-0773-6	Programming Internet Controls	$45.00
0-7615-0780-9	Programming Web Server Applications	$40.00
0-7615-0063-4	Researching on the Internet	$29.95
0-7615-0686-1	Researching on the World Wide Web	$24.99
0-7615-0769-8	VBScript Master's Handbook	$45.00
0-7615-0684-5	VBScript Web Page Interactivity	$40.00
0-7615-0903-8	Visual FoxPro 5 Enterprise Development	$45.00
0-7615-0814-7	Visual J++	$35.00
0-7615-0726-4	Webmaster's Handbook	$40.00
0-7615-0751-5	Windows NT Server 4 Administrator's Guide	$50.00
0-7615-1007-9	Word 97 Visual Learning Guide	$16.99
0-7615-1083-4	WordPerfect 8 Visual Learning Guide	$16.99

To Order Books

Please send me the following items:

Quantity　　　　　　　　　　　　　　　　　　　　　　　　　　　　　Title

____   _____ $ _____ $ _____

____   _____ $ _____ $ _____

____   _____ $ _____ $ _____

____   _____ $ _____ $ _____

____   _____ $ _____ $ _____

Subtotal $ _____

Deduct 10% when ordering 3-5 books $ _____

7.25% Sales Tax (CA only) $ _____

8.25% Sales Tax (TN only) $ _____

5.0% Sales Tax (MD and IN only) $ _____

Shipping and Handling* $ _____

Total Order $ _____

*Shipping and Handling depend on Subtotal.

Subtotal	Shipping/Handling
$0.00–$14.99	$3.00
$15.00–$29.99	$4.00
$30.00–$49.99	$6.00
$50.00–$99.99	$10.00
$100.00–$199.99	$13.50
$200.00+	Call for Quote

Foreign and all Priority Request orders:
Call Order Entry department
for price quote at 916/632-4400

This chart represents the total retail price of books only
(before applicable discounts are taken).

By Telephone: With MC or Visa, call 800-632-8676, 916-632-4400. Mon-Fri, 8:30-4:30 PST.

Orders Placed via Internet E-mail sales@primapub.com

By Mail: Just fill out the information below and send with your remittance to:

Prima Publishing
P.O. Box 1260BK
Rocklin, CA 95677
www.primapublishing.com

My name is _____

I live at _____

City_____ State_____ Zip _____

MC/Visa#_____ Exp._____

Check/Money Order enclosed for $_____ Payable to Prima Publishing

Daytime Telephone _____

Signature _____